THE LIFE AND CRIMES
OF
AGATHA CHRISTIE

CHARLES OSBORNE

The Life and Crimes of
of
AGATHA CHRISTIE

A RAINBIRD BOOK

HOLT, RINEHART AND WINSTON

For Joe Hansen, crime novelist in the Christie mould, in Los Angeles; and Ken Thomson, his sometime accomplice in publishing, in London.

37264

CONTENTS

'Who Cares Who Killed Roger Ackroyd?' was the title of an article by the American critic and novelist Edmund Wilson,[1] who had no taste for crime fiction. It was a silly question, for millions cared.

W.H. Auden began an essay, 'The Guilty Vicarage',[2] with the words 'For me, as for many others, the reading of detective stories is an addiction like tobacco or alcohol', and went on to confess that 'if I have any work to do, I must be careful not to get hold of a detective story for, once I begin one, I cannot work or sleep till I have finished it.'

The Life and Crimes of Agatha Christie is a book for the likes of W.H. Auden, rather than for the likes of Edmund Wilson. It examines not only the crime novels but also everything else that Agatha Christie published, including the non-fiction, the stories for children, the poetry, the plays (both those written by her and those adapted from her novels by other hands), the films based on her works, and the six novels she produced under the pseudonym of Mary Westmacott.

My qualifications for writing this book are slender: (i) I began reading Agatha Christie surreptitiously during a Latin lesson at school in 1943, and I have stopped, temporarily, only because I have read everything she wrote and, blessed with a highly selective memory, have actually read several of the murder mysteries more than once over the years; (ii) I played Dr Carelli in Agatha Christie's *Black Coffee* during a summer season of repertory in Tunbridge Wells in 1955 ('Nearer the Latin temperament was Charles Osborne as the slick Dr Carelli,' said the local newspaper critic, after savaging the leading lady); (iii) I once met Dame Agatha at a party given by her publishers to celebrate the publication of *Passenger to Frankfurt* in 1970. Suddenly and uncharacteristically nervous at finding myself momentarily alone with the eighty-year-old author whom I had admired for so many years, I found myself offering her an engagement to take part in an Arts Council Writers' Tour, and address audiences in the provinces. 'Oh, I'm afraid I couldn't do that,' Dame Agatha replied immediately. 'I wouldn't be any good at it, and in any case, you see, the reason I began to write more than sixty years ago was in order to avoid having to talk to people.'

Let me assure potential readers of this book that they may proceed in perfect safety. Nowhere in these pages do I reveal the identity of any of Agatha Christie's murderers.

Unless otherwise indicated, dates given after the titles of books are those of first publication. In the majority of cases only a few weeks separate American and British publication dates. Where a title was not published in both countries, this is made clear. The notes will be found at the end of each chapter.

My thanks for help of various kinds are due to the following individuals and institutions: Jonathan Barker, Jacques Barzun, Allan Davis, Sebastian Faulks, Joseph Hansen, Jennifer Insull, Sir Peter Saunders, Julian Symons, Kenneth Thomson, John Wells, Philip Ziegler; Arts Council Poetry Library, Brighton Area Library, British Library, British Theatre Institute Library, William Collins Sons & Co., Crime Writers' Association, *Daily Telegraph*, Library of Congress, London Library. I am especially grateful to my editor, Elizabeth Blair.

C.O.

1 Reprinted in *Classics and Commercials* by Edmund Wilson (1950).
2 Reprinted in *The Dyer's Hand* by W.H. Auden (1962).

I

Appearance and Disappearance

The Mysterious Affair at Styles (1920)

It was while she was married to Archie Christie that Agatha Christie, *neé* Miller, wrote and published her first novel, *The Mysterious Affair at Styles*. That marriage lasted for less than fourteen years, ending in divorce at about the time of publication of her ninth book, *The Mystery of the Blue Train*, but her career as a writer of crime fiction continued for a further half-century and a further eighty-five titles (excluding the plays). Having become known to a vast reading public as Agatha Christie, the author continued to use that name for professional purposes throughout the rest of her life, although privately she became Mrs Max Mallowan soon after her divorce from Christie.

Agatha Miller was born in the elegant, sedate seaside resort of Torquay, Devonshire, on the south coast of England, on 15 September 1890, at Ashfield, the home of her parents, Frederick and Clarissa Miller. Frederick Alvah Miller was a well-to-do young American who lived as much in England, where he had relatives, as in America, on an income derived from the family business. After he married Clarissa Margaret Beochmer (his stepmother's niece) he and his wife planned to live in America. However, they first spent some time in Torquay, at the height of the winter season, and Mr Miller, who loved the sea, became enchanted with the town, its attractive bay and the dramatic south Devon coast. The Millers' first child, Marjorie (Madge) was born in Torquay, shortly after which the family left for America where they expected to make their permanent home. It was while they were staying with Frederick Miller's grandparents in New England that their second child, Louis (Monty), was born.

The Millers returned to England for a visit, but Mr Miller was almost immediately recalled to New York by business concerns, and therefore suggested to his wife that she should take the children and rent a furnished house in Torquay until his return. What Clara Miller did, instead, was to buy a house in Torquay from a Quaker family called Brown. Extremely placid by temperament, Mr Miller, though surprised, did not remonstrate. The house could, after all, be sold again in a year's time. The Millers and their two children moved into the house, Ashfield, and Mr Miller found life in Torquay so agreeable that in due course he decided that they may as well settle there. Ashfield, a large and comfortable villa with green lawns, a garden of about two acres, and great beech trees, made a splendid home for Mrs Miller and the children even though it was not in the most fashionable part of Torquay but in Barton Road, in the older, upper-middleclass district of Tor Mohun.

When a third child was born to the Millers, a good eight years after the second, she was christened Agatha May Clarissa. The second and third were family names, but 'Agatha' appears to have been suggested by a friend of Mrs Miller on the way to the christening. A chubby redhead, Agatha turned out to be a quiet, imaginative child who played a great deal on her own or with her elderly nannie, 'Nursy', since her brother and sister were away at school for much of the time and were, in any case, so much older than she. Agatha did not go to school but taught herself to read, and learned something of elementary mathematics from her father. Her formal education did not begin until, at the age of sixteen, she was sent to a finishing school in Paris. Her father had died when she was eleven, and the family income had dwindled. Mrs Miller considered selling Ashfield but was prevailed upon by her two elder children merely to reduce the number of servants and make certain other economies.

The Millers were still able to live comfortably. With Madge married and living in New York, and Monty serving with the army in India, Mrs Miller decided shortly after Agatha's return from finishing school in Paris that she would let Ashfield furnished for three months and take her teenage daughter off to Egypt. Her own health had not been good, but three months with Agatha in and around Cairo, sight-seeing, going to dances and parties and on excursions to the sites of antiquity, seemed to improve her condition and certainly helped Agatha to overcome her childhood and adolescent *gaucherie*. The attractive young lady even received several proposals of marriage from officers serving in the British Army in Egypt, but took none of them seriously. She was still very young, and she was also now her mother's only comfort and companion. When they returned to Torquay, Agatha continued to live at home with her mother, though she also led an active social life with friends of her own age.

Agatha had already begun to write. During her childhood, when she was lying in bed recovering from influenza, her mother had suggested that, instead of telling stories which she enjoyed doing, she should write one of them down. Soon Agatha had produced a number of stories, and began to write poems as well. It was as a poet that she made her first appearance in print, at the age of eleven, with a poem about the new electric trams which she had seen when visiting her grandmother at Ealing, a suburb of London. The poem, which was printed in the local Ealing newspaper, began: 'When first the electric trams did run/In all their scarlet glory,/'Twas well, but ere the day was done,/It was another story.'

Her poems improved, and by the time she was in her late teens Agatha had won a few prizes with them, usually of a guinea or so offered by the Poetry Society, and had had several poems published in *The Poetry Review*. She had also written a number of stories which, as she said later, usually revealed the influence of whomever she had been reading the previous week, as often as not D.H. Lawrence. Under various pseudonyms, among them Mack Miller and Nathanael Miller (her grandfather's name), she would send her stories off to magazines and they would invariably come back to her accompanied by a printed rejection slip. She even attempted a novel, which she called *Snow Upon the Desert*, and at the suggestion of her mother sent it off to Eden Phillpotts, the author of popular novels of Devon rural life in the tradition of Thomas Hardy. (In the twenties and thirties, Phillpotts was to write murder mysteries, both under his own name and as Harrington Hext.)

Phillpotts, who was a neighbour of the Millers and a friend of the family, gave generously of his time and advice. Though he was critical of *Snow Upon the Desert*, and advised its author to cut out the moralizing of which he considered she was much too fond, he thought Agatha had a 'great feeling for dialogue', and introduced her to his literary agent, Hughes Massie. Agatha went to London and was interviewed by Mr Massie, a large, swarthy man who, she said, terrified her. Massie read her novel, and advised her to put it aside and begin another. Instead, she returned to writing her poems and stories.

Agatha was now in her early twenties and fending off young men who wished to marry her. After what she referred to as two near escapes, she became engaged in 1912 to Reggie Lucy, a Major in the Gunners, but while Lucy was serving with his regiment in Hongkong, she fell in love with a handsome young Lieutenant in the Royal Field Artillery, whom she had met at a house party in Chudleigh, not far from Torquay. He was Lieutenant Archibald Christie, the son of a Judge in the Indian Civil Service. They danced together several times at their first meeting, and a few days later Christie arrived on his motorcycle at Ashfield and was allowed by Mrs Miller to stay to supper. Within days, he and Agatha had become engaged, and Agatha eventually plucked up the courage to write to Reggie Lucy in Hongkong ending their engagement.

It was eighteen months later that Agatha Miller married Archie Christie, now a Captain in the Royal Flying Corps. The wedding took place on Christmas Eve, 1914. During the period of their engagement, the Miller family income had been further depleted by the liquidation of a firm in New York, and Britain had declared war on Germany. Captain Christie went off to war two days after the wedding, while his bride went to work at the Torbay Hospital in Torquay, nursing the first casualties who were being brought back from the Front. After two years of nursing, and a number of reunions with Archie when he came home on leave, Agatha transferred to the hospital's dispensary, where she acquired the accurate knowledge of poisons which was later to prove so useful to her.

Years earlier, Agatha and her sister Madge had one day been discussing a murder mystery they were reading, and Agatha had mentioned, idly, that she would like to try her hand at a detective story. Madge was of the opinion that Agatha would find this too difficult a task, an opinion which Agatha remembered in 1916, while working in the hospital dispensary at Torquay. She decided to devote her occasional slack periods at the dispensary to the composition of a detective novel, in the hope of proving her sister wrong.

Her first problem, as Agatha Christie revealed many years later in her autobiography, was to decide what kind of detective story she would write. Since she was surrounded by poisons, it was natural that death by poisoning should be the method she selected. She settled on one particular fact or *donné* which seemed to her to have possibilities, toyed with the idea for a time, and finally decided upon it. Next she turned to the *dramatis personae*. Who should be poisoned? Who would be the poisoner? When? Where? How? Why? It would, she decided, have to be 'very much of an *intime* murder', because of the method chosen. It would have to be all in the family, so to speak.

And, of course, there would have to be a detective to unravel the mystery and unmask the evil-doer. An avid reader of the Sherlock Holmes stories of Sir Arthur Conan Doyle, Agatha pondered upon the personality and methods of Holmes and his relationship with Dr Watson, his friend and the chronicler of his cases. Her detective, she decided, would have to be as different in personality from Sherlock Holmes as possible. However, the device of the friend and helper, the Dr Watson-figure whose obtuseness sets off the brilliant deductive powers of the great detective, was too useful to discard. Her detective would, therefore, have such a figure in attendance, and he could be the narrator of the story.

The budding crime writer now had an idea for the actual crime, and a detective and his aide. But who were the other characters to be? Who was to be murdered? Husbands frequently murdered their wives, of course, but perhaps it would be better to opt for a more unusual kind of murder and for a very unusual motive. But then the whole point of a really good murder mystery was that the criminal should be someone obvious, whose obviousness was not apparent until pointed out in the last chapter by the brilliant detective. At this point in her reasoning, Agatha Christie confessed later, she became confused and went away to make up a couple of extra bottles of hypochlorous lotion, so that she would have more free time the following day to give further consideration to her crime project.

Over the next few days, her plot began to develop in some detail, though in a somewhat unorthodox manner. Having first decided what she wanted her murderer to look like, Agatha next began to search around among her acquaintances for someone who fitted the description, in order to study his physical characteristics. She soon realized, however, that it was pointless to attempt to base a fictional character upon a real person's characteristics. Later, with experience, she would find ways of doing this to some extent, but for the present she was in need of a starting-off point. She found it when, sitting in a tram, she saw exactly what she wanted: 'a man with a black beard, sitting next to an elderly lady who was chattering like a magpie.' As she did not know these people, her imagination was unfettered; she could invent characters for them, and place them in situations of her own invention.

She continued to give consideration to the question of the detective. It was important that he should not be simply an imitation Sherlock Holmes. What other models were there? Arsène Lupin? The young journalist Rouletabille in *The Mystery of the Yellow Room*?[1] Perhaps the detective could be a scientist. Or a schoolboy? A schoolboy would be too difficult, and Agatha was not acquainted with any scientists. Then she remembered the colony of Belgian war refugees who were living in the parish of Tor, in Torquay. Might not one of them be a Belgian police officer? A retired Belgian police officer, not too young:

> I allowed him slowly to grow into his part. He should have been an inspector, so that he would have a certain knowledge of crime. He would be meticulous, very tidy, I thought to myself, as I cleared away a good many untidy odds and ends in my own bedroom. A tidy little man. I could see him as a tidy little man, always arranging things, liking things in pairs, liking things square instead of round. And he should be very brainy – he should have little grey cells of the mind – that was a good phrase: I must remember that – yes, he would have little grey cells. He would have rather a grand name – one of those names that Sherlock Holmes and his family had. Who was it his brother had been? Mycroft Holmes.[2]

Since he was to be a little man, it seemed an amusing idea to name the retired detective Hercules, the hero of Greek myth. Where did 'Poirot' come from? Did Agatha Christie think of her little detective as also being pear (*poire*)-shaped? Later, she was unable to remember. But she liked the sound of 'Hercule Poirot', and enthusiastically set to work on the other characters and on the plot, inventing situations, revelations and false clues during her leisure time at the dispensary and at home. Eventually, she began to write her novel, using a battered old typewriter that had belonged to her sister. Her method was to produce a first draft of each chapter in longhand and then revise the chapter as she typed it.

About halfway through, Agatha began to find herself in difficulties with her complicated plot, at which point her mother suggested that, if she was ever going to bring her novel to a successful conclusion, she should take the typescript away with her on her holiday from the hospital, and work at it with nothing else to distract her. And so, in the summer of 1916, Mrs Archibald Christie took herself off to beautiful, grey, remote Dartmoor, quite near Torquay in distance, but a world away in atmosphere with its rugged moorland, giant granite tors on craggy hills, ancient stone circles, and prehistoric remains.

Much of the 365 square miles of Dartmoor is bleak country, with treacherous bogs. But a few hundred yards from the summit of Hay Tor, the Moorland Hotel is situated, partially hidden by trees, with views over the moor and across South Devon to the sea, and it was there that Agatha Christie lived for two weeks while she finished writing the murder mystery which she had decided to call *The Mysterious Affair at Styles*. The hotel is still there, though it has been closed since fire destroyed some of its rooms in March, 1970. Years later, Agatha Christie described her two weeks' stay at the Moorland Hotel in 1916:

> It was a large, dreary hotel with plenty of rooms. There were few people staying there. I don't think I spoke to any of them – it would have taken my mind away from what I was doing. I used to write laboriously all morning till my hand ached. Then I would have lunch, reading a book. Afterwards I would go out for a good walk on the moor, perhaps for a couple of hours. I think I learned to love the moor in those days. I loved the tors and the heather and all the wild part of it away from the roads. Everybody who went there – and of course there were not many in wartime – would be clustering around Hay Tor itself, but I left Hay Tor severely alone and struck out on my own across country. As I walked, I muttered to myself, enacting the chapter that I was next going to write; speaking as John to Mary, and as Mary to John; as Evelyn to her employer, and so on. I became quite excited by this. I would come home, have dinner, fall into bed and sleep for about twelve hours. Then I would get up and write passionately again all morning.

When Archie Christie came home on leave, he read his wife's novel and enjoyed it. A friend of his in the Air Force was a director of another publishing house, Methuen's, and Archie suggested that if her novel was returned again to Agatha, he would provide her with a letter from his friend which she could enclose with the typescript and send off to Methuen's. This plan was duly followed but, although Methuen's sat on the typescript for about six months, perhaps to prove to Archie's friend that they were giving it their most earnest consideration, they eventually concluded that it was not quite suitable for them, and returned it to its author.

The Mysterious Affair at Styles was submitted to a fourth publisher, again without success, after which Agatha decided to try The Bodley Head, having noticed that they had recently published one or two detective novels. She packed the manuscript off to them, heard nothing, and forgot all about it.

Towards the end of the war, Archie Christie, now a Colonel, was posted to the

Air Ministry in London, so Agatha was able to leave Torquay and live at last with her husband. They took a small flat in St John's Wood, at 5 Northwick Terrace, which was really no more than two rooms on the second floor of a house (now demolished), and Agatha started a course of book-keeping and shorthand to occupy her days. The war came to an end, and a few months later, in 1919, Mrs Christie gave birth to a daughter, Rosalind, at Ashfield, the family home in Torquay.

The Christies now needed a larger London flat, and in due course found what they were looking for on the fourth floor of Addison Mansions (Flat 96), a huge double apartment block behind Olympia in Earl's Court. Archie was de-mobilized, and went to work for a firm in the City. It was towards the end of 1919, nearly two years after she had sent the typescript of *The Mysterious Affair at Styles* to The Bodley Head, that Agatha Christie received a letter from John Lane, the Managing Director of the publishing house, asking her to call and see him. When they met, John Lane explained that several people had read her novel and thought it showed promise. However, the dénouement, which she had written as a court-room scene, did not ring true. If Mrs Christie would rewrite that chapter, in a different setting, and make some other minor changes, The Bodley Head would be willing to publish her book.

After explaining what a risk he was taking by offering to publish a new and unknown writer, and how little money he was likely to make with her novel, John Lane produced a contract from the drawer of his desk, and an excited young author who had given up hope of ever having anything published, other than the occasional story or poem, immediately signed it. She was to receive a small royalty, but only after the first 2,000 copies had been sold. All subsidiary rights, such as serialization and film rights, would be shared fifty-fifty between author and publisher, and there was a clause binding the author to offer The Bodley Head her next five novels, at an only slightly increased royalty rate. A jubilant Agatha rushed home to inform her husband of her good fortune, and that evening they celebrated at the Hammersmith Palais de Danse.

When *The Mysterious Affair at Styles* was published in 1920, it sold nearly 2,000 copies. The £25 which Agatha Christie earned from her first book came, not from royalties, for there were none due to her under the terms of a distinctly unfair contract, but from a half share of the serial rights which had been sold for £50 to *The Weekly Times*. Taking the view that £25 was not a very satisfactory return for all the time and energy she had expended upon the writing of her novel, Agatha did not envisage ever attempting to write another. At least, this is what she was to claim, years later, in her autobiography. She had been dared by her sister to write a detective story, she had done so, and she had got it published. There, as far as she was concerned, the matter ended. She would probably write stories from time to time, but she had no intention of turning herself into a professional writer. To her, writing was fun.

In this, as in one or two other matters, Agatha Christie's *An Autobiography* is less than completely reliable. Writing it over a number of years between 1950 and 1965, she did not always remember with accuracy events which had taken place thirty or forty years earlier. In fact, in a letter to Basil Willett of The Bodley Head, written in the autumn of 1920, she inquired about the publication date of *The Mysterious Affair at Styles*, adding that she was beginning to wonder if it was ever going to appear, as she had already nearly finished a second novel, *The*

Secret Adversary. She also wanted to know what the cover of *The Mysterious Affair at Styles* would look like. After she had seen the cover design, she agreed that it would do as it was 'quite artistic and mysterious'. She also asked that a dedication, 'To my mother', should appear at the beginning of the book.

Most of the qualities which were to make Agatha Christie the most popular crime writer there has ever been were already on display in *The Mysterious Affair at Styles*, and it is astonishing that several publishers turned the novel down before it was accepted by The Bodley Head. Characterization is no more detailed than Agatha Christie needed it to be for her purpose, the setting is an English country house in or near a small village, there is a proliferation of clues which are there for the reader to discover, if he is not dazzled by the author's sleight of hand, and the method used by the murderer is poisoning.

The young Agatha Christie had learned a great deal about poisons through her work at the hospital dispensary in Torquay, and she was to put her knowledge to good use in several of her murder mysteries. Among the many favourable reviews her excellent first novel received, Agatha was especially proud of that in the *Pharmaceutical Journal* which praised 'this detective story for dealing with poisons in a knowledgeable way, and not with the nonsense about untraceable substances that so often happens. Miss Agatha Christie knows her job.'

The 'Styles' of the title is Styles Court, a country house in Essex, a mile outside the village of Styles St Mary. In later novels, Mrs Christie tended not to specify the county, and even in this first novel she avoids using real names of towns. Characters may take the train up to London from the country, but if they have to visit a nearby country town it will not be identified as Chelmsford or Colchester, but will be given a fictitious name. The fictitious village of Styles St Mary is, for instance, seven miles away from the fictitious town of Tadminster, where one of the characters works in the dispensary of the Red Cross Hospital.

The Mysterious Affair at Styles, though not published until 1920, had been written during the First World War, and was set in the summer of 1916. Its narrator, Captain Hastings, is a young officer who has been invalided home from the Front and who, after spending some months 'in a rather depressing Convalescent Home', is still on sick leave when he runs into someone he had known as a boy: the forty-five-year-old John Cavendish who is 'a good fifteen years' Hastings' senior. Hastings, then, is about thirty. Reading *The Mysterious Affair at Styles* now, the reader interests himself more in Captain Hastings' personal details than Agatha Christie's readers would have done in 1920, for they were not to know that Mrs Christie would go on to write scores of crime novels over the years and that Hastings would figure in eight of them (and in numerous short stories) as the associate of her detective, Hercule Poirot.

John Cavendish invites the convalescent Hastings to spend his leave in Essex at Styles Court. Cavendish's stepmother, whom Hastings remembered as a handsome, middle-aged woman, is now an autocratic *grande dame* of seventy or more. After several years of widowhood, she has recently married Alfred Inglethorp, who is about twenty years younger than she, and 'an absolute bounder' in the opinion of John Cavendish because he has 'a great black beard, and wears patent leather boots in all weathers'. Clearly, Alfred Inglethorp is a fortune-hunter, for Mrs Inglethorp has a sizeable fortune to dispose of. When she is found murdered, he is the chief and favourite suspect.

The other inhabitants of Styles Court include John Cavendish's wife Mary, his younger brother Lawrence, a girl called Cynthia who is a protégé of Mrs Inglethorp and who works in the dispensary of the nearby hospital, and Evelyn Howard, a forty-year-old woman who has been the old lady's companion, factotum and general assistant. There is also a tall, bearded and somewhat mysterious foreigner, a Dr Bauerstein, who is staying in the village, recuperating after a nervous breakdown. He is said to be one of the greatest living experts on poisons.

When Mrs Inglethorp's death, at first thought to be due to a heart attack, is found to have been caused by strychnine poisoning, suspicion falls not only upon her husband but, in turn, on most of her nearest and dearest. The local police are called in, but Hastings has encountered in the village an old friend of his, Hercule Poirot, a famous detective now retired, and it is Hastings who persuades his friend John Cavendish to allow Poirot as well to investigate the crime.

Before the First World War, young Hastings had worked for Lloyd's of London. (Not until *The ABC Murders* in 1935 shall we learn Hastings' first name to be Arthur, for Agatha Christie's men habitually address each other in what used to be the approved English upper-middleclass fashion, by their surnames.) It was while he was working for Lloyd's that Hastings had first met Poirot, in Belgium. Poirot had already retired from the Belgian Police Force, after a long career as its most illustrious detective, and had set himself up in private practice as an investigator. Hastings is surprised and delighted to meet him again unexpectedly in the village of Styles St Mary where Poirot, together with a number of other Belgian refugees, is living. Poirot accepts with alacrity the commission to find Mrs Inglethorp's murderer, for, as he explains to Hastings, 'she had kindly extended hospitality to seven of my countrypeople who, alas, are refugees from their native land.' 'We Belgians,' he adds, 'will always remember her with gratitude.'

Poirot, on his first appearance, is described in some detail:

> He was hardly more than five feet, four inches, but carried himself with great dignity. His head was exactly the shape of an egg, and he always perched it a little on one side. His moustache was very stiff and military. The neatness of his attire was almost incredible; I believe a speck of dust would have caused him more pain than a bullet wound.[3]

Later, we shall discover that Poirot is not only fanatically neat but is also obsessed with symmetry. He is forever rearranging the objects he encounters, putting them into straight rows. He probably wished that eggs were square: he certainly, on one occasion, deplored the fact that hens lay eggs of different sizes ('What symmetry can there be on the breakfast table?') It is odd, therefore, that he should habitually carry his head tilted a little to one side. He cannot have been aware that he did so.

Poirot will acquire other personality traits in later books, or at least we shall learn more about him, but already apparent in *Styles* are his genuine affection for Hastings of whose perspicacity he has a justifiably low opinion, his endearing vanity, his odd misuse of the English language and still odder occasional misuse of his native tongue, French (for, despite her Paris finishing school, Mrs Christie's French was to remain obstinately unidiomatic). Incidentally, when he sees his old friend for the first time in several years, Hastings notices that Poirot now limps badly. But the limp is never referred to again: we must assume that it was a temporary disability from which Poirot soon recovered. Indeed, when he inspects Mrs Inglethorp's room at Styles Court, Poirot, we are told, 'darted from one object to the other with the agility of a grasshopper.'

Just as 'Elementary, my dear Watson', (which is not a direct quotation from any story by Sir Arthur Conan Doyle) is the phrase you most associate with Sherlock Holmes, so a habit of constantly referring to 'the little grey cells' of the brain is something closely associated with Hercule Poirot. But, though he is continually having 'little ideas', and recommending order and method to Hastings, Poirot mentions the 'little grey cells' for the first time only towards the end of *Styles*. He makes a point, however, of informing Hastings (and the reader of the book) well before the dénouement that 'I am not keeping back facts. Every fact that I know is in your possession. You can draw your own deductions from them.' Hastings, however, never wins a battle of wits with Hercule Poirot, and it is a reasonable assumption that even the most assiduous reader of Agatha Christie will do so only rarely.

Agatha Christie was conscious of the necessity to make Poirot very different from the most famous fictional detective of his day, Sherlock Holmes. After all, Conan Doyle's Sherlock Holmes adventures were still appearing. *The Valley of Fear* was published in 1915, *His Last Bow* in 1917, and *The Casebook of Sherlock Holmes* in 1927. But it is only physically that Poirot differs greatly from Holmes. The two detectives share a number of qualities, among which vanity is by no means the least noticeable. Still, if Poirot owes something to Conan Doyle and Sherlock Holmes, does he not also owe something to another crime novelist? Mrs Belloc Lowndes, sister of Hilaire Belloc, and writer of a number of historical and mystery novels and stories, was the creator of a detective who, like Poirot, was foreign, retired (in his case, from the Paris Sûreté), and incredibly vain. His name was Hercules Popeau. Agatha Christie must certainly have been aware of him when she began to write her first Hercule Poirot novel, and indeed throughout the nineteen-twenties and -thirties when stories by Mrs Belloc Lowndes, featuring Popeau, appeared in the same anthologies as stories of Hercule Poirot's exploits. In the mid-thirties, Mrs Belloc Lowndes published a Popeau story, 'A Labour of Hercules', which did not deter Mrs Christie in the mid-forties from calling a collection of Poirot stories *The Labours of Hercules*.

Devoted Christieans, who delight in assembling the 'facts' about Poirot in the same manner that Conan Doyle's more fanatical admirers tend to research the great Sherlock Holmes, have somehow convinced themselves that Poirot retired from the Belgian Police Force in 1904, and that this fact is revealed in *The Mysterious Affair at Styles*. It is not. We are told that Poirot 'had been in his time one of the most celebrated members of the Belgian Police.' When, late in the story, Inspector James Japp of Scotland Yard puts in an appearance (he is the Christiean equivalent of Sherlock Holmes's sparring partner, Inspector Lestrade), he greets Poirot and then, turning to a colleague, says: 'You've heard me speak of Mr Poirot? It was in 1904 he and I worked together – the Abercrombie forgery case – you remember, he was run down in Brussels. Ah, those were great days, moosier. Then do you remember "Baron" Altara? There was a pretty rogue for you! He eluded the clutches of half the police in Europe. But we nailed him in Antwerp – thanks to Mr Poirot here.'

Poirot, then, was active in his post in 1904, and the 'Baron' Altera affair may well have occurred after 1904. It is possible that Poirot's retirement did not take place until 1914, in which case he could have been as young as sixty-seven at the time of the Styles murder in 1916. (In *Murder on the Links*, published three years after *Styles*, we learn that Poirot was still active in Ostend in 1909.) Agatha Christie later declared that, if she had realized how long she was going to be saddled with Poirot, she would have made him a much younger man on his first appearance. It is fortunate that fictional chronology can be flexible, for otherwise Poirot would have been at least one hundred and twenty years of age when he came to solve his final case in 1974, after having featured in thirty-three novels and fifty-two short stories. That he was still in his sixties, and not older, when Mrs Christie first introduces us to him in *The Mysterious Affair at Styles* is suggested by a remark of Hastings, when he fails to understand Poirot's train of thought: 'The idea crossed my mind, not for the first time, that poor old Poirot was growing old.' If Poirot had appeared to be in his seventies, the *idea* that he might be growing old would probably not have crossed even Hastings' mind.

One of Agatha Christie's great achievements as a crime writer was to make murder cosy enough to be palatable to refined middleclass tastes. She abhorred violence,[4] and those who see in it the only reality will seek that kind of reality in vain in the Christiean *oeuvre*. Her appeal is incredibly wide – *ça va sans dire*, as Poirot might say – and it is an appeal not to the blood lust but to a civilized delight in the puzzle shared by her readers of all social and intellectual classes. One can discuss Agatha Christie novels with cleaning ladies and classical scholars, with dustmen and dons.

This cosiness is, of course, in itself unreal. *The Mysterious Affair at Styles* has the inhuman remoteness of the puzzle, but it also, curiously, has something of the texture of a social document as well, especially now, more than half a century after it was written, when its social world has all but disappeared. To Agatha Christie, it would seem to have been already disappearing in 1916. The atmosphere in Styles Court and in the nearby village of Styles St Mary is of a country at war. The war may be only a lightly sketched background, but it is there. The servants necessary to staff a large country house are there, too, but only just. Of Dorcus, the faithful old family retainer, Hastings says, 'I thought what a fine specimen she was of the old-fashioned servant that is so fast dying out.'

The values implicitly subscribed to, and the opinions expressed by many of her characters, can reasonably be assumed to be shared by the young author of *Styles*. Evidence in a good many of the early Christie novels seems to point to an unthinking, casual anti-semitism of the kind then prevalent in the English upperclasses. In *Styles*, Dr Bauerstein, a Polish Jew, is suspected of spying. 'A very clever man – a Jew of course,' says Poirot, at which Hastings exclaims, 'The blackguard!' Not too worrying, though there is a suggestion that the doctor's Jewish cleverness is as reprehensible as his espionage activities. In any case, the balance is redressed somewhat with this exchange between a jealous husband and his wife who is infatuated with Bauerstein:

'I've had enough of the fellow hanging about. He's a Polish Jew, anyway.'
'A tinge of Jewish blood is not a bad thing. It leavens the' – she looked at him – 'stolid stupidity of the ordinary Englishman.'

The tactics, though not the actual method of murder, used by the killer of Mrs

Inglethorp were adopted successfully by a real-life murderer about ten years after the publication of Agatha Christie's first novel. It is quite possible that he derived his inspiration from a reading of the book. Other odd facts to be noted about *The Mysterious Affair at Styles* are that the author emphasizes the puzzle-solving aspect of the reading experience by including two plans, one of the first floor of Styles Court and one of Mrs Inglethorp's bedroom, and a number of illustrations of clues, letters, fragments of handwriting and cryptic messages; that Hastings gives evidence of his propensity for redheads, which will continue to be displayed in later stories, by unsuccessfully proposing marriage to one; and that Agatha Christie signals to the reader in the final paragraph of the novel that she is prepared to produce one or more sequels to *Styles*. 'Console yourself, my friend,' Poirot says to Hastings who has failed to capture his redhead. 'We may hunt together again, who knows? And then –'

Though her gift for tight and ingenious plotting and her flair for creating believable characters mainly through convincing dialogue were to develop greatly in the next ten or fifteen years, with *The Mysterious Affair at Styles* Mrs Christie made an extraordinarily successful début as a crime writer. Her novel is a distinct improvement on the average level of the genre as it was then practised, and looking back on it more than half a century later you can see that, in fact, it ushered in a new era for the detective story, an era which Agatha Christie would come to dominate with her engaging and fiendishly ingenious puzzles, an era which lasted for more than three decades and which is referred to now as the Golden Age of crime fiction.

The Secret Adversary (1922)

With Archibald and Agatha Christie living in a flat in London, and Agatha's mother still attempting to keep up Ashfield, the Torquay house, on an inadequate income to which Agatha could not afford to contribute, the question of selling Ashfield was raised by Archie. When Agatha received the suggestion with horror, Archie then proposed that she should try to raise funds towards the upkeep of Ashfield by writing another murder mystery. After all, although she had earned only £25 from *The Mysterious Affair at Styles*, it had been well received and had sold a respectable number of copies. The Bodley Head had presumably not lost money on it, and would no doubt be willing to pay a little more for a second novel.

Agatha, apparently, had already begun a second novel, but was not sure whether The Bodley Head would like it. It was not another detective story, but a thriller, so there was no place in it for Hercule Poirot. The idea for the book had first come to her one day in an A.B.C. teashop, one of a chain of London cafés, when she had overheard two people at a nearby table talking about a girl called Jane Fish. That, she thought, would make quite a good beginning: someone overhearing an unusual name in a café, and then remembering it when it came up again in a different context. Jane Fish, however, was perhaps just a little too comical, so Agatha altered it to Jane Finn, and set to work to invent a plot.

Young people in their twenties were being demobilized from the armed forces after the First World War and finding it difficult to settle down to civilian life. Many were unable to find jobs, or were having to act as door-to-door salesmen. Mrs Christie, who found herself frequently answering the doorbell to ex-servicemen, and buying stockings, household gadgets or even poems from them, decided to have such a pair as the young hero and heroine of her thriller.

When she had finished writing her book some months later, Agatha took it to John Lane of The Bodley Head who had published *The Mysterious Affair at Styles* and who had an option on this and her next four books. Lane was disappointed at finding it was not another murder mystery, thought it would sell less well than *Styles*, and even considered rejecting it. In due course, however, The Bodley Head published the novel, which its author decided to call *The Secret Adversary* having first considered *The Joyful Venture* and *The Young Adventurers* (*The Young Adventurers Ltd*, in fact became the title of Chapter 1). The publishers disposed of serial rights to *The Weekly Times*, as they had done with *Styles*, and sold a reasonable number of copies. This time Mrs Christie 'got £50 doled out' to her by John Lane. It was, she considered, encouraging, though not encouraging enough for her to think that she had as yet adopted anything so grand as a profession. She would have been astonished if anyone had told her she would, from now until the end of her life, publish at least one book a year, sometimes one novel and one collection of short stories, sometimes two novels, and in one year (1934) a total of two crime novels, two volumes of short stories and (under a pseudonym) one romantic novel.

With *The Secret Adversary* in 1922, Agatha Christie introduced her readers to two characters whom she would use again in four later novels: *Partners in Crime* (1929), *N or M?* (1941), *By the Pricking of My Thumbs* (1968) and *Postern of Fate* (1974). It is as well, therefore, that Thomas Beresford and Prudence Cowley, known to their friends as Tommy and Tuppence, are only in their twenties in 1922, for this enabled their creator to allow them to age naturally. In their final adventure in 1974 they are presented as an elderly married couple with three grandchildren. When we first meet them, however, in *The Secret Adversary*, they are young, and just emerging from wartime activities, he as a Lieutenant in the army, who had been in action in France, Mesopotamia and Egypt, and she as a maid-of-all-work in an officers' hospital in London. Tuppence is, perhaps, the author as Agatha Christie liked to fantasize herself, and Tommy is the kind of young man who appealed to the fantasy Agatha.

The relationship of the young couple is lightly romantic, though they refrain from confessing their feelings for each other until the last page of *The Secret Adversary*, and their style of speech is positively Wodehousian. 'Tommy, old thing!' and 'Tuppence, old bean!' they exclaim when they meet unexpectedly for the first time since the war, at the exit to the Dover Street tube station. (This is not a fictitious venue: there used to be a Dover Street station on the Piccadilly line.)

Set in 1920, in the autumn and winter of which year it was written, *The Secret Adversary* is dedicated 'To ALL THOSE WHO LEAD MONOTONOUS LIVES in the hope that they may experience at second hand the delights and dangers of adventure'. If, in her first novel, Mrs Christie had set forth one of her two favourite subjects, the murder committed in (or at least involving the members of) an upperclass or upper-middleclass household, in her second she introduces her other favourite, the master criminal seeking to dominate the world. These two themes, domestic crime and global crime, continue to appear throughout her career, though the domestic crime novels not only greatly outnumber the thrillers involving international criminals or crime syndicates, but also are generally considered to be vastly superior to them.

The Secret Adversary begins with a prologue which takes place at 2 p.m. on the afternoon of 7 May 1915, in the Atlantic Ocean off the south coast of Ireland. The *Lusitania* has just been torpedoed by a German submarine, and is sinking fast. Women and children are lining up for the lifeboats, and a man approaches one of the women, an eighteen-year-old girl, to ask if she will take possession of some 'vitally important papers' which may make all the difference to the Allies in the war. The *Lusitania* settles with a more decided list to starboard as the girl goes forward to take her place in the lifeboat, and then suddenly we are in Mayfair, five years later, with Tommy and Tuppence blocking the exit to the Dover Street underground station, turning themselves into the Young Adventurers.

The Prologue is brief, graphic, and flings the reader *in medias res*: the sudden juxtaposition of a grey, grim Atlantic with the bright sunshine of post-war London and the cheerful optimism of the young adventurers, Tommy and Tuppence, is startlingly effective. In the interests of accuracy, however, it should be noted that Mrs Christie thought the *Lusitania* was sunk by two torpedoes. In fact, the German U-boat fired only one torpedo: those among the survivors who may have thought otherwise were misled by secondary explosions from the *Lusitania*'s boilers.

The story proper concerns the efforts of Tommy and Tuppence to trace the girl, Jane Finn, who survived the *Lusitania* disaster only to disappear immediately afterwards with those secret papers which, if they were made public now, months after the end of the war, would cause great embarrassment to the British Government. Mr Carter, a mysterious individual who is very high up in the British Secret Service, recruits the Young Adventurers to save the country. We are left in no doubt of Agatha Christie's political leanings when Mr Carter points out to the Adventurers, Tommy and Tuppence, how vital it is that the documents should be retrieved and suppressed, for they could discredit a number of Conservative statesmen (– was there really a time when a government of any political persuasion contained 'a number of' statesmen? –) and that would never do. 'As a party cry for Labour it would be irresistible, and a Labour Government at this juncture,' Mr Carter adds, 'would, in my opinion, be a grave disability for British trade.'

During the course of their search, Tommy and Tuppence encounter a number of entertaining characters, some of them engaging but others distinctly unsavoury. They include Julius P. Hersheimmer, Jane Finn's American millionaire cousin; Albert, the cockney liftboy in a Mayfair apartment block; and Sir James Peel Edgerton, a distinguished barrister, 'the most celebrated KC in England', a man likely to become a future Prime Minister. What links *The Secret Adversary*, and later Christie thrillers, with the murder mysteries on which the author's reputation most securely rests is the fact that these and a number of other characters whom Tommy and Tuppence find themselves either collaborating with or pitted against are not only the clearcut 'goodies' and 'baddies' of the usual thriller, but are potential suspects as well. For, although Agatha Christie clearly differentiates the thriller from the murder mystery, she retains an element of the puzzle in her thrillers. The question 'Who?' is asked in the thrillers; it is simply that the question 'How?' becomes equally important.

In *The Secret Adversary*, the puzzle is the identity of the adversary. The Bolshevists, we are informed, are behind the labour unrest in the country, but there is a certain man who is '*behind the Bolshevists*' (the italics are Mrs Christie's). 'Who is he?' Mr Carter asks rhetorically:

'We do not know. He is always spoken of by the unassuming title of "Mr Brown". But one thing is certain, he is the master criminal of this age. He controls a marvellous organization. Most of the peace propaganda during the war was originated and financed by him. His spies are everywhere.'

Tommy manages to eavesdrop upon a meeting of Mr Brown's organization, at which various representatives report on their activities. A Sinn Feiner guarantees to produce, within a month, 'such a reign of terror in Ireland as shall shake the British Empire to its foundations'. Others have infiltrated the trade unions: the report from the miners is thought to be most satisfactory, but 'we must hold back the railways. There may be trouble with the ASE.' It is important that the principal Labour leaders should have no inkling that they are being used by the Bolshevists. 'They are honest men,' says the representative from Moscow, 'and that is their value to us.'

All good clean reactionary fun, and not without a certain absurd relevance to political life in the 1980s! Those who take their politics solemnly, if anyone other than politicians is still able to do so, will probably reflect that *The Secret Adversary* gives an interestingly distorted picture of the social and industrial unrest which followed the First World War and which, during the years which saw the consolidation of the Russian revolution, was to lead to the General Strike in Great Britain, an event which is curiously anticipated in more than one of Agatha Christie's early novels. But Mrs Christie is politically no further to the right in her thrillers than Ian Fleming in his distinctly less amusing James Bond novels of the nineteen-fifties and sixties.

The villain is unmasked at the end of *The Secret Adversary* and the threatened General Strike is averted or, as we now know, postponed. Inspector Japp has made, not an appearance, but a certain effect offstage, and the reader with a knowledge of nineteenth-century French opera will probably spot a certain clue which will leave those who suffer from amusia (the inability to comprehend or produce musical sounds) mystified.

The Secret Adversary was the first Agatha Christie novel to be made into a film. This did not happen until 1928, by which time Mrs Christie was being published in a number of foreign languages. The film, produced by a German company, was called *Die Abenteuer Gmbh* (Adventures Ltd), was directed by Fred Sauer, and starred Carlo Aldini, Eve Gray and a Russian character actor, Michael or Mikhail Rasumny, who was to appear in a number of Hollywood movies in the nineteen-forties and fifties.

The Murder on the Links (1923)

Archie Christie had a friend, Major Belcher, who was a larger-than-life character with the ability to bluff people into giving him positions of responsibility. Belcher came to dine one evening with the Christies at Earls Court, and explained that he was shortly to leave on a grand tour of the British Empire in order to organize 'this Empire Exhibition we're having in eighteen months' time'. 'The Dominions,' Belcher explained to Archie and Agatha, 'have got to be alerted, to stand on their toes and to cooperate in the whole thing,' and it was Belcher's mission to ensure that they did so. He invited Archie to come with him as financial adviser, with all expenses paid and a fee of £1,000. Agatha would be permitted to accompany the party, since most of the transport was being provided free of charge by the ships and railways of the various Commonwealth countries to be visited.

Archie Christie had already grown tired of his job in the City, and when Belcher announced the proposed itinerary, from South Africa to Australia and New Zealand, then on to Canada after a brief holiday in Honolulu, the Christies agreed to go. Agatha longed to travel and see as much of the world as possible, but had expected that, as the wife of a business man, two weeks abroad each summer would be all she was ever likely to get. There was a certain risk to be taken, for Colonel Christie's employer was not willing to guarantee to keep his job open for him on his return, but the Christies did not consider themselves to be people who played safe. Like Agatha's Tommy and Tuppence, they yearned for adventure and were perfectly willing to take risks. Off they went, around the world with Major Belcher, leaving their daughter with Agatha's sister.

The British Empire Exhibition Mission set off in grand style on the *Kildonan Castle*, bound for Cape Town. But Agatha Christie's enjoyment was soon cut short: the weather in the Bay of Biscay was atrocious, the ship was tossed about violently, and for four days Agatha suffered the most appalling seasickness. The ship's doctor became seriously concerned about her, and a woman in a nearby cabin who had caught a glimpse of her was heard, on the fourth day, to ask the stewardess: 'Is the lady in the cabin opposite dead yet?' However, her condition improved when the ship docked at Madeira, and although she subsequently became ill again whenever the weather was rough at sea, it was never quite as bad as those first days. In due course, the ship reached Cape Town, and Agatha was delighted to be back on *terra firma* for a time.

By now, she had come to know Major Belcher quite well, and to realize that travelling around the world with him was not going to be the entirely happy experience she and Archie had anticipated. The Major was very demanding, complained continually about the service, and bullied his secretary, Mr Bates, a serious, somewhat humourless young man and an excellent secretary, though nature had given him 'the appearance of a villain in a melodrama, with black hair, flashing eyes and an altogether sinister aspect'. 'Looks the complete thug, doesn't he?' Belcher said to the Christies. 'You'd say he was going to cut your throat any moment. Actually he is the most respectable fellow you have ever known.' Neither Belcher nor his secretary realized that they were being scrutinized, analyzed and filed away for future reference by a crime novelist always ready to make use of a colourful character or two.

From Cape Town Agatha travelled on to the diamond mines at Kimberley; to Salisbury and the Victoria Falls; to Livingstone where she saw crocodiles swimming about, and hippopotami; to Johannesburg, Pretoria and Durban. She and Archie managed to do a great deal of surfing at Muizenberg, in Cape Province, before facing the, in her case, dreaded sea voyage to Australia.

In Australia she was fascinated by the parrots,[5] blue and red and green, 'flying through the air in great clustering swarms', and by the gigantic tree ferns in the bush outside Melbourne. The food and the sanitary arrangements left much to

22

be desired, but staying on a sheep station in New South Wales was an unusual and enjoyable experience. In the major cities, Belcher made successful public speeches, or rather repeated the same speech which his travelling companions soon knew by heart. After visiting Tasmania, where Agatha fell in love with 'incredibly beautiful Hobart' and decided to go back and live there one day, the party proceeded to New Zealand.

Belcher had, by now, revealed himself in his true colours. The Christies found him for much of the time to be rude, overbearing, inconsiderate and oddly mean in small matters. He was continually sending Agatha out to buy him white cotton socks and neglecting to pay her for them. He behaved, Agatha remembered later, like a spoilt child, but had such immense charm when he was on his best behaviour that he was instantly forgiven. Tasmania forgotten, Agatha now thought New Zealand the most beautiful country she had ever seen, and vowed to go back one day. (However, by the time that air travel had made it possible to get there quickly, an elderly Agatha Christie had decided that her travelling days were over.)

After a lazy voyage, stopping at Fiji and other islands, Agatha and Archie arrived in Honolulu for two weeks' holiday, while Belcher stayed with friends in New Zealand, after which they all embarked upon the last and most gruelling part of their journey, a tour of Canada. It was from the Banff Springs Hotel in Banff National Park, high up in the Rockies, that Mrs Christie wrote on 26 September 1922, to Basil Willett of The Bodley Head thanking him for a cheque for forty-seven pounds, eighteen shillings and ten pence. (But, in December, back in Torquay, she wrote again asking for accounts to be sent to her, and some weeks later had occasion to point out to Mr Willett that, since he had wrongly calculated the selling price of the American edition of *The Secret Adversary*, the exchange rate being $4.45 to the pound, The Bodley Head owed her two pounds, two shillings and three pence.)

Before setting out on her tour of the Commonwealth, Agatha had virtually completed a third novel, *The Murder on the Links*, the idea for which she derived from newspaper reports of a murder in France. Masked men had broken into a house, killed the owner and left his wife bound and gagged. There were discrepancies in the wife's story, and a suggestion that she may have killed her husband. This led Agatha to invent her own plot, beginning several years later and in a different part of France.

Hercule Poirot having been a decided success on his first appearance, he and Captain Hastings were employed again in *The Murder on the Links*. The Bodley Head professed themselves pleased with the novel, but its author quarrelled with them over the jacket they provided for it. She thought its colours ugly and the actual drawing poor. In her autobiography she claims that the jacket was also misleading in that it appeared to represent a man in pyjamas on a golf-links, dying of an epileptic fit, whereas the character had been fully dressed and stabbed in the back. But, in fact, the murdered man, according to Mrs Christie's text, wore only underclothes beneath an overcoat. Whoever was in the right about the jacket, a certain amount of bad feeling was engendered between author and publisher, and Agatha secured her publisher's agreement that, in future, she should see and approve jacket designs for her books. (She had already had another difference of opinion with her publisher, during the production of her first novel, *The Mysterious Affair at Styles*, over the spelling of the hot drink, cocoa, which Miss Howse, an eccentric employee of the firm and described by Mrs Christie as a dragon, insisted should be spelled 'coco'. Agatha produced dictionaries, tins of cocoa, but failed to make any impression on Miss Howse.)

With *The Murder on the Links*, Agatha Christie returned to the murder mystery or puzzle type of novel, and to her team of Poirot and Hastings. Years later, she wrote of it:

> I think *Murder on the Links*[6] was a moderately good example of its kind – though rather melodramatic. This time I provided a love affair for Hastings. If I *had* to have a love interest in the book, I thought I might as well marry off Hastings. Truth to tell, I think I was getting a little tired of him. I might be stuck with Poirot, but no need to be stuck with Hastings too.[7]

The Murder on the Links is a more than 'a moderately good' example of its kind. Until the diabolically ingenious solution, which perhaps fails to convince because of its very complexity, the action moves swiftly, the small seaside resort on the northern coast of France rings true and is not simply an English village in disguise, and the characters, lightly sketched though they are, all come vividly to life. The skill with which Agatha Christie manipulates her plot involving two crimes committed twenty years apart is quite brilliant. Occasionally, however, she displays an odd carelessness in matters of detail. For instance, the corpse of the murdered man is described when it is viewed by Poirot and Hastings. The face is clean-shaven, the nose thin, the eyes set rather close together, and the skin bronzed. We are told that the dead man's 'lips were drawn back from his teeth and an expression of absolute amazement and terror was stamped on the livid features'. The features, it is clear, are at least intact and undamaged. But Poirot finds a short piece of lead piping which, according to him, was used to 'disfigure the victim's face so that it would be unrecognizable'. Poirot's theory of the crime, fortunately, does not hinge upon this point!

Since we are in France, Inspector Japp of Scotland Yard is not available to act as a foil for Poirot. This function is undertaken by Giraud, a young detective from the Sûreté who is already famous and inclined to pour scorn on Poirot's old-fashioned methods. Agatha Christie has confessed that, in writing *The Murder on the Links*, she was influenced less by the Sherlock Holmes stories than by Gaston Leroux's *The Mystery of the Yellow Room*. She must also have been reading A.E.W. Mason's *At the Villa Rose*, for certain events at the Villa Geneviève in *The Murder on the Links* call the 1910 mystery classic to mind.

Since their earlier adventure in Essex, Poirot and Hastings have taken furnished rooms together in London. If you did not learn from *The Big Four* (1927) that their address was 14 Farraway Street, you would have sworn that it was 221B Baker Street, for the ambience is distinctly Holmesian, as is their landlady, who is difficult to distinguish from Sherlock Holmes's Mrs Hudson. Captain Hastings works as private secretary to a Member of Parliament while Poirot pursues a retirement career as private detective, and Hastings finds time to write up Poirot's cases, just as Watson used to chronicle those of Holmes. At the end of *The Murder on the Links*, it seems likely that Hastings will propose marriage to the auburn-haired beauty he has met, and there is even a hint that he, or they, may emigrate to 'a ranch across the seas'. Mrs Christie, it would seem, was already laying her plans for the removal of Hastings from Poirot's life.

The Man in the Brown Suit (1924)

Back in London after their world tour, the Christies for a time found it difficult to settle down. Agatha longed for a cottage in the country, near enough to town for Archie to commute to the city, but far enough away for little Rosalind to be able to breathe air fresher than that of Earl's Court. Archie took some months to find a job that suited him. Eventually, however, he was offered an excellent position with Austral Trust Ltd, a city firm run by an Australian friend, Clive Baillieu. Archie was to remain with Austral Trust Ltd for the rest of his life. Now, while they searched for their place in the country, Agatha proceeded to work on her next novel.

The egregious Belcher had suggested to her, before they went on their trip, that his house, the Mill House at Dorney, would make an excellent setting for a murder. 'The Mystery of the Mill House,' he had said to her one evening when the Christies were dining there. 'Jolly good title, don't you think?' Agatha admitted that it had possibilities, and on their voyage to Cape Town Major Belcher continued to refer to it. 'But mind you,' he added, 'if you write it you must put me in it.' Agatha doubted if she could manage to create a character based entirely on someone she knew, but Belcher continued to pester her throughout their world tour. When he asked her, for the umpteenth time, 'Have you begun that book yet? Am I in it?' she replied 'Yes. You're the victim.'

But Belcher did not see himself as one of life's victims. 'You've got to make me the murderer, Agatha. Do you understand?' And Mrs Christie replied carefully, 'I understand that you *want* to be the murderer.' She had not, in fact, begun writing the book, but she did sketch out its plot while she was in South Africa, and Belcher played a leading role. 'Give him a title,' Archie suggested. 'He'd like that.' So Belcher became Sir Eustace Pedler. Agatha Christie explained later that Sir Eustace Pedler was not really meant to be Belcher,

> but he used several of Belcher's phrases, and told some of Belcher's stories. He too was a master of the art of bluff, and behind the bluff could easily be sensed an unscrupulous and interesting character. Soon I had forgotten Belcher and had Sir Eustace Pedler himself wielding the pen. It is, I think, the only time I have tried to put a real person whom I knew well into a book, and I don't think it succeeded. Belcher didn't come to life, but someone called Sir Eustace Pedler did. I suddenly found that the book was becoming rather fun to write. I only hoped The Bodley Head would approve of it.[8]

The book was written in London and, retitled *The Man in the Brown Suit* since its author thought the title proposed by Belcher too similar to her earlier ones, was delivered to The Bodley Head who 'hemmed and hawed a bit' because it was not a proper detective story but one of those thrillers which Mrs Christie seemed to find easier to write. However, they accepted it.

Agatha Christie, author of four books, was no longer the novice who had grasped eagerly the chance to have her first novel published. As she herself put it, though she had been ignorant and foolish when she first submitted a book for publication, she had since learned a few things. She had discovered the Society of Authors and read its periodical, from which she learned that you had to be extremely careful in making contracts with publishers, 'and especially with certain publishers'. When The Bodley Head, who still had an option on her next two books after *The Man in the Brown Suit*, suggested shortly before its publication that they scrap the old contract and make a new one for a further five books, Mrs Christie politely declined. She considered that they had not treated a young and inexperienced author fairly, but had taken advantage of her ignorance of publishers' contracts and her understandable eagerness to have her first book published.

It was at this point that Agatha Christie decided she needed a literary agent and went back to the firm of Hughes Massie. Massie, who had advised her years earlier, had since died, and she was received by a young man with a slight stammer, whose name was Edmund Cork. Finding him impressive, and considerably less alarming than Hughes Massie himself had been, Mrs Christie placed her literary career, such as it was, in Cork's hands, and left his office feeling that an enormous weight had been lifted from her shoulders. It was the beginning of a friendship which lasted for more than fifty years until her death. Edmund Cork has now retired from Hughes Massie Ltd, but the firm still represents the Agatha Christie Literary Estate.

The Evening News offered what seemed to Agatha Christie the unbelievable sum of £500 for the serial rights of *The Man in the Brown Suit*, which she hastily accepted, deciding not to object that the newspaper intended to call the serial version 'Anna the Adventuress', as silly a title as she had ever heard. That she should receive such a huge amount of money, was, she thought, an extraordinary stroke of luck and, when Archie suggested she buy a car with it, Agatha invested in a grey, bottle-nosed Morris Cowley which, she revealed many years later, was the first of the two most exciting things in her life. (The second was her invitation to dine with Queen Elizabeth II at Buckingham Palace many years later.)

The Man in the Brown Suit, another of the thrillers which Agatha Christie found easier and 'more fun' to write than her detective stories, is one of her best in that genre. The heroine, Anne Beddingfield, is a romantic young woman whose archaeologist father dies, leaving her little more than the opportunity to be free and to seek adventure. Adventure, for Anne, begins when she witnesses the apparently accidental death of a man who falls onto the electrified rails at Hyde Park Corner tube station. Finding reason to suspect that the man's death was not accidental, Anne persuades the great newspaper magnate Lord Nasby, 'millionaire owner of the *Daily Budget*' and several other papers, to commission her to investigate the matter. (For Nasby, we are probably meant to read Northcliffe.) A second death occurs at the Mill House, Marlow, whose owner is Sir Eustace Pedler, MP, and the trail leads Anne to sail to Cape Town on the *Kilmorden Castle*. On board, she meets Sir Eustace, a character whom Agatha Christie, as we know, based largely on Major Belcher, and his secretary, Guy Pagett, who, like the real-life secretary of Belcher, 'has the face of a fourteenth-century poisoner'. Anne, like Agatha herself, proves to be a very poor sailor, and it is not until they reach Madeira that she begins to feel she might possibly recover from her seasickness.

With the exception of a Prologue set in Paris, the entire action of the novel takes place either *en route* to, or in South Africa and Rhodesia, and is presented through the diaries of Anne and Sir Eustace. The villain is a master criminal who organizes crime 'as another man might organize a boot factory'. Jewel robberies, forgery, espionage, assassination, he has dabbled in them all. He is known to his underlings simply as 'the Colonel', and it falls to Anne finally to unmask him, with the aid of two or three friends.

Who Anne's friends are, and who her enemies, is something which Mrs Christie keeps her readers guessing about. Like all Christie thrillers, *The Man in the Brown Suit* incorporates the puzzle element into its plot as well. Thus it retains a hold on the loyalties of those who prefer the murder mystery to the thriller, for it conceals until the last pages the identity of 'the Colonel' (who is, after all, a murderer), while at the same time including all the ingredients of the 'international crime' story: action, violence, suspense. Whether or not the charming old rogue Sir Eustace Pedler is at all like Major Belcher, he is one of Agatha Christie's most convincing and memorable characters, and the author's underestimated ability to convey a strong sense of place is very much in evidence in her discreet but effective description of the exotic African landscape through which Pedler, Anne and the others move.

It might be thought that to present the narrative through the diaries of two characters detracts somewhat from the suspense, or at least from the list of suspects. But with Agatha Christie you cannot always be certain that anyone is above suspicion. Diaries can also be published posthumously. (This is not necessarily a clue.) In *The Man in the Brown Suit* Mrs Christie makes use of a device which, to a certain extent, anticipates her tactics in *The Murder of Roger Ackroyd* (1926), though less spectacularly.

It need not impair enjoyment of the novel to know that one of the characters, a strong silent man called Colonel Race, will appear in three later Agatha Christie novels, ageing over forty years in the process. In fact, enjoyment of *The Man in the Brown Suit* will be impaired only if you take too seriously the African revolution which seems to be trying to foment itself offstage. Mrs Christie, never an acute political observer, rather charmingly recalls in her autobiography that 'there was some kind of a revolutionary crisis on while we were there, and I noted down a few useful facts.' Those facts must have got lost somewhere.

Poirot Investigates (1924)

One of Hercule Poirot's earliest fans was Bruce Ingram, editor of the London illustrated weekly, *The Sketch*. Ingram got in touch with Agatha Christie to suggest that she should write a series of Hercule Poirot stories for his magazine, and a thrilled and delighted Agatha agreed. She was not entirely pleased with the drawing of Hercule Poirot which *The Sketch* commissioned to accompany the first of the stories: it was not unlike her idea of Poirot but it made him look a little too smart and dandified. Agatha Christie wrote eight stories, and at first it was thought that eight would be sufficient. However, it was eventually decided to extend the series to twelve, and the author had to produce another four rather too hastily. When the series of stories began, in the 7 March 1923 issue of *The Sketch*, it was accompanied by a page of photographs of 'The Maker of "The Grey Cells of M. Poirot"', showing her at home with her daughter, in her drawing-room, on the telephone, at her writing table, at work with her typewriter and so on.

The author of 'the thrilling set of detective yarns' made it clear to The Bodley Head that she thought they should publish them quickly as a volume of stories, while the publicity from their appearance in *The Sketch* and from the serialization of *The Man in the Brown Suit* in the London *Evening News* was still current. The Bodley Head agreed, and the stories were collected in a volume which, at first, it was intended should be called *The Grey Cells of Monsieur Poirot*, but which, in due course, appeared as *Poirot Investigates*. The volume was also published in the United States (by Dodd, Mead & Co, who remain Agatha Christie's American hardback publishers), but there is a discrepancy between the British and American editions. The British volume consisted of eleven stories while the American edition contained fourteen. (The three extra stories, 'The Lost Mine', 'The Chocolate Box' and 'The Veiled Lady' eventually appeared in Great Britain, along with several other stories, fifty years later in *Poirot's Early Cases*. 'The Veiled Lady' was also published, together with two other stories, in *Poirot Lends a Hand* [1946: see p. 138].)

Some, though not many, of Agatha Christie's short stories are as satisfying as the best of her novels. In general, however, her talent is not suited to the short story, or at least not to the very short mystery story of which she wrote so many. Her plots are, perforce, skeletal, and her characterization at its most perfunctory. The puzzle element is, therefore, given even greater emphasis than in the novels in which it contributes largely to the reader's pleasure. Many of the stories, including most of the Hercule Poirot adventures collected in *Poirot Investigates*, are little more than puzzles or tricks given 'a local habitation and a name'.

Prior to the emergence of Agatha Christie upon the crime writers' scene, many of the genre's greatest successes were with short stories. It is generally agreed, for instance, that Conan Doyle's Sherlock Holmes stories are superior to the Holmes novels, and most of the other mystery writers who flourished at the same time as Conan Doyle, among them G.K. Chesterton (with his Catholic priest-detective Father Brown), Baroness Orczy, Richard Austin Freeman (whose detective was the physician Dr John Thorndyke), the American Melville Davisson Post (whose mysteries are solved by Uncle Abner, a shrewd Virginian), H.C. Bailey with his Mr Fortune stories, and Ernest Bramah, all produced their most successful work in the form of the short story. However, though she wrote more than a hundred and fifty short stories, Agatha Christie's greatest triumphs were to be achieved with her full-length novels, rather than with short stories or novellas.

That so many of Agatha Christie's stories are little more than puzzles or tricks might not matter so much were the puzzles more varied and the tricks less repetitive. For instance, the first time that Poirot points the accusing finger accurately at the person who engaged him, the reader is surprised and delighted; but M. Poirot and Mrs Christie connive several times at this particular trick, which is also not unknown in the novels.

The stories in *Poirot Investigates* are, on their own level, quite entertaining, but it would be as unwise to read more than one or two at a sitting as it would be to consume a two-pound box of chocolates in one go. Occasionally, Mrs Christie's touch falters, as when, in 'The Adventure of the Italian Nobleman' she is snide about Inspector Japp's French accent and has him refer to the 'boat train to the *Continong*'. Why would he not pronounce 'continent' as an English word? But usually her social placing is exact. In 'The Case of the Missing Will', Poirot's client, a handsome young woman, explains that her father, who came of farming stock, 'married slightly above him; my mother was the daughter of a poor artist.'

'The Adventure of the Egyptian Tomb', in which Poirot investigates a strange series of deaths of people who were involved in the discovery and opening of the tomb of King Men-her-Ra, an event which we are told followed hard upon the discovery of the tomb of Tutankhamun by Lord Carnarvon, is interesting as evidence that Agatha Christie was conversant with the science of archaeology some years before she met Max Mallowan. (She had already introduced an archaeologist into her collection of characters in *The Man in the Brown Suit*.)

One of the best stories in *Poirot Investigates* is 'The Kidnapped Prime Minister'. It is also one in which we learn something more of the author's political opinions, or opinions which it seems reasonably safe to attribute to the author even though she issues them through the mouths of her characters and not by way of authorial comment. It is unlikely that, in 1923, any irony was intended in the opening sentence of the story (even a story narrated by the not very shrewd Hastings), which begins, 'Now that war and the problems of war are things of the past . . .' But pacifism takes a knocking at more than one point in the story, and the statement made by someone meant to be a leading British politician that 'the Pacifist propaganda, started and maintained by the German agents in our midst, has been very active' seems to be accepted by Poirot and Hastings without modification. The politician is 'Lord Estair, Leader of the House of Commons'. Is it, in fact, possible for a nobleman to lead the House of Commons? Apparently, if his is a courtesy title.

It is in 'The Kidnapped Prime Minister' that Poirot most clearly describes his method. He has declined to leap into a military car at Boulogne and set off in pursuit of the kidnappers:

> He shot a quick glance at us. 'It is not so that the good detective should act, eh? I perceive your thought. He must be full of energy. He must rush to and fro. He should prostrate himself on the dusty road and seek the marks of tyres through a little glass. He must gather up the cigarette-end, the fallen match? That is your idea, is it not?'
>
> His eyes challenged us. 'But I – Hercule Poirot – tell you that it is not so! The true clues are within – *here*!' He tapped his forehead. 'See you, I need not have left London. It would have been sufficient for me to sit quietly in my rooms there. All that matters is the little grey cells within. Secretly and silently they do their part, until suddenly I call for a map, and I lay my finger on a spot – so – and I say: the Prime Minister is *there*! and it is so!'

Nevertheless, when it suits him Poirot is not at all averse to snooping about, gathering up the cigarette-end and the fallen match. He has sufficient confidence and vanity to contradict himself whenever he feels like it. In these early stories, he is at his most Holmesian, and the parallels with the minutiae of the Conan Doyle stories are most noticeable. Hastings, similarly, has become more Watsonian than ever, and in some of the stories Mrs Christie treats his relationship with Poirot mechanically. In addition to the stories already mentioned, the volume contains 'The Adventure of "The Western Star" ', 'The Tragedy at Marsdon Manor', 'The Adventure of the Cheap Flat', 'The Mystery of Hunter's Lodge', 'The Million Dollar Bond Robbery', 'The Jewel Robbery at the *Grand Metropolitan*' and 'The Disappearance of Mr Davenheim'.

The Road of Dreams (1924)

Ever since she was a child, Agatha Christie had written poetry. One of her earliest efforts, written at the age of eleven, begins: 'I knew a little cowslip and a pretty flower too,/Who wished she was a bluebell and had a robe of blue.' In her teens, she had occasional poems published in magazines, and by the time she was in her mid-thirties there were enough of them to be gathered into a slim volume which, in 1924, the London publishing house of Geoffrey Bles published, under the title of *The Road of Dreams*. This was also the title of one of the poems in the volume ('The Road of Dreams leads up the Hill/So straight and white/And bordered wide/With almond trees on either side/In rosy flush of Spring's delight! . . .')

Agatha Christie's talent for poetry was genuine, but modest and of no startling originality: the finest poetry is made not out of feelings but out of words, and Agatha Christie was not sufficiently in love with words to become a poet of real distinction. She did, however, enjoy relieving her feelings in verse and, in doing so, occasionally produced a pleasant little lyric poem.

The Road of Dreams is divided into four sections. The first, 'A Masque from Italy', is a sequence of nine poems or 'songs' to be performed by the *commedia dell' arte* characters, Harlequin and Columbine, Pierrot and Pierrette, Punchinello and Pulcinella. Written when Agatha was in her late teens, the Harlequin poems have a certain wistfulness which is appealing. They are of interest, too, in that they anticipate the Harlequin element which was later to creep into some of her short stories, those involving that mysterious character Mr Harley Quin.

The second section of the volume, 'Ballads', consists of six poems, among them 'Elizabeth of England' ('I am Mistress of England – the Seas I hold!/I have gambled, and won, alone . . .'), which is presumably one of the author's teenage efforts, and 'Ballad of the Maytime', a fey little ballad about bluebells which Mrs Christie wrote in 1924 in Sunningdale.

One or two of the eight poems in 'Dreams and Fantasies', the third section of the volume, are romantically death-obsessed – Keats' 'La belle dame sans merci' is not too far away – and one of them, 'Down in the Wood', which forty years later Mrs Christie still liked sufficiently to reprint in her autobiography, is rather good, with a last line that lingers in the memory: 'And Fear – naked Fear passes out of the wood!' The volume's final section, 'Other Poems', consists of thirteen poems written at various times, about the passing of love, the horror of war and the romance of the unknown. Again, there is a certain amount of evidence that the poet is 'half in love with easeful death':

> Give me my hour within my Lover's arms!
> Vanished the doubts, the fears, the sweet alarms!
> I lose myself within his quickening Breath. . . .
> *And when he tires and leaves me – there is Death . . .*

Mystery is never completely absent from any aspect of Agatha Christie's world, and there are one or two minor mysteries connected with this innocuous volume. The crime writer Michael Gilbert in an article on Agatha Christie[9] mentions the volume's title poem, 'The Road of Dreams', and quotes two stanzas from it. But the stanzas he quotes are part of a completely different poem in the volume, a poem called 'In a Dispensary' which Agatha Miller wrote in her mid-twenties when she was working in the hospital dispensary in Torquay.

Mystery number two is provided by the author of a book described as 'an intimate biography of the first lady of crime'[10] who says that Agatha Christie exposed her love for Max Mallowan 'for all the world to see in a poem entitled "To M.E.L.M. in Absence" in *The Road of Dreams* (1924)'. But there is no such poem in *The Road of Dreams*, and Agatha Christie did not meet Max Mallowan until several years after 1924: to be precise, in 1930.

A stanza from 'In a Dispensary' which is not quoted in Michael Gilbert's article clearly reveals the future crime writer's interest in the poisons on the dispensary shelves among which she worked:

> From the Borgia's time to the present day, their power has
>   been proved and tried!
> Monkshead blue, called Aconite, and the deadly Cyanide!
> Here is sleep and solace and soothing of pain – courage
>   and vigour new!
> Here is menace and murder and sudden death! – in these
>   phials of green and blue!

The final poem in the volume is 'Pierrot Grown Old', which reads as though it ought to have been part of the *commedia dell' arte* sequence, 'A Masque from Italy', with which *The Road of Dreams* begins. (When the contents of *The Road of Dreams* were reprinted in *Poems* nearly fifty years later, 'Pierrot Grown Old' was, in fact, taken into the 'Masque' sequence.)

The Secret of Chimneys (1925)

Archie and Agatha did not find the cottage in the country for which they were searching. Instead, they took a flat in a large Victorian country house, which had been divided into four flats. The house, Scotswood, was at Sunningdale in Berkshire, only twenty-four miles from London and close to the Sunningdale Golf Club of which Archie had become a member. Golf was such a passion with Colonel Christie that before long Mrs Christie began to fear she was turning into 'that well-known figure, a golf widow'. She consoled herself by writing *The Secret of Chimneys*, which she later described as 'light-hearted and rather in the style of *The Secret Adversary*'.

Before leaving London for the country, Agatha had taken lessons in sculpture. She was a great admirer of the art, much more than of painting, and was disappointed when she became aware that she possessed no real talent for it. 'By way of vanity', she composed a few songs instead. Her musical education in Paris had been thorough and there had been a moment in her life when she even considered taking up the career of a professional pianist. She also had a pleasant singing voice, so it was appropriate that she should turn, however briefly, to the composition of songs, and equally appropriate that she should set some of her own verses to music. In later years, she continued to profess herself quite pleased with one group of songs in particular, settings of her Pierrot and Harlequin verses. She realized, however, that writing seemed to be the trade to which she was best suited.

After a few months at Scotswood, the Christies decided that they needed a house of their own, and they began to look at properties in the vicinity of Sunningdale. Their choice fell upon a large house with a pleasant garden, and, in 1925, after less than two years in their flat in the country, they moved into their own country house which, at Archie's suggestion, they named Styles after the house in *The Mysterious Affair at Styles*.

Agatha's literary agent, Edmund Cork, had been busy extricating his client from her involvement with The Bodley Head. Cork approached the firm of Collins who had begun to add detective novels to their list, and offered them the first Agatha Christie title which did not have contractually to be offered to The Bodley Head. A three-book contract was signed with Collins as early as 27 January 1924, though there were at that time two volumes still to be published by The Bodley Head. *The Secret of Chimneys* was the last Agatha Christie novel to appear under The Bodley Head's imprint. Collins became her English publishers for the rest of the author's life.

The Secret of Chimneys is one of the best of Agatha Christie's early thrillers. It is, in its way, as typical of its time, the twenties, as Michael Arlen's *The Green Hat* or P.G. Wodehouse's *The Inimitable Jeeves*, both of which were published several months before *Chimneys*. It also owes something to the Ruritanian world of Anthony Hope's *The Prisoner of Zenda*, for its plot is concerned with political events in the fictitious small Balkan state of Herzoslovakia, the character of whose people appears to be of an almost Montenegran fierceness. After a beginning in Bulawayo, however, the events of the novel take place not in the Balkans but in London or at Chimneys, one of the stately homes of England and the seat of the ninth Marquis of Caterham. Chimneys, we are told, is as much a national possession as a grand country house, and history has been made at its informal weekend parties. It was perhaps not unlike Cliveden.

Diplomatic intrigue involving the possible reinstatement of the Herzoslovakian royal family and international crime concerning the attempts of a jewel thief known throughout Europe as 'King Victor' are ingeniously combined in *The Secret of Chimneys*, and at the end two characters are unmasked and revealed in their true colours, though only one of them is a criminal.

It is when she is freed of some of the restrictions of the domestic murder mystery, as in this type of novel, that Mrs Christie seems able to relax into more leisurely, and, therefore, more detailed and believable characterization. Believable, that is, in the context of your willingly suspended disbelief; for, although the reader greatly enjoys making the acquaintance of, for instance, Baron Lolopretjzyl who represents in London the Loyalist Party of Herzoslovakia, it has to be admitted that the Baron's construction of English sentences is a trifle more exotic than it need be. 'Of many secrets he the knowledge had. Should he reveal but the quarter of them, Europe into war plunged may be,' he says of a fellow countryman.

The Baron resides in a suite at Harridge's Hotel. Mrs Christie's London hotels are only lightly disguised. Mr Anthony Cade, who may or may not be the hero of the story, stays at the Blitz, which seems an inappropriate, indeed irreverent, name for an hotel clearly based on the Ritz. The Blitz, however, is oddly situated. Although, at one point, it appears to be where it ought to be, in Piccadilly, when Anthony Cade first arrives he strolls outside for a brief walk on the Embankment, for all the world as though he were staying at the Savoy.

Though it is not he but one of the upperclass amateurs who solves the secret of Chimneys, Superintendent Battle who is in charge of the case is no plodding and unimaginative policeman inserted into the plot to be the butt of the amateur genius's humour. Battle is not at all like Inspector Japp (who is mentally continually trailing along some steps behind Hercule Poirot's thought processes): he is an intelligent and successful officer whose speciality appears to be crimes in which politics or international diplomacy are involved. Outwardly a stolid and impassive figure, Battle reaches his conclusions by a dogged application of common sense. After *The Secret of Chimneys*, he was to appear in four more Christie novels in some of which he would deal with purely domestic crimes.

Occasionally, Agatha Christie carried over from one book to another characters other than her detectives and policemen. Not only Superintendent Battle but also four other characters from *The Secret of Chimneys* appear again four years later in *The Seven Dials Mystery*, as does the house, Chimneys. The house itself, and the kind of life lived in it, plays a lively part in both novels. Chroniclers of a fast disappearing scene will be interested to note that the lavish English breakfast was still very much in evidence in the twenties. On the sideboard in the dining-room were half a score of heavy silver dishes, 'ingeniously kept hot by patent arrangements'. Lord Caterham lifts each lid in turn. 'Omelette,' he mutters, 'eggs and bacon, kidneys, devilled bird, haddock, cold ham, cold pheasant.' Deciding he cares for none of these things, he tells his butler to 'ask the cook to poach me an egg.'

The mandatory racial slurs occur in *The Secret of Chimneys*, though apparently they have been edited out of more recent American editions. 'Dagos will be dagos', 'Like all dagos, he couldn't swim', and other remarks are cheerfully exchanged, and of course all references to Jews are uncomplimentary. People are beginning to be interested in Herzoslovakia, Anthony Cade tells his friend Jimmy, and, when asked what kind of people, he replies, 'Hebraic people. Yellow-faced financiers in city offices.' When we meet one of these financiers, Herman Isaacstein, we are invited to smile at Lord Caterham's references to him as 'Mr Ikey Isaacstein', 'Noseystein', and 'Fat Ikey'. But the true-blue British unemployed are treated with equal contempt. When Anthony Cade disguises himself as an out-of-work ex-serviceman, the upperclass Virginia Revel takes one look at him and decides that he is 'a more pleasing specimen than usual of London's unemployed'.

Her attitude to democracy is so unsympathetic, at least as expressed by a character of whom Mrs Christie evidently approves, that it reveals an unexpectedly authoritarian aspect of the author's nature:

Mind you, I still believe in democracy. But you've got to force it on people with a strong hand – ram it down their throats. Men don't want to be brothers – they may some day, but they don't now. My belief in the brotherhood of man died the day I arrived in London last week, when I observed the people standing in a Tube train resolutely refuse to move up and make room for those who entered. You won't turn people into angels by appealing to their better natures yet awhile – but by judicious force you can coerce them into behaving more or less decently to one another to go on with.

33

It is true that people on the Moscow underground are less surly in their behaviour than those in London and New York, but you would hesitate to use the citizenry of Moscow as a kind of democratic barometer. Even Agatha Christie, one imagines, if she had been offered the choice would have preferred to be bad-tempered in a democracy than polite in a police state.

The danger of pontificating solemnly on the subject of Agatha Christie's politics must, however, be guarded against. The author tells us in *The Secret of Chimneys* that there was nothing that bored Lord Caterham more than politics, unless it was politicians, and one suspects that she shared his Lordship's feelings. No one need be deterred from enjoying *The Secret of Chimneys* by Agatha Christie's politics, nor even by occasional infelicities in her prose style, though prose is more serious a matter than politics. Is there not something endearing about an author who can write the phrase, 'eyeing a taxi that was crawling past with longing eyes'?

In general, Mrs Christie's grasp of style is firm: *The Secret of Chimneys* is enjoyable because its style is light and humorous. It is not, like Anthony Hope's *The Prisoner of Zenda*, an adventure-romance, but a comedy-adventure, which is perhaps a new category.

The Murder of Roger Ackroyd (1926)

It seems now to be generally accepted that the basic idea for *The Murder of Roger Ackroyd* was given to Agatha Christie by Lord Mountbatten. Mountbatten certainly continued to claim, on every possible occasion, that this was so. But a variant of the idea, whether you regard it as an outrageous fraud or remarkably original or both, had earlier been suggested by Mrs Christie's brother-in-law, James Watts, and the author was already mulling it over. It appealed greatly to her, but before starting to write the novel she had to work out just how to make use of the startling suggestion (which will not be revealed in these pages), in such a way that it could not be regarded as cheating the reader. Of course, as Mrs Christie was to admit in her autobiography, a number of people do consider themselves cheated when they come to the end of *The Murder of Roger Ackroyd*, but if they read it carefully they will see that they are wrong, for 'such little lapses of time as there have to be are nicely concealed in an ambiguous sentence'.

It was with *The Murder of Roger Ackroyd*, by far the most ingenious crime novel she had written, that Agatha Christie's reputation took a great leap forward, and so did her sales. The author's solution to the mystery is still debated in books and articles on crime fiction, more than half a century after the novel's first publication, and although its immediate success meant no more than that an edition of approximately five thousand copies sold out, *The Murder of Roger Ackroyd* must by now have sold well over a million copies.

Critics and readers were divided on the propriety of Mrs Christie's brilliant trick. Though the *Daily Sketch* thought it 'the best thriller ever', the *News Chronicle* considered *The Murder of Roger Ackroyd* a 'tasteless and unfortunate let-down by a writer we had grown to admire'. One reader wrote a letter to *The Times* in which he announced that, having been a great admirer of Agatha Christie, he was so shocked by the dénouement of *Roger Ackroyd* that he proposed 'in the future not to buy any more of her books'. Even some of her fellow crime novelists thought she had not played fair, though Dorothy L.

Sayers, author of a number of detective novels featuring Lord Peter Wimsey as investigator, defended Mrs Christie by pointing out that 'it's the reader's business to suspect everybody'.

Agatha Christie herself remained unrepentant. In an interview with Francis Wyndham in 1966, she explained: 'I have a certain amount of rules. No false words must be uttered by me. To write "Mrs Armstrong walked home wondering who had committed the murder" would be unfair if she had done it herself. But it's not unfair to leave things out. In *Roger Ackroyd* . . . there's lack of explanation there, but no false statement. Whoever my villain is, it has to be someone I feel *could* do the murder.'[11]

Lord Mountbatten's claim to be responsible for having given Agatha Christie the idea for *Roger Ackroyd* should probably be taken with a pinch of salt. It is true that, at Christmas in 1969, he received from the author a copy of the book, inscribed: 'To Lord Mountbatten in grateful remembrance of a letter he wrote to me forty-five years ago which contained the suggestion which I subsequently used in a book called *The Murder of Roger Ackroyd*. Here once more is my thanks.' However, this was in response to a letter from Mountbatten reminding her that he had written to her forty-five years earlier.

Whether Agatha Christie thought *Roger Ackroyd* her best book is uncertain, but she usually mentioned it as among her three or four favourites.

In *The Murder of Roger Ackroyd*, dedicated not to Lord Mountbatten but 'to PUNKIE,[12] who likes an orthodox detective story, murder, inquest, and suspicion falling on every one in turn!', Agatha Christie returned to the classical domestic crime novel for the first time since *Murder on the Links* three years earlier, and at the same time reintroduced Hercule Poirot who, apart from the short stories in *Poirot Investigates*, had also been missing for three years.

The story, narrated not by Poirot's usual associate, Hastings, but by the local doctor whose name is Sheppard, begins with the death of someone other than Roger Ackroyd. Mrs Ferrars, a wealthy widow, has been found dead in her bed, and Dr Sheppard has been sent for. He suspects suicide, but sees no point in saying so publicly. The following evening Roger Ackroyd, a wealthy widower whom village gossip had prophesied would marry Mrs Ferrars, is murdered in the study of his house.

We are soon introduced to Dr Sheppard's sister Caroline who keeps house for him, and to the Sheppards' neighbour, a recent arrival in the village of King's Abbot. He is a foreign gentleman with 'an egg-shaped head, partially covered with suspiciously black hair, two immense moustaches, and a pair of watchful eyes'. He has retired from whatever his profession may have been, grows vegetable marrows, and is thought to be called Porrott.

Porrott, of course, is simply the King's Abbot pronunciation of Poirot, and soon the retired detective has introduced himself to Dr Sheppard, has admitted how bored he is with his vegetable marrows, and how much he misses his friend ('who for many years never left my side') who is now living in the Argentine. When Poirot is asked to investigate the murder of Roger Ackroyd, he allows Dr Sheppard to take the place of his old friend Hastings as assistant and part-confidant; and also as Boswell to Poirot's Johnson, for it is Sheppard who writes up the case and is the chronicler of Poirot's eventual success.

It is not a success which comes easily to Poirot, for the suspects are many and varied. Most of them were staying in Ackroyd's house when he was murdered.

Major Blunt, a big-game hunter, is an old friend, and appears to have a romantic interest in Ackroyd's niece, Flora. Flora and her mother, who is Ackroyd's widowed sister-in-law, are poor relations living on a rich man's charity. Geoffrey Raymond, the dead man's secretary, Ursula Bourne, a somewhat unusual parlourmaid, and Ralph Paton, Ackroyd's adopted son who is burdened with gambling debts, all come under suspicion.

Poirot is assisted not only by Dr Sheppard but by the doctor's sister Caroline, a middle-aged spinster who seems to know everything that goes on in the village. Many years later, in discussing the character of Miss Marple, an unconventional solver of puzzles whom she was to introduce in *Murder at the Vicarage*, Agatha Christie said she thought it possible that Miss Marple 'arose from the pleasure I had taken in portraying Dr Sheppard's sister in *The Murder of Roger Ackroyd*. She had been my favourite character in the book – an acidulated spinster, full of curiosity, knowing everything, hearing everything: the complete detective service in the home.'

It is not simply because of its startling dénouement that *The Murder of Roger Ackroyd* has remained one of Agatha Christie's most popular novels. The story is believable, the characters convincing, and Mrs Christie's ear for dialogue is accurate. That she can occasionally be clumsy ought not to obscure the fact that, on form, she writes speech which sounds natural, whether it issues from the mouth of a peeress or a parlourmaid. Even more impressive is her ability to enter into the thought processes of her male characters. Dr Sheppard, the narrator of *Roger Ackroyd*, is a fully rounded and perfectly convincing character, and his loving, exasperated relationship with his sister Caroline, an amusing and acutely observed character, is beautifully conveyed. Another important ingredient in the success of the novel is the background of English village life which Mrs Christie provides. It is never obtrusive but it is there, and it is important.

From *The Murder of Roger Ackroyd* onwards, Agatha Christie's readers knew what to expect, or rather knew that they would never know what to expect. And it is this quality of unexpectedness which makes Mrs Christie unique among crime writers. Dorothy L. Sayers writes more elegantly but also, at times, more ploddingly. Her stories do not move quickly. Ngaio Marsh is in the Christie tradition but can get bogged down in endless interviews with suspects. Patricia Wentworth is pastiche Christie and her villains can usually be guessed. After the trick she played on her public in *Roger Ackroyd* (though some of those who remembered *The Man in the Brown Suit* ought perhaps not to have been taken in), clearly there were no holds barred. It is this realization that no one, absolutely no one, is exempt from suspicion in an Agatha Christie novel that makes reading the finest ones such a delight. Here she will kill off all the characters, there she will make virtually everyone the murderer, somewhere else the crime will be committed by – no, surely not by him? But how could she possibly justify that? Well, she does.

Her puzzles endure to delight and surprise readers towards the end of the twentieth century just as much as they did in the twenties because they are not mechanical but concerned with human character. The locked-room mysteries beloved of John Dickson Carr are of no great interest to Agatha Christie, nor are the fiendish devices, the evaporating ice darts or any of the other paraphernalia used by some of the earlier crime writers. Her tricks are sometimes verbal, sometimes visual. If you listen carefully and watch her all the time, you *may* catch Mrs Christie, but it is highly unlikely that you will. The solution which she has somehow persuaded you quite early in the narrative is *not* the correct one very frequently *is* – but not invariably.

Mrs Christie is at her best throughout *The Murder of Roger Ackroyd*. The occasional Christie carelessness is there, as when she tells us that Ackroyd is nearly fifty years of age, and a paragraph or two later it becomes clear that he could not have been older than forty-three. And Poirot's years in England have caused his command of French to deteriorate. He says 'Je ne pense pas' when he clearly means 'Je crois que non', and in any case is perfectly capable of saying 'I think not' in English. But these are minor quibbles. In Dr Sheppard and his sister Mrs Christie has created a pair of highly engaging characters, and her description of Caroline Sheppard, tempted to gossip, but wavering for a second or two 'much as a roulette ball might coyly hover between two numbers', is especially felicitous.

You can usually expect a little music in her books and, at least in the early Christies, a little anti-semitism. Both are to be found in *Roger Ackroyd*. Oddly, it is the unmusical Major Blunt who provides the two references to opera when he talks of 'the johnny who sold his soul to the devil' and mentions that 'there's an opera about it', and later reveals his knowledge that Mélisande is someone in an opera. Agatha Christie probably saw both *Faust* and *Pelléas et Mélisande* during her period at finishing school in Paris, but you would not have expected Major Blunt to know Debussy's opera though he might just have been aware of the more popular *Faust* of Gounod. Blunt, incidentally, is a name Mrs Christie seems to have been fond of using. Three more Blunts, one of them an Admiral, will turn up in later works.

The mandatory anti-semitic reference occurs when one of the characters receives demands from debt collectors (Scotch [sic] gentlemen named McPherson and MacDonald), and Dr Sheppard comments: 'They are usually Scotch gentlemen, but I suspect a Semitic strain in their ancestry.'

Two years after its publication, *The Murder of Roger Ackroyd* was adapted for the stage by Michael Morton. Mrs Christie much disliked Morton's first suggestion which was to take about twenty years off Poirot's age, call him Beau Poirot, and have lots of girls in love with him. With the support of Gerald Du Maurier who produced the play, she persuaded the adaptor not to change the character and personality of Poirot, but agreed to allow Caroline Sheppard to be turned into a young and attractive girl, in order to supply Poirot with romantic interest. Mrs Christie's agreement was reluctant. She resented the removal of the spinster Caroline, for she liked the role played by this character in the life of the village, and she liked the idea of that village life being reflected through Dr Sheppard and his sister. In the play, Poirot confesses to Dr Sheppard that he loves Caryl, as she is now called, and although at the end the great detective announces his intention to leave 'for my own country', the final moments suggest that he may, one day, come back for Caryl:

POIROT (taking both her hands and kissing them): *Un de ces jours* . . .
CARYL: What do you mean?
POIROT: Perhaps one day . . .
    (Caryl goes out slowly. Poirot turns back to table, takes rose out of

specimen glass which is on table, kisses it, and puts it in his button-hole, looking off towards the garden where Caryl has gone out.)
The curtain falls.

The play, which was called *Alibi*, opened on 15 May 1928, at the Prince of Wales Theatre in the West End of London, with the twenty-nine-year-old Charles Laughton as Hercule Poirot, J.H. Roberts as Dr Sheppard, Basil Loder as Major Blunt, Henry Daniell (who went to Hollywood the following year to play suave villains in countless American films) as Parker, the butler, Lady Tree as Mrs Ackroyd, Jane Welsh as her daughter Flora, Cyril Nash as Ralph Paton, Henry Forbes Robertson as Geoffrey Raymond, Iris Noel as Ursula Bourne, and Gillian Lind as Caryl Sheppard. *The Sketch* said that Laughton 'admirably impersonated' Poirot, and Mrs Christie thought he was a good actor but 'entirely unlike Hercule Poirot'. The play was a commercial success, running for 250 performances in London before being taken up elsewhere and eventually by amateur dramatic societies with whom it is still highly popular.

In 1931, the play became a film, still with the title of *Alibi*. Produced by Julius Hagen, who had already made an Agatha Christie movie in 1928 (see p. 57), and directed by Leslie Hiscott, *Alibi* was filmed at the Twickenham studios near London, with Austin Trevor who was even less like Hercule Poirot than Laughton had been, and who made no attempt at a characterization, but played the role 'straight'. Others in the cast were Franklin Dyall, Elizabeth Allan, Clare Greet and Milton Rosmer. (Max Mallowan in his autobiography, *Mallowan's Memoirs*, wrongly identifies the actor who played Poirot in this film as Francis Sullivan, who played Poirot twice on the stage, but who was not in either the film or the stage version of *Alibi*.)

Retitled *The Fatal Alibi*, the play was staged in New York on 28 February 1932, with Charles Laughton directing and also playing Poirot. It closed after twenty-four performances.

The first of Agatha Christie's books to be produced in Great Britain by Collins and in America by Dodd, Mead & Co who had bought John Lane and Co, *The Murder of Roger Ackroyd* was published in the spring of 1926. Seven months later, on Friday, 3 December, Mrs Christie disappeared in mysterious circumstances worthy of one of her crime novels.

The year 1926 had been far from a happy one for Agatha Christie. It began well enough with a brief holiday in Corsica with her sister, during which she worked on *The Mystery of the Blue Train*, but shortly after the sisters arrived home they learned that their mother was ill and some months later she found herself also having to cope with the realization that her marriage to Archie Christie had badly deteriorated. For some time Colonel Christie had seemed to be more interested in golf than in his wife, and now Agatha discovered that she had a more serious rival for her husband's affections, a young woman called Nancy Neele who lived at Godalming in Surrey and who was also an acquaintance of hers. Archie confessed that he was in love with Miss Neele and wanted to marry her. He asked Agatha to divorce him.

On the morning of Friday, 3 December 1926, after a quarrel with his wife, Colonel Christie packed his bags and left home to spend the weekend with Miss Neele in Godalming. That evening, leaving her daughter Rosalind asleep in the house, Mrs Christie drove off in her car. She left two letters, one addressed to Archie, and one requesting her secretary to cancel her appointments as she was going to Yorkshire. According to the daughter of the then Deputy Chief Constable of Surrey, she posted a letter to the Deputy Chief Constable, in which she said she feared for her life, and appealed for his help. Her car was found next morning by George Best, a fifteen-year-old gypsy lad. It had been abandoned on the embankment at the side of the road at a popular 'beauty spot' called Newlands Corner, near a lake known as the Silent Pool. The bodywork of the car was covered in frost, and the lights were still on. Inside the car the police found a fur coat, and a small case which had burst open and which contained three dresses, two pairs of shoes and an expired driving licence in the name of Mrs Agatha Christie.

For the next few days the newspapers were full of stories about the well-known mystery writer's disappearance, with huge banner headlines announcing new so-called developments, interviews with and comments by several people, and speculation by many more. Suicide was not ruled out, nor was murder.

On 7 December, the *Daily News* offered '£100 reward to the first person furnishing us with information leading to the whereabouts, if alive, of Mrs Christie'. The Deputy Chief Constable of Surrey said, in the best tradition of the detective novel: 'I have handled many important cases during my career, but this is the most baffling mystery ever set me for solution.' Also in the best tradition of crime fiction, suspicion centred for a time upon the husband of the missing woman.

By the following weekend, hundreds of policemen and thousands of members of the general public had joined in the search for Agatha Christie. The Silent Pool was dredged with special machinery, light aircraft scoured the countryside from above, and packs of airdales and bloodhounds went over the ground more closely. Police from four counties, Surrey, Essex, Berkshire and Kent, were brought in. As in an Agatha Christie murder mystery, a number of clues were found, only to be discarded as red herrings: a local chemist said that Mrs Christie had often discussed with him methods of committing suicide; a woman claimed that she had seen someone, whom she identified from photographs as Mrs Christie, wandering about, dazed; and two other people remembered that a woman answering to her description, her clothes covered in frost, had asked them the way to Petersfield, a town in Hampshire. The police guarded Colonel Christie's house, monitored his phone calls, and followed him to his office. Christie told a city colleague, 'They think I've murdered my wife.'

The weekend after her disappearance, in answer to an appeal from the police fifteen thousand volunteers searched the Downs. On the Saturday afternoon, three thousand of their cars were parked on Merrow Downs, and they set off in groups of thirty with a police officer in charge of each group. The *Daily Mail* played its part by publishing an article by the famous thriller writer, Edgar Wallace, in which he expounded his theory of Mrs Christie's disappearance. He did not suspect foul play, but considered it

> a typical case of 'mental reprisal' on somebody who has hurt her. To put it vulgarly her first intention seems to have been to 'spite' an unknown person who would be distressed by her disappearance.
>
> That she did not contemplate suicide seems evident from the fact that she

deliberately created an atmosphere of suicide by abandonment of her car.

Loss of memory, that is to say mental confusion, might easily have followed but a person so afflicted could not possibly escape notice . . . If Agatha Christie is not dead of shock and exposure within a limited radius of the place where her car was found, she must be alive and in full possession of her faculties, probably in London. It is impossible to lose your memory and find your way to a determined destination.

Edgar Wallace's theory was perfectly tenable, and indeed may well have been correct. It was certainly quite proper for him to have suggested it, but perhaps unwise of the chief suspect, Colonel Christie, to put forward the same idea to the *Daily News*: 'My wife said to me, some time ago, that she could disappear at will and would defy anyone to find her. This shows that the possibility of engineering her disappearance was running through her mind.'

During the week in which Agatha Christie remained missing, the banjo player in the band at the Hydropathic Hotel at Harrogate, in those days an elegant spa resort in Yorkshire, informed the Harrogate police of his suspicion that the Mrs Neele who had been staying at the hotel since the previous Saturday was, in fact, Mrs Christie. The police stationed a detective in the hotel for two days to keep an eye on Mrs Neele, and the manager of the hotel (which is now called the Old Swan Hotel) made a statement to the police about Mrs Neele:

> She arrived by taxi on Saturday morning with only a small suitcase and asked for a bedroom on *en pension* terms and was given a good room on the first floor with hot and cold water.
>
> I did not see her myself but I believe that the price quoted to her was seven guineas a week. She accepted this without hesitation. Indeed, from the first day she has been here she seems to have as much money as she wants. From the first her life in the Hydro has been exactly similar to that of our other guests. She takes her meals in the dining-room and only once or twice has had breakfast in bed. She is a very agreeable guest.

When the story that a Mrs Neele at the Hydro Hotel in Harrogate might well be Agatha Christie was leaked to the press, several newspapers sent reporters to Harrogate, and the *Daily Mail* sent a special train with a team of reporters and photographers. It was, however, a *Daily News* reporter, the twenty-year-old Ritchie Calder (the late Baron Ritchie-Calder) who walked up to Mrs Neele in the lounge of the hotel and addressed her as Mrs Christie. 'Mrs Neele' admitted to him that she was Mrs Christie, but, when asked how she had got to Harrogate, said she did not know as she was suffering from amnesia. She then left Calder abruptly, went up to her room and stayed there for the remainder of the afternoon.

On Tuesday, 14 December, the London *Evening Standard* published the news that Agatha Christie had been found. The *Daily News* sent Mrs Christie a telegram, which they also published: 'In view widespread criticism your disappearance strongly urge desirability authentic explanation from yourself to thousands of public who joined in costly search and cannot understand your loss of memory theory.'

No 'authentic explanation' was ever vouchsafed by Agatha Christie. She had registered at the Hydro Hotel as Mrs Teresa Neele, and had let it be known to fellow guests[13] that she was a visitor from Cape Town. On the evening of the day she arrived, Saturday, 14 December, there was a dance at the hotel, and when the band played 'Yes, We Have No Bananas', Mrs Neele got up and danced the Charleston. She spent her week at Harrogate shopping ('she was constantly buying new clothes,' Miss Corbett, the hotel pianist, told the police), taking tea in a local tea shop, and going on long walks. In the evening she played billiards at the Hydro, and on more than one occasion was prevailed upon to sing in her small but sweet soprano, accompanying herself at the piano. Once in the middle of a sentimental song, she faltered and seemed close to tears, but this was attributed to the fact that 'Mrs Neele' was recovering from the loss of a child in South Africa. During the week she posted an announcement to *The Times*, which appeared in the newspaper's personal column on Saturday, 11 December: 'Friends and relatives of Teresa Neele, late of South Africa, please communicate – Write Box R 702, *The Times*, EC4'.

When he accosted her at the hotel, the young journalist Ritchie Calder thought that 'amnesia', which Mrs Christie flung glibly at him, 'was much too clinical a word for someone supposedly surprised into conversation, and if, as her doctor later suggested, she had an "identity crisis", well, by golly, there was no "Teresa Neele" lurking in the self-possessed woman I met.'

Archie Christie arrived in Harrogate at 6.45 p.m. on Tuesday, 14 December, and identified his wife as she walked through the lounge of the hotel wearing an orchid pink dinner gown. She appeared unembarrassed as he walked up to her, merely turning to a group of fellow guests and saying, 'Fancy, my brother has just arrived'. One of the guests who watched the reunion said later that the Christies then sat down in front of the fire in the lounge, but several chairs apart from each other as though they had been quarrelling. They stayed overnight, not in Mrs Neele's room but in a suite. Colonel Christie made an announcement to the press:

There is no question about the identity. It is my wife. She has suffered from the most complete loss of memory and I do not think she knows who she is. She does not know me and she does not know where she is. I am hoping that the rest and quiet will restore her. I am hoping to take her to London tomorrow to see a doctor and specialists.

Two doctors, a neurologist and a general practitioner, issued a statement to the effect that Mrs Christie was 'suffering from an unquestionable loss of memory and that for her future welfare she should be spared all anxiety and excitement.' In other words, ask no questions.

The press accused Mrs Christie of having planned her disappearance merely to obtain publicity. That was a nonsensical accusation, for she was not only a shy woman who avoided publicity as much as possible, she was also in no need of it. But she was certainly not the victim of amnesia. The week before her disappearance, Agatha Christie had lost a diamond ring at Harrods. She wrote to the Knightsbridge department store from Harrogate, describing the ring and asking that, if it were found, it be sent to Mrs Teresa Neele at the Hydro Hotel. Harrods did, in fact, return Mrs Christie's ring to Mrs Neele.

In 1980, in a magazine called *The Bookseller*, a very elderly journalist claimed to remember that, in 1926, on the morning after Mrs Christie disappeared, her publisher Sir Godfrey Collins had told him not to talk to anyone about it, as Mrs Christie was in Harrogate, resting.

The strongest likelihood is that a very unhappy Mrs Archibald Christie had come close to nervous collapse, and that it was in a condition of considerable mental turmoil that she, nonetheless deliberately, staged her disappearance in such a way as to cause the maximum distress to the man whom she loved and who had caused her such anguish. She probably hoped that he would think she had killed herself and would suffer remorse. She may even have hoped that he would be suspected of having murdered her. Perhaps she thought her disappearance would bring Archie to a realization of how much he needed her. Normal, warm-hearted and affectionate a creature though she was, Mrs Christie was not necessarily more so than many another who had been driven by extreme mental anguish to commit actions which seem wildly out of character. Far from disappearing in order to court publicity, she was so distraught at the collapse of her marriage that she was driven to a course of extremely neurotic behaviour despite her fear of publicity. And, her most successful novel having been published seven months earlier and sold extremely well, she had no need of publicity.

In her autobiography, written in old age, Agatha Christie made no direct reference to these exciting events of 1926, contenting herself merely with the observation that after illness came sorrow, despair and heartbreak, and that there was no need to dwell on it. Further clues to the mystery of her behaviour in December 1926 are inextricably embedded in the crypto-autobiographical novel, *Unfinished Portrait*, which she wrote a few years later (see pp. 81–82).

Notes between pp. 8–42

1 Gaston Leroux's *Le Mystère de la Chambre Jaune* (1907) had appeared in English translation in 1909 as *The Mystery of the Yellow Room*.

2 Agatha Christie: *An Autobiography* (London, 1977).

3 Did the teenage Agatha Christie attend in Paris a concert conducted by Pierre Monteux? Poirot, as described, certainly resembled Monteux.

4 But someone, once, must have accused her of a love of violence, for journalists who have clearly not read her still parrot the cry. In *The Times* of 8 December 1981, for instance, Sheridan Morley refers to 'that mix of snobbery with violence which has always been at the heart of Dame Agatha's writing.' Must he not have been thinking rather of Ian Fleming?

5 Which, in her autobiography, she mistakenly refers to as 'macaws'.

6 As also with *The Murder at the Vicarage*, some later editions dropped the definite article from the title.

7 Agatha Christie: *op. cit.*

8 Agatha Christie: *op. cit.*

9 In *Agatha Christie: First Lady of Crime* (ed. H.R.F. Keating, London 1977). Mr Gilbert appears not to have consulted the volume of poems but to have taken this information from an unreliable book, *Agatha Christie: Mistress of Mystery* by G.C. Ramsey (1967).

10 Gwen Robyns: *The Mystery of Agatha Christie* (1978)

11 London *Sunday Times*, 27 February 1966.

12 Agatha Christie's sister, Madge.

13 These included a fourteen-year-old boy who was to become a novelist in later life. 'The only time I saw Harrogate was with my family at the same hotel and historic moment when Agatha Christie checked in without her memory,' wrote Patrick White in *Flaws in the Glass* (1981).

2

The Vintage Years

The Big Four (1927)

Mrs Christie spent the first weeks of 1927 recovering from her December adventure, at Abney Hall in Cheadle, near Manchester, the home of her sister and her brother-in-law, Madge and Jimmy Watts, while Archie Christie continued to live at Styles which he and Agatha had agreed to sell. Archie wanted a divorce as quickly as possible, but Agatha thought it fairer to their child Rosalind to wait for a year, so that Archie could be quite certain that he knew what he wanted. It is from this time in her life that Agatha Christie's revulsion against the press and her dislike of journalists can be dated. She had felt, she said later, like a fox: hunted, her earths dug up, and followed by yelping hounds. She had always hated notoriety of any kind, and now could hardly bear even the kind of publicity consequent upon her successful career as a writer.

With her marriage in ruins, Mrs Christie was forced to give serious thought to that career. She had little money other than that which she earned from her writing; it was important, therefore, that she should continue to produce books at regular and frequent intervals. She had been unable to write since the death of her mother; her brother-in-law Campbell Christie, Archie's brother, now made the suggestion that the last twelve of the Hercule Poirot stories which had been published in the weekly magazine, *The Sketch*, and which had not yet been collected into a book, could with very little rewriting be strung together in such a way that they would make a kind of picaresque crime novel. Campbell Christie helped his sister-in-law with the rewriting, for she was still in no condition to manage it on her own, and the result was *The Big Four*.

In *The Mysterious Affair at Styles*, *The Murder on the Links* and *The Murder of Roger Ackroyd* we were presented with dazzlingly plotted domestic crime novels, their mysteries solved by Hercule Poirot. In the mystery-thriller novels *The Secret Adversary*, *The Man in the Brown Suit* and *The Secret of Chimneys* we were introduced to a world of international crime in which Poirot did not appear. Now, in *The* (hastily patched-together) *Big Four*, the consultant detective who prefers to stay at home finds himself in the wrong kind of novel, forced to chase after the Big Four, an international crime organization 'hitherto undreamed of'. The four would-be rulers of the world heading the organization are Li Chang Yen, an immensely powerful 'Chinaman' (to use Mrs Christie's term which nowadays would be thought offensive), a wealthy American, a mysterious French woman and, the chief executive of the cartel, an Englishman referred to as 'the destroyer'.

Hastings, who has spent the previous year and a half managing a ranch in the

Argentine ('where my wife and I had both enjoyed the free and easy life of the South American continent') arrives in London on a business trip, and of course immediately makes his way to 14 Farraway Street where he had shared rooms with Poirot, only to find his old friend about to set out to visit him in South America, as well as to undertake a commission there on behalf of Abe Ryland, an American who is 'richer even than Rockefeller'. It takes the death of a stranger who bursts into Poirot's rooms in a state of collapse to change the detective's plans and to set him and Hastings on the trail of the Big Four, one of whom had been responsible for offering Poirot the South American commission merely to get him out of the way.

One by one, Poirot picks off the criminals in a series of only loosely connected episodes. In the first, he does not actually catch the real criminal but is at least instrumental in saving an innocent man from the gallows, which, as Poirot remarks to Hastings, is enough for one day. It is in this chapter, 'The Importance of a Leg of Mutton', that Mrs Christie makes unacknowledged use of a brilliant piece of deduction which she, if not Poirot, ought to have credited to Sherlock Holmes.

Throughout *The Big Four*, Poirot is thrust into adventures which require him to resort to a number of uncharacteristic and, indeed, highly unconvincing actions. In his encounter with the female French villain, he threatens her with a blow-pipe disguised as a cigarette and containing a dart tipped with curare. 'Do not move, I pray of you, madame. You will regret it if you do,' he exclaims in his best Sherlock Holmes manner. The wealthy American is the second of the Four to be tangled with, and here Poirot is helped by Inspector Japp of Scotland Yard and by Hastings whom Poirot unkindly uses as an unwitting decoy. The Chinese member of the foursome is never encountered in person.

Some of the episodes in the novel are only tenuously linked with the main plot, and indeed one of them, 'A Chess Problem' (Chapter 11), has appeared separately in short story anthologies. *The Big Four* is packed with incident, including the threatened abduction and torture by 'that Chinese devil' of Hastings' wife in the Argentine, the unexpected appearance of Poirot's brother Achille (whose name causes Hastings to ponder on the late Madame Poirot's classical taste in the selection of Christian names), and, horror of horrors, the apparent death of Hercule Poirot, and his funeral, a solemn and moving ceremony at which Hastings is, not unnaturally, overcome by emotion. Again, has not Mrs Christie placed herself too heavily in the debt of Conan Doyle with these brothers and deaths, even though Achille returns to the land of myths at the end of the story, and Hercule miraculously returns to life? When Hastings says he had no idea that Poirot had a brother, Poirot is somewhat cynically made to exclaim, 'You surprise me, Hastings. Do you not know that all celebrated detectives have brothers who would be even more celebrated than they are, were it not for constitutional indolence?'

At the end of *The Big Four*, at least three of the four are dead. But a slight doubt remains about number four, the Englishman who is a master of disguise and who has played a number of roles throughout the novel. His body has been found, but the head was blown to pieces and it is just possible that the real Number Four has escaped again. Poirot cannot be absolutely certain, but he thinks that he has routed the Big Four, and that he can now retire, having solved the greatest case of his life, after which anything else will seem tame. Perhaps he will grow vegetable marrows, he says. And Hastings will return to his charming wife in the Argentine. So we should assume that the events in *The Big Four* have occurred before those in *The Murder of Roger Ackroyd*, which began with Poirot already in retirement and attempting to grow his marrows.

Though it is entertaining to read, and moves swiftly, *The Big Four* can hardly be counted among Agatha Christie's more successful works. Poirot in *The Big Four* is, like Falstaff in *The Merry Wives of Windsor*, shabbily treated by his creator. Two of the novel's characters, the Countess Rossakoff and Joseph Aarons, are to be met in other Poirot adventures. Aarons, the theatrical agent and friend of Poirot (it is reassuring to know that Poirot has at least one Jewish friend) has already helped the detective in *The Murder on the Links* and will do so again in *The Mystery of the Blue Train*, while the Countess Rossakoff, a flamboyant and exotic Russian beauty who gains Poirot's respect and even affection, remains an acquaintance for many years, appearing in two short stories, 'The Double Clue' in which Poirot first meets her (1925, but not collected in a volume until 1961) and 'The Capture of Cerberus' in *The Labours of Hercules* (1947).

'Those who come to expect subtlety as well as sensation in Mrs Christie's writing will be disappointed,' said the *Daily Mail* of *The Big Four*, and this seems to have been the general opinion. Nevertheless, this hastily assembled 'novel' managed to sell more than 8,500 copies of its first edition. There can be little doubt that the publicity surrounding its author's disappearance a couple of months earlier was largely responsible for the increased sales.

The Mystery of the Blue Train (1928)

In February, 1928, Agatha Christie took her daughter Rosalind for a holiday to the Canary Islands, and while they were there she managed to finish another novel, *The Mystery of the Blue Train*. She did not enjoy writing it, and persevered only because of the contractual obligation to her publisher and the need to continue to earn money. She had worked out what she referred to as a conventional plot, based on one of her short stories, 'The Plymouth Express'; but, although she had planned the general direction of the story, both the scene and the characters resolutely refused to come alive for her. She plodded on, recalling later that this was the moment when she ceased to be an amateur and became a professional writer.

If one differentiates between amateur and professional (writer, actor, musician) on the basis that the professional can do it even when he does not feel like it, while the amateur cannot even when he does, then undoubtedly Mrs Christie was now justified in admitting herself to the professional ranks, for although she did not much like what she was writing and did not think she was writing particularly well (in fact, she later referred to *The Mystery of the Blue Train* as easily the worst book she ever wrote), she nevertheless finished it and sent it off to Collins. It immediately sold a healthy 7,000 copies, which pleased her, although she could not feel proud of her achievement.

Mrs Christie was granted a divorce from her husband in April, 1928, on the grounds of his adultery not with Nancy Neele but with an unknown woman in a London hotel room. This particular act of adultery was purely formal, if it took place at all: in those days, when both parties to a marriage wanted a quick divorce the only course open to them was for one of them to stage-manage an act of infidelity and to arrange for circumstantial evidence to be provided by 'witnesses'. (As soon as the divorce became absolute, Christie married Nancy Neele. They remained married until Nancy died of cancer in 1958. Archibald Christie died in 1962.)

After the divorce, Agatha Christie wished to discontinue using her former husband's name, and suggested to her publishers that she should write her novels under a male pseudonym. However, she was persuaded that her public had become used to her as Agatha Christie and that it would be unwise for her to change her name. So she remained Agatha Christie to her readers, for the rest of her life.

Though it is far from being one of her more brilliant efforts, and is distinctly inferior to *The Murder of Roger Ackroyd*, *The Mystery of the Blue Train* does not deserve the scorn which its author liked to pour upon it. It is, at least, an improvement upon its immediate predecessor, *The Big Four* although, like *The Big Four*, it uneasily combines domestic murder with international crime. In solving the former, Poirot manages also to put a stop to the latter. One marvels at Agatha Christie's objectivity as a writer. There is little trace in *The Mystery of the Blue Train* either of the emotional turmoil which its author had recently undergone or of the reluctance with which she claims to have written it.

The daughter of an American millionaire is found strangled in her compartment on the famous Paris–Nice *train bleu* when it pulls into Nice, and a fabulous ruby, the 'Heart of Fire', which her father had recently given her, is discovered to have been stolen. The plot is an expansion of a short story, 'The Plymouth Express' in which the theft and murder take place on a less glamorous train, the 12.14 from Paddington, and are very swiftly solved by Poirot. 'The Plymouth Express' did not appear in a volume of Agatha Christie stories until 1951 when it was included with eight other stories in *The Under Dog*, published in the United States. This volume was not published in Great Britain, and it was not until 1974 that British readers found 'The Plymouth Express' collected in a volume entitled *Poirot's Early Cases* (called *Hercule Poirot's Early Cases* in the United States).

In its expansion into a full-length novel, Mrs Christie's story acquired sub-plots and a great many more characters. Anyone reading the novel who remembered the story would be able to identify one of the criminals but would still be left with a mystery to solve. Though the novel reveals traces of having been hastily written, its characters are entertaining and not unbelievable, and an atmosphere of the French Riviera in the twenties is still conveyed by its pages today, perhaps even more clearly than when the novel was first published. And scattered among the clumsy syntax and the phrases of bad French are a number of tart Christian *aperçus*. Hastings is absent from the story, presumably on his ranch in the Argentine, and Poirot is a retired gentleman of leisure, travelling with an English valet, George, whom he must have acquired recently. It is only because he happens to be travelling to the south of France on the Blue Train on which the murder is committed that Poirot is drawn into the case.

The Mystery of the Blue Train is the first Poirot novel to be written in the third person. With no Captain Hastings or Dr Sheppard to make ironic little jests at his expense, and thus keep his overweening vanity in check, Poirot tends occasionally to act like a caricature of himself. But he is more like the Poirot Mrs

Christie's readers had come to regard with affection than the cardboard figure of *The Big Four*, though at one point he indulges in an uncharacteristically Wildean epigram, taking to his bed because the expected has happened and 'when the expected happens it always causes me emotion'.

Parts of *The Mystery of the Blue Train* are set in the English village of St Mary Mead which we will later come to know as the home of Miss Marple, a Christie detective we have yet to encounter. A minor character in the present novel is Miss Viner, an elderly inhabitant of the village who, with her curiosity and her sharp powers of observation, is quite as definitely an adumbration of Miss Marple as Caroline Sheppard was in *The Murder of Roger Ackroyd*.

There are one or two inconsistencies in the plot. Why, for instance, does Poirot say of Derek Kettering that he 'was in a tight corner, a very tight corner, threatened with ruin,' when Kettering has, in fact, been offered £100,000 in return for allowing his wife to divorce him?

Agatha Christie told an interviewer in 1966 that *The Mystery of the Blue Train* 'was easily the worst book I ever wrote . . . I hate it'. And her final verdict, in her autobiography, was that it was commonplace, full of clichés, and that its plot was uninteresting. 'Many people, I am sorry to say, *like* it,' she added. And so they should. Third-rate Christie is, perhaps, to be sneezed at, but not second-rate Christie.

The Seven Dials Mystery (1929)

The difficulties which Agatha Christie had experienced in writing during the period of nervous exhaustion which led to her disappearance, and even later, while she was recovering, seemed to evaporate as soon as she and Archie Christie were divorced. She continued to write stories for publication in magazines, especially when she needed ready cash for repairs to Ashfield or for some other unexpected expense. A story brought in about £60, and took a week to write. At the same time, she found that ideas for novels were coming quite easily to her. Having especially enjoyed writing *The Secret of Chimneys* five years earlier, she decided to employ some of the characters and the setting of *Chimneys* in a new light-hearted thriller, *The Seven Dials Mystery*, for she continued to find that thrillers required less 'plotting and planning' than murder mysteries.

The Seven Dials of the title can be taken to mean either the district of Seven Dials in the West End of London, or the dials of seven alarm clocks (Mrs Christie favours the older spelling, 'alarum') which are discovered ranged along the mantelpiece in the room at Chimneys in which a young man is found dead in his bed. The action takes place partly at Chimneys, the country seat of Lord Caterham, and partly in various other places, among them the sinister Seven Dials Club, in Seven Dials, which 'used to be a slummy sort of district round about Tottenham Court Road way'. Seven Dials is actually a block or two southeast of the bottom of Tottenham Court Road, and not noticeably less slummy now than in 1929. (Two of its theatres which stand side by side, the Ambassadors and St Martin's, acquired Christiean connections when, in 1952, Agatha Christie's play, *The Mousetrap*, opened at the Ambassadors, and in 1974 transferred next door to the St Martin's where, at the time of writing, it is still running.)

As usual with Agatha Christie's thrillers, the mystery element is not neglected. Not only does the reader have to discover who killed two of the house guests at Chimneys, he also has to worry about the secret society at Seven Dials and the identity of its leader, referred to by his cronies as 'Number Seven'. Among the characters from *The Secret of Chimneys* who reappear in *The Seven Dials Mystery* are some of the representatives of law and order, including Colonel Melrose, the Chief Constable, and the stolid, reliable Superintendent Battle of Scotland Yard. Lord Caterham's daughter, Lady Eileen Brent, familiarly known as 'Bundle', who had played an important role in *The Secret of Chimneys*, is the amateur sleuth who attempts to solve the Seven Dials Mystery with the aid of a couple of amiably silly young men, one of whom, Bill Eversleigh (also in *Chimneys*), works at the Foreign Office.

The Seven Dials secret society is in many ways similar to the secret organization headed by the mysterious Mr Brown in *The Secret Adversary*, but its aims turn out to be not at all similar to those of Mr Brown's group. The reader is not likely to discover the identity of Number Seven before it is revealed to Bundle Brent, and whether he discovers the identity of the murderer (not the same person) will depend on how he interprets an ambiguous utterance quite early in the piece. The solution to the mystery of the Seven Dials secret society is, in fact, more than usually ludicrous, but such is the air of Wodehousian inconsequentiality and charm with which Agatha Christie has imbued the characters and the atmosphere of her story that it hardly matters. *The Seven Dials Mystery* has not quite the freshness and insouciance of *The Secret of Chimneys* but it is in very much the same mould, and is one of the more engaging of the early thrillers.

As an author, Mrs Christie was not given to making comments *in propria persona*, but you gain a certain amount of information about her attitudes by noting what is said by characters of whom she approves. Superintendent Battle reveals a tough edge to his cosy, bourgeois normality when he speaks contemptuously of those who play safe on their journey through life. 'In my opinion,' he tells Bundle, 'half the people who spend their lives avoiding being run over by buses had much better be run over and put safely out of the way. They're no good.' Even Bundle is shocked by the brutality of Superintendent Battle's sentiments, which will issue a few years later from the lips of kindly Major Despard in *Cards on the Table*, in almost the same words: 'I don't set as much value on human life as most people do . . . The moment you begin being careful of yourself – adopting as your motto "Safety First" – you might as well be dead, in my opinion.' ('I have never refrained from doing anything on the grounds of security,' Mrs Christie was to reveal in her autobiography.)

'Hearts just as pure and fair/May beat in Belgrave Square/As in the lowly air/Of Seven Dials', wrote W.S. Gilbert in *Iolanthe*. Oddly, Mrs Christie said very much the same thing in *The Seven Dials Mystery*, and was rewarded with initial sales of over 8,000 copies. This was thought by all concerned to be highly satisfactory: it was to be a good twenty years before the first printing of a Christie novel reached 50,000 copies.

More than fifty years later, by which time *The Seven Dials Mystery* had become a quaint old period piece without losing its power to entertain and to mystify, a British commercial television company produced a film of Agatha Christie's thriller, in a faithful adaptation by Pat Sandys which was first transmitted in Great Britain on 8 March 1981, and on 16 April in the United States. Sir John Gielgud made a convincing Lord Caterham, with Cheryl Campbell very much in period as Bundle, Harry Andrews as an excellent Superintendent Battle, Christopher Scoular as Bill Eversleigh, and James Warwick, Leslie Sands and Lucy Gutteridge in other important roles. The director was Tony Wharmny. 'The millions around the world,' wrote the television critic of *The Times* the following day, 'on whom television co-productions are regularly foisted will in this case get their vicariously spent money's worth. . . . Mere entertainment? Yes, and why not? There is at present no dearth of Plays for Today purporting to school us in the so-called realities of life.' On its first showing on London Weekend TV the film, which ran for two-and-a-half hours with commercial breaks, topped the London ratings with four million viewers.

Partners in Crime (1929)

In *Partners in Crime*, a collection of short stories, and the second Agatha Christie title to appear in 1929, the author reintroduced Tommy and Tuppence Beresford, the two engaging young sleuths from her second book, *The Secret Adversary*. Tommy and Tuppence have now been married for six years, and life has become a little too dull and predictable for them, at least for Tuppence. Tommy works for the Secret Service, but apparently in an administrative capacity, so there are no thrills to be had from that direction. When Tommy's boss, Mr Carter, the chief of British Intelligence who was responsible in *The Secret Adversary* for starting them off on their adventures, offers Tommy and Tuppence a new assignment, they eagerly accept his offer. They are to take over for six months the running of the International Detective Agency, which had been a front for Bolshevik spying activities. In addition to keeping an eye open for letters with Russian postmarks, they may also take on any genuine cases which happen to come their way.

Having read, as he claims, 'every detective novel that's been published in the last ten years', Tommy decides to adopt the character and methods of a different detective of fiction for each case, thus giving Mrs Christie the opportunity to produce a number of satires on the detectives of her rival crime writers. The Beresfords have acquired Albert, the young Cockney assistant porter from *The Secret Adversary*, who has become their all-purpose domestic servant, and who now takes on the job of office-boy for the International Detective Agency. At least, one supposes it is the same lad, for he has the same name and personality as the earlier Albert. But he is described now as being a tall lad of fifteen, which means that he can have been no more than nine when he was a lift-boy in Mayfair. This, if not impossible, is unlikely; but then, Agatha Christie's chronology was ever inexact. Albert apparently stays in the employ of the Beresfords: we shall meet him in middle-age in *N or M?* and *By the Pricking of My Thumbs*, and as an elderly servant in *Postern of Fate*.

The Bolsheviks make an occasional appearance in *Partners in Crime*, and are routed in the final episode, but most of the stories in the book are self-contained adventures, with Tommy and Tuppence assuming the methods of a different detective of fiction for each case. In 'The Affair of the Pink Pearl', Tommy decides to solve the mystery in the manner of Dr John Thorndyke, the physician-detective hero of the stories of Richard Austin Freeman. In 'The Adventure of the Sinister Stranger' Tommy and Tuppence are the Okewood brothers, Desmond and Francis, who were popular crime solvers of the period. They are American detectives McCarty and Riordan for their next case, and Tommy is Sherlock Holmes in the one after that. For 'Blindman's Buff' Tommy decides, appropriately, to be Thornley Colton, 'the Blind Problemist'. Chesterton's Father Brown, an Edgar Wallace investigator, 'The Old Man in the Corner', A.E.W. Mason's Inspector Hanaud, Freeman Wills Crofts' Inspector French, Roger Sheringham and Dr Reginald Fortune are all impersonated, until the final episode, 'The Man Who Was Number 16', when Tommy has the gall to pretend to be Hercule Poirot and Mrs Christie has a joke at the expense of *The Big Four*. 'You recall do you not,' Tommy-Poirot says to Tuppence-Hastings, 'the man who was No. 4. Him whom I crushed like an egg shell in the Dolomites . . . But he was not really dead . . . This is the man, but even more so, if I may put it. He is the 4 squared – in other words he is now the No. 16.'

When Agatha Christie wrote *Partners in Crime*, all those detectives would have been familiar names to readers of crime stories, but when she came to write her memoirs many years later, she could not even remember who some of them were, for many had faded into oblivion. If they had not been created by Mrs Christie, one feels certain that Tommy and Tuppence would also have failed to survive, for their adventures in *Partners in Crime* are really rather unmemorable. Most of the separate stories are too slight and far too brief for any suspense to be generated, and the reader has to make do with the light comedy of the Tommy-Tuppence relationship, for their 'little grey cells' are by no means the equal of Poirot's. As parodies, the stories are superb; but, since the majority of the writers parodied are hardly known at all today, much of Mrs Christie's skill has to be taken on trust.

The volume entitled *The Sunningdale Mystery*, published by Collins in 1929 as a 6d paperback, is in fact merely Chapters 11 to 22 of *Partners in Crime*.

As no attempt has previously been made by writers on Agatha Christie to identify all of the crime writers parodied in *Partners in Crime*, the following table which lists them all may be of interest:

Chapter	Detective(s) impersonated	Author (and some titles)
3	Dr John Thorndyke	Richard Austin Freeman (1862–1943): *The Cat's Eye; Dr Thorndyke Intervenes*
5	the brothers Desmond and Major Okewood (There is a passing reference to Sapper's Bulldog Drummond stories)	Valentine Williams (1883–1946), writing as Douglas Valentine. The Oakwood brothers appear in *The Secret Hand*, also entitled *Okewood of the Secret Service*
7	(Timothy) McCarty and Riordan	Isabel Ostrander (1885–1924). McCarty and Riordan appear in *McCarty Incog.*

Chapter	Detective(s) impersonated	Author (and some titles)
9	Sherlock Holmes	Sir Arthur Conan Doyle (1859–1930); *The Adventures of Sherlock Holmes; His Last Bow; The Case-book of Sherlock Holmes*
10	Thornley Colton	Clinton H. Stagg (?–?). Thornley Colton is the hero of *Thornley Colton, Blind Detective*
11	Father Brown	G.K. Chesterton (1874–1936): *The Innocence of Father Brown; The Secret of Father Brown; The Scandal of Father Brown*
13	The Busies	Edgar Wallace (1875–1932): *The Clue of the Twisted Candle; The Ringer*
15	The Old Man in the Corner	Baroness Orczy (1865–1947): *The Case of Miss Elliott; The Old Man in the Corner; Unravelled Knots*
17	Inspector Hanaud	A.E.W. Mason (1865–1948): *At the Villa Rose; The House of the Arrow*
19	Inspector French	Freeman Wills Crofts (1879–1957): *Inspector French's Greatest Case; Tragedy in the Hollow*
20	Roger Sheringham	Anthony Berkeley: *The Wychford Poisoning Case; Top Story Murder; Murder in the Basement*
22	Reggie Fortune	H.C. Bailey (1878–1961): *Mr Fortune's Practice; Mr Fortune Objects*
23	Hercule Poirot	Agatha Christie (1890–1976): *The Mysterious Affair at Styles; The Murder of Roger Ackroyd*

The Murder at the Vicarage (1930)

In the autumn of 1929, Agatha Christie decided to take a holiday alone. Rosalind was at school, and would not be home until the Christmas holidays, so Agatha planned a visit to the West Indies and made all the necessary arrangements through Thomas Cook's. Two days before she was to leave, a married couple at a dinner party spoke to her of the Middle East, where they had been stationed, and of the fascination of Baghdad. When they mentioned that you could travel most of the way there on the Orient Express, Agatha became extremely interested, for she had always wanted to travel on the famous international train which went from Calais to Istanbul. And when she realized that, from Baghdad, she would be able to visit the excavations at Ur, the biblical Ur of the Chaldees, the matter was decided. The following morning she rushed to Cook's, cancelled her West Indian arrangements and made reservations on the Orient Express to Istanbul, and further on to Damascus and Baghdad.

The journey on the Orient Express, through France, Switzerland, Italy and the Balkans, was all that she had hoped it would be. After an overnight stay in old Stamboul, Mrs Christie crossed the Bosphorus into Asia and continued her train journey through Asiatic Turkey, entering Syria at Aleppo, and continuing south to Damascus. She spent three days in Damascus at the Orient Palace Hotel, a magnificent edifice with large marble halls but extremely poor electric light, and then set off into the desert by bus (the Nairn Line fleet of buses was operated by two Australian brothers, Gerry and Norman Nairn). After a forty-eight-hour journey which she found both fascinating and rather sinister because of the complete absence of landmarks of any kind in the desert, she finally reached her destination, the ancient city of Baghdad, capital of modern Iraq and of old Mesopotamia.

One of the first things Agatha did was arrange to visit the excavations at Ur, about halfway between Baghdad and the head of the Persian Gulf, where Leonard Woolley was in charge of the joint British Museum and Museum of the University of Pennsylvania Expedition. As Woolley's wife Katharine, a formidable lady, was a Christie fan and had just finished reading *The Murder of Roger Ackroyd* with great enjoyment, the author was accorded special treatment and was not only allowed to remain with the digging team but was invited to join them again the following season. Having fallen in love with the beauty of Ur, and the excitement of excavating the past, Mrs Christie enthusiastically agreed to return. Meanwhile, she enjoyed the rest of her stay in Baghdad until, in November, it was time to go back to England. In March of the following year, 1930, travelling from Rome to Beirut by sea, she made her way back to Baghdad and to Ur.

This time, Agatha Christie met Woolley's assistant, Max Mallowan, who had been absent with appendicitis on her first visit. Of mixed Austrian and French parentage, his father being an Austrian who had emigrated to England, Mallowan was a twenty-six-year-old archaeologist who had been Woolley's assistant at Ur since coming down from Oxford five years previously. At the conclusion of Agatha's visit, the imperious Katherine Woolley ordered young Mallowan to take their distinguished guest on a round trip to Baghdad and to show her something of the desert before escorting her home on the Orient Express. They enjoyed each other's company and, by the time they arrived back in England, Mallowan had decided to ask Mrs Christie to marry him.

When he proposed to her, she was taken completely by surprise. They had become close friends, but that was all, and she was fourteen years older than he, she told him. Yes, he knew that, and he had always wanted to marry an older woman. She agreed to think about it, and although she had grave doubts as to the wisdom of marrying again, let alone marrying a man so much younger than herself, she did like him and they had so much in common. She consulted her daughter, Rosalind, who gave her unqualified approval. At the end of the summer, Agatha Christie said yes, and on 11 September 1930, after she returned from a holiday in the Hebrides, they were married in the small chapel of St Columba's Church in Edinburgh.

The Orient Express took the newly married couple on the first stage of their honeymoon to Venice, whence they made their way to Dubrovnik and Split and then down the Dalmatian coast and along the coast of Greece to Patras in a small Serbian cargo boat. After a tour of Greece with a few idyllic days at Delphi, they parted in Athens, Max to rejoin the dig at Ur, and Agatha to return to London, suffering from an especially violent form of Middle Eastern stomach upset or possibly, as diagnosed by the Greek doctor she consulted, ptomaine poisoning.

In her autobiography, Agatha Christie writes that *Murder at the Vicarage* was published in 1930, but that she cannot remember where, when or how she wrote it, or even what suggested to her that she should introduce a new detective, Miss Marple. (As with *The Murder on the Links*, the title originally began with the definite article, which it lost in some later editions.) Mrs Christie claimed that it was certainly not her intention at the time to continue to use Miss Marple and allow her to become a rival of Hercule Poirot. It merely happened that way. Poirot was to remain her most frequently employed detective, appearing altogether in thirty-three novels, as well as ten volumes of stories, while Miss Marple was allowed to solve no more than twelve full-length mysteries. In the post-Second World War years, Poirot and Miss Marple novels tended roughly to alternate, but Miss Marple titles were thin on the ground in earlier years. After her initial appearance in *The Murder at the Vicarage* in 1930, and in a volume of stories in 1932, Miss Marple is not heard of again until the end of the thirties.

The vicarage in *The Murder at the Vicarage* is in the small village of St Mary Mead, a village in which Miss Marple had always lived and from which she was rarely to stray for the rest of her life. She did not go out into the world in search of murder; it came to her. We are not meant to wonder at the fact that so much violence should be concentrated in so small and, in all other respects, so apparently innocuous a village, and indeed to wonder would be churlish. In her introduction to murder, in *The Murder at the Vicarage*, Miss Marple acquits herself well, although she is not trained to detect crime, but she is inquisitive, has a good memory, a rather sour opinion of human nature (though she would deny this) and a habit of solving problems by analogy. She does not possess little grey cells of the quality of Hercule Poirot's, and when congratulated upon her success is likely to attribute it to the fact that she has lived in an English village all her life and thus has seen human nature in the raw.

The surface cosiness of village life, disturbed by violent crime and then found to be somewhat murky under the surface, is something which Agatha Christie is extremely adept at conveying. In *The Murder at the Vicarage*, one of the vicar's more irritating parishioners, Colonel Protheroe, is found dead in the vicar's study. There is no shortage of suspects, including the vicar himself who narrates the story, his flighty young wife, Griselda, and his teenage nephew, Dennis. The relationship between the vicar and his wife is amusingly presented. More likely suspects are the Colonel's widow, his daughter, a slightly dubious anthropologist, and a mysterious Mrs Lestrange. Dr Haydock, Miss Marple's physician and next-door neighbour, must be above suspicion as he is to appear in a number of later Miss Marple stories, and the same applies, surely, to Miss Marple's nephew, Raymond West, a novelist and poet who writes the kind of novels and poems, all pessimism and squalor, which Miss Marple rather detests, though of course she is proud of her nephew's reputation.

Like Poirot, Miss Marple is elderly when we first meet her in 1930, and over the next forty years she will age some more, but not as much as forty years. Agatha Christie based Miss Marple on the kind of old lady she had met often in west country villages when she was a girl, and described her also as being rather like the fussy old spinsters who were her grandmother's 'Ealing cronies'. With Agatha Christie's grandmother, Miss Marple shared a propensity to expect the worst of everyone and, usually, to be proved right. She was to exhibit this propensity in twelve novels and twenty short stories.

The Murder at the Vicarage provides an auspicious début for Miss Marple, and a mystery which few of her readers will solve before the amateur sleuth of St Mary Mead even though Mrs Christie's tactics are not dissimilar to those she adopted in her first novel. In later years, Agatha Christie professed to be less pleased with *The Murder at the Vicarage* than when she had written it, having come to the conclusion that there were far too many characters and too many sub-plots. But she still thought the main plot sound, and added, 'The village is as real to me as it could be – and indeed there are several villages remarkably like it, even in these days [the early 1960s].'

The domestics in St Mary Mead are a dim lot, and rather unsympathetically described by Mrs Christie. This may be because she wishes her readers not to consider them as 'real people' and therefore potential suspects, but you cannot help observing that Mary, the vicar's all-purpose servant, is presented as a truculent dim-wit and an appalling cook, that the artist, Lawrence Redding, describes his cleaning woman as 'practically a half-wit, as far as I can make out', and that Gladys, kitchen-maid at the Old Hall, is 'more like a shivering rabbit than anything human'. It should also be noted that Mrs Christie, like the Almighty, helps those who help themselves. The vicar is, for the most part, the essence of Christian charity, but he is prone to make cynical remarks about the 'thoroughgoing humanitarian' and to sneer at Dr Haydock's sympathy for what the vicar calls 'a lame dog of any kind'. Sentiments more Christiean than Christian. The police in Agatha Christie novels are not always the comic incompetent butts of the private detective, but Inspector Slack (who also appears in two short stories and in the 1942 novel, *The Body in the Library*) is a satirically characterized stupid police officer disliked by all, rude and overbearing, and foolhardy enough to allow his contempt for Miss Marple's suggestions to show.

There is no formula by which you can forecast guilt in the works of Agatha Christie. Nevertheless, some years after the collapse of the novelist's marriage to Archie Christie, her readers would do well to cast a wary eye upon any handsome young men in the novels, while keeping in mind the fact that resemblances to Colonel Christie do not automatically stamp a character as the murderer!

On 16 December 1949, nineteen years after the novel's first publication, Agatha Christie's *Murder at the Vicarage*, dramatized by Moie Charles and Barbara Toy, was produced in London at the Playhouse or, as it was tautologically called at the time, the Playhouse Theatre. (The Playhouse still stands, at the Thames Embankment end of Northumberland Avenue, but since 1951 it has been used as a BBC studio.)

A reasonably faithful and straightforward adaptation of the novel, *Murder at the Vicarage* simplifies the original plot somewhat, and alters the ending, though not the murderer's identity, in the interests of dramatic effect. The play is set, not in the 1930 of the novel, but in 'the present time', i.e. 1949, with references to American airmen being stationed in the village during the war.

With Barbara Mullen as Miss Marple, Reginald Tate (who also directed the play) as Lawrence Redding, Jack Lambert as the Vicar, and Genine Graham as his wife, Griselda, *Murder at the Vicarage* had a reasonably successful run of four months, and later became popular with repertory companies and amateurs. A production at the Savoy theatre in the West End of London in 1975, with Barbara Mullen returning to her role of Miss Marple, and Derek Bond as the Vicar, ran for two years.

The Mysterious Mr Quin (1930)

1930 was professionally a busy year for Agatha Christie. In addition to *The Murder at the Vicarage*, she had two books published and her first play produced. One of the books was a volume in which were collected a number of stories featuring Mr Quin and Mr Satterthwaite, stories which she had written at the rate of one every three or four months for publication in magazines. Mrs Christie refused to produce a series of Mr Quin stories for any one magazine. She considered them to be something special and apart from her usual crime stories, and preferred to write about Mr Quin only when she really felt like doing so.

Twelve of the stories were collected in *The Mysterious Mr Quin* (published in March 1930). The game is given away almost immediately when one notes that the volume is dedicated 'To Harlequin the invisible' and that, in the opening story, an unexpected visitor who 'appeared by some curious effect of the stained glass above the door, to be dressed in every colour of the rainbow' announces, 'By the way, my name is Quin – Harley Quin'.[1] Whenever Mr Quin makes a first appearance in these stories, some trick of the light makes him seem momentarily to be dressed in the motley costume of Harlequin and to wear the *commedia dell' arte* character's mask. Then the illusion vanishes, as Mr Quin is seen to be merely a tall, thin, dark man – and young, according to a fugitive Mr Quin story not collected in this volume – conventionally dressed.

A by-product of Agatha Christie's youthful interest in the characters of the *commedia dell' arte* and of the sequence of Harlequin and Columbine poems, 'A Masque from Italy', in *The Road of Dreams* (1924), Mr Quin is the friend of lovers, and appears when some crime which threatens the happiness of lovers is committed. Usually, however, he does not himself directly intervene to solve a problem, but works through his intermediary, Mr Satterthwaite, 'a little bent, dried-up man with a peering face oddly elflike, and an intense and inordinate interest in other people's lives'.

Despite the elflike face, there is nothing supernatural about Mr Satterthwaite, a gentleman of means, in his sixties, and someone whom life has passed by, who has always been merely an onlooker. After his first meeting with Mr Quin in 'The Coming of Mr Quin', he discovers within himself an ability to penetrate to the heart of mysteries and to solve problems, but only when Mr Quin is there to act as catalyst, to reveal to him what it is that, unconsciously, he already knows.

Mr Quin and his emissary Mr Satterthwaite were, according to Mrs Christie, two of her favourite characters, so it is hardly surprising that their stories should be among her very best. Sometimes Mr Satterthwaite encounters Harley Quin at the Arlecchino, a Soho restaurant. At other times, they meet, as if by accident, at a country pub, the Bells and Motley. Once, very appropriately, Mr Satterthwaite (who, oddly for such a connoisseur of the arts, thinks the opera *Cavallaria Rusticana* ends with 'Santuzza's death agony') encounters Mr Quin at Covent Garden in the interval between *Cav* and *Pag*. (The clowns in *Pagliacci* perform a Harlequinade, and one of them, Beppe, impersonates Harlequin.)

On one occasion, Mr Quin persuades Mr Satterthwaite to travel all the way to Banff, in the Canadian Rockies, to find a clue which brings a criminal to justice and reunites two young lovers. Not surprisingly, Mr Quin turns up at Monte Carlo at Carnival time to intervene in a story involving a *soi-disant* Countess who consorts with men (of Hebraic extraction, sallow men with hooked noses, wearing rather flamboyant jewellery'!)

One of the most curious stories in the volume is 'The Man from the Sea', which takes place on a Mediterranean island. Mr Satterthwaite muses on the role of Isolde which a young protégée of his is about to sing in Germany, and encounters a young man contemplating suicide. It is a story in which, you sense from the quality of the prose as much as from anything else, Mrs Christie's beliefs concerning the meaning of life, not very original, perhaps, but her own and deeply held, are involved. And there are four paragraphs, not essential to the plot, in which the last moments of a dog's life are described: paragraphs whose observation, imagination and compassion are the equal of many a novelist generally thought vastly superior in literary ability to Agatha Christie.

In his memoirs, Sir Max Mallowan describes his wife's Mr Quin stories as 'detection written in a fanciful vein, touching on the fairy story, a natural product of Agatha's peculiar imagination.' He mentions that there is a Mr Quin story, 'The Harlequin Tea Set', not in *The Mysterious Mr Quin*, but published separately in *Winter's Crimes 3* (1971), an anthology of stories by several writers. Sir Max was apparently not aware of a fourteenth story featuring Mr Quin and Mr Satterthwaite, 'The Love Detectives', which has still to appear in any volume published in Great Britain, but which is to be found in *Three Blind Mice and other stories* first published in America in 1950 and sometimes reprinted as, confusingly, *The Mousetrap*.

In 'The Love Detectives', Mr Quin and Mr Satterthwaite assist Colonel Melrose (whom we remember as Chief Constable in *The Secret of Chimneys* and *The Seven Dials Mystery*) in the investigation of a murder. It is a story which fits easily into the canon, and clearly dates from the period in the twenties when most of the Quin stories were written.

The fugitive Harley Quin story mentioned by Max Mallowan, 'The Harlequin Tea Set', is a pendant to the series, written much later, after the Second World War, containing an oblique reference to the Mau Mau troubles in Kenya in the early 1950s. Mr Satterthwaite, 'now of an advanced age', has a final adventure involving Mr Quin whom he encounters, as always apparently by chance, at the Harlequin Café in a village whose name, Kingsbourne Ducis, suggests that it is in Dorset. It is many years since he last met Mr Quin: 'A large number of years. Was it the day he had seen Mr Quin walking away from him down a country lane' in the final story in *The Mysterious Mr Quin*? It was, indeed, and they were not to meet again after this single late adventure, for Mr Quin who has now acquired a small black dog called Hermes contrives to turn himself into a burning scarecrow at the end of the story. The supernatural has come too close for comfort.

Perhaps the most charming story in *The Mysterious Mr Quin* is the final one, 'Harlequin's Lane', despite the fact that the author sees fit to describe one of its characters as 'a fat Jewess with a *penchant* for young men of the artistic persuasion'. Mrs Christie's fat Aryans, whatever their sexual proclivities, tend to attract their creator's venom neither so fiercely nor so frequently. In general, however, the Mr Quin stories are both unusual and pleasantly rewarding to read. Incidentally, Mr Satterthwaite appears, without Mr Quin, in *Three-Act Tragedy* (1935), a Poirot novel, and 'Dead Man's Mirror', one of the four long Poirot stories which make up *Murder in the Mews* (1937: in the USA the volume itself was called *Dead Man's Mirror*, probably because 'Mews' is a much less familiar word in America than in England).

After its initial magazine publication, but before it had been collected into *The Mysterious Mr Quin*, one of the stories, 'The Coming of Mr Quin', was filmed in Great Britain in 1928. In addition to having its title changed to *The Passing of Mr Quinn* (Did the film makers fear their audiences would read a sexual connotation into 'coming'? And why the additional 'n' in 'Quinn'?), the story underwent such violent changes in the course of its adaptation for the screen that you wonder why the producers of the film bothered to acquire it in the first place. Perhaps their interest was simply in acquiring the name of Agatha Christie. Made by Strand Films, and both produced and directed by Julius Hagen, *The Passing of Mr Quinn* was the first British film to be made from a work by Agatha Christie. (The German film industry had got in a few months earlier, with its adaptation of *The Secret Adversary*: see p. 21). The leading roles were played by Stewart Rome, Trilby Clark and Ursula Jeans, and the script was written by Leslie Hiscott who, three years later, was to direct two Christie films, *Alibi* (see p. 38) and *Black Coffee* (see p. 59).

In 1929, in a cheaply produced series, 'The Novel Library'.[2] The London Book Company published *The Passing of Mr Quinn*, described as 'The book of the film adapted from a short story by Agatha Christie, novelized by G. Roy McRae'. It was prefaced by a note: 'Readers are requested to note that Mr Quinny of this book is the same person as the Mr Quinn of the film.' But neither Mr Quinn nor Mr Quinny is Agatha Christie's Mr Quin, for this Quinn-Quinny reveals himself at the end to be the murderer. The victim is a Professor Appleby, who also bears little resemblance to anyone in 'The Coming of Mr Quin'. Here is a sample of the narrative style of G. Roy McRae's 'novelization':

Such was Professor Appleby, a monstrous figure of ebony and white in his dinner suit, as he wrestled under the soft-shaded lamp with the Haje snake.

There sounded all at once a slight hiss. The Haje's long body wriggled and coiled sinuously, so that its black and white diamond markings seemed to blur. A glass vessel fell to the carpet, knocked over by the snake in its struggles, and Professor Appleby's monocle droppped on its black cord as he smiled grimly.

In Agatha Christie's original story, Appleton (not Appleby) has been dead for ten years, and there is no suggestion that he was given to playing with poisonous snakes when he was alive.

Black Coffee (1930)

Perhaps because of her dissatisfaction with *Alibi*, the play which Michael Morton had made in 1928 out of her Poirot novel *The Murder of Roger Ackroyd*, Agatha Christie decided to try her hand at putting Hercule Poirot on the stage in a play of her own. The result was *Black Coffee*. 'It was a conventional spy thriller,' she said of it later, 'and although full of clichés it was not, I think, at all bad.' She showed it to her agent who advised her not to bother submitting it to any theatrical management, as it was not good enough to be staged. However, a friend of Mrs Christie who was connected with theatrical management thought otherwise, and *Black Coffee* was tried out, in 1930, at the Embassy Theatre in Swiss Cottage, London. (The Embassy is now used as a drama school.) In April the following year, it opened in the West End where it ran for a few months at the St Martin's Theatre (where a later Christie play, *The Mousetrap*, was to run forever).

In 1930, Poirot had been played by Francis L. Sullivan, with John Boxer as Captain Hastings; Joyce Bland as Lucia Amory, and Donald Wolfit as Dr Carelli.[3] In the West End production, Francis L. Sullivan was still Poirot, but Hastings was now played by Roland Culver, and Dr Carelli by Dino Galvani. The London *Daily Telegraph* thought the play a 'sound piece of detective-story writing', and preferred Sullivan's rendering of the part of Poirot 'to the one which Mr Charles Laughton gave us in *Alibi*. Mr Laughton's Poirot was a diabolically clever oddity. Mr Sullivan's is a lovable human being.'[4] Agatha Christie did not see the production. 'I believe it came on for a short run in London,' she wrote in 1972, 'but I didn't see it because I was abroad in Mesopotamia.'[5]

The play, which is in three acts, is set in the library of Sir Claud Amory's house at Abbot's Cleve, about twenty-five miles from London. Sir Claud is a scientist engaged in atomic research and had just discovered the formula for Amorite, whose force 'is such that where we have hitherto killed by thousands, we can now kill by hundreds of thousands.' Unfortunately, the formula is stolen by one of Sir Claud's household, and the scientist foolishly offers the thief a chance to replace the formula with no questions asked. The lights in the library are switched off to enable this to happen, but when the lights come on again, the formula is still missing, Sir Claud is dead, and Hercule Poirot has arrived. By the end of the evening, with a certain amount of assistance from Hastings and Inspector Japp, Poirot has unmasked the murderer and retrieved the formula. However, the way is not thus paved for Hiroshima fifteen years later, and the horror of nuclear war, for something else happens just before the end of the play.

Sir Claud's butler is called Tredwell, but whether he is related to the Tredwell who was the butler at Chimneys in *The Secret of Chimneys* and *The Seven Dials Mystery* is not known. He cannot be the same man, for Lord Caterham would surely not have let his treasure of a butler go. Sir Claud's family are an impressively dubious collection of characters, and the suspects also include the scientist's secretary, Edward Raynor, and a sinister Italian, Dr Carelli.

Black Coffee, which was successfully revived some years after its first production, has remained a favourite with repertory companies and amateurs throughout the world, as have so many plays either by or adapted from Agatha Christie. Though *Black Coffee* lacks the complexity and fiendish cunning of Agatha Christie's later plays, it would probably repay major revival not only as a period piece but, if impressively enough cast, as a highly entertaining murder mystery. The casting of Poirot would, however, have to be very carefully undertaken.[6] Agatha Christie used to complain that, although a number of very fine actors had played Poirot, none was physically very like the character she had created. Charles Laughton, she pointed out, had too much avoirdupois, and so had Francis L. Sullivan who was 'broad, thick, and about 6 feet 2 inches tall'. Austin Trevor, in three Poirot movies, did not even attempt physically to represent the character. A publicist for the film company actually announced that 'the detective is described by the authoress as an elderly man with an egg-shaped head and bristling moustache', whereas 'Austin Trevor is a good-looking young man and clean-shaven into the bargain!'

In 1931, *Black Coffee* was filmed at the Twickenham Studios, with Austin Trevor (who had already played Poirot in the film, *Alibi*) replacing Francis L. Sullivan, Richard Cooper as Hastings, Dino Galvani as Dr Carelli, Melville Cooper as Inspector Japp, Adrienne Allen as Lucia Amory, Philip Strange as Richard Amory, and C.V. France as Sir Claud. The film was directed by Leslie Hiscott, but was generally considered to be inferior to the same director's *Alibi*.

Giants' Bread (1930)

It is no longer a secret that, between 1930 and 1956, Agatha Christie published six non-crime novels under the pseudonym of Mary Westmacott. (It was, however, a well-kept secret until 1949.) As these novels are often referred to as 'romantic' or 'women's fiction', it is important to state that they are not examples of what is generally thought of as the genre of the romantic novel (they are, for instance, much closer to Daphne du Maurier than to Barbara Cartland), and that they are 'women's fiction' only in the sense that they can share that description with the works of Jane Austen or Iris Murdoch. The six Mary Westmacott titles belong to no genre: they are simply novels.

In her autobiography Agatha Christie described how she came to write these books:

> It had been exciting, to begin with, to be writing books – partly because, as I did not feel I was a real author, it was each time astonishing that I should be able to write books that were actually *published*. Now I wrote books as a matter of course. It was my business to do so. People would not only publish them – they would urge me to get on with writing them. But the eternal longing to do something that is not my proper job, was sure to unsettle me; in fact it would be a dull life if it didn't.
>
> What I wanted to do now was to write something other than a detective story. So, with a rather guilty feeling, I enjoyed myself writing a straight novel called *Giants' Bread*. It was mainly about music, and betrayed here and there that I knew little about the subject from the technical point of view. It was well reviewed and sold reasonably for what was thought to be a 'first

novel'. I used the name of Mary Westmacott, and nobody knew that it was written by me. I managed to keep that fact a secret for fifteen years.[7]

Published in March, 1930 and dedicated 'to the memory of my best and truest friend, my mother', *Giants' Bread* is a long novel of 438 pages (approximately 140,000 words), which is about twice as long as a Christie murder mystery.[8] It is also a rather remarkable novel, which is ostensibly about music, as its author claimed it was, but which is really about obsession, friendship, genius, childhood and identity. In other words, it is a novel about real people, in which the author is freed of the requirement to steer her characters along certain paths so that they can be manipulated into making the right moves to establish the necessary pattern that a crime novel must have. She could allow her characters to develop freely, could write about those aspects of them that moved and excited her, and could, in the process, explore and come closer to understanding her own nature and desires.

Without the self-imposed restraints of the mystery novel, Mrs Christie might easily have found herself floundering and confused, but she did not. She found, instead, that she was not only a brilliant creator of puzzles but also a real novelist, with an ability to create fully rounded characters and with the confidence not to worry about the exigencies of plot. *Giant's Bread* is, in a sense, autobiographical, as is all good fiction. And, for that matter, all bad fiction. Human beings are condemned to tell the truth about themselves, though some find oddly devious ways of doing so. Later Mary Westmacott novels will wear their auto-biographical aspects on their sleeves, but those truths about Agatha Christie which exist in *Giants' Bread* are very deeply embedded within the novel, and are not so much factual as psychological or spiritual. The novel examines a number of characters, but concentrates upon its hero, or anti-hero. Vernon Deyre, whom we meet first as a sensitive child in a sheltered, upperclass environment in Edwardian England, and whose development we follow into adult life.

Vernon becomes a composer, and what is most remarkable about *Giants' Bread* is the understanding with which Mrs Christie, despite her disclaiming 'technical knowledge', describes the total possession of Vernon's personality by music. She has created a totally believable composer, believable not simply because Vernon flings the right names about – Prokofiev, Schoenberg, Stravinsky, even 'Feinberg'[9] – but because his own music, experimental and *avant garde*, is convincingly described and because his total absorbtion in music is so clinically and unromantically conveyed. Vernon Deyre could be Bliss or Goossens or an anglicized Scriabin. In fact, although Vernon is not based on any real person, Mrs Christie was helped by Roger Sacheverell Coke, a seventeen-year-old pianist and composer whose parents were friends of her sister. (Roger Coke studied composition under Alan Bush, and went on to compose an opera (on Shelley's *The Cenci*), several symphonies and concertos and a great deal of chamber music. Coke's music, most of which has not been published, is thought to be pre-Debussian in idiom, and so not at all like the music of Agatha Christie's Vernon Deyre.)

Giants' Bread contains fascinating portraits of an opera soprano who loses her voice by insisting on singing Strauss's Elektra, a role too strenuous for her, and of an impresario, Sebastian Levinne, a friend of Vernon's since their childhood, and 'the sole owner of the National Opera House'. Although, in the prologue to the novel in which a new opera is having its première at the National Opera House, Sebastian is referred to by a member of the audience as 'a dirty foreign Jew', Mrs Christie has produced in Levinne and his parents an unexpectedly sympathetic and understanding portrait of a Jewish family coping with genteel English upperclass resentment and prejudice.

It is the apparent ease with which Agatha Christie was able, in *Giants' Bread*, to examine various aspects of human behaviour that is impressive, rather than the actual quality of her writing, though her prose is never less than adequate to convey mood and meaning. She was always too fond of the verb 'to twinkle': Poirot's and Miss Marple's eyes are forever twinkling as they make their little jokes, and in *Giants' Bread* there is a pianist whose hands 'twinkled up and down the keyboard' with marvellous speed and dexterity. But for the most part Mrs Christie's first 'straight' novel reads very smoothly, and indeed grippingly. If the author's attitude to some of her characters is romantic, it is never sentimental, and not even romantic in the diminishing sense in which the word is used to denote a blinkered view of reality. Twice in the course of the novel she quotes that greatest of realists, Dostoevsky, and is fully justified in doing so. She even gets away, towards the end, with a scene in which Vernon, shipwrecked, can drag to the safety of a raft, only one of two drowning women, and has to make a choice between his wife and his ex-lover.

Agatha Christie must have known the real worth of her Mary Westmacott novels, and must surely have been disappointed that they did not arouse more interest in the literary world. But when she was interviewed many years later, after it was known that she had written several non-mystery novels, she merely remarked with an ambiguously arrogant modesty: 'I found with straight novels that they didn't need much thinking out beforehand. Detective stories are much more trouble – even if you have no high ideals in writing them.'

The Sittaford Mystery or Murder at Hazlemoor (1931)

Mr and Mrs Mallowan had bought a house in London, at 22 Cresswell Place, Earl's Court, which Agatha completely redecorated, and which contained a music room on the top floor where she could both write and play the piano. They also kept up the house in Torquay, where Agatha loved to go during the summer holidays when Rosalind was home from school. After their honeymoon, Agatha spent the winter of 1930–31 in London while Max was at Ur, and it was not until March that she joined him at Ur for a few days and then travelled home with him.

The journey back to England was an adventurous one. Having decided to go by way of Persia (Iran), the Mallowans flew from Baghdad to Shiraz, via Teheran, in a small, single-engined plane which 'seemed to be flying into mountain peaks the entire time'. In Shiraz, they visited a beautiful house with a number of medallion paintings on the walls, one of which was of Holborn Viaduct in London! Apparently a Shah of Victorian times, after visiting London, had sent an artist there with instructions to paint various medallions of scenes the Shah wanted to remember, and these included Holborn Viaduct. Agatha Christie used the house as the setting for a short story called 'The House at Shiraz', which she included in a volume, *Parker Pyne Investigates* (1934).

From Shiraz the Mallowans travelled by car to Isfahan, which Agatha maintained to the end of her life was the most beautiful city in the world. Its colours of rose, blue and gold, its noble Islamic buildings with their courtyards, tiles and fountains, the birds and the flowers, all entranced her. They next made a sudden decision to continue their journey home by way of Russia. Hiring a car, they made their way down to the Caspian sea where, at Rasht, they caught a Russian boat across to Baku, capital of the Soviet province of Azerbaydzhan. In Baku, an Intourist agent asked if they would like to see a performance of *Faust* at the local opera house. They declined, and instead 'were forced to go and look at various building sites and half-built blocks of flats'. Their hotel was one of faded splendour, but everything in Baku 'seemed like a Scottish Sunday'. By train, they made their way to Batum on the Black Sea, having been forbidden to break their journey at Tiflis, a town Max Mallowan very much wanted to see. A French ship took them down the Black Sea to Istanbul, where they joined Agatha's beloved Orient Express.

Max Mallowan had arranged not to go back to Leonard Woolley and his dig at Ur, the following season, but instead to accept an invitation from Dr Campbell Thompson to join him in excavating at Ninevah. So, in late September, 1931, Max travelled to Ninevah, and it was arranged that Agatha should join him there at the end of October. Her plan was to spend a few weeks writing and relaxing on the island of Rhodes, and then sail to the port of Alexandretta and hire a car to take her to Aleppo. At Aleppo she would take the train to the Turkish-Iraqi frontier, and then drive on to Mosul where she would be met by Max. But a rough Mediterranean Sea prevented the steamer from putting in at Alexandretta, so Agatha was carried on to Beirut, made her adventurous way by train up to Aleppo, and eventually arrived at Mosul three days late.

The big mound of Ninevah was a mile and a half outside Mosul, and the Mallowans shared a small house with Dr Campbell Thompson and his wife, quite close to the mound which was being excavated. The country was fascinating, with the distant Kurdish mountains to be seen in one direction, and the river Tigris with the minarets of the city of Mosul in the other. At the bazaar in Mosul, Agatha bought herself a table. This cost her £10, according to her memoirs, or £3, according to Max Mallowan's memoirs. Both agree that, on it, she wrote a Poirot detective novel, *Lord Edgware Dies*. When a skeleton was dug up in a grave mound at Ninevah, it was promptly christened Lord Edgware.

The Sittaford Mystery, published in Great Britain in 1931, and in America as *Murder at Hazelmoor*,[10] was written during a few weeks in 1929, and is one of those Agatha Christie crime novels in which the murderer is unmasked not by Poirot or Miss Marple or one of the author's other 'regulars', but by the heroine of the novel, who is usually a courageous and determined young woman with something of the spirit of Tuppence Beresford in her.

Anne Beddingfield in *The Man in the Brown Suit* (1924) is the earliest of these adventurous ladies, and Katherine Grey in *The Mystery of the Blue Train* (1928) is potentially one of them, although she does not develop her potentiality since she has Poirot on hand. In *The Sittaford Mystery* Emily Trefusis is engaged to be married to a young man who has been arrested for the murder of his uncle, Captain Trevelyan. Convinced of his innocence, she sets out to discover the identity of the murderer, and eventually succeeds with the help of the police Inspector in charge of the case. The police, in Christie novels, are not always

Inspector Japp-like incompetents brought into the story merely to set off the brilliance of the private detective.

For the first time, Mrs Christie makes use of Dartmoor, virtually her native heath and the place where she wrote her very first crime novel. Normally, her settings are in less bleak and inhospitable parts of the English countryside, but in *The Sittaford Mystery* she takes advantage of the snow-bound moorland village, using it not simply for atmosphere but making it contribute to the plot as well. You cannot fail to be reminded of Conan Doyle's *The Hound of the Baskervilles*, not only by the setting but also by the fact that, in both novels, a prisoner escapes from Princetown, the prison in the centre of Dartmoor.

Agatha Christie was interested in the supernatural, and indeed was to write some of her finest short stories on supernatural subjects. *The Sittaford Mystery* begins with a seance in which the assembled sitters are informed by the rapping of the table that Captain Trevelyan, six miles away in Exhampton, is dead. And it is discovered that Trevelyan has indeed been murdered, probably at the precise moment that the message was received in the seance six miles away. But *The Sittaford Mystery* is not necessarily a supernatural one. There are, in fact, two mysteries, and Mrs Christie juggles them superbly so that, until she is ready to tell us, we are never sure whether they are connected or even what one of them is. Who murdered Captain Trevelyan? And why have Mrs Willett and her daughter come to live in Sittaford? These would appear to be the mysteries, and presumably they are related.

The Sittaford Mystery is strongly plotted, and the solutions to its puzzles are not likely to be arrived at by deduction on the reader's part. It is also one of Mrs Christie's most entertaining crime novels, and her use of the Dartmoor background is masterly. But you cannot help thinking that, given the characters of those involved, the actual motive for the murder when it is revealed seems rather inadequate. Real life produces murders committed for motives which seem even more inadequate, but that is not the point. Usually the reader is convinced by Mrs Christie's explanations, but on this occasion he may well consider it unlikely that this particular person would have committed that particular crime for the reason given. This reader would have liked a stronger motivation and also to have had loose ends tied up. What, for instance, is the significance of the information given in Chapter 37, that the maiden name of Martin Derring's mother was Martha Elizabeth Rycroft? What is her connection with Mr Rycroft the ornithologist? Why does Rycroft refer to the Derrings as 'my niece . . . and her husband'? There is an irrelevant and unnecessary confusion here.

Mrs Christie, the most objective of authors, who usually keeps herself in the background, intrudes at one or two points in the story: once, inadvertently, when she has Emily think to herself that a tall, blue-eyed invalid looks 'as Tristan ought to look in the third act of *Tristan und Isolde* and as no Wagnarian tenor has ever looked yet', for Emily is not the kind of girl to have been at all interested in the operas of Wagner, and the comment is clearly not hers but her author's; on the other occasion, Mrs Christie describes a character's voice by telling us that it 'had that faintly complaining note in it which is about the most annoying sound a human voice can contain'. The qualifying clause is the opinion not of anyone in the novel but, again, of the author. It is possible to pick up pieces of information about Agatha Christie's personal likes and dislikes in this way, but not often.

In one or two details, there is a similarity between *The Sittaford Mystery* and the long story, 'Three Blind Mice' of about sixteen years later, a story which was subsequently used as the basis of the play, *The Mousetrap*.

Several months before *The Sittaford Mystery* was published, the crime novelist Anthony Berkeley had written, in the preface to one of his Roger Sheringham mysteries, *The Second Shot*:

> I am personally convinced that the days of the old crime-puzzle, pure and simple, relying entirely upon the plot and without any added attractions of character, style, or even humour, are in the hands of the auditor; and that the detective story is in the process of developing into the novel with a detective or crime interest, holding its readers less by mathematical than by psychological ties.

Berkeley would seem here to be looking ahead to Simenon, whose first Maigret stories were soon to appear, or to writers of the type of Patricia Highsmith. But, until the end of her life, Agatha Christie was able to retain and increase a huge readership with precisely the kind of novel which Berkeley thought was on the way out. She did so, of course, by the cunning and subtle injection of those qualities of character, style and humour into a form which, in the hands of some of her rivals, seemed to offer little more than the donnish delights of puzzle-solving.

The Floating Admiral (1931)

An oddity, published in 1931,[11] was the crime novel, *The Floating Admiral*, written by 'Certain members of the Detection Club'.

The Detection Club of London, founded in London in 1928 by Dorothy L. Sayers and Anthony Berkeley, is a private club to which a number of leading crime writers belong. Its first President was G.K. Chesterton.

For many years, the club dinners were held in a private room at *L'Escargot Bienvenu* in Greek Street, Soho. Later, they moved to the more luxurious Café Royal. Agatha Christie was a member of the Detection Club, and from 1958 until her death its Co-President. She was one of fourteen members who combined to write *The Floating Admiral*, a murder mystery to which each of its authors contributed one chapter. The conditions under which *The Floating Admiral* was written were described in Dorothy L. Sayers' Introduction:

> . . . the problem was made to approach as closely as possible to a problem of real detection. Except in the case of Mr Chesterton's picturesque Prologue, which was written last, each contributor tackled the mystery presented to him in the preceding chapters without having the slightest idea what solution or solutions the previous authors had in mind. Two rules only were imposed. Each writer must construct his instalment with a definite solution in view – that is, he must not introduce new complications merely 'to make it more difficult'. He must be ready, if called upon, to explain his own clues coherently and plausibly; and, to make sure that he was playing fair in this respect, each writer was bound to deliver, together with the manuscript of his own chapter, his own proposed solution of the mystery. These solutions are printed at the end of the book for the benefit of the curious reader.

ABOVE: Moorland Hotel on Dartmoor, where a young Agatha Christie completed her first novel, *The Mysterious Affair at Styles.*
BELOW LEFT: A series of Hercule Poirot stories appeared in *The Sketch* in 1923. Poirot's portrait was drawn by W. Smithson Broadhead for the series.
BELOW RIGHT: Agatha Christie in 1926, the year of her disappearance.

ABOVE: The 'Silent Pool' at Newlands Corner. It was dragged by the police at the start of their search for Agatha Christie when her car was found abandoned.
BELOW: Police beaters search for clues which might lead them to Mrs Christie.

ABOVE: There was a large public response to the disappearance of Agatha Christie and many joined the renewed search at Newlands Corner.
BELOW: George Best who discovered Mrs Christie's abandoned car.

ABOVE: The notice that Agatha Christie, using the name of Teresa Neele, placed in the personal columns of *The Times* on 11 December 1926.

BELOW: A huge crowd gathered on the platform at King's Cross to await the arrival of Agatha Christie and her husband, Archie.

ABOVE LEFT: Charles Laughton was the first stage Hercule Poirot in *Alibi* at the Prince of Wales Theatre in 1928. *Alibi* is the stage version of *The Murder of Roger Ackroyd*. A close-up of Charles Laughton's Poirot which appeared in *The Graphic* on 9 June 1928.

ABOVE RIGHT: Agatha Christie's next play, *Black Coffee*, which was first performed in 1930, has remained popular and is often produced by amateur dramatic groups or played in repertory or on tour. Here Kenneth Kent plays Poirot in *Black Coffee* on tour in 1951.

BELOW: A scene from the production of *Alibi* in 1928.

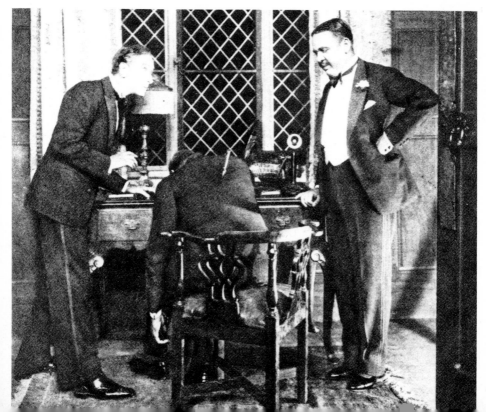

LEFT: Professor C. Woolley. Max Mallowan was Woolley's assistant at the excavations at Ur in the late 1920s.
BELOW: The 'death pit' (*foreground*) containing 74 victims of human sacrifice which were found during excavations at Ur led by Professor Woolley in 1929.

RIGHT: One of the statues uncovered on the dig at Ninevah.
BELOW: The old city of Ninevah excavated by Dr Campbell Thompson in 1931. Max Mallowan was Thompson's assistant.

LEFT: Ruth Draper whose one-woman shows in London suggested to Agatha Christie the character of Carlotta Adams in *Lord Edgware Dies*.

BELOW: The S.S. *Nefertari*. It was such a river-steamer that Agatha Christie used as the setting for *Death on the Nile* which was published in 1937.

RIGHT ABOVE: The Old Cataract Hotel at Aswan where Poirot broke his journey up the Nile.

RIGHT BELOW: Agatha Christie and Max Mallowan in the grounds of Greenway House. They bought Greenway with its 33 acres of ground in 1939 for £6,000.

ABOVE: Francis L. Sullivan played Poirot again in 1940 in *Peril at End House*. Here Poirot helps to concentrate 'the little grey cells' by building a house of cards.
RIGHT ABOVE: A scene from *A Stranger Walked In*, the Hollywood film of the play *Love from a Stranger* which Frank Vosper had adapted from a Christie short story.
RIGHT BELOW: The 1945 version of *Ten Little Niggers* produced by René Clair was one of the most successful Christie film adaptations.

ABOVE LEFT: Agatha Christie checks the proofs of *The Hollow*, published in 1946.
ABOVE RIGHT: Agatha and Max leave for Baghdad to continue archaeological excavations in 1950.
BELOW: Agatha Christie and Max Mallowan look at photographs of archaeological finds.
RIGHT: Agatha Christie writing at her desk at Winterbrook House in 1950, the year *A Murder is Announced* was published.

ABOVE LEFT: A scene from *The Hollow* produced in 1951 by Hubert Gregg. Inspector Colquhoun (Martin Myldeck) shows the murder weapon to Gudgeon (A.J. Brown).
ABOVE RIGHT AND BELOW: Of the four films starring Margaret Rutherford as Miss Marple, *Murder, She Said*, an adaptation of *4.50 From Paddington*, was the best.

ABOVE LEFT: Agatha Christie attends the first night of *The Mousetrap*.
ABOVE RIGHT: The programme for the first night of *The Mousetrap*.
BELOW: Agatha Christie at a dress rehearsal in 1953 of *Witness of the Prosecution* with David Horne (the Defence), Percy Marmont (the Judge) and D.A. Clark-Smith (the Prosecution).

ABOVE LEFT: Margaret Lockwood with Agatha Christie after signing up to play in *Spider's Web*.
ABOVE RIGHT: Poster for *Spider's Web*.
BELOW: Agatha Christie with her grandson Mathew in 1955 as they leave for Christmas in Tripoli.

Set in the classical murder mystery country of southern England, the events in *The Floating Admiral* take place in and near Whynmouth, a fictitious South Coast holiday resort. The corpse of Admiral Penistone is found floating down the river Whyn, in the vicar's boat, and the detective whose task it is to discover the killer is not Poirot or Lord Peter Wimsey or Father Brown or anyone associated with an individual contributor, but Inspector Rudge of the Whynmouth police, 'a tall, thin man with sallow, clean-shaven face'.

The authors of *The Floating Admiral*, in the order of their contributions, are G.K. Chesterton, Canon Victor L. Whitechurch, G.D.H. and M. Cole, Henry Wade, Agatha Christie, John Rhode, Milward Kennedy, Dorothy L. Sayers, Ronald A. Knox, Freeman Wills Crofts, Edgar Jepson, Clemence Dane and Anthony Berkeley. The book is a remarkably successful group effort, and the fact that the story twists and turns even more than it would have done had it been the work of a single writer merely adds to its effectiveness as a mystery. The *New York Times Book Review* said of it: 'The plotting is ingenious, the pace sustained, the solution satisfying'.

In her chapter, Agatha Christie plays one of her typical tricks, and in her proposed solution she attempts to foist the crime upon a young man in drag. She is, however, foiled by the writers who follow her, and who send the plot off in several different directions.

The Floating Admiral, out of print and forgotten for many years, was reissued in the United States in a paperback edition in 1980, and in Great Britain in hardback in the autumn of 1981, fifty years after its initial publication.

Peril at End House (1932)

Agatha Christie published two books in 1932, one a new Poirot mystery and the other a volume of stories featuring Miss Marple. The Poirot novel, *Peril at End House*, was dedicated to Eden Phillpotts 'to whom,' said the author, 'I shall always be grateful for his friendship and the encouragement he gave me many years ago'.

Though it is one of her best murder mysteries, when she came to write her memoirs about thirty years later Mrs Christie had to confess that *Peril at End House* had left so little impression on her mind that she could not even remember having written it. This seems to have led some recent critics to undervalue what is, in fact, one of Agatha Christie's most ingenious puzzle stories with a brilliant plot and some very lively characterization.

The action of *Peril at End House* takes place at 'the Queen of Watering Places' on the south coast of England, a town called St Loo which reminds Hastings forcibly of the Riviera. Although it is supposed to be in the adjoining county of Cornwall, from the author's description of its topography St Loo is obviously her home town of Torquay in Devon, and the Majestic Hotel where Poirot and Hastings are holidaying is the famous Imperial Hotel, lightly disguised. Hastings is in England on one of his periodical visits from the Argentine: reference is made to the murder on the Blue Train two or three years earlier, which Poirot had been forced to solve without Hastings' assistance.

At the Majestic Hotel, Poirot and Hastings make the aquaintance of a charming though somewhat brittle young lady, Nick Buckley, who lives at End

House up on the cliffs, and who, it seems, has recently been having some very narrow escapes from death. Poirot is convinced that someone is trying to kill her, but Nick appears to treat the matter as a huge joke until her cousin is killed at End House, perhaps having been mistaken for her. This is one of those novels in which Mrs Christie behaves most like the stage conjuror who confuses his audience by compelling them to watch his right hand while he deceives them with his left. It is also one of those novels in which she plays tricks with people's names.

The particular deception which she practices in *Peril at End House* is one which Mrs Christie liked so much that she resorted to it again in more than one future novel. Some readers might think it as unfair as the infamous trick she played in *The Murder of Roger Ackroyd*, though no one appears to have objected to it when the novel first appeared. The characters are an especially lively bunch, most of them friends or relatives of the ultra-modern Miss Buckley, and among them is the young Jewish art dealer, Jim Lazarus. Mr Lazarus is marginally less unsympathetically described than others of his race have been in earlier Christie novels. Condescension appears to have replaced active dislike. 'He's a Jew, of course,' someone says of him, 'but a frightfully decent one.' But when he offers fifty pounds for a picture which is worth no more than twenty, the point is made by Poirot, that 'the long-nosed M. Lazarus' has behaved in a manner 'most uncharacteristic of his race'. You are saddened to hear this from Poirot, who must himself frequently have been the butt of other people's xenophobia.

The characters include a mysterious Australian couple who, as Poirot observes, are almost too good to be true, with their cries of 'Cooee' and their not quite properly employed antipodean slang ('And now you tell me you're a bonza detective'). The Australia she had visited some years earlier was perhaps beginning to fade in Mrs Christie's memory. Hastings has a decidedly odd lapse of memory when, in response to a comment by Poirot on the success which he and his wife have made of their ranch in the Argentine, he says, 'Bella always goes by my judgment.' But Hastings' wife is called Dulcie. Bella, one recalls from *The Murder on the Links* in which Hastings met both girls, is the name of Dulcie's sister.

Some years after its publication, *Peril at End House* was adapted for the stage by Arnold Ridley, author of the popular comedy-thriller, *The Ghost Train*. With Francis L. Sullivan as Poirot[12] (whom he had already impersonated in 1930 in *Black Coffee*), the play began a pre-London tour on 2 January 1940, and opened at the Vaudeville Theatre, London, on 1 May. The cast included Ian Fleming (Hastings), Olga Edwards (Nick Buckley) and Brian Oulton (Charles Vyse). As it was 1940, and anti-semitism was no longer fashionable, the 'long-nosed M. Lazarus' of the 1932 novel became Terry Ord, 'a tall good-looking man of about thirty-five' and presumably a gentile.

The Thirteen Problems or The Tuesday Club Murders (1932)

Having successfully introduced her amateur detective, Miss Jane Marple, in *The Murder at the Vicarage* (1930), Agatha Christie wrote for a magazine a series of six short stories featuring Miss Marple. In the first story, 'The Tuesday Night Club', the old lady is entertaining a group of friends at her house in the village of St Mary Mead. Her guests are her nephew Raymond West, the novelist, and his fiancée, an artist named Joyce Lemprière; Dr Pender, the elderly clergyman of the parish (what, one wonders, has happened to the Rev. Leonard Clement, the vicar in *The Murder at the Vicarage?*); Mr Petherick, a local solicitor; and a visitor to St Mary Mead, Sir Henry Clithering, who is a retired Commissioner of Scotland Yard.

The talk turns to crime, and Joyce Lemprière suggests that they form a club, to meet every Tuesday evening. Each week, a different member of the group will propound a problem, some mystery or other of which they have personal knowledge, which the others will be invited to solve. In the first story, Sir Henry is invited to start the ball rolling. Of course, Miss Marple is the one to arrive at the correct solution every time, not because she possesses any brilliant deductive powers but because, as she puts it, 'human nature is much the same everywhere, and, of course, one has opportunities of observing it at closer quarters in a village'.

In a second series of six stories, Mrs Christie repeated the formula, the setting this time being the country house of Colonel and Mrs Bantry, near St Mary Mead, and the assembled company including Sir Henry again, the local doctor, a famous actress and, of course, Miss Marple. A separate, single story, in which Sir Henry visits St Mary Mead yet again, to stay with his friends the Bantrys, and finds himself drawn by Miss Marple into the investigation of a local crime, was added to the earlier twelve, and the collection, dedicated to Leonard and Katherine Woolley, with whom Agatha Christie had stayed in the Middle East, was published in Great Britain as *The Thirteen Problems* and in the United States as *The Tuesday Club Murders*, though only the first six cases appear to have been discussed at meetings of the Tuesday Club.

Some of the stories are especially ingenious, and all are entertaining, though if more than one or two are read at one sitting they can become monotonous, for they are all very sedentary stories whose action is recounted in retrospect. Miss Marple solves most of the mysteries without rising from her chair, and almost without dropping a stitch in her knitting. The exception is the final story, 'Death by Drowning', which is also one of the few occasions when Agatha Christie strayed into workingclass territory. Usually, it is only the crimes of the middle and upperclasses which commend themselves to her investigators.

For all her old-world charm, and the twinkle which is never far from her china-blue eyes, Miss Marple can be stern in her opinions. Talking of a murderer whom she had brought to justice and who had been hanged, she remarks that it was a good job and that she has no patience with modern humanitarian scruples about capital punishment. Miss Marple is speaking not only for herself but also for her creator, for many years later Mrs Christie was to write:

> I can suspend judgment on those who kill – but I think they are evil for the community; they bring in nothing except hate, and take from it all they can. I am willing to believe that they are made that way, that they are born with a disability, for which, perhaps, one should pity them; but even then, I think, not spare them – because you cannot spare them any more than you could spare the man who staggers out from a plague-stricken village in the Middle Ages to mix with innocent and healthy children in a nearby village. The *innocent* must be protected; they must be able to live at peace and charity with their neighbours.

It frightens me that nobody seems to care about the innocent. When you read about a murder case, nobody seems to be horrified by the picture, say, of a fragile old woman in a small cigarette shop, turning away to get a packet of cigarettes for a young thug, and being attacked and battered to death. No one seems to care about her terror and her pain, and the final merciful unconsciousness. Nobody seems to go through the agony of the *victim* – they are only full of pity for the young killer, because of his youth.

Why should they not execute him? We have taken the lives of wolves, in this country; we didn't try to teach the wolf to lie down with the lamb – I doubt really if we could have. We hunted down the wild boar in the mountains before he came down and killed the children by the brook. Those were our enemies – and we destroyed them.[13]

Imprisonment for life, Mrs Christie goes on to say, is more cruel than the cup of hemlock in ancient Greece. The best answer ever found, she suspects, was transportation: 'A vast land of emptiness, peopled only with primitive human beings, where man could live in simpler surroundings.' Well, yes, but of course the price one pays for that is the Australia of today!

Five minor points about *The Thirteen Problems*, two concerned with Christie carelessness and three with Christie parsimony: (i) in one of the stories, 'phenomena' is used as though it were a singular, and not the plural of 'phenomenon'; (ii) in *The Thirteen Problems*, Raymond West's fiancée is called Joyce but, in later Christie stories, after they are married, she is always referred to as Joan; (iii) variations on the plot of one of the stories, 'The Blood-Stained Pavement', will be presented in the story 'Triangle at Rhodes' in *Murder in the Mews* (1937) and in the novel, *Evil Under the Sun* (1941); (iv) the plot of another story, 'The Companion', will be made use of again in the novel, *A Murder is Announced* (1950); (v) an element in the plot of 'The Herb of Death' will re-occur in *Postern of Fate* (1973).

Agatha Christie always considered that Miss Marple was at her best in the solving of short problems, which did not involve her in doing anything other than sitting and thinking, and that the real essence of her character was to be found in the stories collected together in *The Thirteen Problems*.

Lord Edgware Dies or Thirteen at Dinner (1933)

In 1933, Max Mallowan was ready to conduct a dig of his own in the Middle East, and he was fortunate enough to be sponsored by the British Museum to lead an expedition to Iraq to excavate for two months at Arpachiyah, not far from the site of Ninevah where he had worked the previous year. His party consisted only of his wife, Agatha, and a young architect, John Rose. Such was Agatha Christie's fame by this time that the British press announcements of the expedition emphasized her involvement in it.

After the Mallowans had arrived in Iraq, the beginning of the enterprise was unpropitious, for the rain poured down so heavily that it was almost impossible to move about, and finding out who owned the land on which it was proposed to dig proved incredibly difficult. As Agatha explained in her memoirs years later, questions of land ownership in the Middle East were always fraught with difficulty. If the land was far enough away from cities it was under the jurisdiction of a sheikh, but anything classified as a *tell*, that is a hillock or mound thought to be covering the ruins of an ancient city, was considered the property of the government. The *tell* of Arpachiyah was apparently not large enough to have been classified as such, so the Mallowan party had to negotiate with the owner of the land.

This was less simple than it appeared to be, for the huge, cheerful man who assured Max Mallowan that he was the owner was contradicted the following day by his wife's second cousin who claimed ownership, and by the third day of negotiations Mallowan had identified fourteen (according to Agatha, nineteen) owners, who were rounded up in two horse-drawn cabs, conveyed to the Ottoman Bank in Mosul and persuaded to append their thumb-marks to a contract.

The dig produced some extraordinary finds; among them a potter's shop with numerous dishes, vases, cups and plates, a cemetery dating from 4,000 BC which contained forty-five graves, and a rich collection of small objects such as amulets, necklaces, knives and pieces of pottery. Agatha's tasks included washing, labelling and sometimes mending the objects discovered. She loved the work, and soon became highly competent at any job assigned to her. She was to assist her husband on all of his digs in the Middle East throughout the nineteen-thirties, learning in the process a great deal about the sites of antiquity which were being uncovered. At Arpachiyah, Agatha found time to write *Murder on the Orient Express.*

To celebrate the end of the season, the three members of the expedition decided to organize a cross-country race, open to all the Arab workers who had taken part in the excavations. Agatha dignified the proceedings with a name: the Arpachiyah Amateur Athletic Association, or AAAA, and Max Mallowan described the occasion in his memoirs:[14]

> The rules were announced to all would-be competitors on the dig, and it was decreed that the race should be run from the Nergal gate at Ninevah on the Mosul side of the river Khusr, thus involving a river crossing, over a length of about three-and-a-half miles, the finishing point to be just below the *tholos* in Arpachiyah. We offered substantial rewards to the competitors, the first prize to consist of a cow and a calf, second prize a sheep and a lamb, the third prize a goat and a kid and the fourth, as far as I remember, was a substantial sack of dates. The fifth prize was a hundred eggs, and after that in descending denominations there were nine more prizes of eggs in all; moreover, every competitor who finished and did not fall out of the race was to be rewarded by a presentation of as much *helawa*, that is as much sweetmeat as could be covered by the span of two hands – a generous ration. Our cook was kept busy for many days organizing the purchase of these goods in the market at Mosul. He was an Indian; 'Too much work, Memsahib,' he said to Agatha, and I think did not particularly enjoy collecting the prizes, which on the day of the race were motored out to Arpachiyah in our lorry.

According to Agatha, the first thing that happened when the starting pistol was fired was that everyone made a concerted rush forward and most of them fell flat on their faces into the river. There had been a great deal of betting on the race, and when it was over a huge feast was held at night at which most of the prizes were consumed in a very short time. It was a great day for the AAAA.

It was early in May when the expedition departed first for Baghdad, where an equitable division of the objects found was made at the Baghdad Museum, and it was then back home to England. The Director of Antiquities in Baghdad, Dr Julius Jordan, a German, was a Nazi agent who did all he could to undermine British authority in Iraq. Personally, he could not have been more charming to the Mallowans. He was an excellent pianist, played Beethoven sonatas for them, and seemed always a gentle, considerate and cultured human being. But, at tea one day in his house, someone mentioned Jews. Agatha noticed that the expression on Dr Jordan's face changed suddenly, 'in an extraordinary way that I had never noticed on anyone's face before'. 'You do not understand,' said the Doctor. 'Our Jews are perhaps different from yours. They are a danger. They should be exterminated. Nothing else will really do but that.'

Agatha stared at him unbelievingly. It was, she wrote later, the first time she had come across any hint of what was soon to happen in Germany. She had met her first Nazi, and she discovered later that Dr Jordan's wife was an even more fanatical Nazi than her husband. It must have been, you cannot help thinking, a salutary experience for Agatha Christie, for the casual anti-Semitic comments which disfigure most of her earlier books are not to be found in such profusion in those published after the mid-thirties. Probably, too, her outlook was broadened by her contact with the more cosmopolitan mind of Max Mallowan.

After the Mallowans arrived back in England, Max spent a busy summer writing up his account of the expedition. An exhibition of some of their finds was held at the British Museum, and Max's book on Arpachiyah was published several months later. But on the actual day of their return to London from the Middle East, it was the novelist, not the archaeologist, whom the journalists were most concerned to interview.

The novel which Agatha Christie had written in the autumn of 1931 at Ninevah, on the table she purchased at the Mosul bazaar, was published in the spring of 1933 in Great Britain as *Lord Edgware Dies* and in the United States as *Thirteen at Dinner*, and dedicated to Dr and Mrs Campbell Thompson, the leader of the Ninevah expedition and his wife.

Poirot, who has solved murders in English villages and French seaside resorts, finds himself this time investigating a crime in the West End of London, supping at the Savoy, interviewing suspects in a mansion in Regent's Park, and venturing no farther from the metropolis than Sir Montagu Corner's house on the river at Chiswick, which is where the dinner party for thirteen takes place.

When Lord Edgware, a thoroughly unsympathetic character, is murdered, suspicion falls upon his wife, the beautiful actress, Jane Wilkinson. An important character in the story is Carlotta Adams, an American actress who has taken the West End by storm with her one-woman show in which she impersonates a number of different characters. 'Her sketch of an evening in a foreign hotel was really wonderful. In turn, American tourists, German tourists, middleclass English families, questionable ladies, impoverished Russian aristocrats and weary discreet waiters all flitted across the scene.' Carlotta Adams includes in her performance an amazingly accurate impersonation of Jane Wilkinson.

Agatha Christie revealed in her autobiography that the idea for *Lord Edgware Dies* had first come to her after she had been to a performance by the famous

American entertainer, Ruth Draper. 'I thought how clever she was and how good her impersonations were; the wonderful way she could transform herself from a nagging wife to a peasant girl kneeling in a cathedral.' Carlotta Adams was clearly based on Ruth Draper, whom older playgoers in London will remember, for, although she first appeared in London in 1920 with her dramatic monologues at two matinées at the Aeolian Hall in Bond Street (Carlotta Adams in *Lord Edgware Dies* 'had given a couple of matinées which had been a wild success' before doing a three weeks' season the following year), Ruth Draper continued to visit London for the following thirty-six years, giving her final performance at the St James's Theatre (now, alas, demolished) in July, 1956, the year of her death. She possessed, to an extraordinary extent, the ability to alter her appearance with the minimum of help from props or costumes, merely by thinking herself into the character she wished to impersonate.

In *Lord Edgware Dies*, there are witnesses willing to swear that the woman who visited the victim shortly before his death was his estranged wife, Jane Wilkinson, who had rather melodramatically announced her intention of killing him. Of course, it is possible that Jane Wilkinson was impersonated by Carlotta Adams. On the other hand, there are several other hands involved. Agatha Christie is not one to make life easy for her detectives, or for her readers, and this particular Poirot murder mystery is one of her most brilliantly plotted. The characterization, too, is richly enjoyable, for Mrs Christie seems as much at home with these peers, actresses, and Jewish financiers as with the villagers of St Mary Mead.

The anti-Semitism is still to be found, not so much in the portrait of Sir Montagu Corner who does no worse than show off his knowledge of 'Japanese prints, of Chinese lacquer, of Persian carpets, of the French impressionists, of modern music and of the theories of Einstein' before allowing Poirot to get a word in, but in a young and impoverished aristocrat's comments on the wealthy Rachel Dortheimer, with whom he flirts in a box at the opera, but of whom he later comments that 'her long Jewish nose is quivering with emotion'. This is by no means the last Christie novel which will be disfigured by what Jacques Barzun[16] has called 'the usual tedious British anti-Semitism', which will continue to surface in her pages until the war years, though less frequently than heretofore.

Hastings is at Poirot's side throughout this adventure. Why he is not at home with his wife in the Argentine is not explained: he is recalled home at the end of the story. Incidentally, it is in this novel that we discover Hastings to have a small 'tooth-brush' moustache, for Poirot contrasts it scornfully with his own ludicrously luxuriant waxed creation. We discover, too, that young men, if they are too good-looking ('It isn't natural for a man to have good looks like that') are likely to have very dubious morals. 'Not the usual thing. Something a great deal more recherché and nasty,' says Inspector Japp of a suspect's sex-life, though probably all he means is 'Not girls but boys'.

Poirot's investigation is interrupted by his being called away to solve the case of 'The Ambassador's Boots'. This is an example of Mrs Christie's occasional absent-mindedness, for the case in question was solved not by Poirot but by Tommy and Tuppence Beresford. 'The Ambassador's Boots' is an episode in *Partners in Crime*.

In 1934, *Lord Edgware Dies* was filmed by Read Art Films, with Austin

Trevor playing Poirot for the third and last time, Richard Cooper as Hastings and Melville Cooper as Inspector Japp, roles they had played in the film of *Black Coffee*. Jane Wilkinson was played by Jane Carr, and the film was produced by Julius Hagen and directed by Henry Edwards. Though well acted, it did only moderately well at the box office, and was dismissed by one unsympathetic reviewer as 'just another conventional mystery play'.

The Hound of Death (1933)

It was in the thirties that Agatha Christie was most productive, for between 1931 and 1943 there was not a year in which she did not publish at least two titles. In 1933, her second title was 'The Hound of Death', a volume of twelve stories, the majority of which defy classification as murder mysteries or crime stories but which could perhaps be collectively described as stories about mental or psychic disturbance.

Some are about the supernatural world. Mrs Christie throughout her life retained a healthy respect for phenomena not susceptible to rational explanation, though her natural scepticism led her to seek first an explanation in rationalism. But, as a devout Anglican, in an age when the Church of England still adhered to most of its traditional beliefs, she did not find it necessary to shy away from problems of the spirit or the psyche: in *The Hound of Death* she tackled one or two such problems head-on. Some of these stories of the bizarre, the occult and the macabre are among her most interesting, whether they are concerned with apparently genuine psychic phenomena or with dishonest manipulation.

The title story, 'The Hound of Death', if it were written today would be classified as science fiction, although at the time of its publication it must have seemed to be more in the tradition of M.R. James and his tales of the occult. In an interview with Nigel Dennis in 1956, Agatha Christie professed a keen interest in science fiction. Had she been a few years younger, she would probably have made major contributions to that particular genre. What today is scientific was yesterday considered occult, and 'The Hound of Death' concerns itself with a phenomenon which could be either, and with a Belgian nun who is able to harness thought, or prayer, to unleash destructive forces.

'The Red Signal', though a crime story, involves a genuine case not necessarily of spiritualism but certainly of extra-sensory perception, and introduces Mrs Thompson, a plump, middle-aged medium, 'atrociously dressed in magenta velvet' who, with her Japanese spirit control and her fondness for Welsh rarebit, is a forerunner of Madame Arcati in Noël Coward's play, *Blithe Spirit* (1941). Extra-sensory perception is also the basis of 'The Gypsy'; a moving little ghost story, 'The Lamp', has echoes of Henry James and *The Turn of the Screw*; and 'Wireless' (known in the United States as 'Where There's a Will') brings an ironic twist to crime and the spirit world.

'The Call of Wings', in which a phrase from Wagner's *Rienzi* exemplifies the mystical, transforming power of music, is one of the earliest short stories Agatha Christie wrote, dating from before the First World War. Towards the end of her life, the author herself still thought it 'not bad'. You wish she had pursued this particular vein of fantasy more thoroughly, for 'The Call of Wings' is a fascinating little parable about the nature and perhaps the purpose of art.

The most ingenious story in the volume is a piece of crime fiction, 'The

Witness for the Prosecution' which, twenty years later, Agatha Christie turned into a play with (almost) the same title, and which subsequently became a film (see p. 174). This is one of her finest stories. It is interesting to note that, in the story, the criminal escapes justice, but that, by the time she came to write the stage adaptation, Mrs Christie wanted her murderer punished, if not by the law then by some other agency. She altered the ending accordingly, and fought successfully to have her new ending accepted, for those concerned with the production of the play apparently would have preferred the original ending.

'The Fourth Man', which is about dual personality, and 'The Last Seance', a powerful and frightening supernatural tale, are among the other very successful stories in *The Hound of Death*, but there is really not one failure among the entire twelve.

The Hound of Death was not published as a collection in the US. All twelve stories have appeared in America, but spread, together with other stories, between three volumes. 'Witness for the Prosecution', 'The Red Signal', 'The Fourth Man', 'Wireless' (under the title 'Where There's a Will'), 'The Mystery of the Blue Jar' and 'S.O.S.' are to be found with three other stories in a volume published only in the United States, *Witness for the Prosecution* (1948). 'The Last Seance' is in a volume of eight stories, *Double Sin*, published in the United States in 1961, its contents drawn from several English collections. The remaining stories, 'The Hound of Death', 'The Gypsy', 'The Lamp', 'The Strange Case of Sir Arthur Carmichael' and 'The Call of Wings' are in *The Golden Ball*, a volume of fifteen stories published in the United States in 1971. (All but two of the other stories in *The Golden Ball* come from a 1934 English volume, *The Listerdale Mystery*.)

Why Didn't They Ask Evans? or *The Boomerang Clue* (1934)

For most of the nineteen-thirties, until shortly before the outbreak of the Second World War, the Mallowans spent part of every year on archaeological excavations in Syria. Agatha helped Max in various ways, and managed to write a number of her books at times when she was not washing or marking pottery, taking photographs, or dealing with the expedition's paper work. The usual season for excavation in the Middle East was from October to March, and much of the spring and summer period from April to September was spent happily in Devon, at Agatha's family home in Torquay.

After successfully leading his expedition at Arpachiyah, Max Mallowan turned his attention to another part of Mesopotamia. Syria, which was then under French Mandate, offered generous terms to the archaeological excavator and granted licences for digging with a minimum of red tape. Mallowan's special interests at this time were prehistoric, but he wanted to widen them. Western Syria and the Lebanon were already the scene of intense archaeological activity, so Mallowan decided to conduct a survey in the Habur Valley in the northeast of Syria, and he and Agatha spent November and December of 1934 in the Middle East in connection with this. The preparations for their survey involved a long stay in Beirut, where they found a modest little hotel named Bassoul, with what Max Mallowan described as a delightful terrace overlooking the waterfront. In Beirut they purchased a four-cylinder Ford van for £150, had its chassis raised to make it more suitable for the rough terrain they intended to survey, painted it lavender and christened it 'Queen Mary' because of its great dignity and height. This remarkable vehicle conveyed equipment and four tents, two for the Europeans, one for the servants, and one which housed the lavatory.

On leaving Beirut, the party headed for Homas and then crossed to Palmyra. They established a camp near Hasaka, at the junction of the upper and lower Habur and one of the wadis. Later, they went a few miles south and pitched camp at a place called Meyadin in the courtyard of a huge khan.[17] The pillar of the expedition, according to Mallowan, was a young architect named Robin Macartney, 'a man endowed with a cast-iron stomach and few words'. Agatha at first found Mac extremely difficult to get to know. She was convinced that his taciturnity and monosyllabic replies to her conversational gambits meant that he disapproved of her. It was not until Mac's reserve was broken down when he fell headlong into thick, slimy mud while attempting to put up a tent, and his spontaneous language was discovered to be less stuffy than his usual speech, that the barriers fell and Mac and Agatha became firm friends.

The expedition examined various tells, until finally Mallowan decided to concentrate upon Tell Chagar Bazar and Tell Brak. Chagar Bazar seemed to him the most tempting, rewarding and practical prospect, so this became his immediate objective for the following season, after which he planned to make an attempt on the mighty mound of Tell Brak. Malloway recognized that Tell Brak was probably the most important archaeological site he would have the opportunity to explore, and made a resolution that he would dig there one day. However, he decided to get his bearings by first excavating the lesser but important mound of Chagar Bazar.

In due course, the party made its way back to the Mediterranean coast, Mrs Mallowan electing to travel by train and meet Max and Mac at Aleppo. From Aleppo they all went on by train to Beirut where the Mallowans parted with Mac who was going to Palestine. Max and Agatha spent the winter in Egypt.

1934 was the year in which five titles by Agatha Christie were published: two crime novels, two volumes of short stories and, under her pseudonym of Mary Westmacott, a crypto-autobiographical novel. Both crime novels are among Mrs Christie's best.

The first to appear, *Why Didn't They Ask Evans?* (published in the United States as *The Boomerang Clue*) is in the same category as *The Secret Adversary*, *The Man in the Brown Suit*, *The Secret of Chimneys* and *The Seven Dials Mystery*, in that its characters do not include any one of Mrs Christie's regular detectives. The mystery or crime is solved by one or more of the people involved, with little help from police or other professional investigators. *The Secret of Chimneys* and *The Seven Dials Mystery*, in both of which Lady Eileen Brent, familiarly known as 'Bundle', played a major part, had both been more than faintly Wodehousian. *Why Didn't They Ask Evans?* also has a somewhat bossy young lady of the aristocratic class, Lady Frances Derwent (Frankie) who helps her middleclass chum, Bobby Jones, the vicar's son, to investigate a murder, but its tone is more akin to the early novels of Evelyn Waugh than to Wodehouse. At moments, the world of *Vile Bodies* (published in 1930) is not far away. As a team, Frankie and Bobby have much in common with Tommy and Tuppence Beresford, and like the Beresfords they are motivated as much by a desire for adventure as by any pressing need to become involved with the mystery which confronts them.

The title, both in its English and American versions, derives from the cryptic question uttered shortly before he dies by a man who has apparently fallen over a cliff on the west coast of Wales. He has been found by Bobby who stays with the dying man while his golfing companion, the local doctor, goes off for help. The man opens his eyes, murmurs 'Why didn't they ask Evans?', and dies. It is, as we shall discover more than thirty chapters later, a boomerang clue, indeed. But Bobby and Lady Frances undergo a number of adventures before the meaning of the question is revealed to them, adventures which include being bound and gagged by the villain and left in an attic to die, and all related in the light-hearted style which Agatha Christie adopted for her thrillers. A certain economy with plot devices becomes apparent, when Bobby climbs a tree to look through a window into a nursing home and falls from the tree. Julius P. Hersheimmer had done exactly the same in *The Secret Adversary* twelve years earlier. Frankie's trick, in *Why Didn't They Ask Evans?*, of deliberately crashing her car, will be imitated by Oliver Manders in *Three-Act Tragedy*, and for the same reason.

Why Didn't They Ask Evans? is both thriller and mystery, and is thoroughly satisfying as either. In 1980, it was filmed by a British TV Company, London Weekend. A faithful adaptation of the novel, it was impeccably directed by Tony Wharmby and John Davies. A first-rate cast included Francesca Annis as Frankie; James Warwick as Bobby; John Gielgud as Bobby's father, the vicar; Eric Porter, Bernard Miles, Leigh Lawson, Madeline Smith, Connie Booth and Robert Longden in other leading roles.

Why Didn't They Ask Evans? was shown on television in Great Britain, America and several other countries.

Murder on the Orient Express or *Murder in the Calais Coach* (1934)

Written on the dig at Arpachiyah in 1933, and dedicated to her husband, *Murder on the Orient Express* is one of Agatha Christie's most popular and, in the audacity of its solution, most outrageous murder mysteries. Almost the entire action takes place on the famous train on which, by the time she came to write the novel, Mrs Christie had travelled a number of times. For years before she set foot on the Orient Express, she had longed to travel on it. 'When I had travelled to France or Spain or Italy,' she wrote much later,[18] 'the Orient Express had often been standing at Calais, and I had longed to climb up into it.' She had travelled most of the way to and from Arpachiyah in 1933 on the Orient Express and, as she told an interviewer much later, was able to ensure that her details were accurate: 'On the way back I was able to check on things I had thought about on the way out. I had to see where all the switches were. After he had read my book, one man actually made the journey to check up on this.'

The confidence trick Mrs Christie plays on her readers this time is even more dazzling than the one in *The Murder of Roger Ackroyd*. The plot must by now be well known, especially since the very successful 1974 film of the novel; but Christie fans tend to play fair and not reveal dénouements to the uninitiated, and so future generations will probably still be able to enjoy pitting their wits against the cunning authoress. It gives little away to reveal that Mrs Christie clearly was inspired to write *Murder on the Orient Express* not only by the romantic image of the train which had intrigued her for years before she travelled on it for the first time but also by the tragic Lindbergh kidnapping. (The American aviator Charles Lindbergh had made the first solo flight across the Atlantic in 1927. In March, 1932, his infant son was kidnapped and killed.) The startling solution to the problem posed by *Murder on the Orient Express* was first suggested to Agatha Christie by her husband Max Mallowan, to whom the novel is dedicated.

The murder is committed in one of the sleeping compartments in the Istanbul-Calais coach of the train, and much of the subsequent action takes place in that coach and the adjoining one, which is the restaurant car. Hercule Poirot is on the train, returning from a visit to Syria where he has solved a difficult problem for the government of France. Shortly after the murder has been committed the train is brought to a halt in the middle of Yugoslavia by a snowstorm, and Poirot is prevailed upon by his old friend, M. Bouc, a Director of the Compagnie Internationale des Wagons Lits, to investigate, in the hope that, by the time the train reaches the Italian border, the murderer will have been apprehended and can be handed over to the Yugoslav police.

The suspects are a colourful and international collection of travellers: Mrs Hubbard, a loquacious American who has been visiting her daughter in Smyrna; the Princess Dragomiroff, an exotic Russian accompanied by her German maid; the Count and Countess Andrenyi, a Hungarian diplomat and his wife; a young English governess; a British Colonel on his way home from India on leave; Greta Ohlsson, a Swedish missionary ('Poor creature,' someone says of her, 'she's a Swede'); and two or three others. The murder victim is an American businessman named Ratchett. At least some of these individuals are not what, at first sight, they appear to be.

The famous American crime novelist Raymond Chandler was known to have despised Agatha Christie's solution to the Orient Express mystery, but he was one of a very small minority. Oddly, Agatha Christie revealed the ending by referring to it in a Poirot novel, *Cards on the Table*, two years later. All that will be said here of the solution is that, though perhaps improbable, it does explain an earlier improbability in the story.

Poirot, in fact, propounds two theories, one of which is more likely than the other, and allows M. Bouc of the Wagon Lit company to choose between them. The question of whether to allow the criminal to escape is raised, and it becomes clear that Poirot is, under certain circumstances, not averse to allowing someone to take the law into his own hands, if justice cannot be achieved by legal means. Mrs Christie appears to condone this, not only in *Murder on the Orient Express* but also, a quarter of a century later, in a play, *The Unexpected Guest*. In other words, not only did she not disapprove of capital punishment, she was also willing, under certain circumstances, for that punishment to be inflicted by agencies outside the legal system.

The murder mystery is usually at its best when a group of people are isolated from the world at large, on an ocean liner, in a snow-bound country house or, as in this instance, on a train. The train has a fascination of its own, especially the glamorous international train, and none more so than the Orient Express which is now only a memory, though a London-Venice rail service, calling itself Venice Simplon-Orient Express Ltd and using four of the old Pullman carriages, recommenced in 1982.[19]

Agatha Christie's murder mystery is not the first novel of adventure to have been set on the famous train. *La Madonne des Sleepings* by Maurice Dekobra

(1925) had appeared in an English translation in 1927 as *The Madonna of the Sleeping Cars*, and Graham Greene's *Stamboul Train* was published in 1932, two years before Agatha Christie's novel. It is curious that Greene's title was changed for American publication to *Orient Express*, since Agatha Christie's *Murder on the Orient Express* was published in America as *Murder in the Calais Coach*. Could it have been that the Christie title was changed in order to avoid confusion in the United States with Graham Greene's novel?

On its first publication, *Murder on the Orient Express* was widely and favourably reviewed. The distinguished novelist Compton Mackenzie, writing in the London *Daily Mail*, called it 'a capital example of its class', and even Dorothy L. Sayers, Agatha Christie's rival in the field of crime fiction, wrote in the *Sunday Times* that it was 'a murder mystery conceived and carried out on the finest classical lines'. Reviewing the American edition, *Time Magazine* said: 'Basing the tale on America's great kidnapping, the author brings the arch-criminal on a snow-bound Yugoslavian express. Coincidentally, the rotund, penetrating Poirot is aboard. Clues abound. Alibis are frequent and unassailable. But nothing confounds the great Hercule who, after propounding alternative solutions to his jury of two, retires modestly.'

Murder on the Orient Express was made into a film, but not until 1974 when it became the most successful British film ever made, with gross profits of more than £20,000,000. EMI was the production company, the producers were John Brabourne and Richard Goodwin, and the director was Sidney Lumet. All the roles were played by stars or very well-known feature actors: Albert Finney (Poirot), Richard Widmark (Ratchett, the victim), Lauren Bacall (Mrs Hubbard), Wendy Hiller (Princess Dragomiroff), Rachel Roberts (Hildegarde Schmidt, the German maid), Michael York and Jacqueline Bisset (the Andrenyis), Vanessa Redgrave (Mary Debenham, the English governess), Sean Connery (Colonel Arbuthnot), Ingrid Bergman (Greta Ohlsson), Martin Balsam (M. Bouc, whose name was changed, presumably for reasons of euphony, to Bianchi), John Gielgud (the victim's valet, with again a change of name from Masterman to Beddoes), Anthony Perkins, Colin Blakely, Denis Quilley, and Jean Pierre Cassel.

This was altogether a different affair from the cheaply made Agatha Christie movies of the thirties. Expensively and stylishly produced in colour, it was highly entertaining, though the profusion of famous faces on the screen tended to detract from the dramatic effect. Albert Finney took great pains to sink himself into the character of Poirot, with the help of an excellent make-up artist, but the other stars were instantly recognizable. Recreated at the studio in Elstree by the designer Tony Walton, who had managed to borrow parts of the old Orient Express from the museum of the Compagnie des Wagons Lits in Paris, the train almost stole the show.

Paul Dehn's screenplay was highly respectful to the novel. Max Mallowan revealed that Agatha Christie, who generally disliked the film versions of her books, 'gave a rather grudging appreciation to this one', which was described in the London *Times* as 'touchingly loyal' to its source. *The Times* critic added, 'It stays precisely at the level of Agatha Christie, demands the same adjustments, the same precarious suspension of disbelief'.

Agatha Christie said of the film: 'It was very well made except for one mistake I cannot find in my heart to forgive. It was Albert Finney as my detective

Hercule Poirot. I wrote that he had the finest moustache in England – and he didn't in the film. I thought that a pity. Why shouldn't he have the best moustache?'[20]

On 3 May 1981, the London *News of the World* reported a murder in Bamberg, West Germany, which it called 'a carbon-copy crime of Agatha Christie's thriller, *Murder on the Orient Express*'. The method by which a sixteen-year-old girl was killed certainly suggested a knowledge of the novel or the film.

The Listerdale Mystery (1934)

Of the twelve stories which comprise *The Listerdale Mystery*, no more than seven are concerned with crime, although deception of one kind or another is practised in most of them. They are, with one or two exceptions, frivolous and amusing in tone, agreeable though rather slight. The 'romantic interest' which Mrs Christie tended to minimize in her crime novels is indulged in several of the stories in which young couples are thrown together because of crimes or swindles of some kind, and fall in love. This happens in the title story, 'The Listerdale Mystery', though the 'swindle' is a charitable one and the couple are not exactly in the first flush of youth. There is a snobbishly slighting reference to 'half-castes'.

In 'Sing a Song of Sixpence', the old nursery rhyme is used in the detection of a crime. It must have been one of Agatha Christie's favourite nursery rhymes, for it was later to feature in a Miss Marple novel, *A Pocket Full of Rye* (1953) as well as in the short story 'Four-and-Twenty Blackbirds' (in *Three Blind Mice*, USA, 1948, and *The Adventure of the Christmas Pudding*, UK, 1960).

The hero of 'The Rajah's Emerald' is a resourceful young man named James Bond, who is almost as adept in the apprehension of criminals as Ian Fleming's less agreeable character of the same name who flourished in the 1950s. The final story in the volume, 'Swan Song', will appeal to opera buffs, for it concerns a prima donna who gives a charity performance of *Tosca*, at which her Scarpia dies in earnest. The plot is rather obvious, but at least Agatha Christie is familiar with Puccini's opera, and the references to Maria Jeritza suggests that the author may have attended that temperamental prima donna's sole performance in *Tosca* at Covent Garden on 16 June 1925, when Jeritza sang the aria, 'Vissi d'arte', lying on her stomach on the floor. ('And why not?' is the response of Agatha Christie's soprano, Paula Nazorkoff. 'I will sing it on my back with my legs waving in the air.') Since Agatha Christie retained a love of music throughout her life, it is odd that 'Swan Song' should be her only story, apart from *Giants' Bread*, to concern that art, and odder still that she should not know that Radames in *Aida* is a tenor role.

'Mr Eastwood's Adventure' has caused some bibliographical confusion amongst writers on Agatha Christie. In it, Anthony Eastwood, a young writer, is attempting to produce a story called 'The Mystery of the Second Cucumber'. Eventually, he changes his mind and begins another story which he intends to call 'The Mystery of the Spanish Shawl'. Agatha Christie's story, 'Mr Eastwood's Adventure', has appeared in the United States in the volume, *Surprise! Surprise!* under the title of 'The Mystery of the Spanish Shawl'. 'The Mystery of the Spanish Shawl' is the same story as 'Mr Eastwood's Adventure', and has no connection with another Christie story which exists not only under

78

two titles but in two versions (one with and one without Hastings): 'The Mystery of the Spanish Chest' and 'The Mystery of the Baghdad Chest' (see p. 114).

The two best-known stories in *The Listerdale Mystery* are 'Accident' and 'Philomel Cottage'. The former, a clever and chillingly ironic little tale about a murderer who is *not* caught at the end, has been reprinted in several anthologies of crime stories, while the latter, a first-rate story of suspense with a dénouement which is open to more than one interpretation, was expanded in 1936 by the actor and playwright, Frank Vosper, into a play, *Love from a Stranger*, (see p. 94).

The Listerdale Mystery was not published in the United States. Two of its stories, 'Philomel Cottage' and 'Accident', first appeared in America in 1948 in the collection *Witness for the Prosecution* (which also contained 'Witness for the Prosecution' and five other stories from the 1933 English collection, *The Hound of Death*, and 'The Second Gong', a shorter, earlier version of a long story which is to be found in the 1937 collection published in England as *Murder in the Mews* and in the USA as *Dead Man's Mirror*). With the exception of 'Sing a Song of Sixpence' and 'Mr Eastwood's Adventure', the remainder of the stories in *The Listerdale Mystery* are to be found in the American collection, *The Golden Ball*, which did not appear until 1971. 'Mr Eastwood's Adventure' is to be found in *Surprise! Surprise!* (1965), a collection of stories which have all appeared in other volumes, but 'Sing a Song of Sixpence' has not been published in the USA.

Parker Pyne Investigates or *Mr Parker Pyne, Detective* (1934)

The American title of Agatha Christie's only volume in which the character of Parker Pyne is introduced is inappropriate, for in one of the stories Mr Pyne states quite categorically: 'You must remember I am not a detective. I am, if you like to put it that way, a heart specialist.' The British title is not quite accurate either, for Mr Parker Pyne does not so much investigate as arrange. But Mrs Christie seems to have been in two minds about her new character, for the twelve stories in the volume divide neatly into two categories, with six stories in each category.

In the first six, all of whose titles begin 'The Case of. . .', Mr Parker Pyne[21] is presented as a retired civil servant who, after thirty-five years of compiling statistics in a government office, has decided to use in a novel fashion the experience he has gained. Engaging a secretary, Felicity Lemon, he rents a small office in London and inserts an advertisement in the Personal column of *The Times*: 'ARE YOU HAPPY? IF NOT, CONSULT MR PARKER PYNE, 17 Richmond Street.' The unhappy begin to trickle in to him with their problems: 'The Case of the Middle-Aged Wife', 'The Case of the Discontented Soldier', and four others.

In the remaining half-dozen stories in the volume, Mr Parker Pyne is on holiday and reluctant to accept cases. However, he finds himself involved in acting as an adviser and occasionally as an investigator when odd things happen or crimes are revealed or contemplated. In these six stories, he behaves rather as Poirot or Miss Marple might. Mr Parker Pyne's holiday takes him via the Orient Express to the Middle East, ground which Mrs Christie had covered more than once and which she knew rather well by this time. 'Have You Got Everything You Want?' is set mainly on her favourite train, and the other five stories take us

79

to Baghdad, Shiraz, Petra, Delphi, and on a cruise up the Nile.

Parker Pyne is an engaging character, plump, bald and probably in his sixties. His theory is that there are five principal types of unhappiness, and that once the cause of the malady is known, a remedy should be possible. His cures are arrived at by unconventional means, but he guarantees them. In cases where no treatment can be of any avail, he says frankly that he can do nothing and refuses to accept the client. Mr Parker Pyne has one or two part-time helpers as well as his secretary, Felicity Lemon, who will later become Hercule Poirot's secretary. There is, for instance, a young man named Claude Luttrell, 'one of the handsomest specimens of lounge lizard to be found in England'. He is used in 'The Case of the Middle-Aged Wife' to make a straying husband jealous of the wife he has been neglecting. In 'The Case of the Distressed Lady', which is about the theft of an emerald ring, Claude Luttrell and another of Mr Parker Pyne's regulars, Madeleine de Sara, 'the most seductive of vamps', are required to pose as internationally famous exhibition dancers at a huge party given by the wealthy Dortheimers. This particular case proved more complex than at first seemed to be, and Mr Parker Pyne revealed a startling investigative talent.

The first six stories are the more unusual, but the second six, in which the author draws on her own experience of the Middle East, are especially interesting. 'The Pearl of Price' was written after a visit Agatha and Max Mallowan made to the temples and rock tombs of Petra; 'The House at Shiraz', an imaginative and psychologically penetrating little tale, is set in the house they saw at Shiraz; and the potted crime novel which is encapsulated in 'Death on the Nile', a story which gave only its title, none of its plot, to the 1937 Christie novel, *Death on the Nile*, is a gem. Prodigal in the almost wasteful ease with which she threw plots away, Mrs Christie parsimoniously stored up fragments of experience with which to garnish those plots. The minor incident of Mr Parker Pyne's bug powder is found to have its basis in fact when one reads *Come, Tell Me How You Live* (1946), Agatha Christie's account of her visits to Syria in the thirties. In one of these stories, the criminal is an archaeologist.

Critics of Agatha Christie are divided on the merits of the Parker Pyne stories, opinions ranging from Robert Barnard's 'mediocre'[22] to the view expressed by Barzun and Taylor[23] that, 'On rereading, the collection holds up very well'. The Parker Pyne stories, slight though they are, are well worth seeking out, for their hero is a delightful and unusual character, whom Agatha Christie wrote about again only in two further stories, 'Problem at Pollensa Bay' and 'The Regatta Mystery', both of which are to be found in the 1939 American collection, *The Regatta Mystery* (see p. 114).

One of Mr Parker Pyne's occasional helpers, whom we meet in 'The Case of the Discontented Soldier', is Mrs Ariadne Oliver, 'the sensational novelist'. Ariadne Oliver is an amusing and satirical self-portrait of Agatha Christie. Like Mrs Christie, she is addicted to munching apples as she types her stories, and she is agreeably untidy. As we come to know Mrs Oliver better in seven novels written between the mid-thirties and the early seventies we shall discover other similarities to her author. We find in 'The Case of the Discontented Soldier', in which she presents Mr Parker Pyne with a plot, that Mrs Oliver is the author of 'forty-six successful works of fiction, all bestsellers in England and America, and freely translated into French, German, Italian, Hungarian, Finnish, Japanese and Abyssinian'. If this was not true of Agatha Christie in 1934, it certainly would be a decade or two later. Mrs Ariadne Oliver is referred to in a second Parker Pyne story, 'The Case of the Rich Woman', but does not put in an appearance. We next encounter her in the 1936 novel, *Cards on the Table*, when she makes the acquaintance of Hercule Poirot. Her involvement with Poirot in six of his most celebrated cases provides Mrs Christie with numerous opportunities to poke fun at herself, which she does with unfailing good humour. It is in *Cards on the Table* that Ariadne Oliver is revealed to be not simply a bestselling novelist but a bestselling crime novelist!

A minor inconsistency, due either to Mrs Christie's well-known occasional carelessness in matters of detail or to that of her editors, occurs in 'The Case of the City Clerk' when the client is introduced as 'a man of forty-five' on the first page only to age three years on the following page.

Unfinished Portrait (1934)

The last of Agatha Christie's 1934 publications, *Unfinished Portrait* appeared under the name of Mary Westmacott, the *nom de plume* Mrs Christie had first adopted for *Giant's Bread* in 1930. This second Mary Westmacott novel differs from the other five which Agatha Christie published under that name in that it is much more overtly and directly autobiographical than the others. There is something of autobiography in the work of every writer of fiction, however slight or however disguised that element of autobiography may be. Some novelists reveal themselves in more devious ways than others, some use more and finer filters than others. Some, perhaps the majority, progress from lightly disguised autobiography in their earlier works to imaginative reworking of their spiritual if not their physical lives and experiences. Agatha Christie was a novelist of skill and imagination. Her acceptance of a certain discipline of the creative imagination in her crime novels should not lead one to the belief that she was incapable of exploring the psychology of character much more deeply than in those murder mysteries. In most of her Mary Westmacott novels, Mrs Christie can be seen to revel in the lifting of restraints, as she pursues character and motivation and allows her personages to develop in a more complex way than would be suitable in a Poirot or Miss Marple story.

In *Unfinished Portrait*, however, Agatha Christie's aim was to produce a fictionalized and necessarily unfinished portrait of herself. The story is told by Larraby, a portrait painter who meets the heroine, Celia, on an island (which could be one of the Canary Islands) when Celia is on the point of committing suicide. He is instrumental in saving her life or at least in delaying her decision, becomes fascinated by what she tells him of herself, and proceeds to create her portrait. For a reason which becomes clear only at the end of the novel, Larraby elects to produce his portrait of Celia in words instead of in paint.

The story of Celia is remarkably similar to the story of Agatha as readers were eventually to be offered it in *An Autobiography* more than forty years later. Several incidents are common to *An Autobiography* and *Unfinished Portrait*, and the novel is quite clearly a fictionalized, more detailed, and emotionally more forthcoming version of the first third of the autobiography. The portraits of Celia's mother and her grandmother are really of young Agatha Miller's mother and the grandmother with whom she stayed in Ealing. The men in Celia's life are the men in Agatha's life, and Dermot, whom Celia marries, is Archie Christie.

Writing only a few years after the end of her first marriage, Agatha Christie in *Unfinished Portrait* was concerned to produce her own portrait, perhaps in order to attempt to understand herself and her behaviour. In the novel, Celia makes a first suicide attempt during a period of nervous collapse, and is rescued by a young cockney from the river into which she has jumped. On the island, having surveyed the mess she has made of her life, and fearful that she may not even be able to continue as a novelist since she can no longer summon up much interest in other people or in herself, Celia intends to attempt suicide a second time. Much of what we learn about her throws light upon Mrs Christie's nervous breakdown and her disappearance in 1926.

Agatha Christie's second husband, Max Mallowan, wrote of *Unfinished Portrait*: 'The book is not one of her best because, exceptionally, it is a blend of real people and events with imagination. Only the initiated can know how much actual history is contained therein, but in Celia we have more nearly than anywhere else a portrait of Agatha.' Mallowan wrote those words after having read his wife's autobiography. You can therefore confidently accept Celia as a recognizable portrait of Agatha, and a much more candid and revealing portrait than that which she chose to present to the readers of her autobiography. Wearing the protective cloak of fiction, she was able to confess to aspects of herself which she could not bring herself to acknowledge in a non-fiction format.

Unfinished Portrait, as a novel, is the least satisfactory of the six Mary Westmacott titles, though it is thoroughly readable, and interesting in its account of a woman trying to come to terms with her own nature. It is most valuable for what it tells us about Agatha Christie, who was both a conventional middleclass wife and mother and a cold-blooded artist adept at posing as middleclass wife and mother. She was equable of temperament, yet curiously ill-balanced. She contained, and somehow depended upon, her opposites. In *Unfinished Portrait*, Larraby says of Celia: 'Like all people who live chiefly by the inner vision, Celia was peculiarly impervious to influence from outside. She was stupid when it came to realities.' This, we should remember, is also Agatha Christie talking of Agatha Christie.

The next Westmacott novel was not to appear until ten years later.

Three-Act Tragedy or *Murder in Three Acts* (1935)

It was in 1935 that Max Mallowan began his excavations at Chagar Bazar in Syria. Agatha accompanied him, and the party also included Robin Macartney (Mac) and Richard Barnett, a 'mine of esoteric learning'. They employed approximately one hundred and forty-five workmen, described by Mallowan as 'a mixed gang of Arabs and Kurds, with a sprinkling of Yezidis, the mild devil-worshippers from the Jebel Sunjar, and a few odd Christians.' Some of their best men, however, proved to be Turks who had entered the country illegally. They were usually tougher physical specimens than the Arabs, and the expedition was happy to employ them.

As they were to spend two seasons at Chagar Bazar, the party set about building a mudbrick house, to designs by Mac. They were proud of it when it was completed, and somewhat annoyed when the local Sheikh bespattered all four corners with the blood of a newly slain sheep, an act of propitiation towards supernatural forces which spoiled the appearance of the freshly plastered brickwork. The seven-roomed house had cost about £150 to build, including labour and all the woodwork fittings.

The archaeological significance of his work in Syria in the thirties is described in non-technical terms by Max Mallowan in *Mallowan's Memoirs*, while the details of life on the digs is brought to life admirably by Agatha Christie in *Come, Tell Me How You Live*, which she was not to publish until 1946, although she began keeping a diary in Syria, with a view to expanding her notes eventually into a book. The life suited her. Max would depart every morning at dawn to work at the mound, and on most days Agatha would accompany him, though occasionally she would stay at home to deal with various chores. There was pottery to be mended, there were objects to be labelled, and of course there was usually an Agatha Christie novel to be created on the typewriter.

In addition to her other duties, Agatha was given the job of developing photographs, for which purpose a dark room was allotted to her which she considered rather similar to the 'Little Ease' of mediaeval times. Unable either to sit or stand in what was, in effect, a small cupboard, she would crawl in on all fours, develop plates, and emerge almost asphyxiated with heat and unable to stand upright. Though her husband occasionally murmured, 'I think you're wonderful, dear', he was interested much less in her account of her sufferings in the dark room than in the negatives she brought out of it. Small wonder that, although she enjoyed her Middle East experience every year, toward the end of each season Agatha would begin to daydream of Devon, of red rocks and blue sea, of her daughter, her dog, bowls of Devonshire cream, apples, and bathing.

1935 saw the publication of three Agatha Christie crime novels, all of them featuring Hercule Poirot: *Three-Act Tragedy* (whose American title was *Murder in Three Acts*), *Death in the Clouds* (or, in America, *Death in the Air*) and *The ABC Murders*. Hastings is absent from the first two but makes an appearance in the third.

The first five chapters of *Three-Act Tragedy* constitute the 'First Act: Suspicion', the next seven are 'Second Act: Certainty', and the remaining fifteen are 'Third Act: Discovery'. As in a theatre programme there are credits at the beginning of the book:

Directed by
SIR CHARLES CARTWRIGHT

Assistant Directors
MR SATTERTHWAITE
MISS HERMIONE LYTTON GORE

Clothes by
AMBROSINE LTD

Illumination by
HERCULE POIROT

There is no 'cast of characters', but if there were it would have to include the same people, for Sir Charles Cartwright, a famous actor living in retirement in Cornwall by the sea, not only directs the proceedings or at least sets them in motion by giving a dinner party at which one of the guests dies, but also plays a leading role in the subsequent events, as do the somewhat callow but engaging

Miss Lytton Gore, Cynthia Dacres who is the proprietress of Ambrosine Ltd, Mr Satterthwaite who makes here the first of his only two appearances outside a Harley Quin story (see p. 57) and, of course, Hercule Poirot. Other guests at the fateful dinner party, not all of whom survive to the end of the story, include Sir Bartholomew Strange, a distinguished Harley Street physician; Angela Sutcliffe, a well-known actress; Freddie Dacres, husband of Cynthia; Miss Wills, better known as the playwright Anthony Astor, and 'cut off by success', as Mrs Christie rather bitchily puts it, 'from her spiritual home – a boarding house in Bournemouth'.

Also at the dinner party is Oliver Manders; 'A handsome young fellow, twenty-five at a guess. Something, perhaps, a little sleek about his good looks. Something else – something – was it foreign? Something unEnglish about him.' It is only when Miss Lytton Gore jokingly calls him a 'slippery Shylock' that Mr Satterthwaite realizes 'that's it – not foreign – Jew!' But this is 1935, and Oliver's semitic ancestry is not held against him. Even the snobbish Mr Satterthwaite admits that Hermione Lytton Gore and Oliver Manders make an attractive pair. 'Both so young and good-looking . . . and quarrelling, too – always a healthy sign.'

The particular kind of deception played by the author on her readers in *Three-Act Tragedy* is one which some of them might on this occasion see through, for this is by no means one of the best examples of it. The novel is a delight to read, for the characters are a more varied lot than usual. However, few of them are brought to life as fully as you would wish them to be. Mrs Christie seems this time to have been so interested in her murderer that she has neglected to round out some of the other characters. A minor mystery is that, when some of the suspects are entertained by Poirot in London, it is 'in his slightly florid suite at the Ritz'. Why does he need to stay at the Ritz? Is his apartment being redecorated? We are never told.

Though the characters of the actor (Sir Charles Cartwright) and the female playwright with the male *nom de plume* (Anthony Astor) are certainly not based upon real people in those professions, Mrs Christie surely intended her readers to note a light-hearted superficial resemblance to certain personality traits of the celebrated actor-manager, Sir Gerald du Maurier, and the playwright, Gordon Daviot. Du Maurier, 'a great exponent of natural acting and of the art that conceals art, was virtually the leader of the English stage.'[24] He died in 1934 at the age of sixty-one. The pseudonym of Gordon Daviot (in whose *Richard of Bordeaux* John Gielgud achieved his first big success in 1932) concealed the identity of Elizabeth MacKintosh (1896–1952) who also wrote detective fiction, first as Gordon Daviot and later as Josephine Tey.

Though it is no longer likely to be thought one of the best of Agatha Christie's crime novels of the thirties, *Three-Act Tragedy* was initially very favourably received, and became the first Christie novel to sell more than 10,000 copies within a year of publication.

The *New English Weekly* thought *Three-Act Tragedy* 'her wittiest novel so far', *The Times Literary Supplement* was of the opinion that 'very few readers will guess the murderer before Mr Hercule Poirot reveals the secret', the *Manchester Guardian* thought the author 'in great form' and found 'the characters (as always with Mrs Christie) . . . lifelike and lively', and Ralph Partridge in the *New Statesman* was enormously impressed:

Mrs Christie can be trusted to turn out at least one book a year up to her own impeccable standard. *Three-Act Tragedy* has given scope for all her art. The power to wrap up clues in the easiest and most natural conversation; the choice of contrasting characters, each outlined with just sufficient sharpness to give them all individuality; the steady pulse of events in chapter after chapter; the originality of the murder plot itself, and the dramatic suspense of the solution hold you until the latest possible minute. These are the characteristics of a Christie novel in the *Roger Ackroyd* tradition, and it is here that *Three-Act Tragedy* takes its place in the succession, a worthy descendant of *Lord Edgware Dies* . . . Nothing could be more baffling to any reader or detective than the opening crime. Even Poirot could find nothing to suggest foul play.

And even the famous drama critic, James Agate, writing in the *Daily Express*, succumbed to Mrs Christie's 'tender strokes of art':

In my opinion, *Three-Act Tragedy* succeeds, because as a hardened reader of crime stories I have ceased to care who murders anybody so long as up to the last chapter the story has held me. Here Mrs Christie succeeds abundantly for the simple reason that she is an amusing writer.

The ending of *Three-Act Tragedy* is certainly an amusing example of Poirot's endearingly childlike egotism. When Mr Satterthwaite remarks that he might accidentally have drunk the poisoned cocktail, 'There is an even more terrible possibility that you have not considered,' said Poirot. 'Eh?' 'It might have been ME,' said Hercule Poirot.

Death in the Clouds or *Death in the Air* (1935)

The title of *Death in the Clouds*, the second of the 1935 Hercule Poirot crime novels, was changed for publication in the USA to *Death in the Air*, presumably to avoid confusion with some other novel of the same or similar title. However, Barzun and Taylor list no other 'Death in the Clouds', but another 'Death in the Air', a short story by the American crime writer, Cornell Woolrich.[25]

Hastings is absent from this inventively plotted Poirot mystery, in which the murder is committed on the aircraft 'Prometheus', during the midday Universal Airlines flight from Paris (Le Bourget) to London (Croydon). The murderer can therefore only be one of the eleven passengers in the rear compartment of the plane, or one of the two stewards. Since one of the passengers is Hercule Poirot, he has to be considered a suspect along with everyone else. But surely Agatha Christie wouldn't dare – or would she? The reader may relax, for Hercule Poirot is not the murderer. But, as usual with Mrs Christie, hardly anyone else is to be trusted.

The point has been made that the most satisfying Agatha Christie crime novels are those in which a group of people is somehow isolated from the world at large, and one of them is killed. The country house party, the international express train, a remote archaeological site in the Middle East, the small village community in which a stranger would certainly be noticed, each of these Mrs Christie used more than once. Now the modern method of travelling, the air flight, is also put to nefarious use. Poirot does not succeed in solving the mystery before the plane touches down at the old, pre-Heathrow airport (or aerodrome to use the thirties term) of Croydon, for not until the plane is about five minutes' flying time away from its destination is it realized that Madame Giselle is not asleep but dead. The investigation takes place in London and Paris, and Poirot works in co-operation not only with his old friend and colleague, Inspector Japp, but also with M. Fournier of the Sûreté, a more sympathetic French police officer than Giraud (from *The Murder on the Links*). 'I have also heard of you from M. Giraud,' says M. Fournier, as he is introduced to Poirot.

It is not quite clear, at first, how Madame Giselle has been murdered. There is a minute puncture mark on the side of her throat, and speculation encompasses a blowpipe containing 'the famous arrow poison of the South American Indians' with which Poirot makes much satirical play, an injection of some kind, and even a wasp which had been buzzing about the cabin at the time until it was killed by one of the other passengers. Those other passengers vary widely in character and class, with two types of aristocracy (landed gentry and ex-chorus girl), two young whitecollar workers who appear to be supplying 'romantic interest', the middleclasses (a doctor, a business man) and a French middle-aged father and adult son whom Inspector Japp mistakes for a pair of toughs. This is Agatha Christie's little joke at the expense of her husband's profession, for Poirot has to explain to Japp that the two men are not the toughs or cut-throats suggested by their appearance and manner, but 'two very learned and distinguished archaeologists'.

There is also what at the time of publication was a strictly private joke at the expense of Max Mallowan personally, for Mrs Christie's readers would not have known of the occasion when Mallowan abandoned his sick wife in Athens because it was important for him to get to Syria by a certain date. In *Death in the Clouds*, the younger of the two Frenchmen, in support of his thesis that the English care more for their work than for their wives, recounts the story of an Englishman whose wife had been taken ill while they were staying in a little hotel in Syria. 'He himself had to be somewhere in Iraq by a certain date. *Eh bien*, would you believe it, he left his wife and went on, so as to be "on duty" in time. And both he and his wife thought that quite natural; they thought him noble, unselfish. But the Doctor, who was not English, thought him a barbarian.'

Mrs Christie also satirizes her own profession of crime novelist in the character of Daniel Clancy, a writer of detective stories and the creator of the fictional detective, Wilbraham Rice. Clancy is Inspector Japp's favourite suspect: 'This is just the sort of damn-fool murder that a scribbler of rubbish would think he could get away with.' Incidentally, the French detective is seen to be distinctly superior to Japp in intelligence and imagination. Between them, Fournier, Japp and Poirot suspect everyone, including the two stewards, and the clues are fairly presented and discussed. Poirot, of course, plays fair with no one, but if he is watched closely throughout the investigation he may inadvertently reveal something of his thought processes earlier than he intended.

The murder is an audacious one, committed in full view of a cabin full of passengers, and the fact that none of them seems to have noticed it happening is commented upon more than once. As a puzzle, *Death in the Clouds* must be rated highly, though it is less exciting than Mrs Christie at her very best. Read now, fifty years or more after its publication, it retains a marvellous period flavour: the old Le Bourget-Croydon run is as richly nostalgic, surely, as the route of the

Orient Express. Two minor points: there is a careless mistake – and it *is* a mistake, not a significant clue – in Chapter 1, where a sentence about 'the passengers in the forward compartment' thinking their various thoughts clearly should refer to the passengers in the *rear* compartment, the one in which the murder takes place. The second point concerns a minor character, met briefly during the investigation in London. He is M. Antoine the hairdresser, the employer of Jane Grey, one of the passengers. M. Antoine's real name, we are informed, was Andrew Leech, and his only claim to foreign nationality lay in his 'having had a Jewish mother'. Sad to say, Mrs Christie allows him to be referred to by his employees as 'Ikey Andrew'. Her old prejudices, (or those of her characters, and many of her readers), though dying, are dying hard!

The ABC Murders (1935)

Having been absent from the three most recent Poirot novels, Hastings is allowed to make a reappearance in *The ABC Murders*, which in fact he narrates in his capacity as occasional chronicler of the adventures of Hercule Poirot. He begins by explaining that in June, 1935 he came home from his ranch in South America for a stay of about six months: 'It had been a difficult time for us out there. Like everyone else, we had suffered from world depression. I had various affairs to see to in England that I felt could only be successful if a personal touch was introduced. My wife remained to manage the ranch.' This is by no means the first time, nor will it be the last, that Hastings has persuaded himself he has business in London, and stayed away from home for months on end. This is 'staying late at the office' carried to extraordinary lengths.

Hastings finds that Poirot has moved from the rooms they used to share in Farraway Street, and is now installed 'in one of the newest type of service flats in London' which Hastings accuses his old friend of having chosen entirely on account of its strictly geometrical appearance and proportions. Poirot, who does not deny that he was influenced by 'the most pleasing symmetry' of the apartment block (whose name, we learn later, is Whitehaven Mansions), admits that he is 'like the prima donna who makes positively that farewell performance'. That farewell performance repeats itself an indefinite number of times.

In a Foreword 'by Captain Arthur Hastings, OBE', the narrator explains that he has departed from his usual practice of relating only those incidents and scenes at which he himself was present, and that certain chapters are written in the third person. He assures his readers that he can vouch for the occurrences related in those chapters. He is referring to his descriptions of the thoughts and actions of Mr Alexander Bonaparte Cust.

The ABC murders begin a few days after Poirot receives this letter:

Mr Hercule Poirot, – You fancy yourself, don't you, at solving mysteries that are too difficult for our poor thick-headed British police? Let us see, Mr Clever Poirot, just how clever you can be. Perhaps you'll find this nut too hard to crack. Look out for Andover on the 21st of the month.

Yours, etc.

ABC

At Andover, in Hampshire, an old woman who keeps a tobacco shop is murdered on the 21st. A second letter invites Poirot to direct his attention to

Bexhill-on-Sea on the 25th of the following month, and on that day a young waitress is murdered. Churston, in Devon, is the next town chosen by ABC who taunts Poirot in his third letter: 'Not so good at these little criminal matters as you thought yourself, are you? Rather past your prime, perhaps?' There is a fourth murder, in Doncaster.

There appears to be no connection between the victims, and Poirot's task is rendered almost impossible for this apparent madman would seem merely to be making his way through the alphabet, not only with places but also with people. The Andover victim was a Mrs Alice Ascher; in Bexhill, the murdered waitress was Betty Barnard; in Churston, Sir Carmichael Clarke; and in Doncaster – in Doncaster, something goes wrong, and the killer strikes at a man named Earlsfield. In each case, a copy of the monthly railway timetable, the *ABC Rail Guide* (still published monthly in Great Britain), open at the page listing the town of the murder, is found close by the victim. Poirot arrives at the truth before a fifth murder can be committed.

The truth is that there is method in ABC's madness or pretended madness. Poirot does not simply foil a madman, he solves a mystery: the mystery of why the murderer is proceeding through the alphabet. Would he have continued to Z, if Poirot had not arrived at the truth? Probably not. And who is Alexander Bonaparte Cust? He would appear to be the murderer. But is he? And who is he?

The plot of *The ABC Murders* is positively brilliant in its imagination and originality, and its characters are splendidly brought to life in what is one of Agatha Christie's masterpieces. The apparently motiveless murders certainly perplex Hercule Poirot, but it is he alone who arrives at the truth, and he does so through the application of logic to the problem, and through the exercise of the little grey cells of the brain.

The ABC Murders was serialized in a London newspaper, the *Daily Express*, in the autumn of 1935, and the newspaper published simultaneously a column of 'Readers' Guesses' at the solution. One reader accused Poirot of not making intelligent use of the *ABC Rail Guide*: 'He is anxious to reach Churston, and so takes the midnight train from Paddington, arriving at 7.15. Had he looked more carefully, he would have found that by leaving nearly two hours later – 1.40 a.m. – he would have arrived an hour earlier – at 6.10 a.m.' But it is Hastings, not Poirot, who chooses that particular train from the *ABC*, and he may well have been choosing the most convenient, rather than the fastest train. 'There's a midnight train – sleeping-car to Newton Abbot – gets there at 6.8 a.m., and to Churston at 7.15,' Hastings tells Poirot, adding that the *ABC Rail Guide* identifies Churston as a small town in Devon, 204¾ miles from Paddington, and with a population of 656. (The *ABC Rail Guide*[26] no longer deals in fractions of a mile. It now lists Churston as being 205 miles from Paddington Station, London, with a population of 1,582. Sadly, it reveals that trains no longer run to Churston, and that the nearest British Rail station is three miles away, at Paignton. From Paignton, there is a bus service to Churston which takes fourteen minutes. The midnight train gets to Newton Abbot at 4.17 a.m., knocking 1 hour, 51 minutes off its 1935 time.)

A number of crime writers have more or less plagiarized various aspects of *The ABC Murders*. In *Greenmask!* by the American novelist, Elizabeth Linington, one of a pair of homosexuals is an Agatha Christie fan. He and his partner decide to make use of her ABC plot in the murders they commit: they place a copy of the relevant California county guide on the body of each victim. Ellery Queen's *Cat of Many Tails* leans heavily on *The ABC Murders*. A French novel, *The Sleeping Car Murders* (filmed in 1966 with Simone Signoret and Yves Montand), was obviously inspired by Mrs Christie's Hercule Poirot adventure.

In Chapter 3 of *The ABC Murders* Poirot curiously adumbrates the plot of a later Agatha Christie novel which, although she did not write it until several months after *The ABC Murders*, must already have been clearly formed in the author's mind:

> 'Supposing,' murmured Poirot, 'that four people sit down to play bridge and one, the odd man out, sits in a chair by the fire. One of the four, while he is dummy, has gone over and killed him, and intent on the play of the hand, the other three have not noticed. Ah, there would be a crime for you! *Which of the four was it?*'

No one can say that Agatha Christie made things easy for herself.

'Shouldn't wonder if you ended by detecting your own death,' Inspector Japp says to Poirot, laughing heartily. In due course Poirot was to do precisely this, in his last and, in many ways, most extraordinary case, *Curtain*.

In 1966, more than thirty years after the novel's initial publication, a film version of *The ABC Murders* was made by Metro-Goldwyn-Mayer at their English studio in Elstree, near London. It was released as *The Alphabet Murders*. The American director of the film, Frank Tashlin, had made his name with comedies such as *The Paleface*, starring Bob Hope, and *Will Success Spoil Rock Hunter?*, and had also worked on Bugs Bunny cartoons. He turned the film into an exercise in visual comedy, aided and abetted by a cast which included Tony Randall as Poirot, Robert Morley as Hastings, Anita Ekberg, Maurice Denham, and Austin Trevor (who had played Poirot in films in the thirties), and by an adaptation by David Pursall and Jack Seddon which was a travesty of the novel. Guest appearances were made by Margaret Rutherford and Stringer Davis who had appeared in M-G-M's four Miss Marple movies earlier in the sixties, three of which had also been scripted by Pursall and Seddon.

The film was originally to have been directed by Seth Holt, a British director, with the American comedian Zero Mostel as Poirot, but this project came to grief on what should have been the first day of shooting when Agatha Christie took strong objection to the script which included a bedroom scene for Poirot. It could hardly have been further removed from the style of the novel than the script of Frank Tashlin's *The Alphabet Murders*.

Murder in Mesopotamia (1936)

Agatha Christie returned to the archaeological dig at Chagar Bazar with Max Mallowan and his party in the spring of 1936, 'and a pretty wet season and a most enjoyable one it was,' wrote Mallowan. They enjoyed residing in their 'lovely airy and light house' which, somewhat to their surprise, showed no signs of collapsing upon them. In addition to Agatha, Mallowan's assistants in the spring were a retired Colonel from the Indian army and a young architectural assistant who was nicknamed 'Bumps' since he referred to the ancient tells scattered about the plain as bumps and was astonished to learn that they represented the formerly inhabited places that the mission had come to dig. The retired Colonel 'was inclined to be a trifle military and expect [the Arab workers] to keep orderly ranks and line up in columns of four for their pay, but this they seemed to enjoy and looked on with amused tolerance.[27]

One day, when the team was digging near the town of Mosul, their old foreman approached Mallowan in great excitement, saying 'You must take your wife to Mosul tomorrow. There is to be a great event. There will be a hanging – a woman!' When Agatha expressed her repugnance at the thought, the old Arab was stupified. 'But it is a *woman*,' he repeated. 'Very seldom do we have the hanging of a woman. It is a Kurdish woman who has poisoned three husbands! Surely the *Khatun* would not like to miss *that*!'

Their last season at Chagar Bazar was in the autumn when they were joined by 'Mac', their companion from the previous year. It was now that they achieved their goal, seventy cuneiform tablets, mostly written within a single year about a decade before 1800 BC 'when Shamshi-Adad I was king of Assyria and his younger son Iasmah-Adad was in charge of the district'. These tablets gave a chronological orientation and established the dating of the painted Harbur pottery which the team had dug up. The connection of Chagar Bazar with the royal house of Assyria, as asserted by the tablets, was of extraordinary interest to archaeologists and historians, and fully justified Mallowan's choice of the site for excavation. He now decided to turn his attention the following season to the great mound of Tell Brak, 'much the most important centre in the Habur, and one that cried out for excavation'.

Hercule Poirot novels continued to pour from Agatha Christie's typewriter, and as so many were conceived and partly written in the Middle East it was hardly surprising that Mrs Christie should begin to set some of them in that part of the world. The first of these was *Murder in Mesopotamia*, which takes place on an archaeological dig in that part of Iraq formerly known as Mesopotamia, and is dedicated to 'my many archaeological friends in Iraq and Syria'. The murder victim is the wife of the archaeologist. It is possible that Mrs Christie's concentration upon Poirot throughout the middle and late thirties, and her consequent neglect of Miss Marple, are due to the fact that she herself was engaged in travelling with her husband and thus tended to make increasing use of foreign locations, into which it was considerably easier to fit Poirot than Miss Marple who would have seemed out of place away from her English village. In *Murder in Mesopotamia*, for example, Poirot's presence in the Middle East is explained on the grounds that he has been 'disentangling some military scandal in Syria' and happens to be passing through Hassanieh, the site of the dig, on his way to Baghdad. This military scandal, presumably, is the affair referred to at the beginning of *Murder on the Orient Express* (1934). Indeed, we are informed by the narrator at the end of *Murder in Mesopotamia* that 'M. Poirot went back to Syria and about a week later he went home on the Orient Express and got himself mixed up in another murder'.

The narrator is not Hastings, whom we must presume to be spending a little time at home with his wife in the Argentine, but Nurse Amy Leatheran who had travelled to Iraq to look after a mother and child, and who is engaged by Dr Leidner, the leader of the archaeological expedition, to care for his wife Louise. Nurse Leatheran is encouraged, after it is all over, to write her account of the case. A Foreword by one of the other characters explains that the events took place 'some four years ago', thus explaining the chronology in relation to *Murder on the Orient Express*: not that Agatha Christie ever gave an undertaking to her readers that she would present Poirot's cases in chronological order.

The murder victim, Louise Leidner, wife of the leader of the archaeological dig, has a number of characteristics in common with Katharine Woolley, the overbearing wife of Leonard Woolley, who had been in charge of the archaeological expedition to Ur of the Chaldees in 1929–30 with Mallowan as his assistant. The real Dr Woolley and the fictional Dr Leidner also have points of similarity. In his memoirs, Max Mallowan described Katharine Woolley:

> His wife, Katharine Woolley, who always accompanied him, was a dominating and powerful personality of whom even at this time[28] it is difficult to speak fairly. Her first marriage had been a disaster, for not long after the honeymoon her husband shot himself at the foot of the Great Pyramid and it was only with reluctance that she brought herself to marry Woolley – she needed a man to look after her, but was not intended for the physical side of matrimony. Katharine was a gifted woman, of great charm when she liked to apply it, but feline and described by Gertrude Bell, not inaptly, as a dangerous woman. She had the power of entrancing those associated with her when she was in the mood, or on the contrary of creating a charged poisonous atmosphere; to live with her was to walk on a tightrope.

It was through Leonard and Katharine Woolley that Agatha Christie had met Max Mallowan, at Ur, but Mrs Christie found Mrs Woolley as difficult and infuriating a personality to cope with as did virtually everyone else who came into contact with her. A comparison of the reference to Katharine Woolley in the Christie autobiography with the character of Louise Leidner in *Murder in Mesopotamia* clearly reveals the latter to be based on the former. Whatever her feelings about Katharine Woolley may have been, Agatha Christie relieved or sublimated them by turning her into Louise Leidner and having her murdered. By whom? Like Mrs (later, Lady) Woolley, Mrs Leidner has a dead first husband in her past, but there is some doubt as to whether he is really dead, for Mrs Leidner has been receiving threatening letters purporting to come from him, for quite some time before she is murdered.

Mrs Christie obviously enjoyed herself writing *Murder in Mesopotamia* and turning Katharine Woolley into a murder victim, though, as Max Mallowan revealed, 'here perhaps Agatha touched rather near the bone and for once was apprehensive about what this *dramatis persona* might say'. Fortunately, the Woolleys appeared not to recognize any character traits which might have been taken as applicable to them. They were, in any case, not the only victims of the crime novelist. Max Mallowan was aware that he was the original of David Emmott, the quiet assistant archaeologist who 'seemed to be the best and most dispassionate judge of Mrs Leidner's personality'. And at least one other member of Woolley's team provided a starting-point for Mrs Christie's imagination in *Murder in Mesopotamia*. It is, perhaps, not too fanciful to discern elements of Christiean self-portrait in the character of Nurse Leatheran.

Murder in Mesopotamia is fascinating for its seemingly authentic picture of life on an archaeological dig in the Middle East, and for its description of passions which fortunately do not very frequently lead to murder, as well as for its amusing fictionalization of the dominating Katharine Woolley. It must be said, however, that the more than usually extravagant plotting is at times rather too far-fetched to be convincing even on the level of the murder mystery novel, though the novel as a whole is undeniably entertaining.

Here, at the end of a discussion of archaeologists and their wives, fictional and real, is probably as good a place as any to dispose, once and for all, of the frequently quoted remark which Agatha Christie insisted she never made: 'An archaeologist is the best possible husband, for the older you get the more interested he is in you.' Nigel Dennis[29] claimed that Mrs Christie was 'fond of quoting' this, but she herself insisted on more than one occasion that she had 'neither made the remark nor did she consider it particularly complimentary or amusing'.[30]

Cards on the Table (1936)

In Chapter 3 of *The ABC Murders* (1935), Poirot asks Hastings, 'If you could order a crime as one orders a dinner, what would you choose?' Hastings reveals a preference for a body, preferably that of some highly important personage, discovered in the library, and suspicion falling upon a houseful of guests. Poirot disdainfully comments that what Hastings has described is 'a very pretty resumé of nearly all the detective stories that have ever been written'. He, Poirot, would prefer 'a very simple crime. A crime with no complications. A crime of quiet domestic life . . . very unimpassioned – very *intime*.' As he might have said, *un crime pas passionel!* Then, as his imagination warms to the task, he proceeds to describe the kind of crime he would most like to investigate. Four people in a room are playing bridge, while a fifth reads in a chair by the fire. At the end of the evening, it is discovered that the man by the fire has been killed. No one has been in or out of the room, and the murderer must have been one of the four players while he or she was dummy. 'Ah, there would be a crime for you! *Which* of the four was it?'

It is well known that life frequently imitates art, and a year or so after imagining such a crime, Poirot finds himself actually investigating it. Mr Shaitana, an exotic connoisseur of the bizarre, who exists 'richly and beautifully in a super flat in Park Lane', gives a supper party to which he invites four people who, in one way or another, are detectives or investigators of crime, and four people who have each, according to him, at some time in the past committed murder and got away with it. After dinner, two games of bridge are set up: the four investigators play in one room, and Mr Shaitana's four successful murderers in another, while their host, a non-player, sits by the fire to read or observe. When the four investigators finish their five rubbers of bridge, and go into the next room to say goodnight to their host, they find the other game still in progress. Mr Shaitana is sitting by the fire, but he has been stabbed in the chest with an ornamental dagger, one of a number of 'knick-knacks' displayed in the room. Mr Shaitana is dead.

In a Foreword to *Cards on the Table*, her account of Poirot's investigation of the murder of Mr Shaitana, Agatha Christie makes reference to the usual type of murder mystery in which, nine times out of ten, the least likely person is the criminal, and then goes on to describe her new novel:

Since I do not want my faithful readers to fling away this book in disgust, I prefer to warn them beforehand *that this is not that kind of book*. There are only *four* starters and any one of them, *given the right circumstances*, might have committed the crime. That knocks out forcibly the element of surprise. Nevertheless there should be, I think, an equal interest attached to four persons, each of whom has committed murder and is capable of committing further murders. They are four widely divergent types; the motive that drives each one of them to crime is peculiar to that person, and each one would employ a different method. The deduction must, therefore, be entirely *psychological*, but it is none the less interesting for that, because when all is said and done it is the *mind* of the murderer that is of supreme interest.

Mrs Christie ends her Foreword by informing the reader that Hercule Poirot considered the Shaitana murder one of his favourite cases but that, when he described it to Captain Hastings, his friend thought it very dull.

The four bridge players, one of whom murdered Shaitana, are a young woman who may once have poisoned her employer, a doctor who may have removed one or two troublesome patients, a widow whose husband died under suspicious circumstances, and a Major who may have killed a noted botanist during an expedition up the Amazon. The other four guests, the investigators of one kind or another whom it had amused Shaitana to invite along with his collection of murderers, were Superintendent Battle of Scotland Yard, whom Agatha Christie introduced to her readers in *The Secret of Chimneys* and who also appeared in *The Seven Dials Mystery*; Colonel Race, the Secret Service agent who is 'usually to be found in one of the outposts of the Empire where trouble was brewing', and who was first encountered in *The Man in the Brown Suit*; Mrs Ariadne Oliver, the famous author of detective stories, here beginning an association with Poirot which was to endure through six novels; and, of course, Hercule Poirot himself.[31]

Cards on the Table is one of Agatha Christie's finest and most original pieces of crime fiction: even though the murderer is, as the author has promised, one of the four bridge players, the ending is positively brilliant and a complete surprise. The novel is of particular interest to bridge enthusiasts, and it has been said that by carefully studying the players' scores (reproduced in the volume) alongside the text it is possible to come up with the right answer. But those with no knowledge of bridge need not feel at a disadvantage, for the superb construction of the plot and the detailed characterization make this a positively gripping novel. Until the exciting conclusion, it is the puzzle that grips, for Poirot is here at his most cerebral.

Mrs Ariadne Oliver, the celebrated crime novelist, one of Agatha Christie's most endearing characters, is a satirical self-portrait, as Max Mallowan confirms in his memoirs. Mallowan also points out that, in *Cards on the Table*, there is a very good description of the pain and toil of writing and that some of Mrs Oliver's remarks must have been written with a view to debunking those of Agatha Christie's fans 'who so often wrote saying what a wonderful pleasure writing must be'. Just as Mrs Christie became somewhat bored with Hercule Poirot, Mrs Oliver detested her Finnish detective, Sven Hjerson. 'I only regret one thing,' she exclaims to Superintendent Battle, '– making my detective a Finn. I don't really know anything about Finns and I'm always getting letters from Finland pointing out something impossible that he's said or done.' Mrs Christie must have received a good many letters criticizing Poirot's French!

One of the suspects from *Cards on the Table* survives to reappear twenty-five years later, and married to another character from the same book, in *The Pale Horse*, the only novel in which Ariadne Oliver appears without her friend Hercule Poirot. Poirot, incidentally, in *Cards on the Table* quite gratuitously reveals the solution to the *Murder on the Orient Express* mystery. It is difficult to understand why Agatha Christie allowed this to happen. Perhaps she imagined at this stage of her career that, after its initial sales, each of her books would die a natural death and would not be likely to be reprinted. Although Poirot does not mention the title of the earlier novel, his comment on a gift presented to him by the Compagnie Internationale des Wagon Lits really does give the game away. Readers of *Cards on the Table* who have not already read *Murder on the Orient Express* should get a friend to block out the sentence beginning 'A knife, mademoiselle' which will be found near the end of Chapter 23. Their enjoyment and understanding of *Cards on the Table* will in no way be impaired.

Nearly six years after the death of Agatha Christie, Peter Saunders presented a dramatization of *Cards on the Table* by Leslie Darbon (who had been responsible for the other posthumous Christie adaptation, *A Murder is Announced*, in 1977). *Cards on the Table* opened at the Vaudeville Theatre, London, after a short provincial tour, on 9 December 1981. Taking a leaf from the author's book where adaptations of Poirot novels were concerned, Darbon removed Poirot from the plot, but in so doing ruined the symmetry of the two groups of bridge players in the novel. Colonel Race is also absent from the proceedings, which leaves the burden of detection to be shared by Superintendent Battle and Mrs Ariadne Oliver.

Cards on the Table is one of the Christie novels least suited to stage adaptation, and it must be said that the task defeated Leslie Darbon. His plodding first act, in which Battle conducts formal interviews with each of the four suspects in succession, would never have been passed by Dame Agatha; in Act II the murders committed in the past by the various suspects are mentioned too perfunctorily to be properly understood by an audience. The West End first-night audience was never certain when it ought to laugh; it is clear that some of the lines were meant to be funny but probably not, for instance, this exchange:

POLICE SERGEANT: He's been seen driving along Piccadilly in the direction of Green Park.
BATTLE (excitedly): Then he's travelling West!

A first-rate cast was headed by Gordon Jackson (Battle), Margaret Courtenay (Mrs Oliver), Derek Waring (Dr Roberts), Pauline Jameson (Mrs Lorrimer), Belinda Carroll (Anne Meredith), Mary Tamm (Rhoda Dawes) and Gary Raymond (Major Despard). The play was directed by Peter Dews. It received generally dismissive reviews, but was still running at the Vaudeville Theatre in the spring of 1982.

Love from a Stranger (1936)

The play, *Love from a Stranger*, is not an original work by Agatha Christie, but an adaptation by Frank Vosper of the Christie short story, 'Philomel Cottage', from the volume entitled *The Listerdale Mystery* which was published in 1934.

Frank Vosper, a popular leading man in British theatre in the twenties and thirties, was also the author of several plays. He disappeared, mysteriously, from an ocean liner in 1937.[32] Vosper preserved the plot of the story in his play, merely adding scenes and characters to deliver in dialogue on the stage information embedded in the expository prose of the story.

The play, like the story, is a thriller rather than a mystery, in that it becomes clear well before the end precisely who is planning to do what and to whom. The question is, will the murder plot succeed? Vosper wrote the leading male role of Bruce Lovell (the names are different from those of Agatha Christie's characters) for himself to play, though, as it happened, on the try-out tour it was played by Basil Sydney, with Edna Best as Cecily Harrington (Gerald Martin and Alix King are the characters' names in the Christie story).

When the play opened in the West End of London, at the New Theatre, St Martin's Lane, on 31 March 1936, Frank Vosper and Marie Ney headed the cast. The play was directed by Murray Macdonald. The final scene was so thrilling that some members of the audience literally fainted with fright. 'The climax was brilliantly handled by Miss Ney and Mr Vosper, and brought down the curtain to a storm of applause,' wrote the critic of the *Daily Mail*. 'Thanks to Miss Agatha Christie who wrote the story, to Mr Frank Vosper who adapted it . . . *Love from a Stranger* is first-class entertainment.'

The other critics agreed. 'Brilliant terror play. Our blood was gloriously curdled last night by Frank Vosper,' reported the *Daily Herald*, while W.A. Darlington in the *Daily Telegraph* prophesied that 'quite obviously it is going to hit the present taste for cleverly manipulated horror and will have an enormous success'. In *The Times*, the play was reviewed by the distinguished novelist Charles Morgan:

> This final act is very sure of its effect. The suspense is maintained; each turn of the story is clear and striking; the terror-stricken self-control of the girl and the man's gross and abominable insanity are depicted by Miss Marie Ney and Mr Frank Vosper with every refinement of a murderous thriller . . . a successful thriller it certainly is.

Love from a Stranger clocked up a respectable 149 performances in London, but when Vosper took it to New York, where it opened on 29 September with Jessie Royce Landis as his co-star, it closed after 31 performances. It has remained popular with repertory, summer stock and amateur theatres through the years. Other writers on Agatha Christie have described the play as having been adapted jointly by Christie and Vosper. This is incorrect: it was the work of Frank Vosper alone, and the credit for its shape and dialogue must be entirely his. But the plot and indeed the suspense of that final scene are all there in Agatha Christie's story.

In 1937, *Love from a Stranger* was filmed in England by United Artists, with an American director, Rowland V. Lee (whose successes had included such films as *The Count of Monte Cristo* and *The Three Musketeers*), and the leading roles played by Basil Rathbone and Ann Harding. The screenplay was by Frances Marion. This was the first film from an Agatha Christie work to be released in the United States of America. The suavely sinister performance of Basil Rathbone was greatly admired, and the final scene, superbly directed and acted, is still effective. *Love from a Stranger* occasionally surfaces on television, or at special screenings by film societies.

The film was remade in 1947 in Hollywood, by Eagle Lion, when it was directed by Richard Whorf. The leading roles were played by John Hodiak and Sylvia Sidney, and others in the cast included Ann Richards, John Howard and Isobel Elsom. The screenplay this time was by the American crime novelist, Philip Macdonald. The name of the leading male character was changed from Bruce Lovell to Manuel Cortez, presumably because John Hodiak looked more like a Manuel than a Bruce, and the ending of the play was changed, not for the better. Because the earlier and better film of the play was still occasionally shown in Great Britain, the title of the 1947 version was changed to *A Stranger Walked In*[33] for its British release.

At one point in the 1947 Hollywood film, the heroine is made to say: 'We're going to places nobody ever heard of – India, the Persian Gulf, Baghdad.' Nobody in Hollywood, perhaps.

Death on the Nile (1937)

In the spring of 1937 Agatha Christie accompanied her husband to Syria again, to his new archaeological dig at Tell Brak. The great mound of Brak dominates the plain around it, standing three hundred miles east of the Mediterranean and one hundred and thirty miles west of the Tigris, the nearest towns being Nisibin about twenty-five miles to the north, and Hasaka about the same distance to the south. As usual, Agatha subjugated her own life to that of the archaeological expedition, taking on a variety of tasks, and fitting her writing in as best she could. When they first arrived at Brak, she and Mallowan lodged in a high, bat-infested tower: later, a huge, empty caravanserai, consisting of ten rooms, servants' quarters and kitchen, was put at the team's disposal.

The discoveries made at Tell Brak were of extraordinary interest, archaeologically, historically and artistically, and are fully described in *Mallowan's Memoirs*. Agatha, in her book about life as an archaeologist's wife,[34] fills in the domestic background: entertaining local Sheiks, and being entertained by them; outwitting dishonest Arab workmen by the use of superior cunning; preventing, and sometimes failing to prevent, acts of violence. Reading both accounts of life in Syria, you sense that she came to grips more easily than he with the Arabs' indifference to death and consequent lack of respect for life.

Agatha Christie's interest in the Middle East as a locale for her novels and stories was not confined to those parts where she and Max Mallowan had been engaged in archaeological endeavours. They had also travelled in Egypt for pleasure, and the first fruits of her interest in Egypt, both ancient and modern, began to appear in 1937. She wrote a Poirot murder mystery set in modern Egypt, and a non-mystery play, set in the Egypt of the Pharoahs. The novel was published in 1937; the play, written during that year, was neither performed nor published until more than three decades later.

Many years after she had written it, Agatha Christie said of *Death on the Nile*, 'I think, myself, that the book is one of the best of my "foreign travel" ones. I think the central situation is intriguing and has dramatic possibilities, and the three characters, Simon, Linnet, and Jacqueline, seem to me to be real and alive.'[35] It is, in fact, the favourite Christie novel of many readers, and certainly one of her very finest.[36] Not only is it one of the most splendidly plotted of her mysteries, with a superb exposition, colourful and engaging characters, and a masterly dénouement, it also benefits from its exotic setting, on an old river-steamer, the S.S. *Karnak*, cruising between the First and Second Cataracts on the Nile. Again, as in *Murder on the Orient Express* and *Death in the Clouds*, Mrs Christie has isolated a group of travellers and placed one or more murderers among them. Unlike those two earlier novels, however, the travel experience itself need not be viewed by modern readers merely as something from the nostalgic pre-war past. At least until very recently, in addition to the modern, air-conditioned boats which ply the Nile, two old steamers of the S.S. *Karnak* type still carried passengers on the river.[37] Some of those passengers still break their journey at the Cataract Hotel at Aswan, as Poirot and his fellow travellers do, though the attractive old colonial-style hotel is now called the Old Cataract to distinguish it from the modern horror adjacent to it.

In the first chapter of *Death on the Nile*, the leading characters (amongst them the murderer) are introduced and you discover the reasons why they will all be found, in the second chapter, in Egypt. The experienced reader of Agatha Christie will, of course, be on his guard, but Mrs Christie seemed uncannily to know her readers better than they knew her: she manipulated them as Pavlov his dogs, and here she plays upon her knowledge of how her readers will react to certain situations drawn, if not from life, then at least from popular romantic literature's view of life. In a curious kind of way, *Death on the Nile* is more of a love story than are most murder mysteries.

The wealthy and beautiful Linnet Ridgeway has lured handsome but penurious Simon Doyle away from her best friend, Jacqueline, and has married him. Jacqueline reacts by turning up at all the places the couple visit on their honeymoon, not to threaten or harass, but simply to establish a presence. Linnet and Simon are surprised and dismayed to find Jacqueline amongst the fifteen or so passengers on the *Karnak*. During the cruise, Linnet is murdered. The other passengers, not all of whom are what they appear to be, include, in addition to an ostensibly retired Poirot moodily travelling for pleasure, an American *grande dame* and her mousy paid companion (rather like Mrs Van Hopper and companion in Daphne du Maurier's *Rebecca* which was published the following year), a lady novelist and her daughter, an upperclass Englishwoman and her son, Linnet Ridgeway's American solicitor who would have Linnet believe his presence to be a coincidence, an eccentric Italian archaeologist, a fierce young socialist, and an equally young English solicitor.

Also on board is Colonel Race, the member of the British Secret Service who was 'usually to be found in one of the outposts of the Empire where trouble was brewing' and who was involved in the events of *The Man in the Brown Suit* (1924) and *Cards on the Table* (1936). Poirot is surprised to find Race on board. They had met only once before when they were fellow-guests 'at a very strange dinner-party' in London (a reference to *Cards on the Table*). Race has reason to suspect that a certain political agitator and murderer is travelling, incognito, on the *Karnak*. It is interesting to note that, as Europe approaches its second world war, spies and agitators begin to invade Mrs Christie's pages. (*Akhnaton*, her play about ancient Egypt, written simultaneously with *Death on the Nile*, can be read as a parable of the dangers of twentieth-century saintly pacifism.)

As so often in the works of Mrs Christie, a murderer is presented as being in some ways a sympathetic character. The victim in *Death on the Nile*, Linnet Ridgeway, is physically attractive but not very likeable: the unsympathetic victim is another Christie characteristic. The fact that so many of her victims are either nasty or merely ciphers with whom the reader can in no way identify suggests that she planned this deliberately as a means of keeping sordid reality at bay. The novels remain puzzles; they are never violent descriptions of brutal slayings. The victim becomes 'the body' as soon as possible. As often as not, within minutes of the discovery of a murder the victim's nearest and dearest will be found referring to the dear departed not by name but as 'the body' or 'the corpse'. We are rarely in danger of mourning the passing of an Agatha Christie victim.

The author's sense of place always emerges particularly strongly in those of her novels with un-English settings. The Nile and its banks, and the oppressive feeling that the awesome past of the Pharaohs co-exists with the present in the extraordinary well-preserved temples, are conveyed with a confident touch. The morning sun striking the colossal figures at the great temple of Abu Simbel, the cool stealth of the temple's interior, these pervade the chapter in which the first attempt on Linnet's life is made. The atmosphere on board the *Karnak* is no less convincingly suggested.

In Chapter 1, when Poirot visits the restaurant *Chez Ma Tante* in London, he is greeted by the proprietor, M. Blondin, and remembers 'that past incident wherein a dead body, a waiter, M. Blondin, and a very lovely lady had played a part'. Usually, such a reference would be to one of Poirot's past cases already known to Agatha Christie's readers. But whatever the incident involving M. Blondin may have been, it forms no part of the Christie *oeuvre*. An example of the kind of cross-reference which you find quite frequently in Agatha Christie occurs in Chapter 11 when the elderly American lady, Miss Van Schuyler, tells Poirot that she has heard about him 'from my old friend Rufus Van Aldin'. Rufus Van Aldin was an American millionaire whose daughter's murder was investigated by Poirot in *The Mystery of the Blue Train* (1928). Van Aldin must have been extremely impressed by Poirot, for he is mentioned in *Murder in Mesopotamia* (1936) as having recommended the Belgian detective to the American archaeologist, Eric Leidner.

In 1945, Agatha Christie adapted *Death on the Nile* for the stage, changing the title slightly to *Murder on the Nile*. This was the second[38] of four Poirot novels she was to adapt for the stage, and in each case she removed her great detective from the proceedings. She had begun her playwriting career with *Black Coffee* (1930) in which Poirot is the leading character. At that time, she had already seen her eccentric little Belgian on the stage in *Alibi* (1928), Michael Morton's adaptation of *The Murder of Roger Ackroyd*. By the time she came to adapt *Appointment with Death* and *Death on the Nile* for the stage, she had also seen Poirot portrayed in Arnold Ridley's dramatization of *Peril at End House* (1940). She may have come to the conclusion that Poirot simply did not work on stage, perhaps because he was too overwhelming a personality and thus tended to dwarf the other characters, or perhaps because he was nothing but a collection of mannerisms and was all too clearly revealed as such when impersonated on stage. Many years later, Agatha Christie told Lord Brabourne, producer of the film version of the novel, *Death on the Nile*, that she had taken Poirot out of the play because he was too difficult to cast satisfactorily.

The alterations made to *Death on the Nile* to turn it into *Murder on the Nile* are less far-reaching than those made in the dramatization of *Appointment with Death*. The plot of *Murder on the Nile* remains the same as that of *Death on the Nile*. There are differences of detail, and there are fewer characters in the play than in the novel. Gone are several of the novel's choicest suspects. The Otterbournes, mother and daughter, are replaced by a Miss ffoliot-ffoulkes and her niece, though there is also something of the Van Schuyler duo in these two. Linnet and Simon Doyle are renamed Kay and Simon Mostyn for no obvious reason, and Jacqueline de Bellefort has become Jacqueline de Severac. Kay Mostyn's legal guardian is not Uncle Andrew Pennington from New York, but a man of the cloth, Canon Pennefather, and it is he who brings the guilty to justice, and perhaps to repentance. There is a significant difference between the endings of novel and play.

Murder on the Nile opened at the Wimbledon Theatre in 1945 and came to the West End of London where it opened at the Ambassadors Theatre on 19 March 1946. It opened in New York on 19 September 1946, under a new, and surely less effective title, *Hidden Horizon*, with David Manners and Halliwell Hobbes in the leading roles, but lasted for only twelve performances.

EMI had done so well with their film of *Murder on the Orient Express* in 1974 that in 1977, a year after Agatha Christie's death, they made a second star-studded colour film based on a Christie novel. This was *Death on the Nile* (the film reverted to the original title of the novel), which was released (by Paramount Films) in 1978. The producers were again John Brabourne and Richard Goodwin. A British director of no particular distinction called John Guillermin was engaged, the playwright Anthony Shaffer (who wrote *Sleuth*) provided the screenplay, and the stars whose names helped to sell the film were Peter Ustinov (as Poirot), Bette Davis (Miss Van Schuyler), Angela Lansbury, David Niven, Maggie Smith, Jack Warden, and Mia Farrow. Less 'starry' names in the cast included I.S. Johan, Simon McCorkindale, Jane Birkin, Jon Finch, George Kennedy, Lois Chiles and Olivia Hussey. The name which dominated the posters and credit titles, however, was, quite rightly, that of Agatha Christie. Much of the film was made on location in Egypt, over a period of seven weeks, at the places referred to in the novel. It was the first time in many years that a foreign film had been made in Egypt. The interior scenes were shot in England.

Akhnaton (written in 1937; published in 1973)

The vast majority of Agatha Christie's works reached her public shortly after they were written: usually, no more than a few months separate the completion of a novel from its publication or a play from its production. Exceptions are the 'final cases' of her major detectives, Poirot and Miss Marple, which she wrote during the Second World War and deliberately set aside for posthumous publication; these will be dealt with in chronological sequence related to their publication dates. Though written in 1937, the play *Akhnaton* was not published until 1973. However, in this case, no particular significance attaches to the year of publication, whereas the period of the play's conception and creation does throw some light on the work itself. Exceptionally, therefore, *Akhnaton* is dealt with here instead of later.

Written at about the same time that its author was at work on *Death on the Nile*, *Akhnaton* is a play in three acts and an epilogue (eleven scenes in all), with a cast of twenty-two characters plus such 'extras' as peasant men and women, soldiers, guards, and young artists. It is set in ancient Egypt, spanning a period of seventeen years from 1375 to 1358 BC, the years of the reign of the Pharaoh, Akhnaton. The leading characters are Akhnaton, his wife Nefertiti, his mother Tyi, Nefertiti's sister Nezzemut, a young army officer named Horemheb, and Akhnaton's successor, the teenage Tutankhaton.

The play is concerned with the attempt of Akhnaton to persuade a polytheistic Egypt to turn to the worship of one deity, Aton, the Sun God. Son and successor of Amenhotep III, the Pharaoh had changed his name to Akhnaton, son of Aton, to indicate his devotion to the sun god. As presented by Agatha Christie, he is a man whose gentleness is not offset by strength but undermined by a weakness of character; a ruler whose attempts to lead his people along paths of peace and amity have the unfortunate effect of delivering an enervated and demoralized country into the hands of its enemies. Akhnaton's closest friend is the young soldier Horemheb, a follower, though not a fanatical one, of the sect of Amon, the most powerful of the old gods. The affection of Akhnaton and Horemheb for each other survives their differences of temperament and even, for many years, survives Horemheb's conviction that Akhnaton's saintly, other-worldly idealism will lead to the subjugation of Egypt by its enemies. Akhnaton's dream of 'a kingdom where men dwell in peace and brotherhood, foreign countries given back to rule themselves, fewer priests, fewer sacrifices,' a dream of the triumph of reason, wisdom and goodwill over the baser attributes of human nature, leads him to neglect the defence of his country, and to become increasingly obsessed with the view that the only evil in the land is, as he explains to Horemheb,

> the power of the priesthood of Amon. I know – none better – I grew up in its shadow. This is the war, Horemheb, the real war that must be fought. Between Light and Darkness, between Truth and Falsehood – between Life and Death. Amon and the priests of Amon are the dark power that strangle the land of Egypt. I will deliver my land. I will bring it from darkness into light – the Eternal Light of the everliving God. From now on the battle is between me and the priests. And Light shall conquer Darkness.

As Akhnaton retreats further into his vision of universal peace, refusing to fight the enemies of his country, preferring instead to exhort them to change their warlike ways, Egypt's situation deteriorates until Horemheb, a simple soldier who has always loved his king and his country, is forced to realize that the interests of king and country have diverged, and that he must, while loving both, betray one. Finally, Akhnaton is deposed, and when Tutankhaton succeeds to the Pharaoh's throne, he swears to the High Priest of Amon that he will abandon the name of Tutankhaton and take instead that of Tutankhamun.

Whether or not Agatha Christie intended her play to be seen as a comment on the opposing forces of aggression and appeasement in the 1930s, a comment pointing, albeit ironically and sadly, to the folly of pacifism, it is clear that such a comment is firmly embedded in this play about the Pharaohs. A few years later, their country overrun by the invading Germans, such dramatists of the French resistance as Camus, Sartre, Giraudoux and Anouilh wrote plays in which they used the classical past to make statements about the present condition of their country. Whether consciously or not, Agatha Christie had done so as well. More than thirty years later, Agatha Christie said of *Akhnaton*:

I like it enormously. John Gielgud was later kind enough to write to me. He said it had interesting points, but was far too expensive to produce and had not enough humour. I had not connected humour with Akhnaton, but I saw that I was wrong. Egypt was just as full of humour as anywhere else – so was life at any time or place – and tragedy had its humour too.[39]

This is a generous reaction to criticism, but *Akhnaton* would not necessarily have been improved by injections of humour, nor was it by any means a bad play as it stood. Agatha Christie's literary agents probably did not try very hard to place it, for it clearly was not commercial, and it was also not the kind of thing expected from Agatha Christie. She had, at the time, written only one other play, *Black Coffee*, a Poirot murder mystery, and her agents no doubt considered it in their best interests that their author should confine herself to the steady production of crime fiction.

Akhnaton is, in fact, a fascinating play. It deals in a complex way with a number of issues: with the difference between superstition and reverence; the danger of rash iconoclasm, the value of the arts, the nature of love, the conflicts set up by the concept of loyalty, and the tragedy apparently inherent in the inevitability of change. Yet *Akhnaton* is no didactic tract, but a drama of ruthless logic and theatrical power, its characters sharply delineated, its arguments humanized and convincingly set forth.

No doubt it was when she visited the tomb of Tutankhamun at Luxor in 1931 with Max Mallowan, and met Howard Carter, the Egyptologist who in 1922 had been associated with Lord Carnarvon in discovering the tomb, that Agatha Christie became particularly interested in Ancient Egypt. According to Mallowan, she was also helped, when she began to plan her play, by another renowned Egyptologist, Stephen Glanville, who 'discreetly fed Agatha with the ancient literature . . . until she became deeply versed in the subject'. Mallowan himself can hardly be considered an objective commentator on Agatha Christie but, as an archaeologist with some knowledge of Ancient Egypt, his comment on *Akhnaton* is surely not without value:

The treatment comes as near to historical plausibility as any play about the past can be. The Egyptian court life and the vagaries of Egyptian religion come alive. This is the way to learn painlessly about Ancient Egypt and to become imbued with an interest in it. It seems to me that the characters themselves are here submitted to exceptionally penetrating analytical treatment, because they are not merely subservient to the dénouement of a murder plot, but each one is a prime agent in the development of a real historical drama. The play is studded with some lovely passages of Ancient Egyptian poetry . . .

For thirty-five years *Akhnaton* was forgotten, until one day in 1972 Agatha Christie came across a typescript of it, in the course of spring-cleaning. Although the play had never been performed, she decided that she would at least like to see it in print, so *Akhnaton* was duly published by her regular publishers, Collins, in 1973, thirty-six years after she had written it.

Though it bears some of the marks of theatrical inexperience, among them a certain self-indulgence as far as sets and numbers of characters are concerned, *Akhnaton's* failure to achieve production in the late nineteen-thirties may also have been due, to some extent, to its anti-appeasement stance. Many people in positions of authority in England at that time thought that 'peace in our time' had, at any cost, to be maintained. The contemporary Akhnatons failed, and Great Britain went to war. After that, there was even less chance than before, of Agatha Christie's *Akhnaton* being produced on the stage.

The play still awaits a professional production. It was first seen on the stage when performed by amateurs.

Dumb Witness or Poirot Loses a Client (1937)

In addition to *Death on the Nile*, two other Agatha Christie titles were published during 1937.

Dumb Witness, published in the United States as *Poirot Loses a Client*, is known in some of its reprint editions as *Mystery at Littlegreen House* or *Murder at Littlegreen House*. Littlegreen House is in the small country town of Market Basing in the county of Berkshire in the south of England, about an hour and a half by car from London. This is the heart of the Christie country which stretches from London in the southeast to the moors and coastal resorts of Devon and Cornwall in the southwest. Market Basing (a fictitious name) has been mentioned in several earlier works of Agatha Christie: it is near both the famous house, Chimneys, which is the setting of two novels,[40] and the village of St Mary Mead, home of Miss Marple.

It was from Littlegreen House in Market Basing that Emily Arundell, an elderly spinster, wrote to Hercule Poirot a long and rambling letter, asking him to undertake an investigation for her, but failing to outline its nature. Oddly, the letter is not received by Poirot until two months after the date on which it was written. He and Hastings pay a visit to Littlegreen House, only to discover that Miss Arundell has died of a heart attack several weeks earlier. Poirot investigates: a commission is a commission.

Dumb Witness may not be among the 'top ten' Christies, but dog owners have a special place in their affections for it, because a leading character, the dumb witness of the title, is a charming wire-haired terrier called Bob, and the novel is dedicated to the author's own wire-haired terrier: 'To Dear Peter, most faithful of friends and dearest of companions. A dog in a thousand.' Bob plays an important and quite feasible role in the plot. He is also given a certain amount of dialogue to speak, but this is simply Agatha Christie indulging herself. Those who do not care for dogs will agree with Robert Barnard that 'the doggy stuff is rather embarrassing, though done with affection and knowledge',[41] but those who number wire-haired terriers among their friends will enjoy making Bob's acquaintance as much as Captain Hastings did:

> His feet were planted wide apart, slightly to one side, and he barked with an obvious enjoyment of his own performance that showed him to be actuated by the most amiable motives.
>
> 'Good watchdog, aren't I?' he seemed to be saying. 'Don't mind me! This is just my fun! My duty, too, of course. Just have to let 'em know there's a dog

about the place! Deadly dull morning. Quite a blessing to have something to do. Coming into our place? Hope so. It's durned dull. I could do with a little conversation.'
'Hello, old man,' I said and shoved forward a fist.

In addition to Bob, the terrier, *Dumb Witness* contains all those ingredients which are to be found in so many of the finest Christie novels: the small village, the domestic murder with a relatively small number of suspects, and death by poisoning. The beginning of *Dumb Witness*, with Poirot arriving on the scene in response to a vaguely expressed request for help, only to discover that the elderly lady who had written to him has since died, is the same as the beginning of a short story, 'How Does Your Garden Grow?', which will be found in the collection, *Poirot's Early Cases*. The characters and plots, however, have nothing in common. The astute reader may be fortunate enough to solve the mystery in *Dumb Witness* before Poirot announces the solution, for a major clue given by the author is really quite helpful, if not obvious.

Hastings, who narrates the events, and who has most of the conversations with the wire-haired terrier, ends by happily accepting custody of the dog, and presumably takes him back to Argentina. We shall not encounter Hastings again until *Curtain*, Poirot's final case, in 1975.

In Chapter 18, the author allows Poirot to mention the names of four 'delightful personalities' all of whom were murderers. In other words, she reveals, to those whose memories are retentive enough to keep the names in mind, the identity of the criminal in the following four books: *The Mysterious Affair at Styles*, *The Murder of Roger Ackroyd*, *The Mystery of the Blue Train* and *Death in the Clouds*. She surely would not have done this had she realized that generations to come would continue to buy and read these earlier titles. She must have assumed that the earlier books had already reached and been read by everyone likely to read them. In this modest assumption Agatha Christie was, as we now know, mistaken. Had her agent or someone in her publisher's office drawn the matter to her attention, surely she would have agreed to delete Poirot's remark. The danger could be avoided by deleting five or six lines from 'I am reflecting . . .' to '. . . delightful personalities', and substituting the following sentence for Poirot to speak: 'I am reflecting on various people, all of whom were delightful personalities, and all of whom were also murderers.' Why do not her publishers, as an act of charity, make this slight editorial change? The Christie Estate could have no good reason to object.

Murder in the Mews or Dead Man's Mirror (1937)

Murder in the Mews, the last of the 1937 Christies, is a volume of Hercule Poirot stories, unusual in that there are only four stories (three in the American edition, *Dead Man's Mirror*, which omits 'The Incredible Theft') and that each is much longer than the average Christie short story. The title story of the English edition, 'Murder in the Mews', and that of the American edition, 'Dead Man's Mirror', are both novella-length. The fourth story, 'Triangle at Rhodes' is shorter, but even so is about twice the length of most stories by Agatha Christie.

In all four stories, Poirot is functioning on his best form. 'Murder in the Mews' finds him and Inspector Japp collaborating more closely than has often been the case, to solve a murder disguised as suicide in a mews house, presumably somewhere in Mayfair. (At the beginning of the story Japp and Poirot have been dining together, and find themselves walking through Bardsley Garden Mews, taking a short cut to Poirot's flat.) The characterization is superb, and the plot clever and convincing, though the author had already used the central device in 'The Market Basing Mystery'.[42]

'The Incredible Theft' is an earlier story, 'The Submarine Plans', expanded to more than three times its original length, and much improved in the expansion. The submarine has now become a bomber, and Poirot retrieves the plans by an especially brilliant exercise of his little grey cells. (In its expanded version, this story has not been published in the United States.)

Mr Satterthwaite of the Harley Quin stories and *Three-Act Tragedy* (or *Murder in Three Acts*) is among the characters in 'Dead Man's Mirror', another expanded retelling of an earlier tale, in this case 'The Second Gong',[43] and a first-rate example of the conventional murder mystery with a body in the library, a collection of suspects the most unlikely of whom turns out to be the murderer, and the obligatory plan of study and hall as an aid to comprehension. One of the characters quotes from Tennyson's 'The Lady of Shalott' the lines which twenty-five years later will provide the title of a Christie novel:

The mirror crack'd from side to side;
'The curse is come upon me,' cried
The Lady of Shalott.

Agatha Christie was, throughout her long career, not well served by her editors. No doubt she would have resisted having her spelling or grammar changed, but surely she would have been grateful for the opportunity to get rid of careless errors as, for instance, in 'Dead Man's Mirror' where she allows Poirot to show to one suspect a bullet-shaped pencil he had earlier relinquished to its owner, another suspect.

Incidentally, Poirot has been known to sneer at the type of detective who races about the lawn, measuring footprints in the wet grass, but in 'Dead Man's Mirror' we find him doing precisely this with every appearance of relish.

'Triangle at Rhodes', the final story in the volume, must have been in Agatha Christie's mind when she came to write *Evil Under the Sun* (1941), for there are distinct similarities in the relationships of the leading characters to one another. It is, in some ways, the most interesting story in the volume, for it reaches out beyond the murder mystery genre. It has correspondences, although no similarities of plot, with an earlier story, 'The Bloodstained Pavement' in Miss Marple's *The Thirteen Problems* (or *The Tuesday Club Murders*).

Appointment with Death (1938)

The Mallowans spent what was to be their final pre-war season in the Middle East in 1938, when they moved from Tell Brak 'because of the blackmailing pressure of the Sheikhs of the Shammar tribe who were obviously bent on inducing our workmen to strike',[44] and set up camp more than a hundred miles to the west, in the Balikh Valley, remote marsh-like country but a paradise for the archaeologist. There they spent a profitable and enjoyable few months, until at the beginning of December it was time to pack up and return to England.

In *Come, Tell Me How You Live*, Agatha Christie described her mood of nostalgic regret as she and Max Mallowan left Beirut by ship. She stood looking over the rail at the lovely coastline 'with the mountains of the Lebanon standing up dim and blue against the sky', breathing in the romance of the scene. Then, suddenly, a cargo vessel crossed her line of vision, its crane accidentally dropped a load into the water, and a crate burst open. The surface of the sea before her was now dotted with lavatory seats. 'Max comes up and asks what the row is about. I point, and explain that my mood of romantic farewell to Syria is now quite shattered!'

Two crime novels were published in 1938: *Appointment with Death* and *Hercule Poirot's Christmas*.

The setting of *Appointment with Death*, a novel which begins in Jerusalem and moves to Petra, the 'rose red city, half as old as time', is one of Agatha Christie's most exotic, and the characters, the majority of whom are one large family of Americans touring the Holy Land, are among her most colourful. The Boynton family consists of old Mrs Boynton, fat, grotesque and a mental sadist, her four offspring, and the wife of one of them. The party of tourists who make the excursion to Petra also includes a French psychiatrist, a young English woman who is a medical student, and Lady Westholme, a formidable British Member of Parliament described as 'a big, masterful woman with a rocking-horse face'. It also includes M. Hercule Poirot. Poirot is travelling for pleasure, like the others, but he also has an introduction from his old friend Colonel Race to Colonel Carbury, who is with the British army in Transjordania. When Mrs Boynton is murdered at Petra, Poirot is asked to help with the investigation.

It was in 1938, the year in which *Appointment with Death* was published, that Agatha Christie said of Hercule Poirot in an interview she gave to the London *Daily Mail*,

> There are moments when I have felt: 'Why – why – why did I ever invent this detestable, bombastic, tiresome little creature? . . . eternally straightening things, eternally boasting, eternally twirling his moustache and tilting his egg-shaped head. . . .' Anyway, what *is* an egg-shaped head. . . .? I am beholden to him financially . . . On the other hand, he owes his very existence to me. In moments of irritation, I point out that by a few strokes of the pen . . . I could destroy him utterly. He replies, grandiloquently: 'Impossible to get rid of Poirot like that! He is much too clever.'[45]

Clearly, the author still had a very soft spot for her famous detective, however much she may have become exasperated with him, and her affection for the childishly arrogant but nonetheless endearing Poirot is evident throughout *Appointment with Death*. This is an especially well-plotted novel, and the atmosphere of the various places described, the Dome of the Rock in Jerusalem, the Judean desert, the Dead Sea, the brooding, timeless beauty of Petra, is conveyed with an easy economy.

It was not often that Agatha Christie modelled a character on a recognizable person in real life. However, you are tempted to identify Lady Westholme, the overbearing Member of Parliament in *Appointment with Death* who is 'much respected and almost universally disliked', with Lady Astor. Like Lady Astor, Lady Westholme is an American who married into the English aristocracy and successfully stood for election to Parliament. The French psychiatrist's comment on Lady Westholme ('that woman should be poisoned . . . It is incredible to me that she has had a husband for many years and that he has not already done so') puts one in mind of the often-quoted exchange between Lady Astor and Winston Churchill:

> If you were my husband, sir, I would poison your coffee.
> If you were my wife, madam, I would swallow it.

Seven years after publication as a novel, Agatha Christie turned *Appointment with Death* into a play. In doing so, she made a number of significant changes. Chief among these is the deletion of Poirot from the cast of characters. (She had done this once before, in her dramatization of *Death on the Nile*.) The investigation of Mrs Boynton's death is now undertaken alone by Colonel Carbery (formerly 'Carbury', but then Agatha Christie was often careless about spelling), but it is one of the suspects, and not Carbery, who discovers what really happened. Also, the ending of the play is different from that of the novel. The character who, in the novel, turned out to be the murderer, is, in the play, perfectly innocent. More than this it would not be proper to reveal, though it is probably safe to add that the play has a new character: not a substitute for Poirot, but a comical local politician called Alderman Higgs (or, as he pronounces it, 'Halderman 'Iggs'). 'Ah coom from Lancashire – same as you do', he says with a chuckle to Lady Westholme. He is, of course, of a different political colour from the Conservative Lady Westholme, and intends to oppose her as an Independent candidate at the next by-elections. The role of the Arab guide or Dragoman has also been built up to provide the conventional comic relief which used to be thought necessary in plays of this kind.

After a short, pre-London tour which opened in Glasgow, *Appointment with Death* came to the Piccadilly Theatre, London, on 31 March 1945. Mary Clare was greatly liked as the evil Mrs Boynton, and other leading roles were played by Ian Lubbock (Lennox Boynton), Beryl Machin (Nadine), John Wynn (Raymond), Carla Lehmann (Sarah King), Owen Reynolds (Colonel Carbery), Janet Burnell (Lady Westholme) and Percy Walsh (Alderman Higgs). The play was directed by Terence de Marney.

Hercule Poirot's Christmas or *Murder for Christmas* (1938)

Murder for Christmas is the title under which *Hercule Poirot's Christmas* first appeared in the United States, some months after its British publication. When it was reissued in paperback in the USA in the forties, the title was changed to *A Holiday for Murder*. All the titles seem to promise one of the cozier Christie murders, with perhaps a dash of arsenic in the Christmas pudding, but the epigraph from *Macbeth* which prefaces the volume – 'Yet who would have thought the old man to have had so much blood in him?' – suggests something more violent, as does the author's dedicatory note to her brother-in-law, James Watts:

My dear James,
    You have always been one of the most faithful and kindly of my readers,

and I was therefore seriously perturbed when I received from you a word of criticism.

You complained that my murders were getting too refined – anaemic, in fact. You yearned for a 'good violent murder with lots of blood'. A murder where there was no doubt about its being murder!

So, this is your special story – written for you. I hope it may please.

Your affectionate sister-in-law,

Agatha.

The reader of *Hercule Poirot's Christmas* would do well to think carefully about the *Macbeth* quotation. (Shakespeare is the writer most quoted in the works of Agatha Christie, and there are more allusions to *Macbeth* than to any other Shakespeare play. The English poets of the nineteenth century are also frequently quoted, and so is Lewis Carroll, author of *Alice in Wonderland* and *Through the Looking Glass*. But it is traditional English nursery rhyme that Agatha Christie most frequently turns to: there will be occasion to mention this in a later chapter.)

Two themes are combined in *Hercule Poirot's Christmas*: the traditional murder in the English country house party, in this case a house in the Midlands with the family of a wealthy, unpleasant old man assembled at Christmas from far-flung outposts; and the locked-room mystery, more a feature of John Dickson Carr than of Agatha Christie who preferred to humanize her puzzles. Though the action takes place over Christmas, there is as little Christmas atmosphere in the novel as there is Christmas feeling in the hearts of its characters: the old patriarch is brutally murdered on Christmas Eve. The family suspects are, for the most part, stereotypes of the exotic foreigner, the strong, silent colonial prodigal son, the sympathetic, understanding wife, and so on. One of them is explored in more detail, his weakness of character, his artistic interests, his dependence on a strong-willed wife delicately and sensitively presented, but not to such an extent that the conventional form of the mystery novel is endangered. Agatha Christie maintains the perfect balance. She is also invariably two steps ahead of the reader, especially that reader who imagines he is one step ahead of her.

The clue to the locked-room mystery is an oddly unsatisfactory one. When it proves to be part of something larger, you are tempted to ask 'Where's the rest of it?' If you do, you will receive no answer. The clue to the murder, on the other hand, lies buried in the family and in family resemblances. The diabolically cunning author makes great play with this, and appears to be making things rather easy for the reader. References to a sense of *déjà vu* abound. At one point, Tressilian, the butler, says, 'It seems sometimes, sir, as though the past isn't the past! I believe there's been a play on in London about something like that.' He is right: it is not mentioned by name, but the play Tressilian is thinking of is J.B. Priestley's *I Have Been Here Before*, produced in London in 1937.

Hercule Poirot's Christmas is one of the least realistic but most ingenious Christies, and Poirot performs brilliantly. He is on the scene because he has been staying with the Chief Constable of Middleshire, Colonel Johnson. Middleshire is a fictitious county: when Poirot last encountered Colonel Johnson, in *Three-Act Tragedy*, Johnson was Chief Constable of Yorkshire, which is generally thought not to be fictitious. Incidentally, the reader is warned that, in Johnson's conversation with Poirot in section 5 of Part III, the identity of the murderer in *Three-Act Tragedy* is taken for granted and, by implication, revealed.

An example of the way in which the author fooled her readers as a conjuror does his audience occurs when Poirot indicates a large calendar hanging on a wall, 'with tear-off leaves, a bold date on each leaf', and asks why the date has been left as it is. The elderly butler, Tressilian, 'peered across the room, then shuffled slowly across till he was a foot or two away'. Tressilian informs Poirot that the leaf has been torn off, and that the date is correct. 'It's the twenty-sixth today.' Poirot then asks whose responsibility it is to keep the calendar up to date, and is told. We are encouraged to assume that Poirot has some complex theory connected with the calendar. In fact, as will become apparent only much later, in the dénouement, he has simply been testing Tressilian's eyesight, and has satisfied himself that the old butler is extremely short-sighted.

Hercule Poirot's Christmas received generally favourable reviews, the poet and critic Edwin Muir in *The Listener* asserting that 'even the corpse is meritorious'. But the novelist Howard Spring, reviewing it in the *Evening Standard*, did not play fair, and John Dickson Carr (at that time Secretary of the Detection Club) was moved to protest: 'Mr Spring has carefully removed every element of mystery. He discloses (a) the identity of the murderer, (b) the murderer's motive, (c) nearly every trick by which the murder was committed, and (d) how the detective knew it. After this massacre, it is safe to say that little more harm to the book could possibly have been done.'

Murder is Easy or *Easy to Kill* (1939)

Ashfield, Agatha Christie's childhood home in Torquay, had over the years become hemmed in by new building developments. By 1938, its view of the sea had been completely cut off by a noisy secondary school, and the house next door had become a nursing home for mental patients. The Mallowans decided to sell the house in order to buy another in the country outside Torquay. This was Greenway House, a property which Agatha had known when she was young: 'a white Georgian house of about 1780 or 90, with woods sweeping down to the (river) Dart below, and a lot of fine shrubs and trees,'[45] about four-and-a-half miles up river from Dartmouth.

Under Agatha Christie's supervision, certain Victorian additions were removed and Greenway House was restored and decorated in time for them to move into it in the autumn of 1939, just as the Second World War broke out. Max Mallowan later recalled listening on the radio in the kitchen to the proclamation of war, while their kitchen help wept into the vegetables.

1939 saw the publication of three volumes by Agatha Christie: two novels, in neither of which Hercule Poirot was among the characters, and a volume of short stories. The first of the three to appear was *Murder is Easy*, whose title was changed for its American publication to *Easy to Kill*.

One of the quintessential Christies in that it deals with a series of murders in an ostensibly sleepy village thirty-five miles from London, *Murder is Easy* nevertheless differs from most of its predecessors in having as its chief investigator someone who, although he is a policeman, involves himself in the village murders simply out of curiosity. Luke Fitzwilliam is a youngish policeman who has just returned to England after several years' service in the Far East. A chance conversation with an old lady in a train in which she tells him that she is on her way to Scotland Yard to report a number of unexplained deaths, and that she thinks she knows who the next victim will be, is brought back to Luke's mind when he reads in his newspaper the following day that the old lady was run over and killed by a hit-and-run driver. When some days later he discovers from another news item that the village doctor whom the old lady prophesied would be the next to die, has indeed died, Luke decides to go to Wychwood-under-Ashe and investigate.

The characters, most of them potential suspects, are a varied and colourful lot, and include one of Agatha Christie's rare homosexuals, Mr Ellsworthy, who keeps the local antique shop and also dabbles in witchcraft: 'a very exquisite young man dressed in a colour scheme of russet brown. He had a long pale face with a womanish mouth, long black artistic hair and a mincing walk.' As this is pre-war England, Mr Ellsworthy's sexual tastes are not explicitly revealed; but, although doubtless no double entendre is intended, the sour comment made by a female character that 'there will be gay doings in the Witches' Meadow tonight' is probably not far off the mark.

The murderer in *Murder is Easy* kills not for gain or out of hatred but from a lunatic compulsion, though several people in the village have perfectly sane motives for most of the murders committed. If the exposition of this highly entertaining novel is superb, the dénouement is hardly less so. In the penultimate chapter Scotland Yard is called in, in the person of Superintendent Battle, one of Agatha Christie's most sympathetic policemen, but it is still Luke Fitzwilliam who arrives first at the truth, and, excitingly, just in time to prevent another murder.

Murder is Easy is the kind of novel into which Miss Marple would easily have fitted. Indeed, Lavinia Pinkerton,[47] the old lady who is killed off at the beginning of the story, is very like Miss Marple. And, rather oddly, so is Miss Pinkerton's friend in the village, Honoria Wynflete. 'We women are good observers, you think?' Miss Waynflete asks Luke, who answers 'Absolutely first-class'. It must have been the presence of these Marple-like ladies which led Barzun and Taylor in *A Catalogue of Crime* to commit one of their rare errors in describing *Murder is Easy*. 'Miss Marple,' they say, 'is credible and does not irritate by fussiness.' But Miss Marple is nowhere to be found in *Murder is Easy*. Her presence was not needed; nor, for that matter, was Superintendent Battle's appearance at all necessary. The credit for solving an especially difficult mystery is due entirely to Luke Fitzwilliam, formerly of the Mayang Straits Police Force.

A TV movie version of *Murder is Easy* was made in Great Britain in 1981, with Olivia de Havilland as Honoria Waynflete and Bill Bixby as Luke Fitzwilliam.

Ten Little Niggers or And Then There Were None (1939)

There can be few readers of this book who do not know, at least in outline, the plot of what is probably Agatha Christie's best-known and most popular novel: ten people, from various walks of life, are lured to a house on an island where, one by one, they are murdered. Each one dies in a manner related to the appropriate verse about one of the 'ten little niggers' of the nursery rhyme which hangs in a gleaming chromium frame over the fireplace in every bedroom in the house:

Ten little nigger boys went out to dine;
One choked his little self and then there were Nine.

Nine little nigger boys sat up very late;
One overslept himself and then there were Eight.

Eight little nigger boys travelling in Devon;
One said he'd stay there and then there were Seven.

Seven little nigger boys chopping up sticks;
One chopped himself in halves and then there were Six.

Six little nigger boys playing with a hive;
A bumble bee stung one and then there were Five.

Five little nigger boys going in for law;
One got in Chancery and then there were Four.

Four little nigger boys going out to sea;
A red herring swallowed one and then there were Three.

Three little nigger boys walking in the Zoo;
A big bear hugged one and then there were Two.

Two little nigger boys sitting in the sun;
One got frizzled up and then there was One.

One little nigger boy left all alone;
He went and hanged himself and then there were None.

In 1939, the title *Ten Little Niggers* gave little or no offence, at least in Great Britain. In today's violent world, it appears to be thought by many to be more reprehensible to refer to niggers, yids,[48] wops, wogs, poms, poofs, dagos, japs, dykes, and so on, than to murder representatives of such categories of people. 'Nigger', an English or Irish dialect pronunciation of 'negro' is no longer acceptable; nor, for that matter is 'negro', though it simply means 'black'. 'Black', which means 'negro', is not objected to at present.

Current reprints of the Christie novel are still published in Great Britain under the original title, though American reprints have for some years been entitled *Ten Little Indians*. The American title is inappropriate, for it refers to a children's counting song which has nothing to do with the plot of the novel:

One little, two little, three little Indians,
Four little, five little, six little Indians,
Seven little, eight little, nine little Indians,
Ten little Indian Boys.

'Nigger' has been considered an offensive term in the United States since before the Civil War, so it is hardly surprising that Agatha Christie's title should not have found favour there. Preferable to *Ten Little Indians*, however, is the title under which the novel was first published in the USA in 1940, some months after the original British publication. This was *And Then There Were None*,[49] the final words of the nursery rhyme. (The title of the French edition, *Dix petits nègres*, offends no one.)

So much for irrelevant etymological detail. Whatever you choose to call it, Agatha Christie's novel is one of her masterpieces, with a stunningly original plot, varied and believable characters, and strongly generated suspense as the guests of an unknown host die one by one. Even when only two of the ten are left, there are still surprises to come.

Ten Little Niggers carries the 'closed society' type of murder mystery to extreme lengths. Nigger Island, a mile or so off the coast of Devon, 'had got its name from its resemblance to a man's head – a man with negroid lips'. It is not much bigger than the house built on it by an eccentric millionaire, so there is no possibility of a killer being hidden elsewhere on the island, and in stormy weather no boat from the mainland can approach it. The arrogant Mrs Christie this time set herself a fearsome test of her own ingenuity, passed it with flying colours, and was well aware that she had written a really brilliant murder mystery:

> I had written the book *Ten Little Niggers* because it was so difficult to do that the idea had fascinated me. Ten people had to die without it becoming ridiculous or the murderer being obvious. I wrote the book after a tremendous amount of planning, and I was pleased with what I had made of it. It was clear, straightforward, baffling, and yet had a perfectly reasonable explanation; in fact it had to have an epilogue in order to explain it. It was well received and reviewed, but the person who was really pleased with it was myself, for I knew better than any critic how difficult it had been.[50]

Nursery rhyme frequently proved a source of inspiration to Agatha Christie. Among later titles which derive from nursery rhymes are *One, Two, Buckle My Shoe, Five Little Pigs* ('This little piggy went to market . . .'), *Three Blind Mice, A Pocketful of Rye* and *Hickory, Dickory, Dock*, and in several of these novels the murderer, too, seems to have been inspired by the old rhymes. But nowhere is a nursery rhyme put to more brilliant use than in *Ten Little Niggers*.

When four little nigger boys sailed out to sea, 'a red herring swallowed one, and then there were three'. The astute reader will leap on the 'red herring' as a possible clue: the three surviving 'niggers' certainly considered it to be one, at the time. But finally there are, as the murderer all along intended, no little niggers left. How can that be? There is an epilogue, signed by the murderer, which gives the answers, but it ends with these words (and, with it, the novel): 'When the sea goes down, there will come from the mainland boats and men. And they will find ten dead bodies and an unsolved problem on Nigger Island.'

When *Ten Little Niggers* was published, the reviews, not surprisingly, were without exception wildly adulatory. The *New Statesman* critic wrote:

> Mrs Christie's name again heads the list, but it is no use trying to compare her with other writers of detection. She stands *hors concours*, in a class of her own. No one else in the world would have attempted seriously to manipulate a plot like that of *Ten Little Niggers* without a hopeless presentiment of failure. To show her utter superiority over our deductive faculty, Mrs Christie even allows us to know what every character present is thinking – and still we can't guess! The book must rank with Mrs Christie's previous best – on the top notch of detection.

The Observer thought it 'one of the very best, most genuinely bewildering

Christies yet written', while the *Daily Herald* acclaimed it as 'the most astonishingly impudent, ingenious and altogether successful mystery story for fourteen or fifteen years – since *The Murder of Roger Ackroyd*.' Of the American edition, *And Then There Were None*, *Time Magazine* said, 'One of the most ingenious thrillers in many a day.' One person, however, was not taken in. Max Mallowan[51] revealed that he especially liked his wife's *Ten Little Niggers* because it was

> one of the few novels in which I have guessed the culprit with a feeling of certainty for purely psychological reasons. This novel was read ... and tried out at a house-party in Devon, and great was Agatha's indignation when I won the prize for spotting the murderer – for the wrong reason.

When Agatha Christie decided to turn *Ten Little Niggers* into a play, sometime after the outbreak of the Second World War, she was not an experienced playwright. She had written two plays, only one of which, the Poirot murder mystery, *Black Coffee*, had been produced: and she had seen three of her works adapted for the stage by other hands. *Ten Little Niggers* would surely prove impossible to adapt; but, since she dealt in impossibilities in her books, Mrs Christie accepted her own challenge:

> I thought to myself it would be exciting to see if I could make it into a play. At first sight that seemed to be impossible, because no one would be left to tell the tale, so I would have to alter it to a certain extent. It seemed to me that I could make a perfectly good play of it by one modification of the original story. I must make two of the characters . . . come safe out of the ordeal. This would not be contrary to the spirit of the original nursery rhyme, since there is one version of 'Ten little nigger boys' which ends: 'He got married and then there were none'.[52]

The necessary changes were made, and the new ending, with its own last-minute surprise, proved startlingly successful in the theatre. But not immediately: the first theatrical managements to whom the play was submitted rejected it on the grounds that it would be too difficult to produce, and that audiences would laugh at the multiplicity of murders. The impresario C.B. Cochran liked the play and was willing to take it on, but could not persuade his backers to agree. Eventually the Bertram Meyer management, who had put on *Alibi* in 1928, accepted the play, which was put into rehearsal under the direction of Irene Hentschel and which began a short tour at the Wimbledon Theatre before coming in to the St James's Theatre in the West End of London, in November, 1943.

The reviews of the play were no less favourable than those the novel had collected. 'You see what a task Mrs Christie sets herself,' wrote W.A. Darlington in the *Daily Telegraph*. 'She must play fair because her reputation depends on it. She must stick to her pattern. And she must somehow contrive to keep you and me guessing, even when the choice of suspects has narrowed down. Well, she succeeds.' With an excellent cast, which included Henrietta Watson (as Emily Brent), Linden Travers (Vera Claythorne), Percy Walsh (William Blore), Terence de Marney (Philip Lombard), Allan Jeayes (Sir Lawrence Wargrave), Eric Cowley (General Mackenzie) and Gwyn Nichols (Dr Armstrong), *Ten Little Niggers* ran until the St James's Theatre was closed by bombing, and then continued for several more months at another West End Theatre, the

Cambridge. When it was produced in New York on 27 June 1944, tactfully retitled *Ten Little Indians*, directed by Albert de Courville and starring J. Pat O'Malley, Estelle Winwood and Halliwell Hobbs, the play had a very successful run of 426 performances.

Although the novel is still known in Great Britain as *Ten Little Niggers*, the play is now usually called *Ten Little Indians* when revived by repertory companies or by amateurs, and the island on the Devon coast on which it is set is no longer Nigger Island but Indian Island.[53] The change of title in Great Britain came about when the play was revived in Birmingham in 1966, and more than twenty members of the Co-ordinating Committee Against Racial Discrimination paraded in front of the theatre while customers waited in a queue to purchase tickets. One demonstrator carried a placard giving the Oxford English Dictionary definition of 'nigger': 'a contemptuous reference to coloured people.' 'The Committee's Chairman pointed out that the title had been changed in the United States and demanded the same in England. Without argument, the Producers quietly complied.'[54]

Ten Little Indians was not considered an acceptable title in Nairobi, where the play was staged as *Ten Little Redskins*!

In the spring of 1976 a small, charming, unpretentious musical, *Something's Afoot*, opened in New York where it played for a few weeks at the Lyceum Theatre. Its plot was very loosely and distantly based on that of *Ten Little Indians*: ten people are marooned on an island estate, Rancour's Retreat, and murdered one by one. One of the characters Miss Tweed, a kind of amalgam of Mrs Christie and Miss Marple, was played by the English music-hall performer, Tessie O'Shea, one of whose songs was 'I Owe It All to Agatha Christie'. The show had first been concocted in 1973, and tried out in a tour which opened in Washington, but had undergone a great deal of revision before being presented in New York. It was later seen in London, but achieved only a short run.

Three films have been made of *Ten Little Niggers*, all of them based not on the novel but on the play, with its comparatively happy ending.

The earliest film version was *And Then There Were None*, made in Hollywood by Twentieth Century-Fox, in 1945. Directed by René Clair, this is one of the most successful of the Christie movies, and a remarkable and highly exciting film. The cast was made up of ten of Hollywood's finest character players, among them Louis Hayward, Barry Fitzgerald, Walter Huston, C. Aubrey Smith, Judith Anderson, Roland Young and Richard Haydn. Anthony Marston, the upperclass young man-about-town of the play, was turned into an expatriate Russian prince so that he could be played by the Russian actor, Mischa Auer, who specialized in eccentric comedy roles. In general, however, the film stayed reasonably close to its source, except when it substituted a conventionally sinister old mansion for the streamlined contemporary house of the play. For its release in Great Britain and the Commonwealth countries, *And Then There Were None* reverted to the old title, *Ten Little Niggers*.

The second film, this time called *Ten Little Indians*, was made in England by Seven Arts Films in 1965, and directed by George Pollock who had in the previous three years directed four Miss Marple films. The ten victims, among them Wilfrid Hyde White, Stanley Holloway, Dennis Price, Fabian, Shirley Eaton, Leo Genn, and Hugh O'Brien (TV's Wyatt Earp), are assembled not on an island off the coast of Devon but in an isolated hotel in the Austrian Alps in winter. Why? No one knows. Badly directed and cheaply produced, this was a waste of its cast's talents. Several of the characters were changed from the original, for no good reason. An oddity is the film's 'Who-done-it' break, just before the dénouement, in which the audience is given a chance to guess the solution before it is revealed on the screen.

In 1975, *Ten Little Indians* was remade again by Avco-Embassy in Great Britain. Ploddingly directed by Peter Collinson, this was even worse than the 1965 version. More changes were introduced in the characters, presumably in order to accommodate an international cast which included Oliver Reed, Elke Sommer, Richard Attenborough, Gert Frobe, Charles Aznavour, Adolfo Celli and Herbert Lom. The action takes place neither on a Devonshire island nor in the Austrian Alps, but in the Shah Abah Hotel, in Isfahan, Iran. The voice of Orson Welles is heard as the assembled company's mysterious host, Mr U.N. Owen.

Agatha Christie is said to have been appalled at the liberties taken with her play by the 1965 and 1975 films. The latter film received universally unfavourable reviews, that in the *New York Times* appearing under the headline, 'Global disaster in Iran'.

The Regatta Mystery (1939)

The Regatta Mystery, a volume of short stories which takes its title from the first story, was published in the United States of America in 1939. It has never been published in Great Britain; but, with the exception of 'Yellow Iris', the stories have appeared in other volumes published in Great Britain since 1939. Five of the stories are mysteries solved by Poirot, one is told by Miss Marple, and two are the only Parker Pyne stories which are not included in the 1934 volume, *Parker Pyne Investigates* (*Mr Parker Pyne, Detective* in the USA). The remaining story is one of Mrs Christie's odd crypto-supernatural fragments.

In the title story, 'The Regatta Mystery', Mr Parker Pyne clears someone from suspicion of having stolen a valuable diamond from Isaac Pointz, a Hatton Garden diamond merchant. The theft is a cleverly organized affair, and takes place not in the City of London but in a restaurant at Portsmouth, overlooking the harbour where Isaac Pointz and his partner Leo Stein are entertaining a party of friends who have come ashore from Pointz's yacht. 'The Regatta Mystery' is also to be found in *Poirot Lends a Hand* (see p. 138) and 'Thirteen for Luck',[55] a selection of Agatha Christie mystery stories for young readers, published in the USA in 1961 and in Great Britain in 1966.

'The Mystery of the Baghdad Chest', an excellent Poirot story narrated by Hastings, was expanded to almost twice its original length and given a new title, 'The Mystery of the Spanish Chest', when it appeared in Great Britain in 1960 in a volume of short stories entitled *The Adventure of the Christmas Pudding*. The plot remains the same, but the later version of the story is told in the third person, and Hastings' role has been usurped by Poirot's efficient secretary, Miss Lemon.[56] Some of the characters' names are slightly changed in the second version of the story: Lady Alice Chatterton becomes Lady Abbie Chatterton, Edward Clayton becomes Arnold Clayton; Marguerita Clayton changes the spelling of her name to Margharita, and Major Jack Rich becomes Major Charles

Rich. These slight alterations can hardly have been for copyright reasons: you wonder why the author bothered to make them, and almost suspect monumental carelessness!

'It is indeed the irony,' Poirot says to himself in 'The Mystery of the Spanish Chest', having asked his secretary to make a precis of some newspaper reports, 'that after my dear friend Hastings I should have Miss Lemon. What greater contrast can one imagine? *Ce cher Hastings* – how he would have enjoyed himself. How he would have walked up and down talking about it, putting the most romantic construction on every incident, believing as gospel truth every word the papers have printed about it. And my poor Miss Lemon, what I have asked her to do, she will not enjoy at all!'

The title of 'How Does Your Garden Grow' is taken from the nursery rhyme,

> Mary, Mary, quite contrary,
> How does your garden grow? With silver bells, and cockle-shells,
> And pretty maids all in a row.

Poirot has one of his sudden insights when he remembers the rhyme. How fortunate that his education as a child in Belgium was wide enough to include a course in old English nursery rhymes! The beginning of the story is similar to that of the novel, *Dumb Witness* (*Poirot Loses a Client*), discussed on pp. 102 to 103. 'How Does Your Garden Grow' is also to be found in the collection of stories, *Poirot's Early Cases*, published in both the United Kingdom and the United States in 1974. (The American title is *Hercule Poirot's Early Cases*.)

'Problem at Pollensa Bay' is set on the Spanish island of Majorca, where the problem facing an English tourist is solved in a most engaging fashion by Mr Parker Pyne. The tourist, a middle-aged, middleclass mother, at one point in the story utters words which Mrs Christie might well have been prepared to speak *in propria persona*:

> What are the years from twenty to forty? Fettered and bound by personal and emotional relationships. That's bound to be. That's living. But later there's a new stage. You can think, observe life, discover something about other people and the truth about yourself. Life becomes real – significant. You see it as a whole. Not just one scene – the scene you, as an actor, are playing. No man or woman is actually himself or herself till after forty-five. That's when individuality has a chance.

'Problem at Pollensa Bay' will also be found in the volume, *Thirteen for Luck* (see footnote, p. 114).

'Yellow Iris', a first-rate Poirot story, has never appeared in any volume of stories published in Great Britain; nor is it likely to, for it is virtually *Sparkling Cyanide* (a novel published in 1945) in embryonic form. At least, it adumbrates the central premise of *Sparkling Cyanide* (whose American title is *Remembered Death*). Poirot does not appear in the novel, whose investigators are Colonel Race and one other. 'Yellow Iris' includes the texts of two songs performed by a girl in a night-club, which reveal Agatha Christie to have had a pleasant, sub-Cowardish talent for popular lyrics. The story ends with a pair of lovers dancing to the second of the songs:

There's nothing like Love for making you miserable
There's nothing like Love for making you blue
Depressed
Possessed
Sentimental
Temperamental
There's nothing like Love
For getting you down.

Mrs Christie would have been perfectly capable of composing the tune as well.

In 'Miss Marple Tells a Story', the only Miss Marple adventure which that good lady narrates herself, we are told that the name of her nephew Raymond's wife is Joan. It appears to be the same girl that we knew when they were merely engaged, but her name then was Joyce. Readers in Great Britain will find 'Miss Marple Tells a Story' in the volume of stories entitled *Miss Marple's Final Cases* (1979). Its publication in this American volume *The Regatta Mystery* (1939) marks Miss Marple's first appearance since the stories of *The Tuesday Club Murders* or *The Thirteen Problems* in 1932. She is not encountered again until *The Body in the Library* (1942). Two Miss Marple novels appeared in the nineteen-forties, four in the fifties, three in the sixties, and one in the seventies. (The Poirot novels continued to be more numerous: seven in the nineteen-forties, four in the fifties, four in the sixties, and two in the seventies.)

'The Dream' is a somewhat far-fetched but highly entertaining Poirot story which later appeared in the British volume, *The Adventure of the Christmas Pudding* (1960). 'In a Glass Darkly', a chilling little tale of the supernatural, seems to have strayed into the wrong volume. It would have fitted perfectly into *The Hound of Death* in 1933: actually it did not find its way into a volume published in the UK until 1979 and *Miss Marple's Final Cases* into which it fitted most imperfectly, not being one of Miss Marple's cases!

The final story in *The Regatta Mystery* is 'Problem at Sea', in which the problem solved by Poirot is that of discovering who plunged a dagger into the heart of one of the passengers of an ocean liner while the ship was at berth in Alexandria. The story was reprinted in (*Hercule*) *Poirot's Early Cases*, published both in the UK and the US in 1974. It is also known as 'The Mystery of the Crime in Cabin 66' and 'Crime in Cabin 66'. Under the latter title, it was published in 1944 by Vallency Press Ltd, London, as a sixteen-page booklet, one of a series of fourpenny 'Polybooks'.

Notes to pages 43–116

1 In 1972 a pop singer named Harley Quinne reached the British 'best-seller' charts with a song, 'New Orleans'.

2 Other titles in the series are by Hardy, Flaubert, A.E.W. Mason and H. de Vere Stacpoole.

3 A role played by the present author in a repertory company's revival in Tunbridge Wells in 1955.

4 *Daily Telegraph*, 10 April 1931.

5 Introduction to Peter Saunders: *The Mousetrap Man* (1972).

6 A first-class production of the play which toured very successfully in Great Britain in 1981 starred Patrick Cargill as a delightful and convincing Poirot.

7 Actually, for nineteen years.

8 In Agatha Christie's view, as expressed in her autobiography, 50,000 words was 'the *right* length' for a detective story. However, at the urging of her publishers, she usually wrote between 60,000 and 70,000 words.

9 This is probably Mrs Christie's transliteration of the Russian composer whose name is usually westernized as Weinberg. Jacob Weinberg (1879–1956) taught at the Odessa Conservatory for several years before emigrating first to Palestine and then to the USA. His opera *Hecha Rutz*, was staged in New York in 1934 as *The Lioness of Israel*.

10 Sittaford is the village in which much of the action takes place. Hazelmoor is the name of the house in which the murder is committed.

11 By Hodder and Stoughton in Great Britain and Doubleday in America.

12 In his survey of crime fiction, *Bloody Murder* (1972), Julian Symons mistakenly asserts that Agatha Christie refused to allow Poirot to be impersonated on the stage after the nineteen-thirties. Other Christie commentators guilty of occasional errors include Jeffrey Feinman who in *The Mysterious World of Agatha Christie* (1975) thinks that Hastings does not appear in *Peril at End House*, and Gwen Robyns who, in *The Mystery of Agatha Christie* (1978), gets so many things wrong that it would be pointless to list them, and who appears not to realize that *Black Coffee* is an original play by Agatha Christie and not an adaptation by another hand.

13 Agatha Christie: *op. cit.*

14 Max Mallowan: *Mallowan's Memoirs* (London, 1977).

15 The London *News-Chronicle*, 7 June 1933.

16 In *A Catalogue of Crime* (1971).

17 A wadi is a ravine or valley which in the rainy season becomes a watercourse; a khan, a caravanserai or inn.

18 In *An Autobiography*.

19 For a history of 'the world's most famous train', from its beginning in 1883 to near the time of its demise, the reader is referred to *Orient Express* by Michael Barsley (London, 1966).

20 Quoted in Gwen Robyns: *The Mystery of Agatha Christie*.

21 Close textual examination will reveal his first name to be Christopher, the son of Charles and Harriet Parker Pyne, even though in 'Have You Got Everthing You Want?' his pigskin bag is marked 'J. Parker Pyne'.

22 In Robert Barnard: *A Talent to Deceive* (London, 1980).

23 In Jacques Barzun and Wendell Hertig Taylor: *A Catalogue of Crime* (New York, 1971).

24 *The Oxford Companion to the Theatre* (third edition, Oxford, 1967).

25 In *A Catalogue of Crime*.

26 The edition consulted was that of July, 1981.

27 Max Mallowan: *Mallowan's Memoirs*.

28 Mallowan was writing about forty years later in *Mallowan's Memoirs*.

29 In an article, 'Genteel Queen of Crime', in *Life* (14 May 1956).

30 See Gordon C. Ramsey: *Agatha Christie: Mistress of Mystery* (N.Y. 1967).

31 Superintendent Battle was to appear in two later novels, *Murder is Easy* and *Towards Zero*; Race assists Poirot later in *Death on the Nile* and plays a leading part in *Sparkling Cyanide*; Mrs Oliver, *pace* Robert Barnard (*op. cit.*) who thinks she is making her first appearance in *Cards on the Table*, was introduced in *Parker Pyne Investigates*.

32 Vosper was homosexually inclined. It is generally believed that he committed suicide. In *Flaws in the Glass* (London, 1981), Patrick White refers to his having 'thrown himself off a liner after finding his lover flirting with a beauty queen'!

33 Not (*pace* Philip Jenkinson in *Agatha Christie, First Lady of Crime*) *A Stranger Passes*.

34 *Come, Tell Me How You Live.*

35 Quoted in Feinman: *op. cit.*

36 However, the American critic Edmund Wilson said of it (in *Classics and Commercials*, 1950) that the writing is 'of a mawkishness and banality which seems to me literally impossible to read. You cannot read such a book. You run through it to see the problem worked out'.

37 See illustration between pp. 64–65 showing the S.S. *Nefertari*.

38 The first was *Appointment with Death*, also staged in 1945. (See p. 106).

39 *An Autobiography*.

40 *The Secret of Chimneys* and *The Seven Dials Mystery*.

41 In *A Talent to Deceive*.

42 Collected in *The Under Dog* (1951) and *Poirot's Early Cases* (1974), as was 'The Submarine Plans'.

43 Collected in *Witness for the Prosecution* (1948), a volume published in the USA but not in Great Britain.

44 Max Mallowan: *op. cit.*

45 Quoted in Earl F. Bargainnier: *The Gentle Art of Murder* (1980).

46 Agatha Christie: *An Autobiography*.

47 In the American edition, she is called Lavinia Fullerton, perhaps because of the well-known American Pinkerton Detective Agency, though in the English edition Luke makes the comment that Miss Pinkerton is very suitably named, which bewilders her.

48 A 'little Jew' is referred to sneeringly in *Ten Little Niggers* ('that was the damnable part about Jews, you couldn't deceive them about money – they knew'), but you would expect the character in question to hold such an attitude.

49 Gwen Robyns in *The Mystery of Agatha Christie* claims that the novel now has a new title in the USA, *The Nursery Rhyme Murders*. This is not so. *The Nursery Rhyme Murders* is the title of an omnibus volume (1976) which contains *A Pocket Full of Rye*, *Hickory, Dickory Death* and *Crooked House*.

50 Agatha Christie: *An Autobiography*.

51 In *Mallowan's Memoirs*.

52 Agatha Christie: *An Autobiography*.

53 An excellent production at the Churchill Theatre, Bromley (a London suburb), in the spring of 1981 revealed the play to be as effective as ever. The cast included Ewen Solon, Willoughby Gray, Barbara Bolton and David Warbeck.

54 Jeffrey Feinman: *op. cit.*

55 The thirteen stories in *Thirteen for Luck* are 'Accident', 'The Bird with the Broken Wing', 'The Blue Geranium', 'The Face of Helen', 'The Four Suspects', 'The Girdle of Hippolyta', 'The Market Basing Mystery', 'The Nemean Lion', 'Problem at Pollensa Bay', 'The Regatta Mystery', 'The Tape-Measure Murder', 'The Unbreakable Alibi', and 'The Veiled Lady'. All the stories had been previously published. (See the alphabetical list of stories on pp. 246–50 for details.)

56 Before coming to Poirot, Miss Lemon had worked for Mr Parker Pyne (see p. 80).

3

War and Peace

Sad Cypress (1940)

Soon after the outbreak of war the Mallowans agreed to allow Greenway House, their newly acquired home on the river Dart, to become a nursery for children evacuated from London. For some months, however, they themselves continued to live there. Max joined the Home Guard which, according to Agatha, 'was really like a comic opera at that time'. He soon tired of their pointless inactivities and took himself off to London, hoping to be sent abroad on some useful mission, while Agatha remained in Devon and went back to work in the dispensary at the hospital in Torquay. The chief dispenser, glad to have someone with her knowledge and experience of poisons, brought Agatha up to date with the various new drugs then in use, and found her to be an invaluable assistant.

After some months, Agatha decided to join her husband in London where, after living briefly in service flats, first in Half Moon Street and then in Park Place, 'with noisy sessions of bombs going off all around us', they were about to move into their house in Sheffield Terrace, the people to whom they had rented it having asked if they could be allowed to relinquish the lease, as they wished to leave London. Max, to his great joy, managed to get a job in the Intelligence branch of the Royal Air Force, and went off to work every day at the Air Ministry. When the Sheffield Terrace house was bombed, the Mallowans moved to a modern block of flats in Lawn Road, Hampstead, not far from the Heath. Agatha went to work as a dispenser again, this time at University College Hospital, and Max was sent to the Middle East, where his knowledge of Arabic could be put to good use. He was seconded to the British military authorities in North Africa, to act as Adviser on Arab affairs in Tripolitania.

Unable to travel, and unhappy at her husband's absence, Agatha spent all her free time writing: detective novels and stories, plays, Mary Westmacott novels, and memoirs of the archaeological expeditions she and Max had been on together. She had agreed to allow her Poirot novel, *Peril at End House*, to be dramatized by Arnold Ridley. The play (see p. 66) opened on tour early in 1940, and came to the Vaudeville Theatre, in the Strand, London, on 1 May, with Francis L. Sullivan as Poirot. Larry Sullivan was an old friend of Agatha Christie, and had first played Poirot in *Black Coffee* in 1930.

Two Poirot novels were published during 1940: *Sad Cypress* and *One, Two, Buckle My Shoe*.

The song in Shakespeare's *Twelfth Night* from which *Sad Cypress* derives its title is printed at the beginning of the novel:

Come away, come away, death,
And in sad cypress let me be laid;
Fly away, fly away, breath:
I am slain by a fair cruel maid.
My shroud of white, stuck all with yew,
Oh! prepare it.
My part of death no one so true
Did share it.

Surely the reader is not being given a clue, is not being told to scrutinize closely every fair cruel maid he encounters in the course of the novel?

A prologue describes Elinor Carlisle in court, pleading not guilty to the charge of having murdered Mary Gerrard. As the prosecuting attorney for the Crown begins his case, and the ghoulish spectators lean forward, 'listening with a kind of slow, cruel relish to what that tall man with the Jewish nose was saying about her', Elinor allows her mind to go back to the day she received an illiterate anonymous letter warning her that 'there's Someone sucking up to your Aunt and if you're not kareful you'll get Cut out of Everything'.

A melodramatic and unpromising beginning, but it is the beginning not only of an engrossing Hercule Poirot case but also of a novel which could easily have become not a Christie but a Westmacott. In few other Agatha Christie murder mysteries does harsh reality intrude as frequently as in *Sad Cypress* with its very real and curiously sympathetic characters, and its moving descriptions of the pain and indignity of old age and illness. Elinor's elderly Aunt Laura is a helpless invalid after suffering a stroke, mentally alert but physically incapable of looking after herself. Told that she might live on for many years, she replies: 'I'm not at all anxious to, thank you! I told [the doctor] the other day that, in a decently civilized state, all there would be to do would be for me to intimate to him that I wished to end it, and he'd finish me off painlessly with some nice drug.' Aunt Laura is finished off by someone, with morphine. Another death follows soon afterwards.

The arguments for and against euthanasia are fleetingly but fairly rehearsed: our impression is that Mrs Christie's sympathies are with the doctor, who says that 'one's got an instinct to live. One doesn't live because one's reason assents to living. People who, as we say, would be better dead, don't want to die.'[1] The distress of Laura Welman's relatives at the old lady's helplessness, the ashamed inability of one of them to face visits to her sick-room, and, after her death, the conflicting feelings of sadness, relief and cupidity felt by more than one of the surviving friends and relatives, all are skilfully conveyed.

If *Sad Cypress* has a flaw, it is in the weakness and clumsiness of the exposition, immediately after the Prologue. But once it gets into its stride, this is one of the most real, least schematic of crime novels. It is also unusual in that it employs the device of the possible miscarriage of justice, a miscarriage averted, in this case, by Hercule Poirot. British justice, in the works of Agatha Christie, is rarely allowed to be thought likely to make a mistake.

In addition to those qualities which might seem to place it outside the genre of the traditional crime novel, *Sad Cypress* also works, and works superbly, as a murder mystery. The clues are most ingeniously placed, Mrs Christie's veneniferous knowledge is well to the fore but is never used to daunt the reader who is less well up in poisons, and the rather sad but very real mood which permeates the entire novel in no way weakens the mystery element. The characters are convincing, and stay in the memory, and the actual writing is, as almost invariably with Agatha Christie, easy and natural. A comparison with *Strong Poison* by Dorothy L. Sayers, a 1930 murder mystery which is also about a young woman charged with murder by poison, and which also contains court-room scenes, reveals Christie to be far ahead of Sayers in pace, atmosphere, credibility, and sheer readability.

Interviewed by Francis Wyndham a quarter of a century later, Agatha Christie said: '*Sad Cypress* could have been good, but it was quite ruined by having Poirot in it. I always thought *something* was wrong with it but didn't discover what until I read it again sometime after.'[2] Perhaps she regretted not having written it as a Mary Westmacott novel. Nevertheless, Poirot does not seem an excrescence. He is called in by Peter Lord, the young doctor, to prove Elinor Carlisle innocent: 'I've heard Stillingfleet talk about you; he's told me what you did in that Benedict Farley case,' Lord says to Poirot. The reference is to the short story, 'The Dream',[3] in which Poirot discovered the murderer of Benedict Farley, an eccentric millionaire. (Stillingfleet is known to Peter Lord, presumably because they are in the same profession. At the end of 'The Dream', Dr John Stillingfleet, 'a tall, long-faced young man of thirty', appeared to be contemplating the courtship of the millionaire's daughter. He will be en-countered again in *Third Girl* (1966). In that novel he marries someone else.)

One, Two, Buckle My Shoe or *The Patriotic Murders* (1940)

A highly successful example of the murder mystery inspired by nursery rhyme, the category which Agatha Christie virtually invented and certainly made her speciality, *One, Two, Buckle My Shoe* is prefaced by the rhyme itself:

> One, two, buckle my shoe,
> Three, four, shut the door,
> Five, six, pick up sticks,[4]
> Seven, eight, lay them straight,
> Nine, ten, a good fat hen,
> Eleven, twelve, men must delve,
> Thirteen, fourteen, maids are courting,
> Fifteen, sixteen, maids in the kitchen,
> Seventeen, eighteen, maids in waiting,
> Nineteen, twenty, my plate's empty.

Each of the novel's ten chapters corresponds, loosely, to a line of the verse: the shoe buckle of the first line is not without significance. The first person to die is an apparently harmless London dentist, with a fashionable practice in Harley Street. He is at first thought to have committed suicide, but he seemed in good spirits when Hercule Poirot was a patient in his chair an hour or so before his death, and so Poirot joins his old colleague Chief Inspector Japp in investigating the affair which soon proves to have wider ramifications than were at first foreseen. International politics may be involved, hence the change of title for US publication to *The Patriotic Murders*. (An American paperback reprint in 1953 used a third title: *An Overdose of Death*.)

This is one of those Christie crime novels whose *donnée* the reader would be wise to scrutinize very closely, for things are not necessarily what they seem. The plot is a particularly complicated one but is clearly and unconfusingly presented, except at moments when Mrs Christie intends to confuse. References to politics and to international intrigue abound, but they are both more specific and somewhat more sophisticated than in such Agatha Christie thrillers of the twenties as *The Seven Dials Mystery* and *The Big Four*. Left-wing agitators are more lightly satirized, conservative financiers no longer have to be treated as sacrosanct, both 'the Reds' and 'our Blackshirted friends' (Mosley's Fascists) are seen as threats to democracy, and there is even a mention of the IRA. References are to the real world of 1939, teetering on the brink of war, and not to a cosily recalled, more stable past.

It is odd, surely, that Poirot, who has elsewhere described himself as *bon catholique*, should have known his way around the Anglican forms of service sufficiently to take part, even if 'in a hesitant baritone', in the chanting of Psalm 140 when he accompanies a family to morning prayers in the parish church. 'The proud hath laid a snare for me,' he sang, 'and spread a net with cards; yea, and set traps in my way,' and suddenly he sees clearly the trap into which he had so nearly fallen. It is comforting to think that Poirot has derived some benefit from his visit, for this is the only church service he is known to have attended in the course of his abnormally long career.

Walking through Regent's Park at one point in the story, Poirot notices young lovers sitting under 'nearly every tree'. He compares the figures of the 'little London girls' unfavourably with that of the Countess Vera Rossokoff, a Russian aristocrat and thief whose path had crossed his many years earlier in *The Big Four*, and who has lingered in his thoughts and dreams ever since. The Countess plays no part in *One, Two, Buckle My Shoe*, but she will appear again, seven years later, in *The Labours of Hercules*.

Elsewhere during his investigation Poirot recalls another of his cases, one 'that he had named the Case of the Augean Stables'. This, along with the other labours of Hercules, had not yet been collected into a volume, but will be found in 1947's *The Labours of Hercules*.

Evil Under the Sun (1941)

The work routine of Mrs Christie, or Mrs Mallowan as she was known to her colleagues at University College Hospital, was an exhausting one. Officially she worked a two-day week at the hospital ('three half-days and alternate Saturday mornings'), but whenever other members of the dispensing staff were unable to get to work because of the bombing, she was ready to put in additional days.

In the evenings, the dispenser reverted to being an author. There was, after all, very little else to do. A break in the monotony was provided when she was informed by her daughter Rosalind of her intention to marry Major Hubert Prichard a few days later. Not at all disconcerted by this, Mrs Christie commented later: 'There was something oyster-like about Rosalind that always made one laugh, and I couldn't help laughing now.'[5]

Two novels were published in 1941: *Evil Under the Sun* and *N or M?*

In *Evil Under the Sun*, Hercule Poirot enjoys a few days away from his West

End apartment in Whitehaven Mansions, London W1. Relaxing on a holiday resort island off the coast of Devon, he feels certain that there will be a murder committed. But, 'as he had said once before in Egypt', if a person is determined to commit murder it is not easy to prevent them. He does not blame himself for what happened. It was, according to him, inevitable.

This is one of Mrs Christie's emotional triangle affairs and, as such, it has affinities with the stories, 'The Blood-Stained Pavement' (in *Thirteen Problems*: 1932) and 'Triangle at Rhodes' (in *Murder in the Mews*: 1937). There are also certain correspondences with *Death on the Nile*. To say that *Evil Under the Sun* is good average Christie would be fair, but misleading unless one made it clear that Mrs Christie's average standard is a remarkably high one, and that it is only her very few below-average novels which are not thoroughly entertaining to read. The victim in *Evil Under the Sun* is someone envied and disliked by many, and the suspects, the other guests at the Jolly Roger Hotel, Smuggler's Island, are a well-varied assortment of characters.

Characterization in the crime novels of Agatha Christie tends to be of three kinds: there are the fully-rounded characters who are conceived in great detail, others who are merely sketched in lightly, and a third category of comic characters sometimes presented satirically, and sometimes farcically. Usually, though not necessarily always, the function of this type of character is to provide comic relief, like the Porter in *Macbeth*. In *Evil Under the Sun*, the American couple, Mr and Mrs Odell C. Gardener, would appear to be examples of this third category.

Given Mrs Christie's occasional vagueness in matters of unimportant detail – she is never vague in matters of important detail – to delve too deeply into topographical questions would no doubt be pointless and unproductive. However, it is interesting to note the presence of Colonel Weston, as Chief Constable. As Dartmoor is said to be easy to get to from Smuggler's Island, we are presumably off the coast of Devon, and not Cornwall.[6] Also, Poirot had met the Colonel in his official capacity, a few years earlier, in *Peril At End House*, which takes place in St Loo, a thinly disguised Torquay, and therefore also in Devon. So far, so good. But, in the Mary Westmacott novel *The Rose and the Yew Tree* (1947), St Loo will give the distinct impression that it is further down the coast, in Cornwall. If we must accept that Agatha Christie's St Loo is in Devon and Mary Westmacott's St Loo is in Cornwall, then so be it.

Evil Under the Sun was enthusiastically greeted by reviewers. It 'will take a lot of beating . . . she springs her secret like a land-mine', said *The Times Literary Supplement*. 'As gratifying as anything that peace-time standards could require,' said the *Sunday Times* somewhat inscrutably, adding less equivocally that 'her characters are vivacious and entertaining'. In the judgment of the *Sunday Chronicle*, Mrs Christie was 'still the best of all detective story writers', while the *Daily Telegraph* assured its readers that the author had 'never written anything better than *Evil Under the Sun* which is detective story writing at its best'. Not to be outdone by London literary critics, a native cult in New Guinea used the front cover of the paperback edition of *Evil Under the Sun* as an object of veneration.

In 1981, the British team of film-makers who had done so well with *Murder on the Orient Express* and *Death on the Nile*, though less well with *The Mirror Crack'd*, made a film version of *Evil Under the Sun*, which was released the following year. The film had been planned as early as the mid-1970s, when it was intended as a follow-up to *Murder on the Orient Express*. In the event it became the fourth in the series of lavishly cast Christie movies made by EMI Films. The plot has undergone certain changes and the island is no longer English but somewhere in the Adriatic, although filming of the exterior scenes actually took place in Majorca. As in *Death on the Nile*, Poirot is played by Peter Ustinov. The cast includes Maggie Smith, Diana Rigg, Dennis Quilley, Colin Blakely, James Mason, Sylvia Miles, Roddy McDowall, Nicholas Clay and Jane Birkin.

N or M? (1941)

On one or two occasions, Mrs Christie went to stay with the actor Francis L. Sullivan and his wife in their house in the country at Haslemere, Surrey. Most of her spare time, however, she continued to spend in Lawn Road, Hampstead, writing and attempting to ignore the falling bombs and the flying glass:

> I had decided to write two books at once, since one of the difficulties of writing a book is that it suddenly goes stale on you. Then you have to put it by, and do other things – but I believed that if I wrote two books, and alternated the writing of them, it would keep me fresh at the task. One was *The Body in the Library*, which I had been thinking of writing for some time, and the other one was *N or M?*, a spy story, which was in a way a continuation of the second book of mine, *The Secret Adversary*, featuring Tommy and Tuppence. Now with a grown-up son and daughter, Tommy and Tuppence were bored by finding that nobody wanted them in wartime. However, they made a splendid come-back as a middle-aged pair, and tracked down spies with all their old enthusiasm.[7]

What their author saw as Tommy and Tuppence's 'old enthusiasm' was described by one of her critics[8] as 'their intolerable high spirits'. Mr and Mrs Thomas Beresford had appeared not only in *The Secret Adversary* in 1922 but also in *Partners in Crime* in 1929. Some Agatha Christie enthusiasts acquire a taste for them, while others do not: they are an engaging though occasionally somewhat too ebullient a couple.

The events in *N or M?*, the first Christie novel to be set in the Second World War, take place in 1940, and it must be said that something has gone wrong with Mrs Christie's chronology. At the end of *Partners in Crime* in 1929, Tuppence Beresford was pregnant for the first time. It is revealed in *N or M?* that she must have given birth to twins, Derek and Deborah, for these two young people are now playing their part in helping to win the war – Deborah in the coding and code-breaking department of British Intelligence, and Derek in the RAF – though they can surely be no more than eleven years of age at the most!

Albert, whose full name we now discover to be Albert Batt, has aged more normally. Fifteen when last heard of in *Partners in Crime*, he married in 1934 when he was twenty, and is now, in 1940, the proprietor of a pub in Kennington, a south London suburb. Albert enthusiastically agrees to help the Beresfords who have been informally asked by the Secret Service to join them in rounding up a group of Fifth Columnists. Too old in their mid-forties for official war service, Tommy and Tuppence leap at the chance to do something useful, and in due course they triumph over various dangers and near-disasters to discover the identity of the chief spy and foil the enemy's plans.

It has been a long time since the last Tommy and Tuppence adventure: it has also been a long time since the last thriller, as distinct from domestic crime story. *N or M?* is a trifle less silly than the thrillers of the twenties, and it comes as a relief to find Jews mentioned as victims of Hitler rather than as objects of British racial prejudice. If, finally, *N or M?* is less convincing on its level than the Poirot murder mysteries of the war years are on theirs, it is nevertheless easy to read, undemanding and, unless one is temperamentally allergic to Tommy and Tuppence, rather enjoyable. The Christiean obsession with nursery rhyme raises its interesting head again, for a child's Mother Goose picture book plays its part in the scheme of things. When Tuppence utters the phrase, 'Goosey, goosey, gander', a certain German spy goes quite purple with rage.

A distinctly less sophisticated, home-made British equivalent of Dashiell Hammett's husband-and-wife team of Nick and Nora Charles,[9] the Beresfords share with the American couple a habit of being able to change moods with swiftness and ease from light-hearted insouciance to deadly seriousness. *N or M?* has its fair quota of detection, excitement and humour, though it is not the best of the five adventures of Tommy and Tuppence.

The Body in the Library (1942)

A prolific author in peacetime, Agatha Christie found herself producing even more during the war. Among the twelve books she wrote during the war years were two, completed in the early forties, which were not intended for immediate publication. These were crime novels featuring Miss Marple and Hercule Poirot, and they were written as her two most popular detectives' final cases. Mrs Christie's intention at the time was that these two novels should be published after her death. The Poirot, which she wrote first, was a gift to her daughter Rosalind, and the Miss Marple was for her husband Max. The typescripts were deposited in the vaults of a bank, heavily insured against destruction, and were made over formally by deed of gift to Rosalind and to Max Mallowan. (Although the Miss Marple novel, *Sleeping Murder*, did appear posthumously, Agatha Christie changed her mind in the case of the Poirot novel, *Curtain*, which she allowed to be published in 1975, the year of her eighty-fifth birthday.) Two novels were published in 1942: *The Body in the Library* and *The Moving Finger*.

It was in *Cards on the Table* (1936) that Hercule Poirot had occasion to answer a question about Mrs Ariadne Oliver. Is she the woman who wrote *The Body in the Library?* he was asked, to which he replied, 'That identical one'. Agatha Christie enjoyed indicating the resemblances between herself and Mrs Oliver, so it must have amused her to appropriate the title of her creation's non-existent novel when, five years later, the idea for a new Miss Marple novel came to her. Or perhaps she remembered the title first, and then invented a plot to fit it. The body in the library is such a cliché of detective fiction, she might well have thought, but can it be stood on its head, gently satirized and at the same time made to work as a serious murder mystery? If those are the questions Mrs Christie asked herself, she certainly answered them conclusively in this superb story, the first full-length Miss Marple mystery since that lady's novel début in *Murder at the Vicarage* twelve years earlier.[10]

Several years later, Mrs Christie told an interviewer that she thought the opening of *The Body in the Library* the best first chapter she had ever written. In their country house, Gossington Hall, in the village of St Mary Mead, Colonel Bantry's wife, Dolly, is abruptly awakened from her early morning dream, not by the usual calm arrival of early morning tea, but by her maid rushing in, sobbing hysterically, 'Oh, ma'am, oh, ma'am, there's a body in the library', and rushing out again.

Many of the characters from *Murder at the Vicarage* and from the 1932 volume of Miss Marple stories (*The Thirteen Problems* or *The Tuesday Club Murders*) reappear in *The Body in the Library*, which is hardly surprising, as St Mary Mead is only a small village. One thinks of some of the regulars as a kind of Miss Marple repertory or summer stock company: the Reverend Leonard Clement, he in whose vicarage the murder of the 1930 novel had been committed; his wife, Griselda, now blessed with an infant child who can crawl, but only in reverse; the rude and overbearing Inspector Slack; Dr Haydock, Miss Marple's own physician and the Police Surgeon in St Mary Mead; Colonel Melchett, Chief Constable of 'Radfordshire'; Mrs Price Ridley, 'a rich and dictatorial widow' the village gossip and busy body; Colonel and Mrs Bantry, in whose house the body is found; and Sir Henry Clithering, former Commissioner of Police at Scotland Yard, and a friend of the Bantrys.[11] Several of these characters will turn up again in later adventures of Miss Marple. The criminal element must therefore be looked for among other inhabitants of the village, or among transients.

There are, fortunately, a large number of candidates for suspicion in *The Body in the Library*. The body is that of a young woman unknown to the Bantrys, or so they claim. It is soon identified by the police as that of Ruby Keene, an eighteen-year-old 'dance hostess or something at the Majestic', the leading hotel at Danemouth, a large and fashionable watering-place on the coast not far away. The activities of a number of people at the Majestic are investigated before the reason for the body being found in Colonel Bantry's library is firmly established. Finally it is, of course, not the universally disliked Inspector Slack who solves the case, or any of his official colleagues, but Dolly Bantry's friend, Jane Marple. Miss Marple's cosiness and conventionality mask an inner steeliness of mind not unlike that of her creator. 'Really, I feel quite pleased to think of [the murderer] being hanged,' says this sweet old pussy with the cold blue eyes, at the end of *The Body in the Library*.

How old is Miss Marple? In 1930, in *Murder at the Vicarage*, she is described as a white-haired old lady. She appears to be the same age in *The Body in the Library*: at least, she reveals no signs of becoming decrepit. In *They Do It With Mirrors* (1952) she is, disconcertingly, only in her mid-sixties, but in *4.50 From Paddington* (1957) she says, 'I shall be ninety next year.' Miss Marple may be lying, but it has to be a plausible lie, surely? In *Nemesis* (1971), the last Miss Marple to be written, the old lady is thought to be 'seventy if she is a day – nearer eighty perhaps'. By the time she reaches these last cases in the 1970s, Miss Marple has become extremely frail, though her mind still functions as clearly as ever. This is quite a feat, as she ought to have been well over a hundred years old by then.

The Bantrys' house, Gossington Hall, features in more than one Jane Marple adventure, and of course the country house in general is one of Mrs Christie's favourite settings. 'The one thing that infuriates me,' the author said to Francis

Wyndham in 1966,[12] 'is when people complain that I always set my books in country houses. You *have* to be concerned with a house, with where people *live*.' Ten years later, explaining that she wrote about the world she knew, she added to this: 'I could never manage miners talking in pubs, because I don't know what miners talk about in pubs.' She confined herself to what she knew and, by extension, what she could most easily imagine: hence, in her novels, many more deaths by poison than by, for instance, shooting.

The Moving Finger (1942)

The events of *The Moving Finger* take place, not in Miss Marple's village of St Mary Mead, but in Lymstock, a small backwater of a market town somewhere in the south of England. It is only when an outbreak of poison-pen letters in Lymstock leads to two deaths, the first apparently suicide but the second definitely murder, that the vicar's wife, Maud Dane Calthrop, decides to call in an expert. She invites her friend Miss Marple to come and stay at the vicarage: thus it is that, about three-quarters of the way through the novel, 'an amiable elderly lady who was knitting something with white fleecy wool', appears at tea at the vicarage, and begins to make her views known, along with those of the local citizenry and the police.

The story is narrated by Jerry Burton, a young man who has come to Lymstock with his sister, Joanna, in order to recuperate after an unspecified flying accident. The Burtons first become aware of Lymstock's poison-pen letters when they receive one which expresses, in extremely coarse terms, the opinion that the Burtons are not brother and sister. Other Lymstock residents, they soon discover, have had similar letters, accusing the recipients of the most unlikely illicit sexual activities.

This is one of those Christie crime novels which could easily have become novels of a different, non-generic kind. The nastiness of the anonymous letter activity is graphically conveyed, and the characterization is strong and convincing. Megan Hunter, the twenty-year-old, tall, awkward stepdaughter of the solicitor, Richard Simmington, is an especially well-drawn character, far removed from the faceless piece of 'romantic interest' a more conventional crime novelist might have made of her. And, as the author herself later remarked, '*The Moving Finger* had good misdirection. There is a trap set at the very beginning and, as arranged by the murderer, you fall right in it.'[13]

In her autobiography, Mrs Christie mentioned *The Moving Finger* as one of her novels that she was 'really pleased with'. 'It is a great test,' she added, 'to re-read what one has written some seventeen or eighteen years later. One's view changes. Some do not stand the test of time, others do.'

Two mild and minor comments on the text of *The Moving Finger* are perhaps worth making. The first is that, even in the middle of the Second World War, a skerrick of the old attitude remains: 'Mary Grey was being firm with a stout Jewess who was enamoured of a skin-tight powder-blue evening dress' (Chapter 11). The second is that, near the beginning of Chapter 1, a doctor tells his patient to take life slowly and easily, adding 'the *tempo* is marked *legato*': to a musician, or for that matter, to any one who remembers his school Latin, this verges on the solecistic, for *legato* tells you how to phrase, not how quickly or slowly to play, and is thus not a quality of *tempo*. It is an odd mistake for Mrs Christie to have made; but then Beethoven in his time made even sloppier use of Latin, so one should perhaps be no more than lightly censorious.

Sidney and Mary Smith, to whom *The Moving Finger* is dedicated, were close friends of the Mallowans with whom Agatha Christie was able to keep in touch during the war years, for Sidney Smith was Keeper of the Department of Egyptian and Assyrian Antiquities at the British Museum. His wife, Mary, 'was an extremely clever painter, and a beautiful woman'. Sydney Smith enjoyed Agatha Christie's crime novels, though his criticisms of them were, according to the author herself, unlike anyone else's. 'About something that I didn't think good he would often say, "That's the best point in that book of yours." Anything that I was pleased with he would say, "No, it's not up to your best – you were below standard there."'

Usually, New York publication of the Christie novels followed shortly after London publication. *The Moving Finger*, however, was published first in New York, in 1942, and in the UK in the spring of the following year.

Five Little Pigs or Murder in Retrospect (1943)

Stephen Glanville, a Professor of Egyptology working at the Air Ministry, was another friend of the Mallowans whom Agatha kept in touch with during the war years in London. It was Glanville who, in 1943, suggested to her that she should write a crime novel set in ancient Egypt, which, after a certain amount of persuasion, Agatha agreed to attempt (see pp. 134–37). She had also completed an adaptation for the stage play of her novel, *Ten Little Niggers*, and this ran successfully in London throughout most of 1943, first at the St James's Theatre and later at the Cambridge (see pp. 112–13).

Greenway House, the Mallowan's Devonshire home, ceased to be a home for evacuated children when it was taken over at short notice by the Admiralty, and used as accommodation for United States Navy personnel. The Americans took good care of the house, and apparently appreciated its beauty. Many of the officers who were billeted in the house came from Louisiana, and the big magnolia trees in the grounds made them feel at home.

During the year, after she had completed her ancient Egyptian murder mystery *Death Comes as the End*, Agatha Christie produced another of her Mary Westmacott novels, the first for ten years. This was *Absent in the Spring* (see pp. 132–34), which she wrote one weekend, 'in three days flat'. On the third day, a Monday, she sent an excuse to University College Hospital, 'because I did not dare leave my book at that point – I had to go on until I had finished it':

I was so frightened of interruptions, of anything breaking the flow of continuity, that after I had written the first chapter in a white heat, I proceeded to write the last chapter, because I knew so clearly where I was going that I felt I must get it down on paper. Otherwise I did not have to interrupt anything – I went straight through.

I don't think I have ever been so tired. When I finished, when I had seen that the chapter I had written earlier needed not a word changed, I fell on my bed, and as far as I remember slept more or less for twenty-four hours straight through. Then I got up and had an enormous dinner, and the following day I was able to go to the Hospital again.[14]

At a nursing home in Cheshire on 21 September 1943, Mrs Christie's daughter Rosalind gave birth to a son, Mathew.

The Agatha Christie title to be published during the year was *Five Little Pigs* or, as it was more sensibly retitled for American publication, *Murder in Retrospect*. This is the earliest and by far the best of those novels in which Poirot or another investigator is called upon to solve a crime committed some years in the past. References to the nursery rhyme recalled by the English title, 'This little pig went to market, this little pig stayed at home . . .', are injected awkwardly and unnecessarily into the text; the five characters whom Mrs Christie chooses to identify with the little pigs, to the extent of heading each of five consecutive chapters of the novel (chapters 6 to 10) with the appropriate line of the nursery rhyme, do not have any light thrown upon them by being so identified. The author's obsession with nursery rhyme has run away with her, though she pretends it is not hers but her detective's:

> A jingle ran through Poirot's head. He repressed it. He must *not* always be thinking of nursery rhymes. It seemed an obsession with him lately. and yet the jingle persisted.

Once the nursery rhyme is forgotten, *Five Little Pigs* or *Murder in Retrospect* can be seen for what it is: an excellent novel which happens also to be a first-rate murder mystery, more complex in structure than the majority of Poirot's cases, and containing much vivid yet subtle characterization. The murder victim, a famous painter named Amyas Crale, is no romanticized artist-figure, but a real and convincing personality, some of whose less attractive traits suggest that they might have been borrowed from Augustus John. (Had Joyce Cary's novel, *The Horse's Mouth*, been published not in 1944 but a year or two earlier, you would have suspected that a trace of Cary's artist-hero, Gulley Jimson, had crept into Mrs Christie's Amyas Crale.)

The unusual psychological depth and complexity of *Five Little Pigs*, and the fact that, written in 1942, it investigates a crime committed sixteen years earlier in 1926 (the year of Mrs Christie's celebrated 'disappearance'), taken together suggest that, whether consciously or not, she was somehow commenting upon herself and her marriage to Archie Christie, whose initials, incidentally, are the same as those of Amyas Crale. In the novel, Caroline Crale contemplates suicide by poison: 'I had received a bad shock. My husband was proposing to leave me for another woman. If that was so, I didn't want to live.' Crale had said to her, 'Do try and be reasonable about this, Caroline. I'm fond of you and will always wish you well – you and the children. But I'm going to marry Elsa.'

But it is Crale who is poisoned. Caroline is found guilty of his murder and dies in prison. Sixteen years later her daughter, now a young woman in her early twenties, asks Hercule Poirot to clear her mother's name. The other five principal suspects are still alive, and Poirot not only interviews them but also persuades each of them to write his or her own memoir of those events of sixteen years ago. The five different interpretations of those events, and the tensions between the characters as they are in the present and as they were in the past, are set forth in masterly fashion. Agatha Christie is not generally praised for her ability to create character through dialogue, but she should be. A comparison of her minor characters and their speech with, for instance, that of Conan Doyle's in the Sherlock Holmes stories reveals Mrs Christie to have by far the keener ear, the more fluent style.

The solution of the mystery in *Five Little Pigs* is not only immediately convincing but satisfying as well, and even moving in its inevitability and its bleakness. The murderer is identified, but it is doubtful if prosecution will follow. There are some crimes which can be atoned for only by being lived with.

Some minor points of interest: the Mallowans' Greenway House would appear to have been used as model for Amyas Crale's house; the novel is dedicated to Stephen Glanville who had amiably bullied the author into writing *Death Comes as the End* (see p. 134); *Five Little Pigs* was the first Christie novel to reach a sale of 20,000 copies in its first edition; Lady Mary Lytton Gore, mentioned briefly at the beginning of Chapter 7, is someone whom Poirot had encountered in *Three-Act Tragedy* (1935).

Many years later, Agatha Christie adapted *Five Little Pigs* for the stage, under the title, *Go Back for Murder*. The play opened in Edinburgh, and came to the Duchess Theatre, London, on 23 March 1960. Poirot was banished from the story, and it is a personable young solicitor, Justin Fogg, who helps Miss Crale establish her mother's innocence. The thoroughness with which the author has completely refashioned her material for stage presentation is impressive, but the play limps badly, and the flashback scenes of the second act are unsatisfactory. Robert Urquhart played Justin Fogg, Ann Firbank was both Caroline Crale and Caroline's daughter, and other leading roles were played by Anthony Marlowe, Laurence Hardy and, as the painter Amyas Crale, Nigel Green. Hubert Gregg directed. The play closed after 31 performances, and has rarely been revived. 'It has the usual Christie ingredients,' said the critic of the London *Daily Mail*, 'and is well acted, well produced and thoroughly enjoyable. But for the first time I left a Christie play actually annoyed that I had not guessed whodunit. Normally one is perfectly happy to have theories and suspicions proved wrong by Mrs Christie's logic. But I felt cheated by this one.'

Towards Zero or *Come and Be Hanged* (1944)

One day in 1944 Agatha Christie in London received a telephone call from her daughter Rosalind in Wales, who told her that Rosalind's husband Hubert Prichard had been reported missing in action, and was believed killed. It was not until several months later that Prichard's death was confirmed.

A happier event in the same year was the New York opening of the stage adaptation of *Ten Little Niggers*, called in America *Ten Little Indians*.

One Christie and one Westmacott novel were published during 1944.

Dedicated to the poet Robert Graves, *Towards Zero* is a superb, intricately plotted and somewhat sinister piece of work, in which Superintendent Battle, last encountered in *Murder is Easy* (1939), is the investigator. Poirot does not appear, but is mentioned on two occasions by Battle who wishes his erstwhile colleague were present, and who to some extent adopts Poirot's method.

Detective stories, says one of the characters in *Towards Zero*, begin in the wrong place, with the murder. 'But the murder is the *end*. The story begins long before that – years before, sometimes – with all the causes and events that bring certain people to a certain place at a certain time on a certain day.' In other words, destiny manipulates us, moving us towards a decisive zero hour. This is Agatha Christie's assertion in *Towards Zero*, and the reader's opinion of the novel will depend largely upon whether he is willing to accept pre-destination, or at least to suspend, while reading it, his non-acceptance.

Most of the action takes place at Gull's Point, a large country house on a steep cliff overlooking the estuary of the river Tern. A map of the area is provided, and the curious may like to compare an imagined world with the real world, by consulting a map of the estuary of the Yealme at Salcombe. All the landmarks in the novel are discernible, and the area is, as Max Mallowan suggested,[15] 'a place of pilgrimage for those who are disposed to identify the setting of a most ingeniously planned crime.' It is amusing to note that, in the map of the fictitious area provided in the novel, Mrs Christie helpfully includes an arrow indicating the direction of St Loo, which would appear to support the identification of that town as Torquay.

An unusual feature of *Towards Zero* is that the murder, or what perhaps ought to be called the principal murder, occurs late, which gives the characters and the characterization a chance to breathe, to expand. Nevile Strange, 'first-class tennis player and all-round sportsman', is an especially fascinating and well-developed character, but so are several others, including the old lawyer, Mr Treves, and the suicidal Angus MacWhirter. The prologue, in which the strands of fate begin to be woven together, and in which Treves, MacWhirter, Battle, Mr and Mrs Nevile Strange, Lady Tressilian and her household, Audrey Strange, Thomas Royde, Ted Latimer, and an anonymous murderer who may be one of the above, are introduced, is a masterpiece of technique. So is the entire novel, whether considered as a murder mystery or as a portrait of a certain type of psychopathic mentality.

At one point in the narrative, a character looks straight ahead of him, over the shoulder of the person addressing him, and is affected by what he sees. The reader is not told what has been seen, but is given a clue elsewhere. This is a device which Mrs Christie has used before and will use again: it is a tantalizingly effective one.

An example of the occasional Christie carelessness occurs in *Towards Zero*: it is helpful to the police when they discover puddles of water on the floor of a certain person's room the morning after the murder. But Superintendent Battle a few paragraphs later remarks that the person 'had all night to clear up his traces and fix things'. Why, then, did he leave the tell-tale water on the floor?

Angus MacWhirter, whom we discover in the first pages of the novel to have failed in a suicide attempt, is instrumental much later in rescuing another would-be suicide. This, the author appears to be telling us, is why he was prevented (by fate or God) from taking his own life.

Three minor points: 'old Depleach', mentioned in the fifth paragraph of the prologue, is clearly the distinguished lawyer, Sir Montague Depleach, whom Poirot interviewed in *Five Little Pigs* (1943); Agatha Christie's fondness for wire-haired terriers leads her to introduce into her narrative 'Don, a wire-haired terrier of amiable and loving disposition', who finds an important clue; the alternative title *Come and Be Hanged*, was not that of the first American edition, which retained the British title, but that of a post-war American paperback reprint.

Ten years later, working in collaboration with Gerald Verner, Agatha Christie adapted *Towards Zero* for the stage. Directed by Murray MacDonald, the play was presented by the Peter Saunders management at the St James's Theatre, London, on 4 September 1956. A London evening newspaper reviewer churlishly revealed the name of the murderer in his final sentence, which cannot have helped at the box office, but *Towards Zero* nevertheless managed to survive for six months. One evening, Queen Elizabeth paid a surprise visit, having booked seats through a ticket agency for the front row of the circle. Peter Saunders years later described[16] the problems this presented:

> It was a night when business was quite terrible, and I hastily brought the gallery circle and the upper circle down into the dress circle and virtually filled it. I was rather pleased with myself, and when the play started quietly walked to the side of the dress circle, and then to my horror realized that the Queen could see the stalls from where she was sitting, and there, in splendid isolation, were about fifty people.

The entire action of the play passes in the drawing-room of Lady Tressilian's house, Gull's Point, which is said to be 'at Saltcreek, Cornwall', though, as we know, it was the neighbouring county, her own Devon, which Agatha Christie had in mind. The suicidal MacWhirter of the novel has been dispensed with, and his most important function is now fulfilled by Mr Treves, the elderly solicitor. The first and minor death of the novel does not occur: that particular character stays alive to the end. People do not pair off in quite the same way, and the play offers an additional thrill just before the final curtain, for which there is no precedent in the novel. Unless the acting edition of the play contains a misprint, the co-authors are not too sure of their Latin genders: 'Mens sana in corpore sana', they allow Thomas Royde to say in Act I.

The cast of the première of *Towards Zero* was a strong one. Leading roles were played by Cyril Raymond (Thomas Royde), Mary Law (Kay Strange), George Baker (Nevil Strange), Gwen Cherrell (Audrey Strange), Michael Scott (Ted Latimer) and William Kendall (Superintendent Battle).

Mary Law recalled later that Mrs Christie, who had been present at the auditions and a number of the rehearsals, was painfully shy and ill at ease socially, but that her personality toughened up as the rehearsals progressed. 'We all found her lines very difficult to say, and if someone in the cast said to her, "Do you mind if I alter this line?" Agatha Christie replied from the stalls, "Yes, I do mind. I want you to say, 'I hate her, I hate her, I hate her.'"'

Absent in the Spring (1944)

Written in three days,[17] Agatha Christie's first Mary Westmacott novel in ten years is a *tour de force*. It is not a long novel, no more than about 50,000 words, but it is set down on the page with such intensity, and indeed inevitability, that its effect is out of all proportion to its length. Joan Scudamore, a middleclass English woman in her late forties, has been visiting her married daughter whose husband is employed in the Public Works Department in Iraq. Delayed by floods for several days at a small rest house at Tell Abu Hamid on the Turkish border, she soon finishes reading the two books she has brought with her, tires of writing letters, and is forced into a mood of introspection which is alien to her.

Mrs Scudamore has always considered herself to be a good wife to her husband, a solicitor in an English country town, and an understanding and sympathetic mother to their three children, now all grown up and leading their own lives. But when she brings herself to think deeply about her life and her family, she comes to realize that, underneath her surface of sweet reasonableness she has, in fact, been a destructive force, and that her relationship to those most dear to her has been quite different from what she had always thought it to be.

Most of the novel consists of Joan Scudamore's thoughts and memories as she now painfully reinterprets the past: her husband's friendship with another woman, his unhappiness in his profession, his youthful wish to become a farmer. The events in Mrs Scudamore's life, unlike those experienced by the heroine of *Unfinished Portrait*, bear no especially close resemblance to the events in the life of Agatha Christie. This is, perhaps, spiritual or emotional autobiography; but that, to the reader, should be irrelevant. In Joan Scudamore, Mrs Christie has created a thoroughly believable character, whose identity crisis, brought on by silence, loneliness, the desert sun, and middle-age, is presented with imaginative power and a certain wisdom.

Eventually, the Turkish train which will take Joan Scudamore to Aleppo and on to Istanbul and the Orient Express, arrives. For part of the journey between Aleppo and Istanbul she shares a compartment with a cosmopolitan Russian woman to whom she unburdens herself and then, in embarrassment, regrets having done so.[18] Resolving to confess to her husband her knowledge that, though conventionally she has been a good wife to him, she has essentially failed him, Mrs Scudamore finally arrives in London at Victoria Station.

The ending of the novel is neither happy nor unhappy, unless you are made happy or unhappy by, on the one hand, self-deception or, on the other, self-knowledge. Mrs Christie understands both states, and knows something about alienation as well. Her novel derives its title from the Shakespeare sonnet which begins 'From you have I been absent in the spring,/When proud-pied April, dress'd in all his trim,/ Hath put a spirit of youth in every thing.' The essence of the novel, however, could be more accurately summed up by two lines from Shakespeare's contemporary, Francis Quarles: 'No man is born unto himself alone;/Who lives unto himself, he lives to none.' The human dilemma, so simply and unpretentiously presented by Agatha Christie in *Absent in the Spring*, lies in the necessity and the impossibility of sharing your skin, your prison and protection, with those you love.

The American novelist and critic, Dorothy B. Hughes, reviewing a reprint of the novel some years later, wrote in the *New York Times*: 'I've not been so emotionally moved by a story since the memorable *Brief Encounter . . . Absent in the Spring* is a *tour de force* which should be recognized as a classic.' And, in an article on the Westmacott novels which she contributed to a symposium on Agatha Christie,[19] Dorothy Hughes suggests that this, of all the books created by either Christie or Westmacott, is the one which must have given the writer the most satisfaction, 'possibly even the exaltation which comes so rarely to a writer'. A cooler look at the novel by Robert Barnard[20] also recognizes its achievement: 'That Christie was also capable of casting a typically cold stare at her own class is suggested by the Mary Westmacott novel *Absent in the Spring*, in which the central character – a managing, middleclass woman, cold, interfering, emotionally undeveloped – is seen very much as a representative of the worst kind of middleclass values. It is an analysis of considerable skill.' It is also a more sympathetic and understanding portrayal of character than that comment would suggest. It is not, nor are any of the other Westmacott books, one of those 'somewhat juvenile romantic novels' which is how they are described by a recent Christie commentator[21] who, it must be assumed, has not read them.

In *Deadlier Than the Male*, sub-titled 'an investigation into feminine crime writing',[22] Jessica Mann praises *Absent in the Spring* for being 'well organized technically', but says that 'it gives the impression of being about a type of person, if not an actual person, whom Agatha knew and hated'. Others have been convinced that, on the deepest level, it is about the author herself. Here is what Agatha Christie wrote about it in *An Autobiography*:

> Shortly after that, I wrote the one book that has satisfied me completely. It was a new Mary Westmacott, the book that I had always wanted to write, that had been clear in my mind. It was the picture of a woman with a complete image of herself, of what she was, but about which she was completely mistaken. Through her own actions, her own feelings and thoughts, this would be revealed to the reader. She would be, as it were, continually *meeting* herself, not recognizing herself, but becoming increasingly uneasy . . .
>
> It is an odd feeling to have a book growing inside you, for perhaps six or seven years, knowing that one day you will write it, knowing that it is building up, all the time, to what it already *is* . . .
>
> . . . I don't know myself, of course, what it is really like. It may be stupid, badly written, no good at all. But it was written with integrity, with sincerity, it was written as I meant to write it, and that is the proudest joy an author can have.

She might well have taken pride, also, in the fact that it was written in three days.

Death Comes as the End (1945)

In 1941 the novelist Graham Greene, who worked for the Foreign Office for most of the war, wrote to Agatha Christie asking if she would be interested in doing some propaganda work. She refused, because she thought she would have no aptitude for it. 'I lacked the single-mindedness to see only one side of the case,' she wrote later. 'Nothing could be more ineffectual than a lukewarm propagandist. You want to be able to say "X is black as night" and *feel* it. I didn't think I could ever be like that.' She was of more use to the war effort, in her view, working as a dispenser in a hospital.

Towards the end of the war, however, she began to feel restless. The situation at University College Hospital had changed, many of the patients had moved out of London, and Mrs Christie became bored with spending half her working time handing out 'large quantities of pills to epileptics'. It was, she realized, necessary work, but it lacked that involvement with the war which she felt she needed. Through a young friend in the WAAF, she was given the opportunity to do some intelligence photographic work, and was interviewed by a grave young lieutenant in an office deep underneath the War Office. Shown a number of aerial photographs and asked to comment on or to recognize them, she failed the test. 'I think you had better go back to hospital work,' the lieutenant said gently.

There was, however, another possibility. It was suggested that Mrs Christie might join an ENSA company on a tour of North Africa. She was thrilled by the prospect until, a few weeks before she expected to leave, she received a letter from her husband announcing that he would be returning from North Africa within two or three weeks. Depressed at the thought that she might arrive in North Africa as Max was leaving for England, she went down to Wales to stay with Rosalind for a weekend. Returning to her Hampstead flat late on the Sunday evening, having endured a journey of several hours from Wales in a freezingly cold train, followed by a much shorter though circuitous suburban train ride from Paddington to Hampstead, she had just begun to fry some kippers, when she heard a 'peculiar clanking noise' outside. She went out into the corridor and looked down the stairs:

> Up them came a figure burdened with everything imaginable – rather like the caricatures of Old Bill in the first war – clanking things hung all over him . . . But there was no doubt who it was – it was my husband! Two minutes later I knew that all my fears that things might be different, that he would have changed, were baseless. This was Max! He might have left yesterday. He was back again. *We* were back again. A terrible smell of frying kippers came to our noses and we rushed into the flat . . . What a wonderful evening it was! We ate burnt kippers, and were happy.[23]

Within months, the war in Europe was over.

Professionally, as well as personally, 1945 had been a happy year for Agatha Christie. She had seen two of her plays produced – *Appointment with Death* (see p. 106) and *Murder on the Nile* (see p. 98) – and had published two novels, *Death Comes as the End* and *Sparkling Cyanide*.

It was a friend of the Mallowans, Professor Stephen Glanville, who, over dinner one evening in 1943, persuaded Agatha Christie to write a crime novel set, not in the England of 1943, but in the Egypt of four thousand years earlier. Glanville thought that such a novel would be of interest both to the crime fiction enthusiast and to readers interested in ancient times. Agatha claimed that she was too ignorant on the subject of Egypt in the time of the Pharaohs, but by the end of an evening of argument Glanville had virtually convinced her that she could do it. 'You've read a lot of Egyptology,' he said. 'You are not only interested in Mesopotamia.' This was true: one of her favourite books was *The Dawn of Conscience* by the American historian James Henry Breasted, an authority on Ancient Egyptian history, and she had read widely in the field of Egyptology a few years earlier when she was writing her play, *Akhnaton*. When Glanville drew her attention to certain incidents in Egyptian history, and thrust half a dozen or more books upon her, Agatha realized that the die was cast.

The 'recently published letters' on which *Death Comes as the End* was based were the Hekanakhte Papers, letters from a farmer which had been discovered in a rock tomb opposite Luxor in 1920–21 by the Egyptian Expedition of the Metropolitan Museum of Art. During the writing of the book, Agatha Christie found it necessary to bombard Stephen Glanville with questions, most of which he managed to answer although many of the queries involved him in hours of research. What did the Egyptians eat? How was their meat cooked? Were there special dishes for certain feasts? Did the men and women eat together? What were their sleeping arrangements? Did they eat at a table, or on the floor? Did the women occupy a separate part of the house? Did they keep linen in chests or in cupboards? What kind of houses did they have? Houses were far more difficult to find out about than temples or palaces, for many of the temples remain, whereas domestic buildings were made of less durable material than stone and have not survived.

Glanville read and commented upon the typescript, chapter by chapter. He objected to an important passage in the dénouement, and argued his case so strongly that the author finally gave in to him, and altered it against, as she continued to maintain, her better judgment. Her own ending would have been more dramatic, and, when she came to write her autobiography twenty years or more later, she noted: 'I still think now, when I re-read the book, that I would like to rewrite the end of it – which shows that you should stick to your guns in the first place, or you will be dissatisfied with yourself.' But, of course, she had at the time felt such gratitude to Stephen Glanville for having caused the book to be written and for having taken so much trouble in helping her with it that it would have seemed to her churlish not to take very seriously his objection to the dénouement. Max Mallowan noted that Glanville was, to his knowledge, the only person ever to have persuaded Agatha to alter the end of a book. His comment[24] suggests that he himself may, on occasion, have tried.

There were no equivalents of Hercule Poirot or Jane Marple in Ancient Egypt so the family murders in *Death Comes as the End* have to be solved by the survivors, of whom indeed there are precious few by the end of the novel. Dedicated to Professor Glanville with a letter of thanks from his 'affectionate and grateful friend', and preceded by a note in which some background information is given, *Death Comes as the End* does not require of its reader any special knowledge of Egypt under the Pharaohs. People, beneath changing customs, remain the same, Mrs Christie would appear to be telling us. Certainly this family in Ancient Egypt contrives both to be convincing as such and to suggest parallels with a contemporary middleclass rural household. More specifically, the reader may detect certain similarities with a Poirot mystery, *Hercule Poirot's Christmas* (1938), in which Poirot solves a family murder in a country house in the English Midlands.

One must admire the flair with which Mrs Christie has created and made believable her picture of life in a vanished civilization of four thousand years ago. However, the plot of *Death Comes as the End* is by no means one of her most ingenious; and, although the novel is pleasant to read, the fact that it makes fewer demands on the reader than so many of the author's finest murder mysteries might be thought to render this particular attempt to strike out along new and original paths somewhat disappointing, though worthy. The novel is undoubtedly unique, and it must have the highest number of murders (eight) of any Christie domestic crime novel. But the reader's expectations are pitched high by the prospect of enjoying a cosy English-type murder mystery surrealistically set in the land of the Pharaohs, and the subsequent disappointment is perhaps greater than it has a right to be. *Death Comes as the End*, if you discount the trappings, is no better than average Christie. There is little real detection, and the experienced reader of Agatha Christie may not be surprised when the identity of the murderer is revealed.

Sparkling Cyanide or Remembered Death (1945)

Sparkling Cyanide, or *Remembered Death* as it is called in America, is one of those novels in which a crime is investigated some time after it has been perpetrated: in this case, on its first anniversary. Rosemary Barton had died at a dinner party in a West End restaurant, after swallowing a glass of champagne which happened to be laced with cyanide. After a thorough police investigation, the official verdict was that Rosemary had committed suicide. However, her widower, George Barton, believes Rosemary to have been murdered, and one year later he assembles the same guests at the same restaurant for an experiment the precise nature of which he does not disclose, though clearly its purpose is to apprehend or at least to identify his wife's murderer.

The murder of Rosemary, for such it proves to have been, is, however, not the only crime to come under investigation in *Sparkling Cyanide*, for George's plans go sadly awry and his anniversary party ends with another death. Someone who was invited on both occasions but who failed to put in an appearance at either was Colonel Race. Race, the one-time Secret Service agent who was first encountered in *The Man in the Brown Suit* in 1924, is now over sixty. In *Sparkling Cyanide* he helps another investigator to discover the murderer; this will prove to be the last of Colonel Race's appearances in the works of Agatha Christie.

The reconstruction of a fatal dinner party and the method by which one of the murders is committed had already been used by Mrs Christie in 'Yellow Iris', a Poirot short story published in the USA in *The Regatta Mystery* (1939: see p. 114). In *Sparkling Cyanide* the second murder involves a group mistake which strains the reader's credulity rather dangerously. Up to that point, however, the story has been told with a compulsive ease and a conviction which place the novel among the author's most successful. It is, however, difficult to believe that, after dancing, people would return to the wrong places at their table simply because a purse had inadvertently been moved one place to the left.

Especially impressive though noticeable only if you take the trouble to re-read the passage after having finished the novel, is Mrs Christie's skating on extremely thin ice in the second chapter where she quite blatantly reveals the solution but reveals so much else as well that you fail to notice what is being offered. As the sly author said to an interviewer many years later, 'I don't cheat, you know. I just say things that might be taken two ways.'[25]

It was with *Five Little Pigs*, two years earlier, that an Agatha Christie novel had first achieved sales of 20,000. Now, with *Sparkling Cyanide*, sales in the first year of publication reached 30,000. From this point on, every Christie title would become, to use publishers' jargon, a 'bestseller'.

Come, Tell Me How You Live (1946)

As soon as the war was over, the Mallowans gave up their Hampstead flat, moved into their London house at 22 Cresswell Place, off Old Brompton Road, in South Kensington, and began to resume their pre-war routine, with summers spent in Devon as the Admiralty had relinquished Greenway. Max Mallowan returned, for the time being, to his job at the Air Ministry, and Agatha settled down to invent more adventures for her two most popular sleuths, Hercule Poirot and Jane Marple.

Two slim volumes containing Poirot short stories were published, both in London and in New York, in 1946. *Poirot Knows the Murderer* contained 'The Mystery of the Baghdad Chest', which is also to be found in *The Regatta Mystery* (1939: USA only), and 'The Mystery of the Crime in Cabin 66' which, under another title ('Problems at Sea') was in the 1939 American volume, *The Regatta Mystery*, and will turn up again in *Poirot's Early Cases* in 1974. *Poirot Lends a Hand* consisted of three stories, all of which are also to be found in *Thirteen for Luck*, a selection of Agatha Christie mystery stories for young readers, collected from previously published material and issued as a volume in New York in 1961 and in London in 1966. Two of the stories, 'The Regatta Mystery' and 'Problem at Pollensa Bay' are also to be found in *The Regatta Mystery*, while the third, 'The Veiled Lady' is included in [*Hercule*] *Poirot's Early Cases* (1974).

Also published during 1946 were *Come, Tell Me How You Live* by Agatha Christie Mallowan, and *The Hollow* by Agatha Christie.

It was both appropriate and desirable that *Come, Tell Me How You Live* should have been published under Agatha Christie's married name: appropriate, since it dealt with her adventures on archaeological digs in the thirties with Max Mallowan; desirable because, had it been publicized as being by Agatha Christie, many of her public would no doubt have bought the book on the assumption that it was crime fiction, and might perhaps been disappointed when they discovered that it was not.

Based upon journals which she had kept assiduously during her archaeological expeditions to the Middle East with Mallowan, *Come, Tell Me How You Live* was written by Agatha Christie at odd moments during the Second World War years, and finished in the spring of 1944. She was driven to writing the book by nostalgia for those years of peaceful travel in the thirties, by sadness at her enforced wartime separation from Mallowan, and by a desire to relive past happiness. Sidney Smith of the British Museum's Department of Egyptian and Assyrian Antiquities read the typescript and advised Mrs Christie not to publish it, as he thought that Max Mallowan was likely to find it trivial and unscholarly. Also, according to the author, her publishers, Collins, disapproved of the book. They had 'hated' the Mary Westmacott novels, and were suspicious of anything that enticed Mrs Christie away from the crime fiction which they found so lucrative. Nevertheless, they agreed to publish *Come, Tell Me How You Live*. Paper was scarce, so the edition was a small one. The book, however, was a success, 'and I think they then regretted that paper was so short'.[26]

The title derives from Lewis Carroll,[27] to whom apologies are made by the author for ten stanzas of very poor Carroll pastiche and which describe the first meeting of Mr Mallowan and Mrs Christie. Here are the first three stanzas:

> I'll tell you everything I can
> If you will listen well:
> I met an erudite young man
> A-sitting on a Tell.
> 'Who are you, sir?' to him I said,
> 'For what is it you look?'
> His answer trickled through my head
> Like bloodstains in a book.

He said: 'I look for aged pots
    Of prehistoric days,
And then I measure them in lots
    And lots of different ways.
And then (like you) I start to write,
    My words are twice as long
As yours, and far more erudite.
    They prove my colleagues wrong!'

But I was thinking of a plan
    To kill a millionaire
And hide the body in a van
    Or some large Frigidaire.
So, having no reply to give,
    And feeling rather shy,
I cried: 'Come, tell me how you live!
    And when, and where, and why?'

The dedication of *Come, Tell Me How You Live* reads: 'To my husband, Max Mallowan; to the Colonel, Bumps, Mac and Guilford, this meandering chronicle is affectionately dedicated.' A meandering chronicle it may be, but it is also a perfectly delightful one, in the picture it gives of life on archaeological expeditions in Iraq and Syria in the thirties, and in the good nature and humanity which inform it throughout. The Mallowan team of regulars were clearly agreeable, interesting and amusing people to be with, and Mrs Mallowan's stories of the Arab workmen, the Turks and the desert Sheikhs are colourful, lively, and occasionally touching and thought-provoking:

An old woman comes up to Hamoudi, leading a boy of about twelve by the hand.
'Has the Khwaja medicine?'
'He has some medicines – yes.'
'Will he give me medicine for my son here?'
'What is the matter with your son?'
It is hardly necessary to ask. The imbecile face is only too clear.'
'He has not his proper senses.'
Hamoudi shakes his head sadly, but says he will ask the Khwaja.
The men have started digging trenches. Hamoudi, the woman and the boy come up to Max.
Max looks at the boy and turns gently to the woman.
'The boy is as he is by the will of Allah,' he says. 'There is no medicine I can give you for the boy.'
The woman sighs – I think a tear runs down her cheek. Then she says in a matter-of-fact voice:
'Then, Khwaja, will you give me some poison, for it is better he should not live?'
Max says gently that he cannot do that either.
She stares at him uncomprehendingly, then shakes her head angrily and goes away with the boy.

After this, the stories of Mallowan's attempts to impress upon the Christian Arabs in his employ that they really must refrain from killing Mohammedans read as light relief. Keeping the peace between Mohammedan and Christian Arabs is a major task of the Europeans in the party.

You do not need to have any special interest in the Middle East or in archaeology to enjoy this gentle and charming account of the Mallowans' adventures while digging in Syria and the Mesopotamian area in Iraq between 1935 and 1938. On the other hand, the erudite archaeologist who plays so important a role in it did not think the book at all trivial. 'Agatha's gift for narrative, and for relating humorous exchanges of conversation between all manner of men and women in unusual situations, is rewardingly displayed. There have been many calls for the republishing of this exceptionally entertaining book and it was reissued in 1975. Many have been called to Oriental archaeology, but few have been able to leave so happy a record of it.'[28]

Not even Agatha Christie Mallowan can make Arab indifference to death and thus to life at all engaging, and faced with examples of the more callous behaviour of the followers of Allah she can note only that 'Max says death isn't really important out here'. Agatha Mallowan takes a liberal view, and learns to love 'simple people . . . to whom death is not terrible.'[29]

But Agatha Christie, to whom death is her stock-in-trade, must have been profoundly shocked.

Modestly, the author does not push herself into the forefront of her narrative. That she was a gay and lively participant in the life of the camp, however, is confirmed by the description of Agatha Christie in Iraq given by a London archaeologist who visited the Mallowans there:

It was quite a different Agatha Christie from anyone I had known in England. There was no shy psychological hang-up. Here was a woman in a man's world who knew that she was being accepted at face value. She worked like a beaver, sometimes in heats as high as 120°F, photographing and mending the finds as they were catalogued at the end of the day. No professional could have done it better and the conditions under which she worked were far from easy. Whereas the men could sometimes be tetchy when things went wrong, she always saw the funny side and was mainly responsible for the good humour that prevailed on all the 'digs' organized by her husband.

The Hollow or Murder After Hours (1946)

'The Hollow' in the title is Sir Henry and Lady Angkatell's country house, in which most of the action takes place, though at one point in the narrative Hercule Poirot, displaying an astonishing knowledge of English poetry, quotes the opening lines of Tennyson's *Maud*:

I hate the dreadful hollow behind the little wood;
Its lips in the field above are dabbled with blood red heath,
The red ribb'd ledges drip with a silent horror of blood
And echo there, whatever is ask'd her, answers 'Death'.

One trusts that this was not Agatha Christie's view of the real house on which she modelled 'The Hollow', for that was the home at Hazelmere, Surrey, of the actor Francis L. Sullivan and his wife, to whom the author dedicated her novel: 'For Larry and Danae, with apologies for using their swimming pool as the scene of a murder.' Sullivan later recalled that, on one of the several weekends during the war when Agatha came to stay, he observed the idea for *The Hollow*[30] occurring to the author:

> At the back of the house my wife, in a moment of insane optimism of the English weather, had caused a swimming pool to be made with half a dozen paths leading down to it through the chestnut wood. One fine Sunday morning I discovered Agatha wandering up and down these paths with an expression of intense concentration.[31]

Sullivan asked what she was doing but received no real answer until more than a year later when an advance copy of *The Hollow* arrived in the post.

In some of the earliest Poirot murder mysteries, the plots are highly ingenious but the characterization is negligible: the puzzle is all. The puzzle in *The Hollow* is as important as ever it was, but by now Mrs Christie has amassed years of experience and a consequent building up of confidence in her technique as a novelist. The actual plot-line of *The Hollow* is not one of her best, in the sense that it is not one of her most complex, but the characterization is superb and the writing unostentatiously impressive. Gerda, the slow-thinking but by no means stupid widow of Dr John Christow, the murder victim, is very acutely and sympathetically observed, and there is a delightful portrait of a vague, upperclass lady in Lucy Angkatell, who is slightly reminiscent of Judith Bliss in Noël Coward's play, *Hay Fever*. Lady Angkatell is allowed an anti-Arab joke, which makes a change in the pages of Agatha Christie!

It is not only the characterization that is so commendable in *The Hollow*: the description of the house and grounds, and of that other, larger country estate, Ainswick, mentioned so often by several of the characters, is evocative, and highly important to the narrative. If *The Hollow* is in the top flight of Christie novels, it is as something both more and less than a murder mystery.

Poirot finds himself involved in the proceedings because he is a neighbour of the Angkatells, having purchased a 'weekend' cottage nearby. He is invited to The Hollow for lunch, and arrives to find Lady Angkatell and her guests down by the swimming pool, staring at the body of a dying man who is lying by the pool, with a woman standing over him clutching a revolver. Poirot's first thought is that it is a tasteless, childish, very English kind of joke.

When a character experiences one of those moments of irrational ecstasy in which it seems that 'God's in his heaven, all's right with the world', visionary moments which most of us will have experienced at some time in our lives, moments at which we have the illusion that the gates of perception have been opened, Mrs Christie proves more capable of describing the occasion than a number of novelists classified as literary. No words are adequate to convey the visionary experience: Mrs Christie's, precise, simple and brief, are less inadequate than many another's.

It is disconcerting to find, in a novel written during the Second World War, that the author still cannot resist waving her little anti-Semitic flag. One of the characters, Midge, has a telephone conversation with her employer, the proprietress of a West End dress shop, whose voice, 'the raucous voice of the vitriolic little Jewess', comes angrily over the wires: 'What ith that, Mith

Hardcathle? A death? A funeral? Do you not know very well I am short-handed? Do you think I am going to stand for these excutheth? Oh, yeth, you are having a good time, I dare thay!' Midge describes her employer a few paragraphs later as 'a Whitechapel Jewess with dyed hair and a voice like a corncrake'. Granted that the voice at the end of the phone needed to be that of a mean, money-grasping employer, Mrs Christie might have found some other victim.

Sales of the first edition of *The Hollow* outdid those of the previous year's *Sparkling Cyanide* and reached an impressive 40,000.

Five years later, in 1951, *The Hollow*, a play based by Agatha Christie on her novel, was produced in London. Mrs Christie had written the play simply because it came to her suddenly one day that her novel, *The Hollow*, would make a good play, and she had by this time become somewhat disillusioned with other people's stage adaptations of her books. However, when she mentioned to Rosalind that she was considering such an adaptation, her daughter ('who has had the valuable role in life of eternally trying to discourage me without success'[32]) replied that, although *The Hollow* was a good book, it was completely unsuitable material for the theatre. The undiscouraged writer proceeded with her project and later commented shrewdly on the transition from novel to play:

> It was, of course, in some ways rather more of a novel than a detective story. *The Hollow* was a book I always thought I had ruined by the introduction of Poirot. I had got used to having Poirot in my books, and so naturally he had come into this one, but he was all wrong there. He did his stuff all right, but how much better, I kept thinking, would the book have been without him. So when I came to sketch out the play, out went Poirot.[33]

When the play was completed, it was given to Bertie Meyer who had presented *Alibi* and *Black Coffee*, the earliest Christie plays. However he thought it would be too difficult to cast and, in any case, did not like it sufficiently to make the attempt. It is at this stage that Peter Saunders (now Sir Peter), who was to be associated with the most successful period of Agatha Christie's career as a playwright, enters upon the scene. Saunders, a relative newcomer to theatrical management, had put out a tour of *Murder at the Vicarage*, with which he had done so well that he longed to acquire a new Christie play. He approached her agents, with the result that pressure was placed upon Bertie Meyer either to stage *The Hollow* within six months or relinquish it. Meyer chose to relinquish the play, whereupon Saunders tentatively engaged Hubert Gregg, an experienced light comedy actor and inexperienced director, to stage *The Hollow*.

Saunders, accompanied by Gregg, gave lunch at the Carlton Grill (at the bottom of the Haymarket, on the site now occupied by New Zealand House) to Mrs Christie, who brought along her husband, her daughter and her son-in-law. Despite Gregg's gaffe when he revealed that he thought *Black Coffee* to be an adaptation of *The Murder of Roger Ackroyd*, thus provoking mirthless laughter from the author, Mrs Christie and her advisers sufficiently approved of Saunders as impresario and Gregg as director to allow the venture to proceed. Gregg was even entrusted with the task of rewriting a number of passages, for in its first draft the play too clearly revealed its provenance, the printed page. It had, after all, begun life as a novel of characterization and motive rather than as a mystery full of plot and dialogue.

The play went into rehearsal. A lively picture of Mrs Christie's involvement at this stage was given much later by Hubert Gregg:

We were forever fiddling with the text, trying to take it off the printed page, where it was doggedly at home, and make it come alive. At one rehearsal – in a theatre, with Christie spreading over a seat in the stalls and me walking up and down the centre aisle – my ear was drawn to the Detective Inspector. The word 'peremptory' came into a speech of his. I can't think how I had come to leave it there. But what disturbed me more was his mispronunciation of the word. He wasn't to blame, the word is hardly ever given its correct sound. He plumped for the general mis-stressing of the second syllable. . . . 'It isn't "per*empt*ory",' I said, 'it's "*per*emptory".' The cast all turned in surprise to look at me. So did Christie.

'It isn't, you know,' she said.

'It is, you know,' I said. 'Look it up.'

'I bet you a pound,' she said.

'Done!' said I.

The actor made another stab at the word, getting it right for me but wrong for everyone else.

The following day, Christie inserted herself into her accustomed seat and I began my perambulation as this same scene was played. I was standing beside her – not coincidentally – when the actor came to his verbal Becher's Brook. He sailed over it and turned to me with a 'How's that?' expression on his face. Christie was handing me a pound note. I took it. But, at the same time, I called out to the actor, 'Change the word.' (With a side glance at Christie.) 'I don't think this detective would use it anyway. Make it "short".'

'Why?' asked Christie. By now she was ceasing to object to changes. This question was merely a request for information.

'Apart from anything else,' I said, 'if you and I had a difference of opinion about the pronunciation to the extent of risking a pound on it, the word may fuss an audience. In my view they'll be more fussed if he says it my way because they'll think he's wrong. If he says it your way – which, mainly, will be their way – they'll think he's right but the odd philologist in the audience will know he's wrong and be fussed. Then there's the point that a detective, this kind of detective, even if he used the word, probably wouldn't get it right anyway. Now. For whom is he to make it wrong – you or me?'

'Have a peppermint,' said Christie.[34]

The Hollow began a pre-London tour at the Arts Theatre, Cambridge, on 5 February 1951, and came into the tiny Fortune Theatre in the West End of London (opposite the Drury Lane's stage-door) on 7 June. It subsequently transferred to the Ambassadors Theatre, achieving a very respectable run in London of eleven months (376 performances). On tour, the role of Dr Christow who is murdered near the beginning of Act II was played by the director, Hubert Gregg. In the West End, Gregg having gone off to appear in a Walt Disney film, Christow was played by Ernest Clark. Top billing went to Jeanne de Casalis who, as Lady Angkatell, found all the humour of the part but could not be restrained from adding some of her own. Max Mallowan thought she 'acted throughout as the Queen Bee, to the detriment of the hive.'[35]

The cast at the Fortune Theatre also included George Thorpe (Sir Henry),

Colin Douglas (Edward), Jessica Spencer (Midge), Martin Myldeck (Inspector Colquhoun) and Detective Sergeant Penny (Richard Shaw Taylor).[36] Agatha Christie's instinct in substituting a Scotland Yard detective for Hercule Poirot was a sound one, for the flamboyant Poirot would have drawn attention away from the other characters, whereas the comparatively colourless policeman helps to focus attention upon them. Although the play is necessarily less complex than the novel, its dialogue is lively, and it holds the attention firmly. There is usually a gasp from the audience at the moment just before the end when the apparent situation of murderer and potential second victim is reversed with one line of dialogue, and the identity of the killer thus revealed.

In the play, Midge still has a telephone conversation with her employer, whose voice is heard. It is however, no longer the 'raucous voice of a vitriolic little Jewess' from Whitechapel. 'Allo,' it says, 'This is Madame Henri speaking . . . Why are you not 'ere? You are coming back this afternoon, yes? . . . If you do not return today, you will not 'ave any job. There are plenty of girls who would be 'appy to 'ave it.' This unpleasant French lady may or may not be Jewish: the question does not arise.

With the success of *The Hollow*, Agatha Christie's golden period in the theatre began. In the next three years she was to go on to even greater commercial and artistic success. 'I find,' she said during this period,

> that writing plays is much more fun than writing books. For one thing you need not worry about those long descriptions of places and people. And you must write quickly if only to keep the mood while it lasts, and to keep the dialogue flowing naturally. I didn't care much for what occurred when other people tried to turn my books into plays, so in the end I felt I had to do it myself.

Agatha Christie's plays are, of course, continually being staged throughout the world, in English and in translation. During the year (1981) in which this book was written, the author encountered several productions in the United States and in Great Britain, on tour or in provincial repertory theatres. A production at the Theatre Royal, Windsor, of *The Hollow*, its only major blemish a misguided injection of current idioms or references into the thirty-year-old text ('How does that grab you?'; 'I've been jogging for the past hour'; references to 'The Sweeny' and 'Starsky and Hutch'), revealed the play to be still able to delight audiences.

The Rose and the Yew Tree (1947)

The opportunity to begin travelling abroad again offered itself in 1947, when Max Mallowan became the first Professor of Western Asiatic Archaeology at the Institute of Archaeology in the University of London. His post allowed him to take up work overseas for a period of some months in each year; and thus it was that, in the autumn of 1947, Agatha accompanied him to Baghdad where Mallowan entered into negotiations with the Iraq Department of Antiquities for a resumption of the excavations which had been interrupted by the war.

1947 was also the year in which Queen Mary, mother of the reigning British monarch George VI, celebrated her eightieth birthday. When the BBC enquired how she would like the event celebrated on the radio, Queen Mary's private secretary replied that Her Majesty would like nothing better than a play by Agatha Christie. For many years Queen Mary had been a devoted reader of Mrs Christie's crime novels, and had a standing order with her bookseller for each new title as it was published. She was not the only Agatha Christie fan in the British royal family, for her daughter-in-law, Queen Elizabeth (now the Queen Mother) and her grand-daughters Elizabeth (now Queen Elizabeth II) and Margaret were also Christie readers.

The BBC therefore commissioned from Agatha Christie a half-hour radio play,[37] to be broadcast in celebration of Queen Mary's birthday. Mrs Christie had an idea in mind which she had intended to work up into a story. Instead, within a week she turned it into a radio play, and 'Three Blind Mice' was, in due course, broadcast. Queen Mary with members of her family and friends listened to it in the sitting-room of Marlborough House, and Her Majesty professed to be delighted by it. Agatha Christie subsequently turned 'Three Blind Mice' into a long story, or novella, and it was published in a volume, *Three Blind Mice and Other Stories*, in the United States of America only, in 1950 (see pp. 153–55). The story was not published in Great Britain because, by this time, the author had decided to turn it back into a play, not for radio but for the theatre. This is the play which, retitled 'The Mousetrap', opened in London in 1952, and was still running in 1982 (see pp. 166–69).

During the year 1947, a new Mary Westmacott novel, *The Rose and the Yew Tree*, and a Hercule Poirot volume, *The Labours of Hercules*, were published. Although Agatha Christie's fourth Mary Westmacott novel was written and published in the forties, the idea behind the book had been in her mind, according to the author, since 1929: 'Just a sketchy picture, that I knew would come to life one day.' What that idea was it is not easy to discern, for on one level *The Rose and the Yew Tree* is a simpler piece of story-telling than the earlier Westmacott novels, though on another it can be read as being about time and choice: the mystery of the former, the non-existence of the latter. The title derives from a sentence in 'Little Gidding', the last of the four long, meditative poems which make up T.S. Eliot's *Four Quartets*, and the sentence is placed at the beginning of the novel as an epigraph: 'The moment of the rose and the moment of the yew-tree are of equal duration.'

The story, narrated by a middle-aged man who is crippled after being knocked down by a lorry, concerns a beautiful, high-born maiden who inexplicably forsakes her fairy-tale prince to go off with a coarse workingclass opportunist who, physically brave or perhaps foolhardy, has been awarded a VC during the 1939–45 war and who stands for parliament in the first post-war election. The characters, though closely observed, or at least observed in close-up, seem less real than in the earlier Westmacott novels, and you can quite easily imagine them removed to the middle distance, as it were, and placed in an Agatha Christie murder mystery. The beautiful, somewhat fey girl who lives in the castle on the headland with her grandmother, Lady St Loo; her handsome cousin Rupert, Lord St Loo, whom she is expected to marry; the unpleasant Labour MP, John Gabriel, who undergoes a kind of metamorphosis; the understanding, self-effacing narrator; the artist and his intelligent, articulate wife. The MP would be murdered, Poirot would investigate, and would discover the killer to be, probably, the artist. *The Rose and the Yew Tree* is even set in Agatha Christie country, the seaside resort of St Loo. *Peril at End House* (1932) was set in St Loo which, in the absence of precise information from the author, was identified on page 65 as being in Devon: its leading hotel certainly seemed to be based on the Imperial, Torquay. But, in *The Rose and the Yew Tree*, St Loo is placed further down the coast, in Cornwall.

If the structure of *The Rose and the Yew Tree* appears less complex than that of the earlier Westmacott novels, the quality of the thought, as distinct from that of the creative imagination, is, if not more complex, then certainly very impressive. The full impact of the scene in which the narrator, Hugh Norreys, and the young woman with whom for a time he imagines he is in love go to a concert at the Wigmore Hall and hear Elisabeth Schumann sing a Richard Strauss *Lied*, 'Morgen', will be made only on those readers who know the song and its emotive force, and can identify it from the few words of English translation given in the text. But few will fail to recognize the wisdom and maturity of the narrator's comments on 'nature's last and most cunning piece of deceit', the illusion that accompanies physical attraction. The difference between love and that 'whole monstrous fabric of self-deception' erected by passion disguised as love is not easy to distinguish when you are in the throes of one or the other, but it is real, and it was clearly understood by this most unromantic of novelists.

The Rose and the Yew Tree is also concerned marginally with politics, and a mature disillusion with the political game informs Mrs Christie's outlook. She has travelled a long road since *The Secret of Chimneys*. 'What are politics after all,' Hugh Norreys ponders, 'but adjacent booths at the world's fair, each offering their own cheap-jack specific to cure all ills?' Elsewhere, through her narrator, Mrs Christie reveals a capacity for speculative and abstract thought, and a mystical acceptance of the natural world, which are all the more fascinating because they surface but rarely in her works:

> Across the terrace came running a brown squirrel. It sat up, looking at us. It chattered a while, then darted off to run up a tree.
>
> I felt suddenly as though a kaleidoscopic universe had shifted, setting into a different pattern. What I saw now was the pattern of a sentient world where existence was everything, thought and speculation nothing. Here were morning and evening, day and night, food and drink, cold and heat – here movement, purpose, consciousness that did not yet know it *was* consciousness. This was the squirrel's world, the world of green grass pushing steadily upwards, of trees living and breathing.

Finally, however, *The Rose and the Yew Tree* is about consciousness and the illusory nature of choice. 'Does one ever really have any choice? About anything?' asks Isabella, who would not comprehend any real answer to her metaphysical question. She asks the question, having left her fairy-tale castle in Cornwall to share a degraded life with the rascally and saint-like John Gabriel in a squalid room in the Christie-invented Eastern European town of Zagrade, which is not, as one might expect, in Yugoslavia and equidistant from Zagreb and Belgrade, but in Slovakia.

'Romantically saccharine,' says the unperceptive Jeffrey Feinman.[38] Dorothy B. Hughes, however, understands *The Rose and the Yew Tree* and its companion novels: 'The Westmacotts bear as little relation to women-type novels as to Winnie-the-Pooh. You cannot but wonder if any of those who preferred opinions had ever read her work.'[39] Max Mallowan, not unprejudiced in the matter, thinks *The Rose and the Yew Tree* 'the most powerful and dramatic' of all the novels.

The Labours of Hercules (1947)

Twelve Hercule Poirot stories comprise *The Labours of Hercules*, but they are not simply individual stories collected together to make up a volume: the book has been planned around a theme. In a Foreword, or introductory chapter, in which the celebrated detective is giving dinner in his modern London flat to an old friend, the classical scholar Dr Burton, Fellow of All Souls, the conversation turns to the classics. Poirot, contemplating retirement and the cultivation of vegetable marrows, regrets that a certain richness of the spirit may have eluded him because of his lack of a classical education. A joke is made about his Christian name, Hercule. 'Hardly a *Christian* name,' says Dr Burton. 'Definitely pagan.' And he goes on to make an unflattering distinction between his friend and the Hercules of Greek legend. Burton does not take seriously Poirot's expressed intention to retire from his profession as a private investigator. 'Yours aren't the Labours of Hercules,' he tells Poirot, 'yours are labours of love.' As he leaves, he prophesies that Poirot will make as many farewell appearances as a prima donna.

Burton goes, but he leaves the germ of an idea in the mind of Hercule Poirot who, the following morning, instructs his secretary, the efficient Miss Lemon, to collect for him information about the labours of Hercules. What he reads leads him not to any great admiration of the classical Hercules – 'What was he but a large muscular creature of low intelligence and criminal tendencies!' – but to a determination to accept only twelve more cases, cases which would have to correspond in the modern world to the twelve labours of the classical Greek hero: 'Poirot picked up the Classical Dictionary and immersed himself once more in classical lore. He did not intend to follow his prototype too closely. There should be no woman, no shirt of Nessus . . . The Labours and the Labours only.'

The twelve stories in *The Labours of Hercules* are accounts of the twelve cases which Poirot accepts. But, of course, his friend Dr Burton was right. Poirot continued to bring murderers to justice for many years after completing the last of his twelve labours.

The labours of the Greek Hercules were imposed upon the hero by Eurystheus, king of Tiryns, at the command of the Delphic oracle, as a penance when Hercules killed his own wife Megara in a fit of madness. Poirot's labours were self-imposed, and necessarily involved a certain amount of symbolism, for the dangers of the modern world are not those of classical Greece. Hercules' first task, for instance, was to kill the Nemean lion, a frightful beast which had been ravaging the country. In 'The Nemean Lion', Poirot's first Herculean adventure, he solves a mystery concerning the kidnapping of a beast which could be said to look like a lion, is indeed said by one of the characters in the story to have the heart of a lion, but is, in fact, a Pekingese dog.

The Lernean Hydra, slain by Hercules, was a monstrous snake which inhabited the swamps and which was able to grow replacements of its many heads if they were lopped off. The many-headed monster which Poirot destroys in 'The Lernean Hydra' is malicious gossip. Whereas the earlier Hercules persuaded his friend Iolaus to burn the stumps before new heads could grow, his modern counterpart finds that he has to solve a murder before he can suppress the many tongues of rumour and gossip.

In 'The Arcadian Deer' Poirot functions less as detective than as a sentimental matchmaker, at the request of someone who, 'he thought, was one of the handsomest specimens of humanity he had ever seen, a simple young man with the outward semblance of a Greek god.' He solves a little mystery as well, but his satisfaction is chiefly derived from uniting the Greek God with his stricken Arcadian deer. In the classical legend, it is, surely, an Arcadian *stag* which Hercules captures. It is as well for conventional morality that Poirot gives himself a certain licence in interpreting his brief.

Poirot's equivalent of the fourth labour of Hercules, in 'The Erymanthian Boar', is to achieve the capture not of a wild boar but of a violent murderer and gang-leader. In the course of this adventure, high up in the Swiss Alps whither he had journeyed in search of the Arcadian deer, Poirot indulges in some distinctly un-Poirot-like physical activity, exposing himself to dangerous violence.

In 'The Augean Stables' Poirot averts a political scandal of the greatest magnitude by adopting the methods of Hercules who cleansed the stables belonging to King Augeas by redirecting a river through them. 'What Hercules used was a river,' Poirot exclaims, 'that is to say one of the great forces of nature. Modernize that! What is a great force of nature? Sex, is it not?' And he goes on to argue that scandal allied to sex will divert people's attention from scandal allied to political chicanery or fraud. He is a bit of an old fraud, himself, *n'est-ce pas?*

Poirot's 'man-eating birds' in 'The Stymphalean Birds' are either two middle-aged women with long, curved noses like birds, and loose cloaks which flap in the wind like wings, or they are two other birds of prey and of ill omen. Hercules chased his birds from their hiding-place in the woods by banging a bronze rattle, and then brought them down. Hercule adopts subtler but equally efficacious methods in modern Herzoslovakia. We were last concerned with this small Balkan state (allied, surely, to Ruritania and Pontevedro) in *The Secret of Chimneys* (1925).

'The Cretan Bull', in the story of that name proves not easy to identify. There is, in any case, only the remotest connection between the Poirot story and the legend of Hercules' capture of the bull which may have been the father of the Minotaur. There is also a clue embedded in the sentence before this.

The eighth labour of Hercules was to capture the horses of Diomedes. These animals were fed on human flesh by their owner, the king of the Bistonians. They suddenly became tame when Hercules fed their master to them. Poirot equates them with beasts of another kind who symbolically feed upon humanity, and he seems to expect that at least one of the breed will be tamed.

'The Girdle of Hyppolita' was captured by Hercules after he had defeated the Amazons in battle and either killed their Queen or held one of her generals for ransom. Poirot's 'Girdle of Hyppolita' is a recently discovered masterpiece by Rubens, stolen from a West End art gallery. Inspector Japp appears, and a schoolgirl disappears. Poirot brings all the strands together with ease.

To obtain possession of the flock of cattle of the monster Geryon, Hercules first killed the monster. In 'The Flock of Geryon' Hercule Poirot kills no one. Geryon, the monster, is Dr Anderson, leader of a religious sect, The Flock of the Shepherd, and Poirot investigates Anderson's activities at the instigation of a

Miss Carnaby, who had played a part in the first of the Labours ('The Nemean Lion'). The story ends with the arrest of a murderer, the destruction of a monster.

'The Apples of the Hesperides' grew on a tree guarded by a terrible dragon. There are several versions of the legend: Hercules either plucked the apples himself after killing the dragon, or sent Atlas for them, meanwhile holding the world on his own shoulders. Poirot's apples are a detail of the design on an Italian renaissance goblet, a design representing a tree around which a jewelled serpent is coiled. The apples are formed of very beautiful emeralds. Poirot locates the missing goblet, but there is a twist in the tail of the dragon. (The goblet is *said* to have been made by Benvenuto Cellini and used by Pope Alexander VI, or Roderigo Borgia. This would mean that Cellini made it while he was less than three years old!) At one point in the story Poirot quotes a Spanish proverb: 'Take what you want – and pay for it, says God.' It must have been a proverb which appealed to Mrs Christie, for she also put it into the mouth of Lady Dittisham in *Five Little Pigs* (1943).

The final labour of both Hercules and Hercule is 'The Capture of Cerberus'. To capture the Cerberus of legend, Hercules had to make his way down to Hades, or hell, where Cerberus, a three-headed dog, guarded the gates. Hercule Poirot does likewise, except that Hell is the name of a London night club run by the Countess Vera Rossakoff, whom Poirot had first met more than twenty years earlier (see p. 45), and for whom he had always entertained a tender regard. Cerberus is the 'largest and ugliest and blackest' (one-headed) dog Poirot has ever seen, and it guards the entrance to the club, which is at the bottom of a steep flight of stairs. Entrance is effected by throwing a sop to Cerberus from the basket of dog biscuits provided by the management. Poirot helps Japp foil a dope ring, and emerges from Hell with his affection for the dubious Russian Countess unscathed. He rests from his labours, murmuring contentedly, 'From the Nemean Lion to the Capture of Cerberus. It is complete.'

The Labours of Hercules is generally regarded as the best of Agatha Christie's short story collections. The idea is an amusing one, cleverly implemented, and Poirot is at his most engaging throughout. The parallels between modern reality and ancient myth are wittily and skilfully made, and most of the individual stories are really first-rate. Reviewing the volume in the *Daily Graphic*, Agatha Christie's rival, Margery Allingham, wrote that it was 'as satisfactory as its title'. 'I have often thought,' she continued, 'that Mrs Christie was not so much the best as the only living writer of the true or classic detective story.'

Taken at the Flood *or* There is a Tide (1948)

Max Mallowan returned to his excavations in the Middle East in 1948, which meant that Agatha Christie was able also to return to the way of life she had enjoyed before the war. It was, of course, not quite the same. The Orient Express was no longer the cheapest way to travel to Syria and Iraq, nor was it even possible to make the entire journey on that train which was not what it used to be. This time, as Mrs Christie puts it in her autobiography, it was 'the beginning of that dull routine, travelling by air'. The desert bus service no longer functioned: 'you flew from London to Baghdad and that was that.'

But she enjoyed participating in the life and work of the dig during the excavation season, and equally enjoyed quite different kinds of pleasure in England, such as going to the opera in London, or enjoying summers surrounded by family in Devon. As before, she frequently wrote her crime novels in the Middle East, and now she also began to think about an autobiography, the actual writing of which was to occupy her, on and off, from 1950 to 1965. This took time away from the novels, but from now until the year of her death, she continued to publish at least one title each year. In 1948, there were two, a novel (*Taken at the Flood*) and a volume of stories (*Witness for the Prosecution*).

Both the British and the American titles of the novel came from Brutus's speech in Act IV, scene iii of Shakespeare's *Julius Caesar*, printed as epigraph at the beginning of the novel:

> There is a tide in the affairs of men,
> Which, taken at the flood, leads on to fortune;
> Omitted, all the voyages of their life
> Is bound in shallows and in miseries.
> On such a full sea are we now afloat;
> And we must take the current when it serves,
> Or lose our ventures.

(Poirot carelessly misquotes the first two lines in Chapter XIV of Book Two.)

  Taken in the Flood was written, and is set, in a post-war England whose buoyant 1945 mood of triumph has given way to a certain restlessness and dissatisfaction. The troubles which beset the Cloade family involve murder, suicide and accidental death, but the sense of disillusion felt by Lynn Marchmont, niece of Gordon Cloade (who was killed in an air-raid) and fiancée of her cousin, Rowley Cloade, has more general causes as well, typifying something of the feeling abroad in the country. 'It's the aftermath war has left,' Lynn thinks to herself. 'Ill will. Ill feeling. It's everywhere. On railways and buses and in shops and among workers and clerks and even agricultural labourers. And I suppose worse in mines and factories. Ill will.' Agatha Christie comes dangerously close to a realism which could easily have destroyed her cosy murder mystery world. She flirts with it, emphasizing the irrational pessimism of the forties, and even identifying and listing a number of petty domestic causes of it, as for instance when Superintendent Spence complains of the shortcomings of his local laundry, and describes the difficulties experienced by his wife in coping with the housekeeping.

  It is against this drably realistic background that Mrs Christie with superb confidence and unerring judgment paints her picture of a family of landed gentry who have never been encouraged or even allowed to attempt to make their own way in the world, but have been shackled to family wealth which, it now seems, is about to pass into the hands of a stranger. Questions of identity arise, there is a husband presumed dead and there is the arrival in the village of a stranger calling himself Enoch Arden. Those readers who know Tennyson's narrative poem of that name will have an advantage over those who do not, but only for a few pages. 'Wasn't there a poem, David – something about a man coming back –?' someone asks. It is Hercule Poirot who eventually produces the answer, with the aid of a new police detective, Superintendent Spence, who will appear in three later

Poirot novels. Except for three early stories not collected into volumes until *The Under Dog* (USA: 1951) or *Poirot's Early Cases* (UK: 1974), we shall not encounter again Poirot's old friend and colleague Inspector Japp, whom we must presume to have retired from the force shortly after his involvement in three of *The Labours of Hercules* (1947).

The characters in *Taken at the Flood* are unusually vivid and convincing, and the plot is one of Mrs Christie's most complex. In Chapter I of Book Two, the reader is likely to jump on what seems to be a not sufficiently well hidden clue. The clue is a legitimate one, though it would be unwise to assume that the author has not placed it precisely where she meant to. A minor point of interest: the house, Warmsley Heath, is based on Archibald and Agatha Christie's country house near the golf course, at Sunningdale, remembered and described after many years away from it. It will also serve as model for houses in two later novels.

Favourable reviews of Agatha Christie's novels were by now the rule rather than the exception, and distinguished fellow-novelists were just as impressed as journalist-reviewers. In *The Tatler*, Elizabeth Bowen wrote of *Taken at the Flood* that it was 'one of the best . . . her gift for blending the cosy with the macabre has seldom been more in evidence than it is here.'

Witness for the Prosecution and other stories (1948)

The play, *Witness for the Prosecution*, first staged in 1953, will be discussed on pp. 172–74. The 1948 *Witness for the Prosecution* is a volume, published in the United States of America but not in Great Britain, containing ten stories, all of which had already appeared in collections published in Great Britain, with one exception which is noted below. The title story is still printed with its definite article, as 'The Witness for the Prosecution', though the volume's title anticipates that of the 1953 stage version, *Witness for the Prosecution.*

Of the ten stories in *Witness for the Prosecution*, six come from the 1933 British volume, *The Hound of Death*, and three from the 1934 British volume, *The Listerdale Mystery*, these two volumes having never been published in the United States. The stories from *The Hound of Death* are 'The Witness for The Prosecution', 'The Red Signal', 'The Fourth Man', 'SOS', 'Where There's a Will' (called 'Wireless' in the UK) and 'The Mystery of the Blue Jar' (see pp. 72–73). Those from *The Listerdale Mystery* are 'Philomel Cottage', 'Accident' and 'Sing a Song of Sixpence' (see pp. 78–79). 'Sing a Song of Sixpence' is omitted from the 1956 American paperback edition of *Witness for the Prosecution* which contains only nine stories.

In the remaining story, 'The Second Gong', Hercule Poirot proves that the death of an eccentric millionaire in the study of his palatial country house is not suicide, and unmasks the murderer. This is a much shorter version of the novella, 'Dead Man's Mirror', which is to be found in the 1937 volume entitled *Dead Man's Mirror* (USA) or *Murder in the Mews* (UK). The plot and several characters are common to the two stories, though the characters' names differ, but the stories end differently. The murderer in 'The Second Gong' is not a character who corresponds to the murderer in 'Dead Man's Mirror'. The motives, too, are different. It is fascinating to compare the two stories, one a reworking of the other. 'The Second Gong' has not been published in the UK.

Witness for the Prosecution is a splendid collection of favourite Christie stories.

Crooked House (1949)

Max Mallowan's excavations at Nimrud, the ancient military capital of Assyria, got under way in 1949. For the first season, the supervisory staff amounted to no more than four people: Mallowan, Agatha Christie, Robert Hamilton who had been Director of the Antiquities Department in Palestine, and Dr Mahmud el Amin of the Iraq Antiquities Department. They lodged in a wing of the local Sheikh's mudbrick house in what Mallowan described as near-slum conditions, but they were happy, even when the three men were banished from the living-room by Agatha who occasionally needed it as a dark room for developing negatives. Work was to continue at Nimrud every season for the next ten years.

During the year, the widowed Rosalind married Anthony Hicks, an oriental scholar who later turned his attention to horticulture. It was in 1949, too, that a *Sunday Times* journalist discovered and revealed that the novelist Mary Westmacott was none other than Agatha Christie. This did not, however, prevent Agatha Christie publishing a further two novels, in 1952 and 1956, as Mary Westmacott.

In December, 1949, the play, *Murder at the Vicarage*, a dramatization by Moie Charles and Barbara Toy of the 1930 novel, was staged in London at the Playhouse (see p. 54). It was to be the last dramatization of Agatha Christie by other hands until after the author's death. After 1949, Mrs Christie herself either adapted her novels or wrote new plays for the stage, refusing requests by others for permission to make stage versions of any of her works.

The only volume to be published during 1949 was *Crooked House*, one of those Christie crime novels which makes do without any of the author's regular detectives. There is an investigator of sorts, who is also the narrator: he is Charles Hayward whose father, Sir Arthur Hayward, is Assistant Commissioner of Police at Scotland Yard. It cannot be said, however, that the quality of detection in *Crooked House* is high. This is a novel to be appreciated for its startling dénouement rather than for the intricacy of its puzzle or the skill with which the truth is uncovered.

This is also one of those Christie novels connected with nursery rhymes, though in this case the connection does not extend beyond the title:

> There was a crooked man and he went a crooked mile,
> He found a crooked sixpence beside a crooked stile.
> He had a crooked cat which caught a crooked mouse,
> And they all lived together in a little crooked house.

Aristide Leonides, though enormously wealthy, was no more crooked than anyone else who amasses great wealth. He had a crooked house, though not a little one and his entire family lived in it with him, but the important fact about Leonides was that he was murdered by a crooked member of his family. Charles Hayward, in love with the old patriarch's grand-daughter, unofficially helps the investigating team assigned to the case by his father, the Assistant Commissioner. But it is someone else who arrives first at the truth, and takes drastic steps to deal with the situation.

With the exception of the teenage Linda Marshall in *Evil Under the Sun*

(1941), Mrs Christie has not, until now, produced especially penetrating character portraits of children: but the two children of Philip and Magda Leonides, sixteen-year-old Eustace and eleven-year-old Josephine, are interesting, if not particularly pleasant. The adult inhabitants of the crooked house (a house based on Scotswood in Sunningdale, the old home of Archie and Agatha) are not all equally well characterized, some of them being distinctly more real than others. The actual plot is not one of Mrs Christie's liveliest, but perhaps the solution compensates for any earlier disappointments.

The author herself was not disappointed with *Crooked House*. In fact, on more than one occasion she announced that it was one of her favourites, if not the absolute favourite. 'Of my detective books', she wrote in *An Autobiography*, 'I think the two that satisfy me best are *Crooked House* and *Ordeal by Innocence*.' Elsewhere, she revealed that she had saved up the plot of *Crooked House* for years, thinking about it and working it out: 'I don't know what put the Leonides family into my head – they just came. I feel that I myself was only their scribe.'[40] In 1970, interviewed by Godfrey Winn in the London *Daily Mail*, she said that *Crooked House* was her favourite among her crime novels, while in another interview she is quoted as saying: 'Yes, *Crooked House* is one of my favourites. But I had difficulty with that one. The publishers wanted me to change the end . . . but that's how I'd written it; and some things you *can't* change.'[41] Agatha Christie was right not to change the end, which is the most satisfactory part of a readable but somewhat patchy novel.

One of the characters reminds the narrator of Athene Seyler. Older readers in England will not need to be told that Athene Seyler was one of the most delightful of comedy actresses on the English stage and in films. Now retired, and in her nineties, she was at the height of her career at the time that *Crooked House* was published.

Three Blind Mice and other stories (1950)

For their second season at Nimrud, the Mallowan party were able to move from their portion of the Sheikh's house into a new mudbrick house of their own. Again, Agatha found time both to help with her husband's work and to continue with her own. As she was to explain in her autobiography, their fields of interest differed widely, yet she came to acquire a real interest in and knowledge of many aspects of her husband's work, and he was able to help with hers:

> I am a lowbrow and he a highbrow, yet we complement each other, I think, and have both helped each other. Often he has asked me for my judgment on certain points, and whilst I shall always remain an amateur, I do know quite a lot about his special branch of archaeology – indeed, many years ago, when I was once saying sadly to Max it was a pity I couldn't have taken up archaeology when I was a girl, so as to be more knowledgeable on the subject, he said, 'Don't you realize that at this moment you know more about prehistoric pottery than almost any woman in England?'

In 1950, the 'lowbrow' Agatha Christie was made a Fellow of the Royal Society of Literature. During the year, *A Murder is Announced*, a new Miss Marple novel, was published and, in the USA only, a volume of stories as well. At the time of publication in the USA, none of the nine stories in *Three Blind*

Mice and other stories had appeared in British volumes. Seven of them (four Miss Marples and three Poirots) were in due course to be published in the UK in *Poirot's Early Cases* (1974), the posthumous *Miss Marple's Final Cases* (1979), and *The Adventure of the Christmas Pudding and other stories* (1960). The remaining two stories, 'Three Blind Mice' and 'The Love Detectives', have not appeared in volumes published in the UK.

The title story, is an adaptation of the radio play which Agatha Christie wrote on the occasion of Queen Mary's eightieth birthday (see p. 145), a novella-length murder mystery whose murderer, like so many of Mrs Christie's criminals, likes to find a parallel, or at least a pattern, for his crimes in old English nursery rhyme. He is given to whistling 'Three Blind Mice' which other characters in the story aid and abet him by playing on the piano or singing.

. Set in a remote country guesthouse isolated by a snow storm, 'Three Blind Mice' was to lend itself easily to stage adaptation in 1952 as *The Mousetrap*. The story has not been published in Great Britain, and presumably will remain unpublished there until the play comes to the end of its London run, which after thirty years it shows no sign of doing. 'Three Blind Mice' borrows one element of its plot from *The Sittaford Mystery* or *Murder at Hazelmoor* (1931) and, more significantly, another from *Hercule Poirot's Christmas* or *Murder for Christmas* (1938). *Pace* Jacques Barzun who finds it 'a poor variation of the pattern "Here we are, cut off from help, and a killer is among us"', it is an ingenious tale and well told.

The other stories in the volume are much shorter, and some of them first appeared in magazines as early as the mid-1920s. The four Miss Marple stories present that lady in early rather than late old age, yet they were to be included in the volume entitled *Miss Marple's Final Cases*: perhaps it is best not to inquire too closely. In 'Strange Jest', the problem Miss Marple solves does not involve a crime of any kind. It is, in fact, the most amiable of mysteries. 'Tape Measure Murder' finds her back in familiar and murderous territory, assisting such old friends as Colonel Melchett, Inspector Slack and Constable Palk. (Constable Palk is, perhaps, not such an old friend, but he will be remembered for having behaved courteously to Miss Marple and her friend Dolly Bantry in *The Body in the Library* (1942).) Inspector Slack has reason to be grateful to the spinster sleuth again in 'The Case of the Perfect Maid', one of the best of all Miss Marple stories, and the problem with which Dr Haydock presents the old lady in 'The Case of the Caretaker' adumbrates an important aspect of the plot of the much later novel, *Endless Night* (1967).

The three Poirot cases are 'The Third-Floor Flat', which is first-rate and has extraordinarily well-delineated characters for so short a story; 'The Adventure of Johnnie Waverly (also called 'The Kidnapping of Johnnie Waverly) which asks the reader to accept behaviour from a three-year-old boy which is so good that it is unbelievable, and also to accept a third butler called Tredwell;[42] and 'Four and Twenty Blackbirds' which has very little to do with the nursery rhyme in which blackbirds were baked in a pie, but in which a crime is solved because of Poirot's interest in the eating habits of others.

The remaining story in the volume, 'The Love Detectives', brings Mr Satterthwaite and his mysterious friend Harley Quin back after an absence of many years, in an adventure dating from the twenties, the period in which most of the Harley Quin stories were set (see p. 55).

An excellent collection of Christie stories, *Three Blind Mice* was retitled *The Mousetrap* when it went into a paperback edition in the USA in 1952. Later, it reverted to its original title.

A Murder is Announced (1950)

Those inhabitants of the village of Chipping Cleghorn who had the weekly North Benham News and Chipping Cleghorn Gazette delivered to their homes were able to read, over breakfast one Friday morning in October, a somewhat unsual notice in the Personal column: 'A murder is announced and will take place on Friday, 29 October at Little Paddocks at 6.30 p.m. Friends please accept this, the only intimation.' A number of them turned up at Little Paddocks, where Letitia Blacklock lived with a companion, two young relatives, and a paying guest. They were not disappointed, for there was a murder, although not, it would seem, the right one.

Chipping Cleghorn is not St Mary Mead, so you do not expect to find Miss Marple upon the scene. But the old lady happens to be staying at the Royal Spa Hotel in nearby Medenham Wells, where she is taking the waters for her rheumatism, and it seems that she knows something about the young man who got himself killed at Little Paddocks. She writes to the Chief Constable, who shows her letter to Sir Henry Clithering, ex-Commissioner of Scotland Yard, who of course knows Miss Marple of old. 'George,' says Sir Henry to the Chief Constable, 'it's my own particular, one and only, four-starred Pussy. The super Pussy of all old Pussies.' And the old pussy proceeds to solve a particularly ingenious murder plot, involving past illness, present identity, the expectations of relatives, the sex of certain characters, and perhaps a little too much coincidence for comfort.

Miss Marple, as always, disclaims any special gifts, 'except perhaps a certain knowledge of human nature' and a tendency always to believe the worst, a tendency fostered by her having lived all her life in an English village where human nature, apparently, is seen at its worst. In *A Murder is Announced*, she works in association with a new police detective, Chief Inspector Dermot Craddock, a pleasant and intelligent young man who happens to be Sir Henry Clithering's godson. Craddock will participate in three further Miss Marple cases: 'Sanctuary' from *Double Sin* (1961) and *Miss Marple's Final Cases* (1979); *4.50 From Paddington* or *What Mrs McGillicuddy Saw* (1957); and *The Mirror Crack'd From Side to Side* (1962).

A Murder is Announced is, despite its flaws, one of the most entertaining of the Jane Marple novels. It is also fascinating for the picture it gives of an England still in the throes of post-war muddle and discomfort. A great deal of minor social history can be gleaned from the pages of Agatha Christie: such novels of the twenties and thirties as *The Murder of Roger Ackroyd*, *Murder at the Vicarage* and *Murder is Easy* give a number of details of what life was like in an English village in the years between the wars. The Second World War years themselves are only obliquely chronicled, but England in the immediate post-war period is portrayed in *Taken at the Flood* and *A Murder is Announced*, and the inevitable breaking-up of the old village life is woven into the pages of *The Mirror Crack'd From Side to Side*, several years later in 1962.

The flaws in *A Murder is Announced*, however, are not to be overlooked. The reworking of such old Christie ploys as the ambiguity of names is not exactly a flaw if the author gets away with it, as Mrs Christie does. But she relies on coincidence a little too heavily this time, and she surely is wrong to allow Miss Marple not only to indulge in so unlikely an expression as 'fall guy', even if the old lady does claim to have picked it up from reading Dashiell Hammett, but also to hide in a broom cupboard and imitate a dead person's voice in order to frighten a murderer into a confession. ('I could always mimic people's voices,' said Miss Marple.) And, do people really change so much in ten years that they can reasonably expect not to be recognized by old acquaintances?

Despite these quibbles, it has to be admitted that *A Murder is Announced* is one of Mrs Christie's most successful conjuring tricks. As usual, some of the best and, in retrospect, most infuriating clues are verbal: in this case, you could even say typographical. It is well worth re-reading the earlier parts of the best Christie novels, in the light of the knowledge of the conclusions, to see precisely how you have been misled, how the quickness of the author's hand has deceived the reader's eye. Even though, at the end of *A Murder is Announced*, there are more cases of false identity than there are dead bodies at the end of *Hamlet*, you are likely to finish the novel feeling exasperated with yourself rather than with Mrs Christie. You will also have learned about a cake, known to Miss Blacklock's family as 'Delicious Death'. It is the masterpiece of the temperamental cook Mitzi, who is a refugee from Nazi Germany. The recipe, unfortunately, is not divulged.

Some of the characterization is superb; some is sketchy. The lesbian couple are crudely labelled: one has a 'short, man-like crop' of hair, and a 'manly stance', while the other is 'fat and amiable'. Mrs Christie never progressed beyond the most superficial descriptions of her homosexual characters ('My dears,' says Christopher Wren of the young detective in 'Three Blind Mice', 'he's very handsome, isn't he? I do admire the police. So stern and hard-boiled.').

There is a certain connection between *A Murder is Announced* and an early Miss Marple story, 'The Companion', in *The Thirteen Problems* (1932), which is about 'two English ladies' holidaying in Las Palmas. That Agatha Christie consciously bore the story in mind when she was planning the novel is attested to by the fact that the home address of the two women, as given in the hotel register, is 'Little Paddocks, Caughton Weir, Bucks'. Little Paddocks, the reader may remember, is the name of Letitia Blacklock's house in *A Murder is Announced*.

One of the characters in the novel, an aspiring young writer named Edmund Swettenham, succeeds in having one of his plays produced in London. Its title, *Elephants Do Forget*, is adversely commented upon by another character. More than twenty years later, Mrs Christie was to publish a Poirot novel called *Elephants Can Remember*.

Published on 5 June 1950, *A Murder is Announced* was widely publicized as Agatha Christie's fiftieth murder mystery (which it was, if one discounts volumes of short stories published only in the USA), and a first printing of a record number of 50,000 copies soon sold out. (Sales of her subsequent crime novels were always in excess of that number.) The author's British and American publishers issued a booklet filled with comments on her work by famous people, including the British Prime Minister, Clement Atlee, who claimed Agatha Christie as his favourite writer.

Reviews of the novel were, not surprisingly, highly laudatory. In *The*

Spectator, A.A. Milne wrote: 'A new novel by Miss Agatha Christie always deserves to be placed at the head of any list of detective fiction, and her fiftieth book, *A Murder is Announced*, establishes firmly her claim to the throne of detection. The plot is as ingenious as ever, the writing more careful, the dialogue both wise and witty . . . Long may she flourish.' 'Breathlessly exciting and entirely original', 'a perfect model of construction and enchantingly clever characterization', 'artistry and ingenuity', and 'a heady wine' are but a few of the flattering phrases strewn in the novelist's path by other enthusiastic reviewers. Margery Allingham, one of Agatha Christie's rivals, writing about the novelist in the *New York Times Book Review*[43] on the eve of publication of *A Murder is Announced*, said that Mrs Christie's 'appeal is made directly to the honest human curiosity in all of us. The invitation she gives her readers is to listen to the details surrounding the perfectly horrid screams from the apartment next door . . . In her own sphere there is no one to touch her, and her millions of readers are going to buy her new story, *A Murder is Announced*, and like it.' They did.

It was not until more than twenty-five years later that *A Murder is Announced* was dramatized for the stage. In 1975, not many months before she died, Agatha Christie gave her consent for a stage adaptation to be made by Leslie Darbon and presented by Peter Saunders. In due course, the play was staged, posthumously, first at the Theatre Royal, Brighton, and subsequently at the Vaudeville Theatre, London, where it opened on 21 September 1977. The critic of the *Financial Times* wrote: 'There is no reason, intellectual or dramatic, why it shouldn't run as long as *The Mousetrap*.' In the event, however, it did not run as long as *The Mousetrap*. The adaptation, faithful to the original and with dialogue which was a convincing pastiche of Agatha Christie's style whenever it did not actually quote from her, was competently done, but the complications of the plot were such that they must have proved too perplexing for the average audience. Revelations about the various family relationships, and surprises concerning people's identities come thick and fast in the play, and there is no going back to check that you have got it right! The facetious ending, with Inspector Craddock and Miss Marple tucking into Mitzi's 'Delicious Death' cake cannot have helped. The play ostensibly takes place in 'the present' (i.e. 1977), though the directions in the published acting edition rather whimsically require it to be set in 'Agatha Christie time'. Mitzi, in the novel a refugee from the Nazis, is given snippets of dialogue in Hungarian, and is now presumably on the run from Communist Hungary.

The 1977 production of the play was directed by Robert Chetwyn, and the cast was headed by Dulcie Gray (Miss Marple), Dinah Sheridan (Letitia Blacklock), Eleanor Summerfield (Dora Bunner) and James Grout (Inspector Craddock).

They Came to Baghdad (1951)

At the beginning of 1951, Agatha Christie's dramatization of her novel, *The Hollow*, (see p. 143) opened in Cambridge. After touring for four months, it came into the West End where it played for a further eleven months to large and appreciative audiences.

During the excavation season at Nimrud, a small room was added to the team's house for Agatha Christie's exclusive use and at her expense. For £50 she acquired a square, mudbrick room with a table and two chairs. On the walls she hung two pictures by young Iraqi artists. 'One was of a sad-looking cow by a tree; the other a kaleidoscope of every colour imaginable, which looked like patchwork at first, but suddenly could be seen to be two donkeys with men leading them through the Suq.'[44] On the door, one of the party fixed a placard in cuneiform, announcing that this was the Beit Agatha, or Agatha's house. It was here that she settled down seriously to write her autobiography.

The year 1951 saw the publication of a novel, *They Came to Baghdad*, and, in the United States only, a volume of stories, *The Under Dog*.

With the novel, *They Came to Baghdad*, Agatha Christie returned to the thriller for the first time since the Tommy and Tuppence adventure, *N or M?* (1941). And *N or M?* had been the first since the twenties. Thrillers, as opposed to domestic murder mysteries, are few and far between in the *oeuvre* of Mrs Christie, though she never abandoned the genre because, as she admitted on more than one occasion, she found the thriller not only very satisfying to write but also much easier than the domestic crime story. A major difference between a detective novel and a thriller is the difference between 'who did it' and 'will they get away with it', but Agatha Christie always retained in her thrillers an element of mystery from the domestic murder mystery novel. The question 'Who?' always has to be answered in a Christie thriller, and it is this question which provides most of the interest in *They Came to Baghdad*.

The heroine is another of those idealized young Agathas, intrepid, over-imaginative girls bored with life at home and longing for adventure abroad. Victoria Jones, sacked from an office job in London, gets into conversation on a park bench with an attractive young man. She falls heavily in love with him, and knowing no more than that his first name is Edward and that he is about to leave to take up a job ('Culture – poetry, all that sort of thing') in Baghdad, she determines to follow him. Soon she is involved in helping to foil the plans of a vaguely described authoritarian political group who intend to sabotage the imminent summit meeting of the great nations on which the peace of the world depends.

The plot is engaging and highly readable hokum. What distinguish Agatha Christie's thrillers from most others are not only the traces of mystery which are carried over from her domestic crime stories but also her lightness of touch and an air of self-mocking humour, far removed from the lifeless, mechanical spoofing which passes as humour in the works of Ian Fleming and his followers. An additional enjoyment is derived in *They Came to Baghdad*, from the lively authenticity of the background, and especially the use of Baghdad, a city the archaeologist's wife knew very well. There is also a diverting picture of an archaeological camp in the desert, and of its absent-minded leader, Dr Pauncefoot Jones.

The villains, this time, appear not to be Marxists but fanatical and bloody-minded idealists of the centre, dedicated to destroying both Capitalism and Communism. 'The bad old things must destroy each other. The fat old men grasping at their profits, impeding progress. The bigoted, stupid Communists, trying to establish their Marxian heaven. There must be total war – total destruction. And then – the new Heaven and the new Earth.'

A preposterous plot, a delightful and typical Christiean heroine, and well-drawn minor characters, these are the ingredients which combine to make *They Came to Baghdad* so easy to read. You even forgive Mrs Christie her dreadful French, though surely her editor ought to have corrected (twice) her spelling of *empressement* into which she inserts an unwanted 'é' which must do strange things to the pronunciation of the word. But then, literacy is not what it was, anywhere. The punctuation of the *New York Times* in its praise of *They Came to Baghdad* is such that the intended compliment is impressively multiplied: 'The most satisfying novel in years, from one of the most satisfying novelists!' The London *Times Literary Supplement* thought that *They Came to Baghdad* contained one of the best surprises since the unmasking of the criminal in *The Seven Dials Mystery*. Well, yes, but the assiduous reader might just, this time, find himself prepared for that particular surprise.

The Under Dog and other stories (1951)

Though this volume of Hercule Poirot adventures was published only in the USA, all of the stories in it were later to appear in Great Britain as well: the title-story in *The Adventure of the Christmas Pudding* (1960: Great Britain only: see p. 192) and the others in (*Hercule*) *Poirot's Early Cases* (UK and USA, 1974: see p. 233). All are very early Christie stories, dating from the mid-twenties, but they had not previously appeared in a volume, with the exception of 'The Under Dog' which was first published in 1929 in Great Britain by the Readers Library Publishing Company Ltd, in a volume together with 'Blackman's Wood', a long story by E. Phillips Oppenheim, under the title *Two New Crime Stories* by Agatha Christie and E. Phillips Oppenheim (reprinted by the Daily Express Fiction Library in 1936 as *Two Thrillers*).

Inspector Miller, who appears in the long story, 'The Under Dog' (and three Poirot stories in other volumes), is not one of Hercule Poirot's warmest admirers: in his view, the little Belgian was 'much overrated'. Poirot, of course, proves him wrong and correctly identifies the murderer of Sir Reuben Astwell, a bad-tempered financier, in a conventional story whose length is not entirely justified by its content.

Poirot's other early cases, in three of which Inspector Japp is also involved, are recorded more briefly, perhaps because they are all narrated by Hastings who does not waste words. 'The Plymouth Express' was made use of, and part of its plot recycled when Agatha Christie came to write *The Mystery of the Blue Train* (1928). In a recent American paperback edition of *The Under Dog*, both 'The Plymouth Express' and 'The Affair at the Victory Ball' have their narratives interrupted near the end by an editorial note, inviting the reader to pause at this point, arrive at his own solution to the mystery, and then see how close he comes to that of the author. The characters of the *commedia dell' arte*, or at least their costumes, play a leading part in the Victory Ball murder. This links the story, somewhat tenuously, with the author's Harlequinade poems (see p. 30) and her Harley Quin stories (p. 55).

In 'The King of Clubs' Poirot is able to be of service to Prince Paul of Maurania. The young prince has a weak chin and 'the famous Mauranberg mouth'. We are not told what that is: perhaps it is similar to the prominent Habsburg chin.

'The Submarine Plans' was later expanded into a much longer story, 'The

Incredible Theft' in which form it appeared in *Murder in the Mews* (1937), but not in *Dead Man's Mirror*, the American edition of *Murder in the Mews* (see p. 103). The later version, more than three times the length of 'The Submarine Plans' is more satisfying than the earlier, which leads one to note Mrs Christie's opinion[45] that 'The short story technique . . . is not really suited to the detective story at all. A thriller, possibly – but a detective story, no.' It is certainly true that the average short story length does not allow Agatha Christie to do that which she does best, which is to weave complex strands of mystification. Her longer stories are almost invariably better than her shorter ones.

'The Adventure of the Clapham Cook' finds Poirot investigating a crime in a distinctly lower-middleclass milieu, which makes a change for him as well as for the reader. This and 'The Lemesurier Inheritance' are the outstanding stories in *The Under Dog*, which also contains 'The Market Basing Mystery' and 'The Cornish Mystery'.

Mrs McGinty's Dead or Blood Will Tell (1952)

The year 1952 was an important and memorable one for Agatha Christie. On her sixty-second birthday, on 15 September, it might have seemed to her likely to be memorable only because on that day she fell and broke her wrist. Three months later, however, she knew that her play, *The Mousetrap*, was destined for a very long run at the Ambassadors Theatre in London, for it had opened on 25 November to great acclaim. Even so, she could hardly have guessed that the play would outlast her and still not have come to the end of its first run in London thirty years after.

The dampest journalistic squib of the year was produced by a columnist in the *Daily Mail* who, unaware that, to use an un-Christiean phrase, the author's cover had already been blown three years earlier in the *Sunday Times*, announced, 'I learned yesterday that Miss Agatha Christie has for fifteen years been publishing books under a *nom-de-plume*.' Mrs Christie had, in any case, been doing it not for fifteen but for twenty-two years.

During 1952 Agatha Christie published three titles, two of them detective fiction and the third a Mary Westmacott novel. The first of the crime novels was *Mrs McGinty's Dead*. (*Blood Will Tell* is an alternative American title, but the novel is known in some editions in the United States by its British title.)

At the beginning of *Mrs McGinty's Dead*, Poirot the gourmet is leaving one of his favourite Soho restaurants, having dined alone but exceedingly well. He walks back to his Mayfair flat, a trifle bored, wishing that his old friend Hastings were not on the other side of the world. He glances without interest at a newspaper placard about the McGinty trial, for he recalls a brief paragraph he had read about it. Not a very interesting murder, merely some wretched old woman knocked on the head for a few pounds. But he arrives home to find that he has a visitor. It is Superintendent Spence, whom he had worked with four years earlier (*Taken at the Flood*: 1948), and who wishes to consult him about the murder of Mrs McGinty, an old washerwoman who lived in a cottage in the village of Broadhinny. Her lodger, James Bentley, has been found guilty, but Spence is not satisfied with the verdict, and he manages to persuade Poirot to visit the scene of the crime.

ABOVE: Agatha Christie with Peter Saunders who has presented all her most successful plays.
BELOW: Marlene Dietrich in a scene from the 1957 film version of *Witness for the Prosecution*.

ABOVE: Agatha Christie with John Mills and Richard Attenborough. Mrs Christie holds the gold mousetrap which she presented to the Ambassadors Theatre in 1958.
BELOW: Agatha Christie (*bottom right*) at a party at the Savoy Hotel on 14 April 1958 to celebrate 2,239 performances of *The Mousetrap* which made it London's longest running show.

ABOVE: Mary Law (*left*) watches as Agatha Christie cuts the cake on the sixth anniversary of *The Mousetrap* in 1958.
BELOW: Agatha Christie with Max Mallowan in his study in Greenway House. Greenway was requisitioned during the Second World War.

LEFT ABOVE: Agatha Christie at work in Greenway House.

LEFT BELOW: Agatha Christie with her grandson Mathew in 1962. Agatha made over the rights in *The Mousetrap* to Mathew when the play was first produced.

RIGHT: The boathouse at Greenway House on the river Dart. Agatha Christie used this as a model for the boathouse where 'the body' was discovered on the Murder Hunt in *Dead Man's Folly*.

BELOW: Agatha Christie is helped by Richard Attenborough, one of the original cast of *The Mousetrap*, and Dame Sybil Thorndyke, as she cuts the birthday cake at the tenth anniversary party for *The Mousetrap* at the Savoy Hotel on 26 November 1962.

ABOVE: Margaret Rutherford as Miss Marple in *Murder Ahoy* (1964) with Stringer Davis, Margaret Rutherford's husband.
BELOW: Robert Morley and Tony Randall in a scene from the 1966 film *The Alphabet Murders*, an adaptation of *The ABC Murders*.
RIGHT: Agatha Christie in the library of Greenway House.

ABOVE LEFT: Agatha Christie plays the piano for Max Mallowan at Greenway House.
ABOVE RIGHT: Agatha Christie paints a mantelpiece at Greenway House. She once said that she was always ready to be distracted from her real work, writing, by doing something completely different.
BELOW: Agatha Christie and Max Mallowan in the library of Winterbrook House.
RIGHT: Agatha Christie outside the small Queen Anne Winterbrook House in Wallingford.

ABOVE LEFT: Dame Agatha Christie.
ABOVE RIGHT: Agatha Christie was made a Dame Commander of the British Empire in 1972.
BELOW LEFT: Agatha's hair is matched for the wax model in Madame Tussaud's in 1972.
BELOW RIGHT: An elderly Agatha Christie arrives in Nice in 1972.

ABOVE: Agatha Christie was driven in an unconventional form of transport, a jeep, when she was in the south of France in 1972. She still shunned the publicity which she had always disliked.
BELOW: Suspects on the train discuss the murder in John Brabourne's hugely successful 1974 version of *Murder on the Orient Express*.

LEFT ABOVE: Hercule Poirot (Albert Finney) interviews Countess Andrenyi (Jacqueline Bisset) in *Murder on the Orient Express.*
LEFT BELOW: The Venice Simplon Orient Express was revived in 1982 and now runs from Victoria Station, London to Venice.
ABOVE: St Mary's Church in Cholsey, Berkshire where Agatha Christie was buried in 1976.
RIGHT: The tombstone of Agatha Christie and Max Mallowan in St Mary's Churchyard.

ABOVE: The 1978 film *Death on the Nile*, produced by John Brabourne and Richard Goodwin, was a great box-office success. The star-studded cast was headed by Peter Ustinov as Hercule Poirot.
BELOW: A scene from *A Murder is Announced* with James Grout (Inspector Craddock), Dinah Sheridan (Letitia Blacklock), Dulcie Gray (Miss Marple) and Eleanor Summerfield (Dora Bunner).

When it became obvious that *The Mousetrap* would run for many years, Peter Saunders decided to change the cast each year. A celebration cake has become a tradition as each anniversary passes. ABOVE: the 1978 leading lady Petronella Ford with 1979 new leading lady Patricia Donovan. BELOW: in 1981, Helen Lloyd with Mary Tempest.

ABOVE: Interpreters translate *The Mousetrap* into sign language for a deaf audience during the special matinée performance on 14 May 1981.
RIGHT: Gordon Jackson (Superintendent Battle) and Margaret Courtenay (Mrs Oliver) in a dress rehearsal for *Cards on the Table* which opened at the Vaudeville Theatre on 9 December 1981.

This is one of those rare Christie murder mysteries in which the author steps down a rung or two on the social ladder to concern herself with working people. Some of them may be middleclass, but they are the new post-war impoverished middleclass, the *nouveau pauvre*. There are, for example, Major and Mrs Summerhayes, who run in slovenly fashion the horrid guest house where Poirot stays while he is pursuing his investigations. There is Mrs McGinty's niece, Bessie Burch, who does not grieve for her aunt, and there are, or there may be, a few 'Women Victims of Bygone Tragedies'. There is, of course, languishing in gaol awaiting execution, the unprepossessing James Bentley, 'a deceitful fellow with an ungracious, muttering way of talking'.

The character of Bentley is especially well drawn. He is so unsympathetic that you almost cease to care whether or not he is innocent of Mrs McGinty's murder. Poirot, fortunately, does care, and devotes his attention to discovering why the old lady was killed: it was not for the thirty pounds she had saved and hidden in her cottage. The fact that, unless Poirot discovers the real murderer, James Bentley will soon be hanged does, of course, add an element of tension to the story. But this is 1952 when murder in England could still be punished by sentence of death. No one is executed in England nowadays, which is for the most part a sign of progress. It does, however, make life rather more difficult for the writer of murder mysteries. When murderers are given sentences so light as virtually to encourage the committing of the act, a particular frisson is removed from the literary genre of the crime novel. If James Bentley had been facing not the rope but a suspended two-year sentence, Poirot might still have devoted his energy to proving Bentley innocent, but would the reader have cared? The puzzle element becomes more important as the punishment of the criminal becomes more and more negligible.

The crime novelist Ariadne Oliver is present in *Mrs McGinty's Dead*, making her first appearance since *Cards on the Table* sixteen years earlier (see p. 92). She is now more than ever like her creator, expressing her dislike of the Finnish detective she has created:

How do I know why I ever thought of the revolting man? I must have been mad! Why a Finn when I know nothing about Finland? Why a vegetarian? Why all the idiotic mannerisms he's got? . . . Fond of him? If I met that bony, gangling, vegetable-eating Finn in real life, I'd do a better murder than any I've ever invented.

But she makes it clear that she enjoys the fame and fortune Sven Hjerson has brought her. When Robin Upward, a talented young playwright who is adapting one of Mrs Oliver's crime novels for the stage, suggests that she write a novel to be published posthumously, in which she, Ariadne Oliver, murders the detective, Mrs Oliver replies: 'No fear! What about the money? Any money to be made out of murders I want now.' You can almost hear Mrs Christie's gleeful chuckle as she types that sentence. She probably also took one or two ideas about Robin Upward from Hubert Gregg, who directed her play, *The Hollow*, in 1951, who certainly made suggestions to her for changes in the dialogue, and some of whose conversations with Mrs Christie may well have been similar to those of Robin Upward with Mrs Oliver.

This picture of life and death among the rural proletariat and bourgeoisie is a lively and entertaining one, and the solution is vintage Christie. As the New York

Herald Tribune said, 'We have gone up the garden path, led by the most delicate misdirection in English prose.'

In the early 1960s, a series of four rather poorly made British films featuring Agatha Christie's Miss Marple was released, with the popular English comedy actress Margaret Rutherford as Jane Marple. The first and the best of them, *Murder, She Said*, was based on *4.50 From Paddington* (see pp. 182–84), a Miss Marple adventure. The second, *Murder at the Gallop*, however, was based on a Poirot novel, *After the Funeral*, with Poirot transformed into Miss Marple for the film (see p. 172). And the third, *Murder Most Foul* (1964), is based, very loosely and distantly, on *Mrs McGinty's Dead*, and again turns Hercule Poirot into Jane Marple! Apart from Margaret Rutherford as Miss Marple, who finds herself on a jury and in disagreement with her fellow jurors who think the accused guilty, the cast includes Ron Moody, Charles Tingwell, Megs Jenkins and Margaret Rutherford's husband, Stringer Davis, a mediocre actor who, at his wife's insistence, had a role written into the series for him. The murdered woman is no longer an old charlady but a blackmailing actress. The limp screenplay is by David Pursall and Jack Seddon who wrote three of the four Miss Marple films, as well as two other Christie film adaptations (*Ten Little Indians* and *The Alphabet Murders*, both in 1965), and the director is George Pollock who was responsible for all of the Margaret Rutherford Miss Marple films and for *Ten Little Indians*.

They Do It With Mirrors or Murder with Mirrors (1952)

The second 1952 crime novel was *They Do It With Mirrors*. Presumably the title of this Miss Marple story was considered too ambiguous for the United States. 'What,' American readers might have wondered, 'is it that they do?' The answer has nothing to do with sex but much to do with violence, hence the explicit *Murder with Mirrors* for the American edition. The novel begins with the elderly Miss Marple reminiscing with one of her oldest friends, one of two American sisters whom she had known when they were all girls together at a finishing school in Florence. Ruth is worried about her sister, Carrie Louise, the unworldly one of the two who is now into her third marriage and living in a huge country house in the south of England which her husband, Lewis Serrocold, has turned into a home for delinquent boys. One of Carrie Louise's earlier husbands was Gulbrandsen, he whose name was known internationally through the Gulbrandsen Trust, the Gulbrandsen Research Fellowships and so on. And it is a Gulbrandsen, the brother of Carrie Louise's late husband, who is murdered when he visits the Serrocolds.

No doubt Agatha Christie had the internationally famous Gulbenkian family in mind when she created the Gulbrandsens. Through the utterances of Miss Marple and sundry other characters in the novel, Mrs Christie appears to be sympathetic to the Gulbenkian–Gulbrandsen brand of idealism but less so to that of Lewis Serrocold: 'Another crank! Another man with ideals . . . bitten by that same bug of wanting to improve everybody's lives for them. And really, you know, nobody can do that but yourself.' That observation was made by Carrie Louise's sister, but it could easily have been issued from the lips of Agatha Christie herself, whose ideas about self-help were formed early and were to undergo only slight modification throughout her life. La Fontaine's '*Aide-toi, le ciel t'aidera*' must have come to her mind as frequently as that Spanish proverb she was so fond of, about taking what you want but being prepared to pay for it.

Miss Marple shrewdly comments upon the English fondness for failure, the habit of celebrating defeat (Gallipoli, Dunkirk, the Charge of the Light Brigade) rather than victory, failure rather than success, and she links it to the coddling of failure, the penalizing of success, which is, as she says, 'a very odd characteristic' of the Anglo-Saxon mind. She is not opposed to compassion, but she argues for a sense of proportion. Miss Marple's views are of help to her when she goes to stay with the Serrocolds to keep an eye on her old friend Carrie Louise whose life, she comes to fear, may be in danger. There are three murders before the end is reached.

They Do It With Mirrors is perhaps not one of the most stunning of crime mysteries where complexity of plot is concerned, though the actual solution does indeed display Mrs Christie at the top of her form, performing one of those audacious conjuring tricks which infuriate and delight simultaneously when you go back to see how they were done.

That normally reliable guide to crime fiction, Barzun and Taylor's *A Catalogue of Crime*, gives so inaccurate a description of the plot of *Murder With Mirrors* (*They Do It With Mirrors*), calling it a 'school story' in which Miss Marple goes back as an 'old girl' and investigates 'a fatal accident in a gym', that the authors must have confused it with some other novel of similar title.

Incidentally, in this year of *The Mousetrap* Agatha Christie dedicated *Mrs McGinty's Dead* to her theatrical impresario, Peter Saunders, 'in gratitude for his kindness to authors'.

A Daughter's a Daughter (1952)

It had been five years since the most recent Westmacott novel, *The Rose and the Yew Tree*. In *A Daughter's a Daughter*, Westmacott-Christie did not develop the technique of that novel or pursue the kind of characters she had dealt with there; instead, she reverted to her exploration of various aspects of human relationships with special reference to family life, and to its more destructive aspects.

'*Leicht muss man sein, mit leichtem Herz und leichten Händen*', the Marschallin tells Octavian in Hugo von Hofmannsthal's libretto for Richard Strauss's opera, *Der Rosenkavalier*. ('One must be light, light of heart and light of hand.') 'Know when to grasp, but know when to let go,' she continues. Agatha Christie may have known Strauss's opera, or may have been led to it by her half-Austrian husband Max Mallowan, who certainly knew his Hofmannsthal. '*Die nicht so sind, die straft das Leben, und Gott erbarmt sich ihrer nicht.*' 'Those who are not (light of spirit) are punished by life, and God has no mercy on them.' This is really what *A Daughter's a Daughter* is about.

The plot concerns a widow in early middle-age, still attractive but apparently resigned to her widowhood. However, when the possibility of a second marriage does arise, her nineteen-year-old daughter thwarts it by her possessiveness and jealousy. Placing her daughter's happiness before her own, the mother sends her suitor away, but this leads not only to misery for her but also to a disastrous marriage for her daughter. Eventually, the daughter is able to make a fresh start, but the mother is left alone, sadder and presumably wiser.

Such a synopsis could as easily cover the glib artificiality of a Barbara Cartland as easily as the stylish warmth of a Daphne du Maurier or the psychological commonsense and shrewdness of a Mary Westmacott. Westmacott-Christie, in fact, persuades her reader that she, the author, knows these characters well and that, to a certain extent, she can sympathize with even the least pleasant of them. She does not deal in idealized portraiture: her young lovers have their defects; and even when she invents a character, Dame Laura Whitstable, popular psychologist and television personality who is clearly meant to be as wise as she is witty, we are allowed to see that Dame Laura's admirable trait of refraining ever from giving advice to others can be carried too far.

A Daughter's a Daughter paints so convincing a picture of the destructiveness of sacrificial mother-love that you are tempted to seek in it clues to some of the events in Mrs Christie's earlier life. But the artist has covered her tracks, as artists will, and must, and should be allowed to do. A number of emotional truths which Agatha Christie must have learned from her own family experiences have led her to the imaginative and creative act of inventing a work of fiction embodying them. 'That is all ye know on earth, and all ye need to know.'

Both Agatha Christie and Mary Westmacott occasionally use the same name for two entirely different characters. This is hardly surprising in a writer who is so prolific, and it is probably not in the least significant that Colonel James Grant, a middle-aged army officer in *A Daughter's a Daughter*, should have the same name as a young farmer in *Unfinished Portrait*, which was written nearly twenty years earlier.

Notes to pages 119–164

1 A Q.C., writing to *The Times* in 1980 in support of voluntary euthanasia, claimed that 'information on unusual poisons gleaned from two of Agatha Christie's novels have [sic] been used to kill people in Britain and France'.
2 Francis Wyndham: 'The Algebra of Agatha Christie', in the London *Sunday Times*, 27 February 1966.
3 In *The Regatta Mystery* (1939: USA) and *The Adventure of the Christmas Pudding* (1960: UK).
4 The novel uses the variant, 'Five, six, picking up sticks'.
5 Agatha Christie: *An Autobiography*.
6 In fact, anyone who has visited Burgh Island, off the Devon coast near Bigbury, can have little doubt that it is the unglamourized original of Smuggler's Island.
7 Agatha Christie: *An Autobiography*.
8 Robert Barnard: *op. cit.*
9 In *The Thin Man*.
10 The short stories collected in volume form in 1932 in *The Thirteen Problems* had begun to appear earlier. The very first Miss Marple story, 'The Tuesday Night Club', was published in 1928.
11 Raymond West, Miss Marple's writer nephew, is mentioned in *The Body in the Library*, but does not appear.
12 The London *Sunday Times*, 27 February 1966.
13 Quoted in Jeffrey Feinman: *The Mysterious World of Agatha Christie*.
14 Agatha Christie: *An Autobiography*.
15 In *Mallowan's Memoirs*.
16 In *The Mousetrap Man* (1972).

17 See p. 128.
18 The Russian woman is travelling to Vienna for a surgical operation; 'But they are good surgeons in Vienna. This one to whom I am going – he is very clever – a Jew. I have always said it would be stupid to annihilate all the Jews in Europe. They are clever doctors and surgeons, yes, and they are clever artistically too.'
19 H.R.F. Keating (Ed.): *Agatha Christie, First Lady of Crime* (London, 1977).
20 Robert Barnard's *A Talent to Deceive* (London, 1980).
21 Jeffrey Feinman: *The Mysterious World of Agatha Christie* (New York, 1975).
22 By Jessica Mann (London, 1981): the author uses 'feminine' incorrectly, since she clearly means 'female'.
23 *An Autobiography*.
24 In *Mallowan's Memoirs*.
25 Charleston *Evening Post*, 14 September 1970.
26 Agatha Christie: *An Autobiography*.
27 'The White Knight's Song' from *Alice Through the Looking Glass*: the appropriate line, 'Come, tell me how you live, I cried', is also quoted by a character in *Giant's Bread* by Mary Westmacott (1930).
28 *Mallowan's Memoirs*.
29 Gwen Robyns: *The Mystery of Agatha Christie*.
30 *The Hollow* was also the title of the first American edition of the novel. The alternative title, *Murder After Hours*, was first used for an American paperback edition in 1954.
31 Quoted in Gwen Robyns: The *Mystery of Agatha Christie*.
32 Agatha Christie: *An Autobiography*.
33 *An Autobiography*.
34 Hubert Gregg: *Agatha Christie and All That Mousetrap* (1980).
35 Max Mallowan: *op. cit.*
36 Later to achieve a certain fame on British TV as Shaw Taylor.
37 According to the BBC, it played for 29 minutes, 55 seconds.
38 In *The Mysterious World of Agatha Christie*.
39 In *Agatha Christie, First Lady of Crime*.
40 Quoted in G.C. Ramsey: *Agatha Christie: Mistress of Mystery* (1967).
41 Interview with Francis Wyndham in the London *Sunday Times*, 27 February 1966.
42 Tredwell (Mark I) was in the employ of Lord Caterham in *The Secret of Chimneys* (1925) and *The Seven Dials Mystery* (1929), and Tredwell (Mark II) in *Black Coffee* (1930).
43 4 June 1950.
44 Agatha Christie: *An Autobiography*.
45 In *An Autobiography*.

4

'The Mousetrap' and after

The Mousetrap (1952)

'I knew after I had written *The Hollow*,' Agatha Christie recalled in her autobiography, 'that before long I should want to write another play, and if possible, I thought to myself, I was going to write another play that was not adapted from a book. I was going to write a play as a play.' At this stage in her career, despite the existence of several successful 'Agatha Christie plays', she had written only two as original plays: the Poirot mystery, *Black Coffee* (see p. 58), staged in 1930, and the non-mystery play, *Akhnaton* (see p. 99), which had not been performed. The other plays which she had written, or of which in one instance she had been co-author, were those she had adapted from her novels or stories.

Having resolved to write an original play, one not based on any earlier work, Agatha Christie now proceeded to write the play known to the world as *The Mousetrap*, which was, however, based on her story 'Three Blind Mice', which was, in turn, based on her 1947 radio play of that name (see p. 145). The new play for the stage was written in the autumn of 1951 and called, naturally enough, 'Three Blind Mice'. Shortly after Christmas, Agatha Christie asked Peter Saunders to lunch. 'Over the coffee she handed me a brown paper parcel,' Saunders recalled later, 'and said, "This is a little present for you. Don't unwrap it until you get back to your office."' The present was the script of *The Mousetrap*.

As soon as he had read the typescript, which was stained with innumerable coffee-cup circles, Saunders was keen to stage it. There was a slight difficulty concerning the nursery-rhyme title. It had been used earlier by another West End management for a moderately successful play, and it seemed advisable to choose a completely new title for Agatha Christie's play. The author's son-in-law, Anthony Hicks, made the suggestion that the title of a play mentioned in Shakespeare's *Hamlet* should be lifted out of context and bestowed upon 'Three Blind Mice'. In Act III, sc. ii of *Hamlet*, during the performance which Hamlet causes to be staged before Claudius and Gertrude, the King asks 'What do you call the play?' to which Hamlet replies, 'The Mousetrap'. Later in his speech Hamlet refers to the play as a 'knavish piece of work', but it was very far from Anthony Hicks' mind to imply any criticism of his mother-in-law's play when he suggested that it be called *The Mousetrap*.

With Richard Attenborough and his wife, Sheila Sim leading the cast, and directed by Peter Cotes, who had been recommended by Attenborough, *The Mousetrap* went into rehearsal in September, 1952, and opened at the Theatre Royal, Nottingham, on 6 October. It then toured to Oxford, Manchester,

Liverpool, Newcastle, Leeds and Birmingham, before opening in London at the Ambassadors Theatre on 25 November. The other members of the cast of eight, all of them of equal importance as characters – there are no star parts and no small roles in *The Mousetrap* – were Jessica Spencer, Aubrey Dexter, Mignon O'Doherty, Allan McClelland, Martin Miller and John Paul. (The play which Peter Saunders had read nearly a year earlier contained ten characters, and required two sets. In the interests of economy, one set and two characters were disposed of by the playwright within hours!)

The reviews after the first night in London were almost uniformly favourable. 'Even more thrilling than the plot is the atmosphere of shuddering suspense,' wrote John Barber in the *Daily Express*, adding with more enthusiasm than literary ability, 'No one brews it better than Agatha Christie.' The *Evening Standard* declared: 'What a wily mistress of criminal ceremonies Agatha Christie is. She is like a perfect hostess at a cocktail party. . . . There is none of this hiding of vital facts in Mrs Christie . . . it is this honesty of procedure that puts her so high in the ranks of police novel writers.' 'We have all of us been well and truly diddled,' said the *Weekly Sporting Review*.

Pleased with the reception the play had been given, Peter Saunders told the playwright that he had hopes of a long run of twelve or fourteen months. Mrs Christie was more cautious: 'It won't run that long,' she said. 'Eight months perhaps.'

Set in somewhere in Berkshire, in the depths of winter, in an old manor house converted for use as a guesthouse or private hotel, *The Mousetrap* is good, traditional Christie, presenting a number of people isolated from the outside world, in this case by a blizzard, and faced with the realization that one of them is a killer. The plot does not stray far from its beginnings in the radio play of 1947 and the story of the following year, so anyone planning to see *The Mousetrap* should avoid reading 'Three Blind Mice'. The characters in the play are less fully realized than those in *The Unexpected Guest* or *The Hollow*, but they serve their purpose admirably as pawns in their author's game. There are the young couple, Millie and Giles Ralston, the proprietors of Monkswell Manor who have no previous experience of catering, and there are their guests, expected and unexpected. Among the expected are the effeminate young architect who rejoices in the name of Christopher Wren, and the bossy matron, Mrs Boyle. Unexpected are Mr Paravicini, the somewhat mysterious foreigner whose car has broken down, and Detective Sergeant Trotter who turns up on skis. And there are two other guests. Several of these people are either other or more than they appear to be. A plot linking most of them with certain past events emerges from the circumstances of their apparently chance meeting as fellow-guests.

When Sergeant Trotter announces that a murderer for whom the police are searching is not only among the guests but has come to Monkswell Manor in search of his next victim, the atmosphere of suspicion, distrust and unease is palpable. Tension mounts, relationships waver, and sympathies are readjusted. As always with Agatha Christie at her best, the dénouement is startling and the end, thereafter, comes with the brutal swiftness of an early Verdi opera. Six important pieces of explanatory information are thrust forward in a page and a half of fast dialogue after the murderer is apprehended, and then a final joke brings the curtain down.

Who did it? Those who have seen the play in London have behaved impeccably for thirty years in not spreading the news abroad to spoil the enjoyment of those who have yet to see it. There is one recorded exception: a taxi-driver who delivered a family party to the theatre where *The Mousetrap* was playing is said to have been so disgusted at the smallness of the tip he was given that he took his revenge by shouting after them as they walked towards the entrance, '. . . . . . did it!'

An unusual matinée performance of *The Mousetrap* was given on 14 May 1981, when six interpreters simultaneously translated the dialogue into sign language for the benefit of an audience of 350 deaf people.

Why should *The Mousetrap*, an ingenious, entertaining and well constructed murder mystery but not the best of Agatha Christie's plays, have broken all theatrical records? Agatha Christie, pondering the question after the play had been running for thirteen years, thought that it was ninety per cent luck but that also 'there is a bit of something in it for almost everybody: people of different age groups and tastes can enjoy seeing it'.

The Mousetrap is now, in 1982, in its thirtieth year in the West End of London. Twenty-one years after it had opened at the Ambassadors Theatre, the production transferred, on 25 March 1974, to the slightly larger St Martin's Theatre, next door. After five-and-a-half years, it had broken the record for the longest-running play in London, previously held by the musical play *Chu Chin Chou* (1916). It went on to break whatever other records there were to be broken, and is, beyond any shadow of doubt, the most successful play ever staged anywhere at any time.

After eight years, Peter Saunders began a custom of changing the cast yearly, on the anniversary of the opening, and of having the production restaged by a new director. By 1981, one hundred and seventy-one actors and actresses had appeared in the London production, and the play had been performed in at least forty-one countries, including several in Eastern Europe. (It did no more than reasonably well, however, when staged in New York in 1952, though it ran for six months when revived at an 'off-Broadway' theatre in the 1960–61 theatrical season. In Paris, as *La Souricière*, it lasted for more than two years.)

The success of *The Mousetrap* is, to put it mildly, somewhat disproportionate to its inherent quality. In the first years of its run, Peter Saunders nursed the production along, but for many years now he has merely had to give a party every so often, to celebrate and mark the passing of the years, and more publicity has generated more success which in turn has generated more publicity and so on *ad*, it would seem, *infinitum*. There was a spectacular 1958 party at the Savoy to celebrate the fact that *The Mousetrap* was now the longest-running play. At the tenth anniversary in 1962 when one thousand guests were invited, the doyenne of British theatre, Dame Sybil Thorndike, made a speech which began, 'I have been chosen to make this speech because *The Mousetrap* is the oldest run in the theatre, and I am one of the oldest girls in show business.' She presented Agatha Christie with a copy of the 1952 script of the play, bound in gold.

In 1972, a very frail Agatha Christie attended the twentieth anniversary party, but tried to avoid speaking to anyone except intimate friends because she had left her teeth at home. Nearly two years after her death, *The Mousetrap* celebrated its twenty-fifth birthday in November 1977, again at the Savoy, and in 1982 its thirtieth. There is now no reason why it should ever close. Tourists alone, on whose list of things to see in London it features along with Tower Bridge, Buckingham Palace and Westminster Abbey, could easily keep it alive for as long as the tourist industry survives.

When the company gave a performance of *The Mousetrap* at Wormwood Scrubs, a London gaol, two prisoners in the audience took the opportunity to escape, thus giving the play some additional publicity. In 1968, the journalist Bernard Levin produced some odd statistics relating to the play's run. 'In nearly sixteen years,' he wrote, 'after sixteen leading ladies, twenty-six miles of shirts, four carpets, six thousand cigars, eleven tons of programmes, no one has built a more successful Mousetrap.' The wardrobe mistress who had ironed the twenty-six miles of shirts was interviewed in a popular London newspaper. The figures have now to be regularly updated. The most recent edition of the souvenir programme of *The Mousetrap* sold at the theatre refers to forty-six miles of shirts and one hundred and sixty tons of programmes! When Agatha Christie was once asked, 'Is *The Mousetrap* being kept on to beat more records?' she replied in some bewilderment, 'What records are there to beat?'

To whom do the profits go? When *The Mousetrap* opened in 1952, Agatha Christie gave all her rights in the play to her grandson, Mathew Prichard, who was then nine years old. In 1982, he is approaching forty, and the play has made him a millionaire. As his grandmother tartly observed:[1] 'Mathew, of course, was always the most lucky member of the family, and it *would* be Mathew's gift that turned out the big money winner.'

Authority to negotiate various subsidiary rights in the play was acquired, along with stage production rights, by Peter Saunders, who sold the film rights to Romulus Films in 1956, a condition of the sale being that no film could be released until six months after the end of the London stage run. The rights have changed hands since then, but Peter Saunders has so far been unsuccessful in his attempts to buy them back. Apparently, someone in the film industry believes that somewhere, someday, a film will be made of *The Mousetrap*.

Success breeds jealousy, envy, and a certain crabbedness of the spirit. A journalist on the staff of the London *Guardian*, complained that 'Mr Peter Saunders must have deprived other theatre managers of the opportunity of presenting daring, experimental, or difficult plays.' Neither of the two West End commercial theatres in which *The Mousetrap* has played has ever housed anything remotely resembling a daring, experimental or difficult play. The daring, the experimental and the difficult continue to open and close with monotonous regularity in countless London fringe theatres, completely unaffected by the monstrously unfair success of the undaring, non-experimental and entertaining *Mousetrap*.

A Pocketful of Rye (1953)

With the Mallowan expedition in Nimrud, in addition to writing her novels in the mornings, and helping with the photography, the cataloguing and the repairing of ivories and other items in the afternoons and evenings, Agatha Christie also acquired a reputation as the team's chronicler of events in verses which became known as 'Agatha's Odes'. Max Mallowan had a secretary, Barbara Parker. Good-humoured and hard working, 'a woman of dauntless courage, usually dressed in white, red or blue Kurdish trousers, florally adorned,'² Miss Parker was also, it seems, noisy in the early morning. Agatha dedicated an ode to her:

Is that a fog horn that I hear,
Rising in the morning air?
No, it comes from Barbara's tent;
Up she gets on duty bent,
Dons her Kurdish trousers gay,
Once again it's ladies day!
And once more the trumpet goes
As our Miss Parker blows her nose!

In 1953, Penguin Books reprinted six Agatha Christie crime novels, with prefaces newly written by the author. Two novels, one featuring Poirot and one Miss Marple, were published during the year, and a new Christie play, *Witness for the Prosecution*, was staged.

With the Miss Marple novel, *A Pocketful of Rye*, the reader is plunged again into the Christiean nursery rhyme syndrome: a series of murders committed concurrently with the progress of the images in a nursery rhyme. The rhyme on this occasion is 'Sing a song of sixpence', which must have been one of Agatha Christie's favourites, for she had already made use of it in two short stories, 'Sing a Song of Sixpence' (from *The Listerdale Mystery*, 1934) and 'Four-and-Twenty Blackbirds' (from *Three Blind Mice*, 1948). Miss Marple discerns that the rhyme is the link between a series of rather odd murders, when the third victim, a parlour maid who had at one time been employed by her, is found dead, strangled by a nylon stocking and with a clothes-peg clipped onto her nose. The two earlier victims, she claims, can be seen as the king and queen of the rhyme:

Sing a song of sixpence, a pocketful of rye,
Four-and-twenty blackbirds baked in a pie.
When the pie was opened, the birds began to sing.
Wasn't that a dainty dish to set before the king?

The king was in his counting house, counting out his money,
The queen was in the parlour, eating bread and honey,
The maid was in the garden, hanging out the clothes,
Along came a dicky bird, and nipped off her nose.

The first victim, though not a king, was a financier whose name was Rex (Latin for 'king') Fortescue and the loose grain (rye?) found in his pocket was perplexing. Fortescue's wife was poisoned with cyanide at tea-time. The clothes-peg on the parlour maid's nose no doubt symbolized the dicky bird, but some non-symbolical, real blackbirds are involved in the story as well. 'Have you gone into the question of blackbirds?' Miss Marple asks a puzzled policeman, Inspector Neele. Neele is not one of the Christiean regulars, but an investigating officer who makes his only appearance in *A Pocketful of Rye*, which is a pity for he is an attractive and potentially interesting character.

Most of the action takes place in and around Yewtree Lodge, Rex Fortescue's house in the outer suburban stockbroker-belt, a house whose model was the residence of Mr and Mrs Christie at Sunningdale which had already found its way into the pages of *Taken at the Flood* (1948) and *Crooked House* (1949). The characters are well drawn, and, although the nursery rhyme parallel seems at moments rather forced, there may be a reason for this. Mrs Christie, after all, was by this time quite experienced in juggling rhymes and crimes. She was also, of course, mistress of the ambiguous statement, but did she overreach herself with an especially cheeky sentence in an early chapter of *A Pocketful of Rye*? The really astute reader may well think so, and in consequence may even correctly guess the murderer. An interest in, or at least an awareness of, geography would be an advantage on this occasion.

'How well she nearly always writes, the dear, decadent old death trafficker,' said Maurice Richardson of *A Pocketful of Rye* in the London *Observer*. 'They ought to make her a Dame or a D. Litt.' (In due course 'they' were to do both.) And it was in her review of this novel in *The Bookman* that the distinguished historian C.V. Wedgwood wrote:

> Mrs Christie always plays fair; her puzzles work out with neat plausibility and no loose end; her social settings, her characters and her dialogue are always accurately observed. There is no better all-round craftsman in the field.

After the Funeral or *Funerals are Fatal* (1953)

After the Funeral is the British title, and *Funerals Are Fatal* the American. It was immediately after the funeral of the wealthy Richard Abernethie, when his relatives were gathered in Abernethie's country house in the north of England to hear his will read, that the dead man's sister, Mrs Cora Lansquenet, disconcerted the others by remarking, quite casually, 'But he *was* murdered, wasn't he?' It had been assumed that Abernethie, an elderly man, had died a natural death. When Cora was discovered dead shortly afterwards, the circumstances were such that there could be no doubt that *she* was murdered. The family solicitor, Mr Entwhistle, pursued certain enquiries, and then decided to consult Hercule Poirot.

This time, Christie the conjuror has begun her tricks almost while the audience are still settling into their seats. She is at her best with complicated family relationships, and the Abernethie family is so complicated that a family tree is provided. The reader may or may not be helped by a study of the family tree: he would certainly do well to resist the author's determined attempt to force his attention in a certain direction.

The Delphic ambiguities emanating from the preceding paragraph are as nothing compared with Mrs Christie's mystifications in *After the Funeral*, which is a distinctly above-average example of her tales of soured family relationships. The motive for the crime is very successfully concealed until the author is ready to reveal it; but then it is comparatively easy to conceal a motive from the reader if the reader has also to grapple with the question, 'Motive for what?'

Mr Goby, an eccentric private investigator with whom Poirot had been associated in *The Mystery of the Blue Train* a quarter of a century earlier, comes out of retirement to assist the detective again. He is to make two further appearances in Hercule Poirot novels, in *Third Girl* and *Elephants Can Remember*.

'Women are never kind,' Poirot observes at one point in the narrative, 'though they can sometimes be tender.' The great detective's attitude to the other sex has always been more than slightly perplexing. He is sentimental about mother-love, cynical about romantic attachments (though he carries a tender regard for the Countess Vera Rossakoff with him throughout life), and not, it seems, at all interested in the sexual act *per se*. More than one prurient reader has hinted at homosexual leanings, and even suggested that Poirot and Hastings – but, no, it is inconceivable. Poirot and Hastings were just good friends. We know that Hastings was susceptible to red-haired females, and indeed that he married one. Poirot is one of those admittedly rare beings to whom sex does not appear to have been important at any time in their lives.

The negligence of Mrs Christie's editors has been remarked upon earlier. An example of it occurs in *After the Funeral*, in Chapter VIII, when Dr Larraby is made by the author to say that Abernethie had been suffering from a disease which would have proved fatal within, 'at the earliest', two years, when from the context it is clear that 'at the latest' is meant. What are editors for, if not to prevent readers from discovering that writers are capable of making mistakes?

The series of Miss Marple films made in the 1960s has already been mentioned (see p. 162). The second film, *Murder at the Gallop*, in which Miss Marple joins a riding academy to investigate the death of an old recluse, is based, very distantly, on *After the Funeral*, with Poirot turned into Miss Marple, and the plot turned by a scriptwriter named James Cavenaugh into a pointless jumble. 'I get an unregenerate pleasure when I think they're not being a success,' Mrs Christie said of these films. This one was directed by George Pollock, and featured Margaret Rutherford as Miss Marple. ('To me she's always looked like a bloodhound,' the author is reputed to have said.) Charles Tingwell, Robert Morley, Flora Robson and Stringer Davis play the other leading roles.

Murder at the Gallop was released in 1963, and a new paperback edition of *After the Funeral* was issued in that year by Agatha Christie's British publishers as *Murder at the Gallop*, in order to achieve additional sales as 'the book of the film'.

Witness for the Prosecution (1953)

The Mousetrap had been running for some weeks when Peter Saunders, staying for a few days at Agatha Christie's home in Devon, suggested to the author that she should adapt for the stage one of her short stories, 'Witness for the Prosecution'.[3] Mrs Christie thought this would be too difficult a task, and doubted her ability to write a convincing courtroom scene. Saunders' attempts to persuade her that she could do it finally led Agatha Christie to say to him, 'If you think there's a play in it, write it yourself.' This he proceeded to do, and in due course delivered a first draft of the play to Mrs Christie at her London apartment. When she had read it, she told him she did not think the play, as it stood, was good enough, but that he certainly had showed her how it could be done. Six weeks later, her typescript arrived on his desk, and Saunders immediately made plans to put the play into production. It opened in Glasgow, and toured to Edinburgh and Sheffield, before London.

'It was one of my plays that I liked best myself,' Agatha Christie wrote in *An*

Autobiography. 'I was as nearly satisfied with that play as I have been with any.' She took great pains to get the courtroom scene right, reading several of the *Famous Trials* series of books, and asking questions of barristers and solicitors, until 'finally I got interested and suddenly I felt I was enjoying myself – that wonderful moment in writing which does not usually last long, but which carries one on with a terrific verve as a large wave carries you to shore.' It was, she thought, one of the quickest pieces of writing she had achieved, taking no more than two or three weeks after her preparatory reading had been done. In later years, she was to say that she thought *Witness for the Prosecution* the best play she had written.

On the play's first night at the Winter Garden Theatre, in Drury Lane, London,[4] 28 October 1953, the audience sat spellbound by the ingenuity of the surprise ending. At the curtain call, the entire cast of twenty-eight[5] lined the front of the stage and bowed to the author who was seated in a box. 'So I was happy,' she wrote[6]

and made even more so by the applause of the audience. I slipped away as usual after the curtain came down on my ending and out into Long Acre. In a few moments, while I was looking for the waiting car, I was surrounded by crowds of friendly people, quite ordinary members of the audience, who recognized me, patted me on the back, and encouraged me – 'Best you've written, dearie!' 'First class – thumbs up, I'd say!' 'V-signs for this one!' and 'Loved every minute of it!' Autograph books were produced, and I signed cheerfully and happily. My self-consciousness and nervousness, just for once, were not with me. Yes, it was a memorable evening. I am proud of it still. And every now and then I dig into the memory chest, bring it out, take a look at it, and say, 'That was the night, that was!'

Witness for the Prosecution played for 468 performances at the Winter Garden Theatre, and enjoyed an even longer run of 646 performances in New York, where it opened on 16 December 1954. The leading roles in London were played by David Horne (as Sir Wilfrid Robarts, the QC who defends Leonard Vole), Derek Blomfield (as Leonard Vole) and Patricia Jessel (as Vole's wife, Romaine). The play was directed by Wallace Douglas. In New York the following year, Agatha Christie's old friend and Poirot interpreter, Francis L. Sullivan, played Sir Wilfrid, and Patricia Jessel repeated her London success as Romaine. The director was Robert Lewis. The New York Drama Critics Circle chose *Witness for the Prosecution* as the best foreign play of 1954, with Tennessee Williams' *Cat on a Hot Tin Roof* as the best American play.

The London reviews were almost unanimously enthusiastic. 'Agatha Christie must be happy this morning,' wrote the *Daily Mirror* critic. 'While one thriller, *The Mousetrap*, is packing them in at the Ambassadors Theatre, another play opened with great success last night at the Winter Garden Theatre.' It was left to the legal magazine, *The Magistrate*, to find fault with at least one aspect of Mrs Christie's courtroom scene. Her counsel, *The Magistrate* considered, 'are properly counsel-like in manner and mannerisms, but most unrealistically succinct in speech.' That, however, could be construed as a criticism of the legal profession rather than of the playwright.

In the excerpt from her autobiography two paragraphs above, Mrs Christie speaks of the curtain coming down 'on my ending'. The personal pronoun is important, for the play ends differently to the story on which it is based. The story, written in the early 1930s, has a superb ending which allows the murderer to get away with it. By 1953, however, the author was no longer prepared to see murder (or at any rate this particular murderer) go unpunished. The murderer escapes legal justice but not private retribution. This is meted out in the last moments of the play in an ending which seems 'tacked-on' and which, though morally impeccable, is aesthetically deplorable. Most people concerned with the production of the play had wanted the author to retain the original end of the story. 'I stuck out over the end,' said Mrs Christie. 'I don't often stick out for things, I don't always have sufficient conviction, but I had here. I wanted that end. I wanted it so much that I wouldn't agree to have the play put on without it.'[7] Apart from its expansion for the stage, there are no other significant differences between story and play. Leonard Vole's Viennese wife has become a Berliner, for no obvious reason.

Agatha Christie would not have agreed, and no doubt the Agatha Christie Estate would not agree, but this entertaining and ingenious play would be even better than it is if the final curtain were to come down about a minute and a half earlier, after Sir Wilfrid Robarts says, 'I see no reason to change my opinion.'

In 1957, Agatha Christie having sold the film rights for £116,000, *Witness for the Prosecution* became an expensively made Hollywood film, directed by Billy Wilder for United Artists, and starring Charles Laughton as Sir Wilfrid, Tyrone Power as Leonard Vole, and Marlene Dietrich as Vole's wife, whose name was changed from Romaine to Christine. A number of Hollywood-based British performers appeared in the film, among them Charles Laughton's wife, Elsa Lanchester, for whom a role was written into the film; Henry Daniell, who in London in 1928 had played the butler in *Alibi*, the stage adaptation of *The Murder of Roger Ackroyd*; Ian Wolfe; Una O'Connor; John Williams; and Torin Thatcher. The screenplay was written by Billy Wilder and Harry Kurnitz. A facsimile of a courtroom in London's Old Bailey was constructed on Stage Four on the Sam Goldwyn lot, at a cost of $75,000. Much was made of the surprise ending, and the publicity department placed a huge, framed placard outside the studio while filming was taking place, which all visitors were obliged to sign:

SECRECY PLEDGE

'WITNESS FOR THE PROSECUTION'

No One – But No One – Ever Told the Secret!

In faithful compliance with the conspiracy of silence entered into by everyone who has seen Agatha Christie's remarkable play 'Witness for the Prosecution' which is being produced for the screen by Arthur Hornblow for United Artists release, I agree to continue this silence by promising not to reveal any of the secrets relating to its electrifying climax. Therefore – if, working on or visiting its sets during photography, I discover clues which lead to the disclosure of the surprise ending, I promise to let other people enjoy discovering it for themselves – properly, in a theater.

Among the signatures on the poster are those of Noël Coward, William Holden and Burt Lancaster. Security was apparently strictly enforced: a publicity still issued in advance of the film's release shows the director Billy Wilder denying

Sam Goldwyn entry to his own soundstage. As for the film, it was good enough to survive a flashback scene in post-war Berlin, in which Marlene Dietrich entertains the army of occupation by singing a song entitled, 'I'll Never Go Home Any More'! Miss Dietrich gave a virtuoso performance as Christine Vole, Charles Laughton enjoyed himself hugely as Sir Wilfrid, and that intelligent film star and underrated actor, Tyrone Power, utilized the strain of weakness in his own undoubted charm to offer a convincing portrait of Leonard Vole. Photographed in black and white, this was the best Christie film since the 1945 version of *Ten Little Niggers*, and is still one of the best.

Destination Unknown or *So Many Steps to Death* (1954)

In 1954, the year in which she received the first Grand Masters Award of the Mystery Writers of America, Agatha Christie published one novel and had a new play staged in London. On 16 December, her 1953 play *Witness for the Prosecution* opened on Broadway, and two days later the London *Daily Telegraph* noted that drama critics in New York had been unanimous in finding it one of the most exciting and best acted plays seen in New York for years, and that Patricia Jessel and Francis L. Sullivan had collected a number of very favourable reviews for their performances.

The 1954 novel was *Destination Unknown*, which was not published in the United States until the following year, when it appeared as *So Many Steps to Death*. This is one of the Christie thrillers. In fact, it could be said to form the central part of a trilogy of post-Second World War thrillers which also includes *They Came to Baghdad* (1951) and *Passenger to Frankfurt* (1970), for these three novels share a basic plot premise concerning the existence of a wealthy megalomaniac determined on world domination or anarchy, and they also resemble one another in that their author's personal opinions intrude into the narrative much less circumspectly than in her domestic crime novels.

These opinions, as we have seen earlier, range from the cautiously liberal to the conservative. A tolerance of 'misguided' reformers of the left oddly increases as the years go by, and is certainly more easily discernible in the works written in the fifties than those written thirty years earlier, but the general message emanating from Agatha Christie is that which she puts into the mind of Hilary Craven, the heroine of *Destination Unknown*:

> Why do you decry the world we live in? There are good people in it. Isn't muddle a better breeding ground for kindliness and individuality than a world order that's imposed, a world order that may be right today and wrong tomorrow? I would rather have a world of kindly, faulty human beings, than a world of superior robots who've said goodbye to pity and understanding and sympathy.

Hilary Craven is another of those Christie characters who is saved from suicide by the intervention of a stranger. The stranger, this time, is a British Secret Service agent who cleverly suggests to Hilary that, if she doesn't mind dying, she might like to combine it with doing her country a service in the meantime. Hilary is roped into an adventure involving the mysterious disappearance of promising young scientists, and thus she rediscovers the will to live.

Destination Unknown was written at a time when one or two cases of missing scientists had made international headlines (the Fuchs and Pontecorvo affairs), and the novel postulates not a Soviet Communist plot but something odder. The action moves from England to Casablanca to a remote spot in the High Atlas Mountains of Northwest Africa where a secret scientific complex exists, disguised as a leper colony. The dénouement is unusual for two reasons. One is that it is accomplished without bloodshed and that, in a sense, the evil mind behind the conspiracy (if, that is, it can be called an evil mind) survives to go on to the next *coup*. Another is that embedded in all the international intrigue is a domestic murder mystery, which surfaces only in the final sentence of the penultimate chapter at the point at which it is solved.

This, like so many of Agatha Christie's thrillers, is both a farrago of hokum and a first-rate adventure story. It moves swiftly, but not at the expense of intelligent characterization, and Hilary Craven is one of the most engaging of a long line of mercurial Christiean heroines. Although, like most of the thrillers, *Destination Unknown* is viewed somewhat disparagingly by Christie commentators, but it can safely be said that, if you like this kind of thing, this is the kind of thing you will like. It is, of its kind, excellent and entertaining.

Spider's Web (1954)

With two Agatha Christie successes on his hands, *The Mousetrap* and *Witness for the Prosecution*, Peter Saunders now launched a third. Over lunch at the Mirabelle in Mayfair, he arranged a meeting between Agatha Christie and the popular British film actress, Margaret Lockwood, who ten years earlier had been the top money-making star in British films, but who was now tired of playing *femmes fatales*. She had appeared in one or two plays, among them Barrie's *Peter Pan* and Shaw's *Pygmalion*, and now wanted to play a modern role, preferably in a comedy.

Agatha Christie agreed to write a play for Margaret Lockwood, and to provide her with a role which would display the actress's talent for comedy. She even agreed, at Miss Lockwood's request, to include a role for the well-known light comedy actor, Wilfrid Hyde White, but when the script was completed Hyde White did not like his role, which was played instead by Felix Aylmer.

Spider's Web, directed by Wallace Douglas, and with Margaret Lockwood and Felix Aylmer supported by a first-rate cast including Harold Scott, Myles Eason, Margaret Barton and Judith Furse, opened out-of-town at the Theatre Royal Nottingham, underwent some rewriting on tour, and came to the Savoy Theatre, London, on 14 December 1954, where it stayed for 774 performances, joining *The Mousetrap* and *Witness for the Prosecution* in the West End. Agatha Christie now had three successful plays running simultaneously in London.

The author herself was pleased with *Spider's Web*. She enjoyed writing the role of Clarissa (a form of her own mother's name, Clara) for Margaret Lockwood who, she thought, had 'an enormous flair for comedy, as well as being able to be dramatic'. 'When Margaret Lockwood proceeded to lead the Police Inspector up the garden path she was enchanting,' Agatha Christie wrote in her autobiography. The actress's comedy technique and splendid sense of timing certainly contributed greatly to the success of the play's first production.

Clarissa, the wife of a Foreign Office diplomat, is a delightful character, much given to daydreaming, and to playing a game with herself which she calls 'Supposing':

Supposing I were to come down one morning and find a dead body in the library, what should I do? Or supposing a woman were to be shown in here one day and told me that she and Henry had been secretly married in Constantinople, and that our marriage was bigamous, what should I say to her? Or supposing I had to choose between betraying my country and seeing Henry shot before my eyes? (*She smiles suddenly at Jeremy*) Or, even – (*she sits in the armchair*) supposing I were to run away with Jeremy, what would happen next?

Clarissa has her chance to find out, when she does discover a body, not in the library but in the drawing-room of her house in Kent. For what are made to seem perfectly sensible reasons, it becomes necessary to dispose of the body before her husband Henry arrives home with an important foreign politician, so Clarissa persuades her three house guests to become accessories and accomplices. The murdered man was not unknown to certain members of the house party. Why he was killed is as much a mystery as by whom, and Clarissa's attempts simultaneously to persuade a police inspector that there has been no murder and to discover the identity of the murderer are highly diverting in both senses of the word.

The play is an enjoyable comedy-thriller which does not attempt to rival the complex plots of *The Mousetrap* or *Witness for the Prosecution*, but which is highly successful on its own level. It makes satirical and ironic use of that creaky old device, the secret passage. 'Exit Clarissa mysteriously,' declaimed Margaret Lockwood, disappearing into it as the Savoy Theatre curtain fell on the last act, always to thunderous and delighted applause. Though no one knew it at the time, it was falling also on Agatha Christie's last big success in the theatre. Some of her subsequent plays did better than others, but none was to come anywhere near rivalling the great trio of the mid-fifties: *The Mousetrap*, *Witness for the Prosecution*, and *Spider's Web*.

In 1960, a colour film of *Spider's Web* was made by the Danziger Brothers in England, and released by United Artists. Run-of-the-mill direction by one Godfrey Grayson vitiated perfectly good, necessarily stagey performances by Glynis Johns (Clarissa), John Justin, Ronald Howard and others. That popular British husband-and-wife musical comedy team of the thirties, Cicely Courtneidge and Jack Hulbert, played the roles originally taken on the stage by Judith Furse and Felix Aylmer. Not surprisingly, this unambitious little film was never released in the United States of America.

Hickory Dickory Dock or Hickory Dickory Death (1955)

Agatha Christie celebrated her sixty-fifth birthday in 1955. For some years now, her life and that of Max Mallowan had followed a set pattern, between Nimrud, London and Devon: though not too firmly set, for there were a number of incidental pleasures to vary the routine. One of Mrs Christie's pleasures was buying houses, and furnishing them. At one time she owned eight houses, and, though she was persuaded to part with a number of them, she did so with great reluctance.

A particular pleasure for Agatha Christie in 1955 must have been the occasion when Queen Elizabeth II and the Duke of Edinburgh visited their local repertory theatre, the Theatre Royal, Windsor, to see the company perform *Witness for the Prosecution*. Declining to make use of the Royal Box, the Queen and her party sat in the balcony stalls. After the performance the royal visitors went backstage where the playwright and members of the cast were presented to the Queen.

It was by now customary for a new Agatha Christie title to be published in the summer or autumn of each year: 'A Christie for Christmas' was the publisher's slogan. The 1955 Christie was a Poirot novel, called in Great Britain *Hickory Dickory Dock* after the nursery rhyme ('Hickory Dickory Dock/The mouse ran up the clock/The clock struck one, the mouse ran down/Hickory Dickory Dock') and in the United States *Hickory Dickory Death*, which sounds smart but means nothing.

The British title is almost equally meaningless, for there is no connection between the old rhyme and Agatha Christie's plot. In vain does she allow Poirot to quote the rhyme at the end, merely because he hears a clock strike, or insert a parody of it earlier in the novel ('. . . The police said "Boo", I wonder who/Will eventually stand in the dock') into the mouth of one of the suspects. In vain does she set the scene of the crimes in Hickory Road. The connection refuses to be made, and Mrs Christie ought not to have allowed her fixation on nursery rhymes to land her with so unsuitable a title.

That said, it must be admitted that *Hickory Dickory Dock* is both interesting and entertaining, though the solving of the case involving three murders can hardly be counted as one of Hercule Poirot's greatest triumphs. Poirot is led into the affair through his secretary, the chillingly efficient Miss Lemon. We first met Miss Lemon back in 1934 when she worked for Mr Parker Pyne (*Parker Pyne Investigates*), and later encountered her as Poirot's secretary in some of the short stories in *The Regatta Mystery* and *The Labours of Hercules*. This is Miss Lemon's first appearance in a Poirot novel, and it is only now that we – and, apparently, her employer – discover her first name to be Felicity. Felicity Lemon's usual efficiency is impaired because she is worried about her sister who manages a student hostel where strange things have been occurring.

Foreign students sent to 26 Hickory Road by their Embassies, by the British Council, by the London University Lodging Board? This is not the normal world of Agatha Christie, but she makes a brave and remarkably successful attempt to move, temporarily, with the times, away from the grand country houses or the cosy cottages of St Mary Mead and into the genteel squalor of students' London in the mid-1950s. And she drags Hercule Poirot with her. Poirot even delivers a lecture to the students on some of his past successes, giving away part of the plot of an earlier novel in the process. To most of the students he is hardly known at all, although one of them betrays some knowledge of the events of *Mrs McGinty's Dead*.

Poirot has gone to Hickory Road to look into an outbreak of petty theft, but soon finds himself investigating murder. And why have the thefts led to murder? What is it all about? Those whose memories go back more than a quarter of a century to the episode of 'The Ambassador's Boots' in the Tommy and Tuppence adventure, *Partners in Crime*, may have an advantage.

The students are clearly and sometimes amusingly characterized: the American Sally Finch, the West African Mr Akibombo, the Indians Chandra Lal and Gopal Ram (to find this name, Mrs Christie seems to have overturned Ram Gopal, an Indian dancer well-known in Great Britain in the fifties), and an assortment of British students. One of the female students simulates an odd neurosis in order to attract the interest of an otherwise absent-minded young psychologist, and this makes muddy for a time the waters into which Poirot attempts to peer.

Stronger on characterization than on plot, *Hickory Dickory Dock* has its supporters and its detractors, critical opinion of the novel having been divided from the beginning. The mystery writer Francis Iles, reviewing it in the London *Sunday Times*, wrote: 'It reads like a tired effort. The usual sparkle is missing, the plot is far-fetched and the humour too easy (all foreigners are funny, but coloured foreigners are funnier).' On the other hand, the reviewer in the *Sunday Times*'s rival newspaper, *The Observer*, noted that 'One is pleased, though not in the least surprised, to find her so vociferously sound on the colour problem.'

Hickory Dickory Dock is mentioned in the Diaries of Evelyn Waugh, though not by title. In his entry for 18 July 1955, Waugh enumerates 'the joys and sorrows of a simple life'. Among the joys are 'A new Agatha Christie story which began well', while the sorrows include 'the deterioration of Mrs Christie's novel a third of the way through into twaddle'.[8]

In the early sixties, there were plans to turn *Hickory Dickory Dock* into a lavish stage musical. The idea emanated with the well-known merchant, arts patron and entrepreneur, Sir Nicholas ('Micky') Sekers. Impresarios Peter Daubeny and Bernard Delfont were both involved in the project, a young John Wells (author and star of the 1981 stage success, *Anyone for Denis?*) gave up a safe teaching job to write the script, the music was to be (and some of it actually was) written by an equally young Bulgarian Alexis Weissenberg (a Sekers protegé who went on to become an internationally-known concert pianist). It was expected that Johnny Dankworth would orchestrate Weissenberg's score. Sean Kenny was mentioned as designer, and Peter Sellers as Poirot.

John Wells produced a first draft, entitled *Death Beat*, and he and Weissenberg had more than one meeting with Agatha Christie at which they played and read parts of the show to her. Mrs Christie was enormously impressed with Weissenberg's playing: 'God, it must be wonderful to be you,' John Wells remembers her exclaiming to his collaborator. She was helpful to Wells, and thoroughly professional in her approach to the work in hand. But something, somehow, went wrong, Delfont failed to sustain his interest in the project, and eventually the whole thing fell apart. Presumably Alexis Weissenberg still has the tunes he wrote for the principal numbers. John Wells certainly still has, at the bottom of a drawer, his script.

Dead Man's Folly (1956)

At the beginning of 1956 Queen Elizabeth II made Agatha Christie a Commander of the Order of the British Empire (CBE). The announcement came on New Year's Day, in the New Year's Honours List.

In September, *Towards Zero*, the play which the author and Gerald Verner had fashioned from her 1944 novel, was staged in London (see p. 132).

A news item in the London *Daily Telegraph* on 20 November announced that, because of what the newspaper referred to euphemistically as the 'Suez dispute,'[9] the manager of the Marlowe Theatre in Canterbury, Kent, had decided the previous evening to cancel the production of Agatha Christie's play, *Murder on the Nile*, which the resident company had planned to stage the following week. Although there was nothing offensive to anyone's national or political sensibilities in the play itself, the manager thought its title, in the circumstances, might be considered 'a little unfortunate'.

The 1956 Christie was *Dead Man's Folly*. During the year, *The Burden* by Mary Westmacott was also published.

The first of the murders in *Dead Man's Folly* occurs at one of those typically English affairs, the village fête which is held on a Saturday afternoon in summer in the grounds of the local manor house. At Nasse House, in Nassecombe, on the river Helm in Devon, that celebrated detective-story writer Mrs Ariadne Oliver agrees to take part in the fête and to invent a Murder Hunt, based on the Treasure Hunt game. During the fête, a local girl, cast as 'the body' in the Murder Hunt, is found dead.

The local names are fictitious. For Nasse House and the river Helm, read Greenway House and the Dart, for Agatha Christie has based this 'big white Georgian house looking out over the river' on the house on the upper reaches of the Dart which she and Max Mallowan had purchased in 1939 and had lived in since the end of the war. (The author's daughter and son-in-law now occupy it.) She has even made use of Greenway House's boathouse: 'It jutted out on to the river and was a picturesque thatched affair.'[10] That was where Mrs Oliver intended 'the body' to be discovered, and that is where, despite the presence of Hercule Poirot at the fête, it is discovered.

Poirot was summoned by Mrs Oliver who had vague forbodings that something might go wrong, for she had been staying at Nasse House for a day or two before the fête, and sensed that the atmosphere was some how wrong. *Dead Man's Folly* begins with Mrs Oliver's phone call to Poirot, whose telephone number, trivia collectors will want to note, is TRAfalgar 8137. 'I don't know if you'll remember me,' Mrs Oliver says to Poirot, but of course he does. They first met twenty years earlier (see *Cards on the Table*, 1936) and, again, only four years earlier when Poirot investigated the death of Mrs McGinty (*Mrs McGinty's Dead*, 1952).

And so Poirot takes a train to Devon, and to the riverside house not far from Dartmoor. The moor, one of Agatha Christie's favourite places where in old age she still loved to picnic with family and friends, does not intrude into the narrative but is palpably there in the background as it is in more than one other Christie novel. (The chauffeur who conveys Poirot from the railway station at Nassecombe to Nasse House attempts to draw the great detective's attention to the beauties of the scene – 'The River Helm, sir, with Dartmoor in the distance' – and Poirot makes the proper appreciative noises although he has very little interest in nature and scenery.

More often than not, when characters in a Christie novel refer to previous events which are irrelevant to the plot it will be found that the reference is to an earlier novel. As we have seen, such references can sometimes be irritatingly indiscreet. But, in *Dead Man's Folly*, when Poirot claims to remember the local police investigator, Inspector Bland, from fifteen years ago when Bland was a young Sergeant, he appears to be recalling a case which has not been recorded. The reader has not previously met Inspector Bland.

Dead Man's Folly is a good, average, traditional Poirot novel, entertaining though not outstanding. The colourful Ariadne Oliver, Mrs Christie's good-natured parody of herself and her writing habits, plays a leading part: the story would lack flavour without her. Mrs Oliver's appearances in Christie novels, mostly those also involving Poirot, will become increasingly frequent in future years, and always to splendid effect.

At the end of *Dead Man's Folly*, Poirot announces his solution and identifies the murderer, but the novel ends before the person in question is apprehended by the police. In fact, it is not absolutely certain that an arrest will take place, for Poirot's brilliant guesses are not always supported by the kind of evidence that would stand up in a court of law. Often, he has to trick his criminal into confession or collapse. Here, the question is left open. The feeling, however, is that the killer, 'ruthless . . . without pity . . . and without conscience' as described by a close relative, will not get away with it.

Some critics of this novel have failed to be convinced by the author that an army deserter could return to his local village disguised only by a beard and a change of name, and not be recognized. They have a point.

The Burden (1956)

Agatha Christie was in her mid-sixties when she wrote *The Burden*, the last of her Mary Westmacott novels. Thereafter, her 'extra-mural' writing time was devoted almost exclusively to her autobiography, and her 'official' time devoted with almost as much vigour as she had displayed ten and twenty years earlier to producing her crime novels. She continued to publish at least one each year, approximately a third of them featuring Poirot, a third Miss Marple, and a third making do without either of her most popular characters.

'There is nothing immoral in my books, only murder,' Mrs Christie once said to A.L. Rowse,[11] and you can see what she meant. But, of course, there is much that is immoral in the Mary Westmacott novels, although there are no murders. There is obsessive jealousy, cruelty, greed, hatred, and adultery which, in certain circumstances, qualifies as immorality. In *The Burden*, there is a great amount of guilt which, if it is not immoral, is certainly destructive. The burden, however, is not that of guilt but of love, the over-protective love of an elder sister for a younger, the substitute-mother love of Laura for Shirley which leads to the younger sister's disastrous marriage.

The end of the novel is over-explicit, or perhaps merely too compressed, but, as always with Mary Westmacott, the characters ring true, and you can discern in them traces of people in Agatha Christie's life, though she does not anywhere attempt to place a real person in a fictitious situation. Having known Archie Christie helped her to understand and to describe Shirley's husband, Henry, and to deal ironically with his charm but gently with his abhorrence of responsibility. To love is a burden for Henry, just as to be loved is a burden for Laura, the elder sister, who comes to an acceptance of it only after much pain and distress have been caused by her attempts to protect her younger sister from something against which there can be no protection: life.

Whether writing as Agatha Christie or Mary Westmacott, Mrs Christie was usually able to create believable children in her novels, which is an especially difficult thing to do. To imagine the behaviour of other adults is much easier than to remember thought processes as a child. The child Laura in the early pages of *The Burden* is a remarkable creation, and Laura's scenes with her elderly friend Mr Baldock are particularly impressive. Through Mr Baldock, the author utters words of wisdom about the parent-child relationship without seeming to preach or to be delivering those messages so disliked by Samuel Goldwyn.

Relationships, the future, the nature of time, all are involved in the scheme of this seemingly unambitious novel which is about Kant's three questions, as posed by Dr Llewellyn Knox, an American ex-evangelist: What do I know? What can I hope? What ought I to do? (Dr Knox puts one in mind of the American preacher, Dr Billy Graham, who made evangelistic tours of Great Britain in the early fifties and later.)

'How should I live?' is what not only *The Burden* but all the Westmacott novels are about. *Absent in the Spring* is the only one which is set in the desert, but images of the desert within the soul pervade them all, just as Chekov's three sisters yearning for Moscow pervade the dissatisfied daydreams of Lady Wilding in *The Burden*. These introspective examinations of a way of life she knew, a way of life shared by a great many of her readers, are an oddly and unjustly neglected part of Agatha Christie's *oeuvre*. To a certain extent, they are the victims of publishers' primitive ideas about marketing and about their authors' images. Would Agatha Christie's readers have recoiled in horror if they had been allowed to consider *Giant's Bread* by Agatha Christie? *Unfinished Portrait* by Agatha Christie? . . . *The Burden* by Agatha Christie? Need the author have resorted to a pseudonym which, in the event, robbed the books of much of the critical attention they would surely otherwise have received? It is difficult not to agree with Max Mallowan on the value of these six books:

> The Mary Westmacott novels are of uneven quality, but every one of them is readable and has studies of character easily absorbed, thanks to Agatha's extraordinary gift for telling a story. At best these books are dramatic, and concentrate an interest on the solution to situations which arise out of the high tensions in life. It will be a pity if they are forgotten against the popular achievement of the detective fiction. I do not think that they will be.[12]

4.50 *From Paddington* or *What Mrs McGillicuddy Saw* (1957)

The yearly visits to Nimrud continued, and Agatha Christie was by now a very important member of the team. She was no longer responsible for photographing objects found, for this function had now been assumed by Barbara Parker (the subject of Agatha's Ode on p. 170). She had, however, become a very experienced repairer of ivories, and she also helped her husband pay the local workers each week. She continued to produce Odes on members of the party, visitors, and events.

The film version of *Witness for the Prosecution* (see p. 174) was made during 1957, and Mrs Christie gave her share in the film rights to her daughter Rosalind. It was in this year, also, that Agatha Christie succeeded Dorothy L. Sayers as President of The Detection Club. The 1957 Christie was *4.50 From Paddington*.

4.50 From Paddington was too parochial a title for the American edition of Miss Marple's latest adventure, which became in the USA *What Mrs McGillicuddy Saw*. What Mrs McGillicuddy saw from the window of her train, the 4.50 from Paddington to the west country, was a murder being committed in a train passing on a parallel line. At first, the only person Mrs McGillicuddy could find to believe her story was her friend Jane Marple. It was only after some extraordinarily cunning detective work on Miss Marple's part that the police began to take an active interest. That interest was fully aroused when, as a result of Miss Marple's efforts, a body came to light.

4.50 From Paddington, despite its title, is not one of those thrillers set, like *Murder on the Orient Express* or *The Mystery of the Blue Train*, in whole or in large part on a train. It merely begins on one. The real action takes place in and about Rutherford Hall, an overgrown country estate adjacent to a curve in the railway line, and the majority of the characters involved are members of the Crackenthorpe family. Miss Marple is growing even older and perhaps physically feebler, and at first she is not certain that she can manage to take on the task of tracking down a murderer yet again. But her natural curiosity triumphs over bodily weakness, and she enlists the aid of her nephew Raymond's second son, David, who is grown up and working for British Railways. She also writes to Dermot Craddock, the young policeman who is Sir Henry Clithering's godson. She had made Dermot's acquaintance in *A Murder is Announced*: he is now a Detective-Inspector at New Scotland Yard, and she and he make a good team (as they were to do once again, five years later, in *The Mirror Crack'd From Side to Side*).

Agatha Christie is frequently at her most ingenious when dealing with a large family, its secrets and its tensions. Her first novel, *The Mysterious Affair at Styles*, was very much a family affair, as were such first-rate mysteries as *Appointment with Death* (though here the family is on the move rather than at home), *Hercule Poirot's Christmas* and *Crooked House*. In *4.50 From Paddington* the Crackenthorpes are a family whose past is ripe for investigation, and Miss Marple investigates both at first hand and through Lucy Eylesbarrow, a fascinating young woman whom you would like to have welcomed onto the permanent Marple team. Alas, Lucy does not appear again in the pages of Agatha Christie.

'I specialize in murders of quiet, domestic interest,' Mrs Christie once told an interviewer. And this particular domestic murder is, in its way, quiet and almost cosy, if not in its method then at least in the way in which it is presented to the reader. This cosiness, thought by the writer's critics to be a weakness, is seen by Christie enthusiasts as one of her most endearing attributes. The crimes and attempted crimes in *4.50 From Paddington* are violent ones, but the novel is far from violent, and is full of gentle humour.

To what lengths can the author of a murder mystery go in concealing from the reader the murderer's identity? Many people thought Agatha Christie went too far in 1926 in *The Murder of Roger Ackroyd*, and a few even considered that the author behaved unfairly to her readers in *4.50 From Paddington*. Ambiguity is one thing, those few might have said, but disingenuousness is another. In some of her novels, e.g. *Ten Little Niggers* and *Towards Zero*, there are points at which the murderer's thoughts are given without any identification of the character thinking those thoughts. In other novels, the murderer's thoughts are given and are attributed, but they are not thoughts about the murder. These are not Mrs Christie's only methods of dealing with her murderers before identification. She has several, and most of them are more satisfactory than her tightrope-walking in *4.50 From Paddington*.

The solution to this particular mystery is not in itself unsatisfactory, though the method by which Miss Marple arrives at her discovery of the murderer is by no means clear. Feminine intuition, it would seem, has played a larger role than usual. What is unsatisfactory, surely, is Miss Marple having to resort to unlikely physical action in the course of apprehending the criminal. 'With incredible swiftness Miss Marple slipped' from the villain's grasp, we are told, and, a few lines later, 'again, swiftly, Miss Marple was between' villain and threatened witness. Jane Marple is a very old, rather frail lady and she is extremely fortunate not to have been strangled in Chapter 26 of *4.50 From Paddington*. This incident is almost as embarrassingly unlikely as her hiding in a cupboard and indulging in mimicry in *A Murder is Announced*.

Agatha Christie's strong views on the subject of capital punishment are made to emerge from the lips of Miss Marple in the final chapter. ' "Everything——did was bold and audacious and cruel and greedy, and I am really very, very sorry," finished Miss Marple, looking as fierce as a fluffy old lady can look, "that they have abolished capital punishment because I do feel that if there is anyone who ought to hang, it's ——." ' '

It is all very well for Miss Marple to 'twinkle' at her young police inspector friend a few moments later: in some ways she is a very stern old pussy. And so is her creator.

In 1961, the series of Miss Marple movies made in England by Metro-Goldwyn-Mayer, with Margaret Rutherford as Jane Marple, was begun with *Murder, She Said*, whose screenplay by David Pursall and Jack Seddon was based on *4.50 From Paddington*. This is not only the first, but also the best of the series, despite the fact that, in the interests presumably of economy, Miss Marple takes on the functions of two of the novel's other characters as well: Mrs McGillicuddy, who witnessed the murder on the train, and Lucy Eylesbarrow, who posed as a maid in the Crackenthorpe house.

The director (of this and indeed all the films in the series) was George Pollock, and Margaret Rutherford led a cast which included Muriel Pavlow, James Robertson Justice, Ronald Howard, Arthur Kennedy, Stringer Davis and, as Inspector Dermot Craddock, Charles Tingwell who was to play Craddock in all four films.

Although Margaret Rutherford, a resourceful, eccentric and engaging comedienne, achieved a popular success as Miss Marple, she bore little resemblance to the character as described by Agatha Christie. Asked what she thought of this particular piece of casting, Mrs Christie left it to her secretary to reply:[13] 'Mrs Christie . . . has asked me to tell you that, while she thinks Miss Rutherford is a fine actress, she bears no resemblance to her own idea of Miss Marple.' Nevertheless, a later Miss Marple novel, *The Mirror Crack'd from Side to Side* (1962), was dedicated 'to Margaret Rutherford in admiration'. (When *The Mirror Crack'd* was filmed in 1980, Agatha Christie had been dead for four years. Would she, you wonder, have approved of Angela Lansbury's Jane Marple?)

To coincide with the release of the film, a new paperback edition of the novel was published in the United States in 1961 under the title, *Murder, She Said.*

Verdict (1958)

On 12 April 1958, *The Mousetrap* reached its 2,239th performance at the Ambassadors Theatre, thereby breaking the record for the longest London run of a play. On the following evening, a Sunday, Peter Saunders gave a party at the Savoy Hotel to celebrate, and on Monday, 14 April the London *Daily Mail* published this account of the party:

> A silver-haired middle-aged woman with a motherly smile walked into the Savoy Hotel last night and was stopped by a porter as she approached the banqueting hall where a big theatrical party was about to begin. 'Your ticket, please, ma'am,' said the porter. But she didn't have a ticket. She was the guest of honour. Her name: Mrs Max Edgar Lucien Mallowan – Agatha Christie, Queen of the Thrillers, to you. Shy and reserved, she seldom comes out in public. 'I know many people don't know me. But they did let me in,' she added with a smile.

To commemorate the breaking of the record, Agatha Christie presented to the Ambassadors Theatre a specially designed mousetrap. She was, of course, delighted that her *Mousetrap* had broken all records, and she must have had high hopes for a new play she had written, and of which she thought very highly. This was *Verdict*, which Peter Saunders presented at the Strand Theatre on 22 May. But *Verdict* failed to please, and closed one month later, on 21 June. The resilient Mrs Christie murmured 'At least I am glad *The Times* liked it', and immediately set to work to write another play, which she finished within four weeks: *The Unexpected Guest* opened at the Duchess Theatre on 12 August (see pp. 187–89).

Verdict is unusual in that it is not a murder mystery. A murder does occur in the play, but there is no mystery attached to it for it is committed in full view of the audience and, on this occasion, Mrs Christie is not playing tricks. A middle-European professor, his crippled wife and his secretary, all three of them refugees from some unspecified totalitarian regime, live together in a flat in Bloomsbury. A female student, in love with the professor, kills his wife. Thereafter, the plot becomes, if not more complex, then certainly more complicated. *Verdict*, however, is not really a play about murder but about a certain type of idealist. It is an examination of the character of Professor Karl Hendryk.

In her autobiography, Agatha Christie stated that, although it had not been a success with the public, *Verdict* (a bad title, in her view) had satisfied her completely. She continued:

> I had called it *No Fields of Amaranth*, taken from the words of Walter Landor's: 'There are no flowers of amaranth on this side of the grave'. I still think it the best play I have written, with the exception of *Witness for the Prosecution*. It failed, I think, because it was *not* a detective story or a thriller. It *was* a play that concerned murder, but its real background and point was

that an idealist is always dangerous, a possible destroyer of those who love him – and poses the question of how far you can sacrifice, not yourself, but those you love, to what you believe in, even though they do not.

It is a good theme, and a fascinating one. 'Charity begins at home' is, perhaps, another statement of it. Mrs Christie has fashioned an interesting play around her professor who, for the best of motives, creates havoc, not because his abstract principles are other than admirable, but because he does not have the imagination to envisage the likely outcome of his actions.

The sentence from Walter Savage Landor's *Imaginary Conversations* is quoted in the play, by the Professor's secretary, Lisa Koletzky, though it seems unlikely that a female Middle-European physicist should be well up in Landor in general or his *Imaginary Conversations* in particular. The Strand Theatre programme thought it necessary to print a note on the meaning of 'Amaranth', and so does the published acting edition of the play: 'another name for the plant called "Love-lies-bleeding" – an imaginary flower that never fades. From the Greek *amarantos*, never-fading.'

When Sir William Rollander, a wealthy industrialist, says to Professor Hendryk, 'The Spanish have a proverb, "Take what you want and pay for it"', says God', that particular Spanish proverb is making at least its third appearance in Mrs Christie's *oeuvre*.

Verdict is a serious, worthy play, and not unentertaining. It was booed by the gallery on its first night in London, not because anyone felt cheated at not being offered a mystery to be solved, but because of a lighting-cue misunderstanding which caused the curtain to come down on the final scene about forty seconds too soon. This prevented the 'surprise' re-entrance of an important character, and completely changed the ending of the play! 'So there was no dextrous twist at the end,' wrote the *Daily Telegraph*'s critic, W.A. Darlington, 'instead there was a great scene of renunciation and parting, which rang false and fell flat.' The critic's flurry of metaphors was misplaced, and on the following day the *Telegraph* published this news item:

Verdict, the play by Agatha Christie at the Strand Theatre, was more enthusiastically received last night, when the company took six curtain calls. On Thursday, the first night, there was booing from the gallery.

It was revealed yesterday that on Thursday the curtain was rung down 40 seconds too soon, before the vital two lines between Gerard Heinz and Patricia Jessel. These lines complete a happy and more satisfactory ending to the play. The mistake in lowering the curtain was due to an error by a member of the stage manager's staff.

However, the fact that Agatha Christie had written a murder play which appeared to lack one important ingredient, mystery, was surely the major cause of its disappointingly short run. *Verdict* is occasionally performed, though not as frequently as Mrs Christie's murder mysteries. It may lack mystery: it does not lack suspense.

At the Strand Theatre, London, the leading roles were played by Gerard Heinz (as Professor Karl Hendryk), Patricia Jessel, who had scored a great personal success in *Witness for the Prosecution*, both in London and New York (as the Professor's secretary, Lisa), Viola Keats (as the Professor's wife, Anya),

Moira Redmond (as the student, Helen) and Derek Oldham (as Dr Stoner). The play was directed by Charles Hickman.

The Unexpected Guest (1958)

Undeterred by the failure of *Verdict*, Agatha Christie wrote another play very quickly, and Peter Saunders immediately put it into production. *Verdict* had closed on 21 June 1958. The new play, *The Unexpected Guest*, played for a week at the Hippodrome in Bristol, and then moved to the Duchess Theatre in the West End of London, where it opened on 12 August. It played 604 performances there over the following eighteen months.

The Unexpected Guest could perhaps be described as a murder mystery disguised as a murder non-mystery, for it begins when a stranger, the 'unexpected guest' of the title, runs his car into a ditch in dense fog in South Wales, near the coast, and makes his way to a house where he finds a woman standing with a gun in her hand over the dead body of her husband, Richard Warwick, whom she admits she has killed. He decides to help her, and together they concoct a story and a plan of action.

The murdered man, a cripple in a wheelchair, appears to have been an unpleasant and sadistic character; apart from members of his own family, there are others who might have murdered him if they had been given the opportunity, among them the father of a child killed two years earlier by Richard Warwick's careless and perhaps drunken driving. As the play progresses, the possibility arises that Laura Warwick may not have killed her husband, but may be shielding someone else. Richard Warwick's young half-brother, mentally retarded and potentially dangerous? Laura's lover, Julian Farrar, who is about to stand for Parliament? Warwick's mother, a strong-minded old matriarch who knows she has not long to live? Or, of course, the father of the little boy who was killed?

The investigating policemen who turn up in Act I, scene ii, are a shrewd and sarcastic Inspector and a poetically inclined young Sergeant who quotes Keats. Towards the end of the play's second and final act, they identify and apprehend the real murderer. Or do they? This being an Agatha Christie mystery, there is a further surprise in the play's last lines. Can it be that Mrs Christie allows a killer to escape punishment? If so, might this be because she thinks of the murder of Robert Warwick as a just retribution?

Through the character of Michael Starkwedder, 'the unexpected guest', Mrs Christie makes the interesting assertion that:

> Men are really the sensitive sex. Women are tough. Men can't take murder in their stride. Women apparently can.

The character of the murdered man, as described by his wife, was based, at least in part, on someone whom Agatha Christie had known very well. Here is Laura Warwick, describing one of her late husband's nocturnal habits:

> Then he'd have this window wide open and he'd sit here looking out, watching for the gleam of a cat's eyes, or a stray rabbit, or a dog. Of course, there haven't been so many rabbits lately. But he shot quite a lot of cats. He shot them in the daytime, too. And birds . . . a woman came to call one day for

subscriptions for the vicarage fête. Richard sent shots to right and left of her as she was going away down the drive. She bolted like a hare, he said. He roared with laughter when he told us about it. Her fat backside was quivering like a jelly, he said. However, she went to the police about it and there was a terrible row.

And here is Agatha Christie, in her autobiography, describing her brother Monty, as an invalid towards the end of his life:

Monty's health was improving, and as a result he was much more difficult to control. He was bored, and for relaxation took to shooting out of his window with a revolver. Tradespeople and some of mother's visitors complained. Monty was unrepentant. 'Some silly old spinster going down the drive with her behind wobbling. Couldn't resist it – I sent a shot or two right and left of her. My word, how she ran' . . . Someone complained and we had a visit from the police.

The Unexpected Guest was an original Christie, not only in the sense that it was written by the author herself and not dramatized by someone else from a Christie novel or story, but also in being, like *Spider's Web* but unlike *The Mousetrap* or *Witness for the Prosecution*, completely new and not an adaptation by the author of an earlier work of hers. It is, in fact, one of the best of her plays, its dialogue taut and effective and its plot full of surprises despite being economical and not over-complex. It demonstrates, incidentally, the profound truth that seeing is not believing. The leading roles in 1958 were played by Renee Asherson (Laura Warwick), Nigel Stock (Michael Starkwedder) and Violet Farebrother (Mrs Warwick, senior), with Christopher Sandford (Jan Warwick), Paul Curran (Henry Angell), Roy Purcell (Julian Farrar), Winifred Oughton (Miss Bennett), Michael Golden (Inspector Thomas), Tenniel Evans (Sergeant Cadwallader) and Philip Newman (the corpse). The play was directed by Hubert Gregg.

Reviews were uniformly enthusiastic, many of them contrasting the success of the new play with the recent failure of *Verdict*. 'After the failure of her last play, *Verdict*,' wrote the *Daily Telegraph* critic, 'it was suggested in some quarters that Scotland Yard ought to be called in to discover who killed Agatha Christie. But *The Unexpected Guest*, turning up last night at the Duchess before even the reverberations of her last failure have died away, indicates that the corpse is still very much alive. Burial of her thriller reputation is certainly premature.' The *Guardian* combined reportage and criticism: Only seven weeks after Agatha Christie's last play was booed off the stage, the old lady of 66 [sic] stumped defiantly back into a London theatre last night. She had a new whodunit ready. She watched from the back of the circle, white-faced and apprehensive . . . But no boos came this time. No rude interruptions. At the end she heard the kind of applause that has given her *Mousetrap* a record six-year run.'

Ordeal by Innocence (1958)

The 1958 Christie murder mystery was *Ordeal by Innocence*. 'Of my detective books,' wrote Agatha Christie in *An Autobiography*, 'I think the two that satisfy me best are *Crooked House* and *Ordeal by Innocence*.' In neither novel does any one of Mrs Christie's 'official' investigators appear. Can she really have preferred these two perfectly acceptable murder mysteries to the best of her Poirot and Miss Marple novels of the thirties and forties? Of these two favourites of the novelist herself, *Ordeal by Innocence* is the better. Arthur Calgary, a well-known and respected geophysicist, returns to England from an Antarctic expedition, to find that a young man who had been convicted of the murder of his mother has died in prison. Calgary, who was inaccessible in the Antarctic at the time of the trial and the subsequent events, could have given evidence which would have resulted in the young man being found innocent and acquitted. Feeling that he owed it to the young man's family to reveal this, Calgary visits them in the familiar Christie country, of South Devon. No doubt he hopes also to assuage his own burden of guilt, but he expects that, after the initial shock, the young man's relatives will be relieved to know he was innocent.

Of course, they are not relieved. If Jacko did not kill his mother, someone else did; someone, perhaps a member of the family, who is still living in the house. Until the truth is known, the innocent will suffer with the guilty. Why, the Argyle family wishes fervently, could not Mr Calgary have kept his awkward truth to himself? The police investigation into Mrs Argyle's murder is reopened, and a second death ensues before the real truth is discovered. Arthur Calgary plays his part in that discovery, and is present at the house at Viper's Point at the moment of truth.

All of Mrs Christie's country cottages are the same cottage, all of her 'desirable residences' in the home counties are the same retreat for tired businessmen, and all of her houses on cliffs jutting into the channel from the south Devon coast are the same house. From Torquay southwest along the coast to Salcombe, with Dartmoor in the hinterland, all of this is Christie country, and it is a stronger presence than usual in *Ordeal by Innocence*.

This is one of Mrs Christie's novels of family relationships, a theme which she always handled with confidence and therefore with conviction. By way of epigraph, she places two verses from the Book of Job at the beginning of the novel. They are printed as though they were consecutive verses:

If I justify myself, mine own mouth shall condemn me.
I am afraid of all my sorrows. I know that thou wilt not hold me innocent.

However, the first sentence is part of verse 20 of Chapter 9. The complete verse reads: 'If I justify myself, mine own mouth shall condemn me: if I say, I am perfect, it shall also prove me perverse.' (The second and third sentences of the epigraph are verse 28.) Mrs Christie may consciously have suppressed the phrase after the colon because she thought it irrelevant to her purpose. She may also have subconsciously repressed what an especially perspicacious reader may construe as a clue of sorts, or at least a pointer in a certain direction. We should bear in mind that it is, if not impossible, then at least highly unusual for Agatha Christie to admit any serious imperfection or miscarriage of justice in the English judicial system. On the other hand, Mrs Christie does, to put it mildly, deal in the unusual. The course is a circular one. You may think you are several paces ahead of *her* when she is actually nearly a lap ahead of *you*. From what we learn of the murdered woman, she appears to have had much in common with Professor Hendryk in *Verdict* (p. 185).

What *Ordeal by Innocence* may lack in the way of brilliant detection it compensates for in highly perceptive social observation and lashings of that rare commodity, commonsense, of which Agatha Christie always seemed to have plenty to spare. She was also as greatly concerned with the protection of innocence as with the punishment of guilt. It is as well to bear this in mind when reading *Ordeal by Innocence*. Her implied sneer at Beckett's *Waiting for Godot* may be out of place (in its context, the remark 'You were going to see an amateur performance of *Waiting for Godot* at the Drymouth Playhouse' sounds like a sorrowful reproach), and the ability of a certain member of the family to quote *Phèdre* may not convince (*'Vénus toute entière à sa proie attachée . . .'* runs through his mind: it is identified simply as 'a line of French verse'). However, on the important issues, the Serpent of Old Devon is sound; as long, that is, as you do not trust her for a moment about anything.

Cat Among the Pigeons (1959)

On 15 March 1959, the cast of *The Mousetrap* gave a performance of the play at Wormwood Scrubs prison in London. The set and furniture did not have to be transported to the prison as these were provided, the prisoners having constructed the décor from designs supplied by Peter Saunders. An audience of three hundred prisoners, all men serving long sentences, enjoyed the play and applauded warmly at the end. Or rather, two hundred and ninety-eight of them applauded, for two had taken the opportunity to escape during Act II.

During the year, UNESCO released the information that the Bible had been translated into one hundred and seventy-one languages, Agatha Christie into one hundred and three, and Shakespeare into ninety. The statistics concerning numbers of copies of volumes sold revealed the Bible and Shakespeare to be ahead of Agatha Christie, who came third with something like 400,000,000 copies.

Mrs Christie may have been translated into only one hundred and three languages by 1959. More than twenty years later the number is higher (and the sales figures are considerably higher!) but she was not necessarily admired uncritically in all of them. Under the heading, 'A Slight Case of Poison, Agatha', the London *Daily Express* published this story by its Moscow correspondent on 20 May:

Crime writers in general came under heavy fire at the Soviet Writers' Congress today. And, in particular, Agatha Christie who 'reflects the poisoned air which exists in bourgeois society'.

Seventy-year-old Kornel Chukovsky, a translator, said of her: 'She has talent – but what a waste. If she had written six or seven books in her life instead of seventy they might have been good. As it is, she has become a virtuoso in extermination.

'She makes no attempt to build up pity for her victims – for the child who died because of licking a poisoned postage stamp. She only creates admiration for the murderer's technique. Human interest is excluded from her work. She concentrates on only how to conceal crime, on plot and intrigue, on the intellectual ability of the murderers and the technical excellence of their crimes.

'The extent of inhumanity of the crime writer is frightful. There is a mass psychosis for crime stories. They have poisoned people's brains to such an extent that they cannot absorb normal literary food. People have become incapable of reading books in which there are no ingenious murders.

'Agatha Christie's great stunt is to throw suspicion on everyone. Readers are not allowed to believe in noble virtues like honesty, sincerity, and friendship, in unselfish motives or feelings. She fosters feelings of suspicion, fear, hate, and disbelief in the goodness of people.'

One would like to think that, if her press cutting service landed this news item on the author's desk, she read it with a smile, and murmured, 'Look who's talking!'

The 1959 Christie, a new Poirot mystery called *Cat Among the Pigeons*, is one of the best of the later novels. Agatha Christie is not a writer whose work can be neatly divided into the usual three periods of promise, maturity or achievement, and decline; nevertheless her creative output did alter throughout the years. The thrillers became less light-hearted, while the structure of the mysteries loosened up somewhat, and occasionally to a perilous degree. The plotting of some of the Poirot and Miss Marple novels which Agatha Christie wrote in the last fifteen years of her life is more than a trifle lax. When this happens, there is usually a compensation in the form of especially convincing characterization. *Cat Among the Pigeons*, however, is quite strongly plotted, and its characters, even its minor characters, are more than usually vivid.

The novel is set, for the most part, in a girls' school in England, which has led some critics to compare it to a murder mystery published in 1946 by one of Mrs Christie's rivals: Josephine Tey's *Miss Pym Disposes*, in which certain events in a girls' physical education college lead to a death. The school background apart, however, there is little similarity between the two novels. Agatha Christie's school, Meadowbank, is said to have been based on her daughter Rosalind's school, Caledonia. The school and its staff are certainly described very convincingly, and the crotchety illiberality of outlook which occasionally creeps into the pages of late Christie is completely absent. In fact, the liberal commonsense of the headmistress and founder of the school, Miss Bulstrode, is presented in such a way as to suggest it has the author's wholehearted approval.

The skill with which the summer term at Meadowbank is combined with a revolution in Ramat, a small but rich Arab state in the Middle East, is masterly. Hercule Poirot is required to discover who is busily murdering the staff of the school, and it is not long before a plethora of motives is revealed. Elements of the domestic mystery and the thriller are combined, and two characters whom we shall later meet in the thrillers are first encountered in *Cat Among the Pigeons*: Colonel Pikeaway, who seems to be in charge of intelligence, and is given to remarking 'We know all about things here, that's what we're for' (he will say it again in *Passenger to Frankfurt* and, as an old man in retirement, in *Postern of Fate*); and the enigmatic financier, Mr Robinson, 'fat and well-dressed, with a yellow face, melancholy dark eyes, a broad forehead, and a generous mouth that displayed rather over-large very white teeth'. Mr Robinson will make an appearance in *Postern of Fate* and a Miss Marple adventure, *At Bertram's Hotel*.

For some years, Hercule Poirot has lived in an apartment in Whitehaven Mansions, London, W1. We learn in *Cat Among the Pigeons* that the number of his apartment is 228, but the block of flats is now called Whitehouse Mansions.

Mrs Christie's carelessness again? Or simply a misprint in certain editions? Or has Poirot moved without telling even his creator?

At one point in the narrative a schoolgirl mentions one of the characters from *Mrs McGinty's Dead*, and Poirot reminisces: this time without giving away the solution of the earlier novel. The reader enjoys such harmless and cosy links between novels, but not when vital information is carelessly and unnecessarily revealed.

Julia, the schoolgirl, is taken to a performance of *Faust* at Covent Garden. If Mrs Christie had been in the habit of researching in the interests of accuracy, she would have discovered that Gounod's opera had not been staged at Covent Garden since 1938. Julia was taken either to Sadler's Wells Theatre, or the Welsh National Opera, or the old Carl Rosa Company on tour. Or, of course, to Paris!

The Adventure of the Christmas Pudding (1960)

On 14 March 1960, the London *Daily Telegraph* reported that a survey in Poland had revealed Agatha Christie to be the author most popular with the youth of that country. This information had recently been published in the Polish weekly magazine, *Zycie Literackie*, but the poll itself had been carried out two years earlier and the results suppressed, presumably because they were an embarrassment to Poland and its writers.

Agatha Christie's play *Go Back for Murder*, a dramatization of her novel, *Five Little Pigs* (see p. 128) opened on 23 March at the Duchess Theatre, London, where it ran for no longer than a month. *The Mousetrap* began a six-month run in New York.

The full title of the volume of short stories which was published in 1960, in Great Britain only, is *The Adventure of the Christmas Pudding, and a Selection of Entrées*. In a Foreword, the author described this book of Christmas fare as 'The Chef's Selection', with herself as Chef. There were, she said, two main courses: 'The Adventure of the Christmas Pudding' and 'The Mystery of the Spanish Chest'. The other four stories made up the entrées.

The Foreword ends: 'And a happy Christmas to all who read this book.' The stories themselves, however, with the possible exception of 'The Adventure of the Christmas Pudding', can hardly be described as glowing with seasonal good cheer, for the usual murders abound, to be solved in five of the stories by Hercule Poirot, and in the sixth by Jane Marple. The two 'main courses' are very long stories, and one of the so-called entrées, 'The Under Dog', is even longer.

Only two of the stories are new, in that they appear here in a volume for the first time. They are 'The Adventure of the Christmas Pudding', and the Miss Marple story, 'Greenshaw's Folly'. In the title story, Poirot reluctantly spends Christmas in an English country house, but manages to enjoy a gigantic Christmas dinner of the kind described in Mrs Christie's Foreword, and even copes admirably when a body is discovered lying in the snow. Miss Marple, in 'Greenshaw's Folly', has reason to be 'pleased with her perspicuity', as the author puts it in her Foreword, especially as it is impossible for the reader to discern by what rational steps she arrived at her solution.

Although they had appeared in volumes published in the USA, the other stories were new to Great Britain, with the exception of 'The Under Dog' which had been published together with a story by E. Phillips Oppenheim in a volume, *The New Crime Stories 2* in 1929. It also appeared in the volume of stories, *The Under Dog*, published in the USA in 1951 (see p. 159). 'The Dream' was in the 1939 American volume, *The Regatta Mystery*; and 'Four-and-twenty Blackbirds' was in *Three Blind Mice* (1950). 'The Mystery of the Spanish Chest' will be found in *The Regatta Mystery*, but in a shorter version as 'The Mystery of the Baghdad Chest'. The differences between the two are outlined on p. 114.

The two new stories, 'The Adventure of the Christmas Pudding' and 'Greenshaw's Folly', were to appear in *Double Sin*, a 1961 American collection in which the 'Christmas Pudding' story had its title changed to 'The Theft of the Royal Ruby'.

Double Sin (1961)

In 1961 Agatha Christie received an Honorary Doctorate of Letters from Exeter University, in her native county of Devon. The regular yearly visits to the Middle East had ended the previous year. Max Mallowan was free to take up an academic post in Britain and his wife to spend more time in Devon. Now in her seventy-first year, Mrs Christie continued to keep up her output of at least one book annually. In 1961, two were published, though the first of them, *Double Sin*, appeared only in the USA. *Thirteen for Luck!*, 'a selection of mystery stories for young readers', published in the USA in 1961, contained only stories which had appeared in earlier volumes. When *Thirteen for Luck!* was published in the UK in 1966, Julian Symons in the *Sunday Times* thought it contained 'much dazzling Christie ingenuity'.

Double Sin is a collection of eight stories, four of them dating from the 1920s and four written in the 1950s. Although this title was never published in Great Britain, two of the stories had already appeared in the 1960 British volume, *The Adventure of the Christmas Pudding*, one had been published in 1933 in the British volume, *The Hound of Death*, while the others were to turn up, years later, in *Poirot's Early Cases* (1974) and the posthumous *Miss Marple's Final Cases* (1979).

In the title story 'Double Sin', written in 1929, Poirot and Hastings undertake a journey across Devon from south to north in order to be of service to Poirot's friend, the Jewish theatrical agent, Joseph Aarons. 'If you want to know anything about the theatrical profession,' Poirot had once said, 'there is one person who knows all there is to know and that is my old friend Mr Joseph Aarons.' Aarons had been of assistance to Poirot in *Murder on the Links*, *The Big Four* and *The Mystery of the Blue Train*: in 'Double Sin', Poirot solves Mr Aaron's problem but finds the mystery of a theft from a passenger on the coach in which he and Hastings have travelled across Devon much more intriguing. Hastings, needless to say, finds the auburn-haired young lady who is the victim of the theft equally intriguing. A pleasant little tale, 'Double Sin' is an excellent example of the early Poirot stories which Hastings used to narrate.

Hastings plays no part in 'Wasps' Nest', another 1929 Poirot story in which the great detective confesses to being able to pick pockets, and manages to solve a murder in the planning stage, thus preventing it from taking place.

'The Theft of the Royal Ruby', the longest story in the volume is said by such writers on Agatha Christie as John Barnard and Nancy Blue Wynne[14] to be almost identical with 'The Adventure of the Christmas Pudding'. It is not almost identical: it is, word for word, the same story. Nothing is changed except the title.

Though it was to appear later in *Miss Marple's Final Cases*, 'The Dressmaker's Doll' is not a Miss Marple story but one of Agatha Christie's tales of the supernatural, and a particularly effective one with a wondering half-close rather than a conclusion. 'Greenshaw's Folly', an authentic Miss Marple story, had appeared in the volume, *The Adventure of the Christmas Pudding*, in 1960.

The earliest story in *Double Sin* is 'The Double Clue', a Poirot adventure narrated by Hastings, and dating from 1925. This is the story in which Poirot first encounters the Countess Vera Rossakoff who was to impress him deeply, who would remain in his thoughts for the rest of his life, but who would actually cross his path again only twice: in *The Big Four* (1927) and 'The Capture of Cerberus' from *The Labours of Hercules* (1947). 'What a woman!' Poirot cries enthusiastically to Hastings, after his initial involvement with the Countess in 'The Double Clue'.

'The Last Seance' is the powerful supernatural tale which, written in 1926, was one of the most successful stories in *The Hound of Death* (see p. 72). The final story in *Double Sin* is a Miss Marple adventure, 'Sanctuary', which makes use not only of the village of Chipping Cleghorn, the locale of *A Murder is Announced* (1950), but also of some of the characters from that novel: the Rev. Harmon the vicar with a classical education which he delights in showing off, his wife Bunch who is a friend of Miss Marple, and the vicarage cat, Tiglath Pileser, named after an Assyrian king. Inspector Craddock from *A Murder is Announced* also turns up. (Agatha Christie gave the serial rights in this story to the Westminster Abbey Appeal Fund.)

The Pale Horse (1961)

The title of *The Pale Horse*, the 1961 new Christie novel and one of the most fascinating of the crime novels of Mrs Christie's old age, derives from the New Testament. Chapter 6, verse 8, of The Book of Revelation of St John the Divine, reads: 'And I looked, and behold a pale horse: and his name that sat upon him was Death, and Hell followed with him.'

In the novel, the Pale Horse is the name of an organization which appears to be a group of professional murderers with a difference, the difference being that their method of assassination is based upon black magic. The Pale Horse is also the name of an old house in the village of Much Deeping; a house which in years gone by was an inn and which is now the home of three women who are thought to be the local witches, and who certainly do some very unpleasant things with live cockerels. (There is a great deal of blood: the narrator 'felt horribly sick', and the more squeamish reader may too, at the end of Chapter 17.)

This may sound like distinctly unpromising material for Agatha Christie, but it is not. On the contrary, *The Pale Horse* is an extraordinary study of evil, and if, at some point, it requires our willing suspension of disbelief, this is not for reasons connected with witchcraft, though belief in the efficacy of witchcraft is an important element in the proceedings.

None of Mrs Christie's regular investigators appears in *The Pale Horse*, unless Mrs Ariadne Oliver can be thought a regular investigator, for she plays a leading role. This is, incidentally, the first time since she met Hercule Poirot (in *Cards on the Table*, 1936) that Mrs Oliver appears in a novel in which he does not. Her only other non-Poirot adventures, in fact, were back in the days when she was a freelance employee of Mr Parker Pyne (*Parker Pyne Investigates*, 1934).

Mrs Oliver becomes involved in the mystery of the Pale Horse because she is a friend of the young historian, Mark Easterbrook, who is the narrator of most of the novel. It is, as they say, a small world, for Mark's cousin is Rhoda Dawes who, in 1936, had been involved in the investigation of Mr Shaitana's murder, in *Cards on the Table*. She married Colonel Despard, one of the suspects in that case, and she and her husband play a major part in the investigation of the Pale Horse murders. Oddly, Despard's first name, which was John in 1936, has become Hugh in 1961.

The Reverend Caleb Dane Calthrop and his wife, old friends from *The Moving Finger* (1943), are also on hand. The investigation is an interesting example of the collaboration of amateur with professional. The amateur, Mark Easterbrook, puts in some good work, but he is by no means the brilliant outsider who makes the stolid, local police look stupid, and it is his professional colleague, a somewhat philosophical detective called LeJeune, who arrives at the correct solution to the mystery.

In addition to its extraordinarily ingenious plot, there are many felicities in *The Pale Horse*. Mrs Oliver, for instance, is presented in such a way that her similarity to Mrs Christie is more clearly marked than ever. She really is a delightful piece of amiable self-parody.

There is a curious passage in Chapter 4, in which a character tells a story, not strictly relevant to the plot, of finding himself waiting in the reception room of a mental home,

> and there was a nice elderly lady there, sipping a glass of milk. She made some conventional remark about the weather and then suddenly she leant forward and asked: 'Is it your poor child who's buried there behind the fireplace?'

Mrs Christie was to make more significant use of this same incident seven years later in *By the Pricking of My Thumbs* (and she had already done so in *Sleeping Murder*, written in the 1940s, though not published until shortly after the author's death). Could this little incident, of which she made so much (although not in *The Pale Horse*) have been something from her own experience? Did some little old lady in a waiting room somewhere ask Mrs Christie that disconcerting question?

The character who tells that story in *The Pale Horse*, with no greater relevance to the plot also offers his views on how to produce the witches' scenes in *Macbeth*. Mrs Christie makes Jane Marple in a later novel[15] expatiate upon this as well, and suggest the same approach to the problem. It was, apparently, just one of the many bees in that positive hive of a bonnet.

The Pale Horse is a remarkably fresh and imaginative creation for a writer entering her seventies. As another writer on Agatha Christie has already noticed, she 'makes use of "The Box", a piece of pseudo-scientific hocus-pocus fashionable in the West Country in the fifties (one of the things that drove Waugh to the verge of lunacy, as narrated in *Pinfold*).'[16]

In her autobiography, Mrs Christie describes in some detail someone she knew and worked with during the First World War. 'His memory remained with me so long,' she wrote, 'that it was still there waiting when I first conceived the idea of writing my book *The Pale Horse* – and that must have been, I suppose, nearly fifty years later.' A very long gestation period, but then it produced one of her own favourites among her crime novels.

Life imitates art, and life has plagiarized *The Pale Horse* mercilessly. To the author's distress, a series of murders was committed in Bovington, Hertfordshire, ten years after the publication of the novel, using virtually the same method. The London *Daily Mail* set out the resemblances between the real murderer and Mrs Christie's, and quoted a senior detective as confirming the similarity.[17]

Max Mallowan, in his memoirs, reports a letter which Agatha Christie received in 1975 from a woman in a Latin-American country whose knowledge of *The Pale Horse* led her to recognize and thwart a case of attempted murder. The letter concluded: 'Of this I am quite, quite certain – had I not read *The Pale Horse*, X would not have survived; it was only the prompt medication which saved him; and the doctors, even if he had gone to hospital, would not have known in time what his trouble was.'

The Pale Horse connected with real life a third time, shortly after the death of Agatha Christie, when a nurse, on duty at the bedside of a child dying of an ailment which doctors were unable to diagnose, was passing the time reading Mrs Christie's novel. One of the child's symptoms was paralleled in the novel, a fact which the nurse brought to the attention of the specialists attending her patient. Laboratory tests were made which led to the child's life being saved, thanks to the depth and accuracy of Agatha Christie's knowledge in a certain area. To say more would put the potential reader's enjoyment of *The Pale Horse* at risk.

The Mirror Crack'd from Side to Side (1962)

In March, 1962, a UNESCO report stated that Agatha Christie was now the most widely read British author in the world, with Shakespeare coming a poor second. The tenth year of *The Mousetrap* ended with a huge birthday party at the Savoy. A cake with ten candles was ceremoniously cut by the author. A new novel was published in time to catch the Christmas sale, and three one-act plays were produced on tour and in London. During the year, Colonel Archibald Christie died.

The novel was *The Mirror Crack'd from Side to Side*. This is not the first time that Agatha Christie had occasion to refer to Tennysons's *The Lady of Shalott*:[18]

> Out flew the web and floated wide;
> The mirror crack'd from side to side;
> 'The curse is come upon me,' cried
> The Lady of Shalott.

The lines are quoted in the novel by Miss Marple's old friend, Dolly Bantry. When her husband, Colonel Bantry, had died, Mrs Bantry sold their house Gossington Hall (where the body had been found in *The Body in the Library*) and the land attached to it, retaining for herself what had been the East Lodge. After the huge house had changed hands once or twice, it was acquired by the famous filmstar, Marina Gregg, returning to England after years in Hollywood.

At a fête held in the grounds of Gossington Hall, one of the guests dies after swallowing a poisoned drink. It seems likely that the poison was intended for Marina Gregg, and indeed shortly before the death of the guest, Mrs Bantry had noticed 'a kind of frozen look' come over the face of the famous star. Attempting to describe it later to Jane Marple, she resorted to Tennyson and 'The mirror crack'd from side to side; "The doom [sic] has come upon me," cried the Lady of Shalott.'

The Mirror Crack'd (the shortened form of the title under which the novel was published in the USA) is the last of the Agatha Christie mysteries to be set in Jane Marple's St Mary Mead; in fact, it is the last of the English village mysteries. St Mary Mead is not what it was, Miss Marple thinks to herself as she sits knitting.

The old landmarks were still there, the church and the vicarage and Dr Haydock's house, but the appearance of so many of the shops in the village street had been rendered unrecognizable by modernization, and the new housing development was, to Miss Marple, an eye-sore. Miss Marple was growing old, and so was Agatha Christie, who was now nearly as old as her beloved village sleuth had always been. In *The Mirror Crack'd*, she charts the changes with a not unsympathetic accuracy, but never at the expense of the plot which is kept firmly in the foreground. The first murder is followed by others. Miss Marple's young friend Dermot Craddock, now a Chief Inspector, investigates, but it is she who arrives at the truth. A close reading of Chapter 2 suggests that Miss Marple is thinking along the right tracks well before the first murder has been committed.

Permanently disfigured by progress, St Mary Mead is temporarily either disfigured or adorned by the famous filmstar Marina Gregg, her husband Jason Hudd, who is to direct her new movie, and several other film people. One of Marina Gregg's greatest films had been *Mary, Queen of Scots*: the new film was to be about Elisabeth of Austria. This is not a world in which Miss Marple moves with great certainty, and she is at a further disadvantage in not having been present on the occasion when the first victim died. She has to rely on Dolly Bantry's account of what happened. The final death, after the mystery has been uncovered, is perhaps a suicide, perhaps a compassionate murder. Miss Marple is content not to know for certain.

Some months before publication, Agatha Christie visited a movie studio, where *Murder at the Gallop*, the second of the Miss Marple films, was being made. She visited the set while filming was in progress, and met Margaret Rutherford who played Miss Marple. Mrs Christie had already expressed herself on the subject of the actress's unsuitability for the role, but the two women got on remarkably well and, when *The Mirror Crack'd from Side to Side* was published in the autumn, it was dedicated 'To Margaret Rutherford in admiration'.

When *The Mirror Crack'd* came to be filmed, many years later, in 1980, both Agatha Christie and Margaret Rutherford were dead, and Miss Marple was played by Angela Lansbury. Though it was produced for EMI by the same team which had been responsible for the films of *Murder on the Orient Express* (1974) and *Death on the Nile* (1978), and was, like those films, a star-studded affair, *The*

Mirror Crack'd (the movie used this abbreviated title) was distinctly inferior to them. The blame is to be shared among the script-writers, Jonathan Hales and Barry Sandler, and the director, Guy Hamilton. The writers attempted to jazz up the dialogue with ghastly double-entendres and phrases which one never thought to hear in Agatha Christie. One actress says of another that she entered, 'looking like shit'. There is an embarrassingly coy reference to the police inspector's 'night-stick'. A number of tired old jokes which had been going the theatrical rounds for years are worked into the script as examples of witty Hollywood-type repartee.

Already crippled by its dialogue, the film is finally dealt its death blow by the slow, heavy and cliché-ridden direction. You sympathize with the cast, headed by Elizabeth Taylor (Marina Gregg), Rock Hudson (her husband), Angela Lansbury (Miss Marple), Edward Fox (Inspector Dermot Craddock, here said, for no apparent reason, to be Miss Marple's nephew), Tony Curtis, Kim Novak and Geraldine Chaplin.

Presumably because the mass audience would not be quite certain who Elisabeth of Austria was, the film Marina Gregg is making is about Mary, Queen of Scots. Perhaps a remake of her earlier success?

Rule of Three (1962)

Three short plays, intended to be produced together on one evening, formed Agatha Christie's farewell to her London theatre public. Nearly ten years later, she was to write her final play, but it closed on tour without reaching the West End (see pp. 113–14).

The three one-act plays of 1962 are well contrasted. When they were first produced, under the collective title of *Rule of Three*, they were performed in the following order: (i) *The Rats*, (ii) *Afternoon at the Seaside*, (iii) *The Patient*. However, like the plays which make up Noel Coward's *Tonight at 8.30*, they do not depend upon being produced in any particular order or even being produced together at all. (As separate one-acters, they have proved useful to amateur drama societies.)

Tension is well sustained in *The Rats*, a tautly effective little melodrama set in a flat in Hampstead, and involving only four characters, one of them described by the author as 'a young man of twenty-eight or -nine, the pansy type, very elegant, amusing, inclined to be spiteful'. Though the other three characters are more charitably described, they are all 'rats' of a kind, though only two find themselves caught in a trap. An important element in the plot derives from the story 'The Mystery of the Baghdad Chest' (also known, in an expanded version, as 'The Mystery of the Spanish Chest'), which is to be found in the 1939 volume, *The Regatta Mystery*.

The central play, *Afternoon at the Seaside*, is, in a way, disappointing in comparison with the plays which precede and follow it, though it provides a certain light relief from their more dramatic atmosphere; its weakness of construction is probably more easily disguised when it is performed away from the other two plays. There is a wisp of a plot concerning a stolen necklace, but the real charm of *Afternoon at the Seaside* lies in its curiously old-fashioned, pre-war picture (though it is not specifically set in the past) of the lower-middleclasses relaxing on a crowded beach at a resort called, improbably, Little Slyppingeon-Sea. Both setting and plot owe something to a story, 'The Rajah's Emerald', from *The Listerdale Mystery* (1934) and *The Golden Ball* (1971). Uneconomically, the play requires a cast of twelve, with accents ranging from false genteel to unashamed cockney. Full marks to Agatha Christie for trying something different. As one of the London reviewers said:

> Well, well, Agatha, we never knew. All these years writing serious thrillers and then you come up with *Afternoon at the Seaside*. It is just as if you had sent us a naughty postcard from Brighton. *Afternoon* bears all the marks of that particular brand of rude, breezy humour . . .[19]

The final play, *The Patient*, with a cast of nine, is set in a private room in a nursing-home where ingenious means are found to enable a woman, totally paralyzed and unable to speak after a fall from her balcony, to indicate whether she fell accidentally or was pushed. Those suspected of having pushed her are assembled, and the heavily bandaged patient is wheeled in. Clues abound, but so do surprises, and the name of the would-be murderer, withheld until the final line, will come as the final surprise to most. 'You may come out from behind that curtain now, — —,' says the police Inspector. The murderer comes out from behind the curtain and takes a pace down stage. The lights black out and the curtain falls.

When *Rule of Three* opened its pre-London tour in Aberdeen, *The Patient* ended differently, with the identity of the murderer not revealed to the audience. At this stage of its life, the play ended with the recorded voice of Agatha Christie pointing out that the audience had been given all the clues. Who was the villain?

This did not go down well on the first night in Aberdeen, and Peter Saunders sent a telegram to the playwright who was in Teheran with her husband, informing her that they were reverting to her alternative ending. When *The Patient* arrived in London, on 20 December 1962, it was an excellent mystery thriller, with an unbeatable final line.

Rule of Three received mixed reviews from the London press, ranging from 'as rich and succulent a mixed grill as we've had in the theatre for a long, long time' to 'bricks cannot be made without straw, and this commodity Miss [sic] Christie has surprisingly failed to provide.' Mixed grill *sans* straw, *Rule of Three* survived at the Duchess Theatre for no more than ten weeks. The four leading players who appeared in all three plays were David Langton, Betty McDowall, Mercy Haystead and Raymond Bowers. The director was Hubert Gregg, who had also directed *The Hollow* (1951), *The Unexpected Guest* (1959) and *Go Back for Murder* (1960).

Notes to pp. 168–199

1 In *An Autobiography*.

2 *Mallowan's Memoirs*.

3 The story had appeared in the 1934 volume of stories *The Hound of Death* (UK only) and in *Witness for the Prosecution*, a volume of stories published in the USA in 1948.

4 The splendid, huge old theatre has since been demolished, and a monstrosity of a new theatre, the New London, built in its place.

5 There are thirty roles, but two were 'doubled'. The play can, in fact, be performed with a cast of ten men and five women by doubling some minor roles and dispensing with others.

6 In *An Autobiography*.

7 *An Autobiography*.

8 *The Diaries of Evelyn Waugh* (ed. Michael Davie) (London, 1976).

9 France and Britain had begun to bomb Cairo and the Suez Canal area on 31 October. By 20 November, a United Nations emergency force was supervising a cease-fire.

10 See the photograph of the boathouse at Greenway House, between pp. 64–5.

11 A.L. Rowse: *Memories of Men and Women* (London, 1980).

12 Max Mallowan: *Mallowan's Memoirs* (London, 1977).

13 To Gwen Robyns.

14 In *A Talent to Deceive* (1980), and *An Agatha Christie Chronology* (1976).

15 *Nemesis* (1971). Tommy Beresford in *By the Pricking of My Thumbs* (1968) is also allowed to have views on *Macbeth*.

16 Robert Barnard: *A Talent to Deceive* (1980). The reference is to Evelyn Waugh's *The Ordeal of Gilbert Pinfold* (1957).

17 A forensic specialist's remembrance of *The Pale Horse* led to the identification and capture of the murderer. The London *Daily Telegraph* report of the trial, on 24 June 1972, appeared under the heading, 'Agatha Christie Gave Doctor Clue to Poison'.

18 It was quoted appropriately in *Dead Man's Mirror*.

19 Quoted in Hubert Gregg: *Agatha Christie and all that Mousetrap* (London, 1980)

5

Towards the Last Cases

The Clocks (1963)

When a man is found murdered in the seaside town of Crowdean, in the house of a blind woman, in a room full of clocks most of which do not belong there, the problem is at first one for the local police, and for a young man named Colin Lamb who just 'happened' to be passing by as the body was discovered by a typist who, understandably, screamed and ran out of the house. Colin Lamb, it soon transpires, is not what he at first had seemed to be: he is a British Intelligence agent of some kind, and he is working on a case which involves the nearby Naval Station at Portlebury (for which read, probably, Portsmouth). Colin Lamb takes the problem to his old friend and mentor, Hercule Poirot, for his father and Poirot used to be colleagues.

Colin has changed his name ('My young friend Colin – but why do you call yourself by the name of Lamb?' asks Poirot). His father had been a Police Superintendent ('I thought the good Superintendent was going to write his memoirs?': Poirot again), so it is safe to assume that Colin is the son of Superintendent Battle. In fact, Mrs Christie made the same assumption, for she is quoted [1] as having said of Colin Lamb 'I rather think that he is Superintendent Battle's son'.

The Clocks begins promisingly, with its plethora of those instruments, and although its plot becomes somewhat diffuse and loses impetus well before the end, it is one of the more unusual late Christies. There are, really, two separate plots which the author twists together at the end.

An incidental delight in *The Clocks* is the sequence in which Poirot instructs Colin Lamb in the art of detection, lecturing him on famous murder cases of the past (Charles Bravo, Constance Kent, Lizzie Borden) before turning to the detective in fiction and criticizing the murder mysteries he has been reading. (As we shall discover in a later novel, Poirot is at work on a book of his own on the subject of crime detection.) He finds *The Leavenworth Case* admirable for 'its period atmosphere, its studied and deliberate melodrama'. Modern readers will not have heard of it: it is the first of a number of murder mysteries by Anna Katharine Green (1846–1935), and was published in 1878. Poirot finds vigour and life in *The Adventures of Arsène Lupin*. Arsène Lupin, a character invented by Maurice Leblanc, was the hero of a series of American films in the thirties but is also forgotten today. Nor is *The Mystery of the Yellow Room*, by Gaston Leroux, author of *The Phantom of the Opera*, any longer in circulation, although Poirot thinks it a masterpiece. Agatha Christie read *The Mystery of the Yellow Room* as a teenager, when it first came out in 1908, and found it 'a particularly baffling mystery, well worked out and planned, of the type some call unfair and others have to admit is almost unfair, but not quite: one *could* just have seen a neat little clue cleverly slipped in.[2] It undoubtedly influenced the kind of story she was to write.

Poirot goes on to criticize such fictional writers of crime novels as Cyril Quain, Garry Gregson (a character in *The Clocks*) and Ariadne Oliver, before lashing into the American West Coast school. He ends by picking up *The Adventures of Sherlock Holmes* and uttering reverently the one word, *'Maitre!'* None of this is at all helpful to Colin Lamb who has come to Poirot with his clocks mystery, but it is a delightful interlude for the reader. Poirot sends Colin away with a few lines of verse from Lewis Carroll ('The time has come, the Walrus said, 'to talk of many things . . .') which, he says, is 'the best I can do for you, *mon cher*'. But, in the long run, he does considerably better, even though luck plays its part as well. Poirot might not have arrived at the solution to the problem had he not been engaged upon reading all those murder mysteries. Perhaps the little seminar on crime fiction was not, after all, an irrelevant aside.

A Caribbean Mystery (1964)

During a visit to Torquay in 1964, Agatha Christie 'summoned up the resolution' to drive up Barton Road, where her childhood home, Ashfield, had once stood. Two or three years earlier, when she first learned that the house was to be demolished to make way for a new housing estate, she had attempted to buy it back and perhaps make a gift of Ashfield to an old people's home. But she had been too late, and now she found herself being driven slowly up the hill to the cluster of new houses:

> There was nothing that could even stir a memory. They were the meanest, shoddiest little houses I had ever seen. None of the great trees remained. The ash-trees in the wood had gone, the remains of the big beech-tree, the Wellingtonia, the pines, the elms that bordered the kitchen garden, the dark ilex – I could not even determine in my mind where the house had stood. And then I saw the only clue – the defiant remains of what had once been a monkey puzzle, struggling to exist in a cluttered back yard. There was no scrap of garden anywhere. All was asphalt. No blade of grass showed green.
> I said 'Brave monkey puzzle' to it, and turned away.[3]

By 1981, not even the monkey puzzle[4] remained. The houses may not have deserved Agatha Christie's adjectives, but they were cramped, suburban and ordinary. The view across to the bay was still there, at least from the roadway and intermittently, though probably not from any of the houses which clustered about the space once occupied by Ashfield.

The series of Miss Marple films which had begun two years earlier with *Murder, She Said* (see p. 184) and had continued in 1963 with *Murder at the Gallop* (p. 197), ended in 1964 with *Murder Most Foul* (see p. 203) and *Murder Ahoy! Murder Ahoy!* made a most ignominious conclusion to the series for, unlike the earlier three films, it was not even remotely based on an Agatha Christie novel or story, but had an original screenplay by David Pursall and Jack Seddon which involved Miss Marple in investigating murder and blackmail on a Royal Navy training ship. Margaret Rutherford was again Jane Marple, Charles Tingwell and Stringer Davis were also retained from the earlier films, and Lionel

Jeffries played a leading role. The director, as with the other Miss Marple films, was George Pollock. *Murder Ahoy!* was received so unenthusiastically by audiences that plans for a fifth Jane Marple film, to be based on *The Body in the Library*, were abandoned.

Agatha Christie's attitude to these British MGM movies was unequivocal:

I kept off films for years because I thought they'd give me too many heartaches. Then I sold the rights to MGM, hoping they'd use them for television. But they chose films. It was too awful! They did things like taking a Poirot and putting Miss Marple in it! And all the climaxes were so poor, you could see them coming! I get an unregenerate pleasure when I think they're not being a success. They wrote their own script for the last one – nothing to do with me at all – *Murder Ahoy!* One of the silliest things you ever saw! It got very bad reviews, I'm delighted to say.[5]

A new Jane Marple title, *A Caribbean Mystery*, was published during 1964.

In *A Caribbean Mystery*, one of the best of the later Miss Marple novels, Jane Marple is sent by her affectionate and generous nephew, Raymond West (the 'modern' novelist), on a holiday to the West Indies. Agatha Christie had visited the West Indies in the late fifties, and chose to place Jane Marple's adventure on the fictitious small island of St Honoré. So here is the frail but resilient old dear, 'far from the rigours of the English climate, with a nice little bungalow of her own', friendly West Indian girls to wait on her, and for company a few other guests, among them the elderly and extremely wealthy Jason Rafiel.

One of the guests, a not unpleasant but somewhat boring old ex-Indian Army Major, has been regaling Miss Marple with tales from his repertoire and is about to show what he claims is 'the picture of a murderer' when suddenly he stares fixedly over Miss Marple's shoulder, abandons his story abruptly, blushes in embarrassment and changes the subject. A few hours later he is dead, and Miss Marple finds herself investigating the circumstances of his death. In this she is encouraged by old Mr Rafiel.

The fixed look of surprise or horror, over the shoulder of the person addressed, a hypnotized stare at – what? – has been offered by Mrs Christie more than once previously. There are instances in *Appointment with Death*, *Towards Zero* and *The Mirror Crack'd from Side to Side*. It is a device she was always able to use effectively. What, you wonder can the character have seen? The answer is embedded somewhere in the narrative, or at least a clue will be given, though you may have to search for it, for the author continues to play fair. Or does she?

The concealed relationship is another of Mrs Christie's ploys, and here the reader is really at her mercy. If it is represented to us, as well as to the other characters in the novel, that A detests B but loves C, what can we say when it is subsequently revealed that A and B are, in fact, lovers and have been plotting against C? What but 'Well, who would have guessed it?'. Mrs Christie is fascinated by hidden relationships of this kind; and they do, in some curious and slightly disturbing manner, relate to the kinds of subterfuge that can be encountered in real life, where A and B may, for reasons of politeness or expedience as well as for less innocent reasons, be concerned to conceal the real nature of their relationship.

It is unusual to encounter Miss Marple away from the south of England.

Indeed, this is the only known occasion on which she has ventured abroad. Yet she fits as cosily into the picture at the Golden Palm Hotel, St Honoré, as she does at the vicarage in St Mary Mead. And the relationship she establishes with Mr Rafiel, a character who posthumously will influence a later Jane Marple adventure, *Nemesis*, is both charming and touching. Mr Rafiel is crippled and in ill health. As he takes his leave of Miss Marple who is about to catch her plane back to England, he says to her, paraphrasing Suetonius, '*Ave Caesar, nos morituri te salutamus*'. Though she has no Latin, Miss Marple understands what he is telling her. Little does she realize that she will hear, indirectly, from Mr Rafiel again.

At Bertram's Hotel (1965)

In September, 1965, Agatha Christie celebrated her seventy-fifth birthday. A few weeks later, she finished writing the autobiography which she had been working on, spasmodically, for fifteen years. She decided to end it at the age of seventy-five because, as she put it, 'it seems the right moment to stop. Because, as far as life is concerned, that is all there is to say.' The final paragraph of her typescript reads:

> A child says 'Thank God for my good dinner.' What can I say at seventy-five? 'Thank God for my good life, and for all the love that has been given to me.'

An Autobiography was published posthumously in 1977 (see p. 241).

Surprise! Surprise!, a volume of stories published in the United States during the year, consisted of thirteen stories, all of which had already appeared in earlier volumes. The new Christie title in 1965 was *At Bertram's Hotel*.

In *At Bertram's Hotel*, Raymond and Joan West decide once again to do something for 'poor old Aunt Jane'. Joan West remarks that, 'She enjoyed her trip to the West Indies, I think, though it is a pity she had to get mixed up in a murder case.' (Actually, this leads to an inconsistency in *Nemesis* in which Miss Marple says that she did not tell Joan or Raymond about the murders. Both Agatha Christie and Jane Marple were by now considerably advanced in years. Let us assume that the error was Jane Marple's. Perhaps she did tell the Wests, and later forgot she had done so.)

This time, offered two weeks at one of Bournemouth's best hotels, Miss Marple murmurs that what she would really like is a week at Bertram's Hotel in London. She had stayed there with her uncle, who was Canon of Ely, when she was fourteen. Bertram's, an elegant, though somewhat dowdy hotel in a quiet street in Mayfair, had been patronized over a long stretch of years 'by the higher *échelons* of the clergy, dowager ladies of the aristocracy up from the country, girls on their way home for the holidays from expensive finishing schools.' The more glamorous rich might prefer the Savoy, the Dorchester or Claridges, but, as one of the characters in *At Bertram's Hotel* puts it, 'there are a lot of people who come from abroad at rare intervals and who expect this country to be – well, I won't go back as far as Dickens, but they've read *Cranford* and Henry James, and they don't want to find this country just the same as their own! So they go back home and say: "There's a wonderful place in London; Bertram's Hotel, it's called. It's just like stepping back a hundred years. It just *is* old England!"'

It is an open secret that Agatha Christie used, as the model for Bertram's, Brown's Hotel which has entrances in both Dover and Albemarle Streets. Many have thought that Brown's, whose atmosphere is so restful and agreeable, is simply too good to be true. Mrs Christie may have had this feeling, for her Bertram's Hotel certainly is too good to be true. Miss Marple finds, during her stay, that some very strange things are happening. There is, in due course, a murder, but it does not occur until quite late in the narrative. Murder is not, after all, the only crime in the book, and the great virtue of *At Bertram's Hotel* is that its pace is leisurely enough for Miss Marple's by now somewhat woolly thought processes to be explored in detail, but not so leisurely that your attention is in danger of wandering.

In her mid-seventies, the Miss Marple who stays at Bertram's is much more like her creator Agatha Christie than was the younger (sixtyish) Miss Marple of *Murder at the Vicarage* (1930). This is understandable: Mrs Christie was in her late thirties when she first created the character of Jane Marple. At seventy-five, having allowed Miss Marple to age no more than fifteen years between 1930 and 1965, she is writing now of a woman of her own age. Some of Jane Marple's reflections on comfortable chairs, horrid modern loos, and the latest fashions would not be at all out of place in Mrs Christie's autobiography.

Bertram's itself is the chief character in the novel. It is presented in such a way that you cannot fail to respond warmly to the old place. But, just as Agatha Christie's ostensibly pleasant characters sometimes turn out to be killers, so, too, a favourite place may well not be what it at first appears to be. Bertram's repays close scrutiny. Having encouraged us to indulge in nostalgia, the cynical old crime novelist ends by laughing at our sentimentality.

Not all the human characters are upstaged by the hotel itself. Elvira Blake is one of the most interesting of the elderly novelist's portrayals of modern youth, and the paternal figure of Chief Inspector Davy (nicknamed 'Father' by his staff) is engaging enough for the reader to regret that this is his only appearance in the pages of Agatha Christie. The enigmatic and mysterious Mr Robinson, whom we met in a Poirot novel, *Cat Among the Pigeons*, and who will also appear in *Passenger to Frankfurt* (1970) and *Postern of Fate* (1973), is visited by Chief Inspector Davy to whom he gives some useful information.

In addition to Brown's-Bertram's, another London landmark appears in *At Bertram's Hotel*, but under its own name: the Army and Navy Stores in Victoria Street, a favourite department store which 'had been a haunt of Miss Marple's aunt in days long gone'. It was not, of course, quite the same nowadays, Miss Marple thought to herself, but at least she did not suspect it of having been put to criminal use. This is not the only Christie work in which there is mention of the Army and Navy Stores. Clearly Mrs Christie felt an affection for the old place. Would her affection have survived its renovation and rebuilding in the mid-seventies? Probably.

At Bertram's Hotel collected a number of highly favourable reviews. Elizabeth Smart, author of *By Grand Central Station I Sat Down and Wept*, wrote in *Queen* that it was 'marvellous' and that Miss Marple was 'in cracking form'. In the *New Statesman*, however, Brigid Brophy complained that the author offered nothing like enough signposts to give the reader a chance to beat Miss Marple or the police to the solution. This is a fair comment. *At Bertram's Hotel* is a murder mystery almost by accident.

Star Over Bethlehem and other stories (1965)

In addition to the usual 'Christie for Christmas', in 1965 there was also a 'Christie Mallowan for Christmas' for, under the name Agatha Christie Mallowan, *Star Over Bethlehem*, a slim volume of stories and poems on religious themes, was published in the autumn. Accompanied by decorative drawings, the volume was reviewed by some newspapers in their childrens' book section, and indeed the presentation of the book was such that it seemed to be directed at children. But it was not easy to discern exactly whom the stories (and, *pace* the title, poems) were written for, except, of course, for the author herself. On the surface, the stories and poems are not only religious but also charming and verging on the sentimental. But one or two of the stories are not likely to be understood by any but the most precocious of children.

For the pious adult, perhaps: though piety, too, will find certain aspects of this little book somewhat disturbing. Perhaps the best description of the contents of *Star Over Bethlehem* is that suggested by Max Mallowan[6] who thought that they must 'fairly be styled "Holy Detective Stories"'. 'They were rather fun to do,' Mrs Christie said of these stories. 'It's astonishing how one always wants to do something that isn't quite one's work. Like papering walls – which one does exceedingly badly, but enjoys because it doesn't count as work.'

There are six stories and five poems in the volume.[7] The poems are not very remarkable: 'A Greeting' is conventionally Christmas-like; 'A Wreath for Christmas' and 'Gold, Frankincense and Myrrh' no less so; and 'The Saints of God' is interesting, in context, only because it does in verse what the story preceding it ('Promotion in the Highest') has done in prose. 'Jenny by the Sky', an odd and passionate poem, is the only one which Agatha Christie chose to reprint (with its punctuation improved) in her *Poems* of 1973.

The title-story, 'Star Over Bethlehem', offers what is for the most part a pious gloss on the accounts of the nativity in the Gospels of St Matthew and St Luke, though it has its unconventional aspects, and very few children would be likely to grasp all its implications. The idea of involving Lucifer in the Annunciation is an interesting one. The eponymous hero of the anthropomorphic little tale, 'The Naughty Donkey', is an engaging creature whose story can safely be told to the youngest child: a gentle and poetic invention which is perhaps a little too cloyingly pious. The Holy Family are involved in these two stories and in 'The Island', a story about a reunion between the resurrected Christ and his beloved disciple, John, now an elderly man. Too confusing for children, and probably too naive for most adults.

The remaining three stories, though still religious, are set in modern times. In 'The Water Bus', a somewhat uncharitable woman is touched by the cloak of Christ on a launch going down the Thames to Greenwich. This tale takes abortion in its stride. A backward child encounters God in a country garden in the story called 'In the Cool of the Evening'. 'Promotion in the Highest' brings to life, on 1 January in the year AD 2000, the saints from a fourteenth-century wooden screen.

These are stories and poems which Agatha Christie wrote purely to please herself, and thus they are of interest as an indication of the way she thought about her religion. They show that her views are really conventional Church of England with a twist.

Third Girl (1966)

In 1966 Max Mallowan visited the United States of America, at the invitation of the Smithsonian Institute and the American Institute of Archaeology, to lecture in connection with his two-volume work, *Nimrud and its Remains*, which was published in that year. Enormous public interest in whether or not his famous wife would accompany him was expressed in advance, and in the event she did, appearing with him at interviews and sitting in the front row of the audience at his public lectures.

Mrs Christie herself gave a number of interviews. She told one reporter that it now took her 'six weeks of hard work' to produce a novel, and said to another, 'When I re-read those first books, I'm amazed at the number of servants drifting about. And nobody is really doing any work, they're always having tea on the lawn.'

She accepted a lucrative offer from an American television company to write a three-part script based on Charles Dickens's *Bleak House*, but became so disenchanted with script conferences, discussions, and interference of various kinds, that after having written two parts of the script and received her fee she withdrew from the project. She told her friend A.L. Rowse that she had found the work fascinating but that the constant interference of others had given her 'headaches from worry over her work', which had never happened to her in the past.

The previous year, *The Mousetrap* had celebrated its 5,000th performance, and in 1966 at the August meeting of the Devon and Exeter Steeplechases and Hurdle Races, the 'Mousetrap' Challenge Cup Handicap Steeple Chase was inaugurated, with a prize of £350. This subsequently became an annual event, with a cup donated by Agatha Christie and competed for yearly.

In the autumn, a collection of Jane Marple stories, all of which had previously appeared in other volumes, was published in the United States under the title, *Thirteen Clues for Miss Marple*.

Most published interviews with Agatha Christie are disappointing; she was rarely at ease talking to strangers. She must, however, have enjoyed her conversation with Francis Wyndham, who had visited her at Wallingford in the autumn of 1965, for the long article, 'The Algebra of Agatha Christie', which Wyndham published in the London *Sunday Times* on 27 February 1966, is enlivened by a number of fascinating observations by Mrs Christie, in addition to those which have already been mentioned:

'Modern taste has changed very largely from detective stories to *crime* stories. What are known in America as "gabblers" – just a series of violent episodes succeeding each other. I find these very boring.'

'If I'd known it was for life, I'd have chosen some rather younger detectives: God knows how old they must be by now! I'm afraid Poirot gets more and more unreal as time goes by. A private detective who takes cases just doesn't exist these days, so it becomes more difficult to involve him and make him convincing in so doing. The problem doesn't arise with Miss Marple: there are still plenty of them drifting about.'

'Oh, I'm an incredible sausage machine, a perfect *sausage* machine! I always think it must end soon. Then I'm so glad when the next one comes

207

along and it's not so difficult to think of something new after all. And, of course, as you get older you change, you see things from another angle. But probably I could write the same book again and again, and nobody would notice. Perhaps I'd better keep that up my sleeve, in case I ever run completely out of ideas!'

'A terrible lot of girls write fan letters from America. They're always so *earnest*! And Indians are worse. "I have loved all your books and think you must be a very noble woman". Now what on earth is there in my books to make anybody think I'm *noble*? I'm afraid the fans are sometimes disappointed in my photographs – they write "I had no idea you were so old." I get a good many asking curious questions: "What emotions do you experience when you write?" All a *great* deal too sincere. What I'm writing is meant to be entertainment. I got one rather upsetting letter from a West African: "I'm filled with enthusiasm for you and want you to be my mother. I'm arriving in England next month . . ." I had to write back that I was going abroad indefinitely.'

'Usually you think of the basic design – you know, "That would be an awfully good double-cross or trick." You start with the wish to deceive, and then work backwards. I begin with a fairly complete diagram, though small things may be changed in the writing, of course. One's always a *little* self-conscious over the murderer's first appearance. He must never come in too late; that's uninteresting for the reader at the end of the book. And the dénouement has to be worked out frightfully carefully. The further it comes towards the end, the better. That's even more important in a play, where an anti-climax ruins everything.'

'I was brought up on Dickens. Always loved him and hated Thackeray. I love Jane Austen too – who doesn't?'

'One is very lucky to have writing as a trade. One can work hard at it but also have delicious days of leisure and idleness. Young people nowadays have no time at all for what I call leisure, thinking, and all that. They're overshadowed by education. They're so desperate that they won't get jobs unless they have degrees. At that age they should be really enjoying themselves – kicking up their heels like a filly in the fields. All the people I remember best in my girlhood – the married women of thirty or forty whom I respected most – lived in complete leisure but had good minds, they'd read and studied and were exceedingly interesting to talk to. Now people can very often only talk about one subject. So much education tends to specialize you – it makes you more interested in taking things in than in giving things out. Very few people really stimulate you with the things they say. And those are usually men. Men have much better brains than women, don't you think? So much more originality.'

The new Christie in 1966 was *Third Girl*, a Poirot mystery. Poirot is now incredibly aged. He ought, by rights, to be well over a hundred, but we are probably meant to think of him in the context of the novel as approaching eighty. At the beginning of Chapter I, he is lingering over his breakfast of a brioche and hot chocolate. He had recently completed his *magnum opus*, an analysis of great writers of detective fiction which he had been working on, you realize, during the events narrated in *The Clocks* (1963). At least, he had at that time been doing some preliminary reading and research. We now discover that, in his monograph,

He had dared to speak scathingly of Edgar Allen [sic] Poe, he had complained of the lack of method or order in the romantic outpourings of Wilkie Collins, had lauded to the skies two American authors who were practically unknown, and had in various other ways given honour where honour was due and sternly withheld it where he considered it was not. He had seen the volume through the press, had looked upon the results and, apart from a really incredible number of printer's errors, pronounced that it was good.

All very well, but now he had no task in hand, and he was bored. Thus, when his manservant, George, announces that a young lady has called to consult Poirot 'about a murder she might have committed', the great detective condescends to see her. He is intrigued by that 'might have'. When the visitor, a girl of about twenty, enters, Poirot is disappointed. Here is no beauty in distress, but merely a scruffy modern miss in a state of some perplexity.

His visitor is equally disconcerted by her first sight of Poirot. 'I'm awfully sorry and I really don't want to be rude,' she blurts out, 'but – you're too old. Nobody told me you were so old.' And she rushes away before Poirot has a chance to question her. But his interest has been aroused, he consults his old friend Mrs Ariadne Oliver, and soon they are collaborating on the case of Norma Restarick, the 'third girl' – the third of three girls sharing a flat – who may or may not have committed murder.

The plot of *Third Girl* is not lacking in Christiean complexity or ingenuity, but it is by no means faultlessly constructed, and one or two incidents will not bear close examination. How Poirot manages to ensure that X is on the scene when an attempt is made on Y's life is not revealed, nor is his explanation of the double life led by Z at all feasible. The strength of *Third Girl* lies rather in its elderly author's shrewd and not too uncharitable observation of modern youth, its manners and morals. She has turned a critical eye on the 'hippies' of the sixties:

Long straggly hair of indeterminate colour strayed over her shoulders. Her eyes, which were large, bore a vacant expression and were of a greenish blue. She wore what were presumably the chosen clothes of her generation. Black high leather boots, white open-work woollen stockings of doubtful cleanliness, a skimpy skirt, and a long and sloppy pullover of heavy wool. Anyone of Poirot's age and generation would have had only one desire. To drop the girl into a bath as soon as possible. Such girls, he reflected, were not perhaps really dirty. They merely took enormous care and pains to look so.

The boys get off comparatively lightly:

He was a figure familiar enough to Poirot in different conditions, a figure often met in the streets of London or even at parties. A representative of the youth of today. He wore a black coat, an elaborate velvet waistcoat, skin-tight pants, and rich curls of chestnut hair hung down on his neck. He looked exotic and rather beautiful, and it needed a few moments to be certain of his sex.

Later, Poirot likens this youth to a Van Dyke portrait, and defends him against a charge of effeminacy. It is not that Poirot is unnaturally interested in young men, simply that his author is more sharply critical of her own sex. She is critical, too, of modern craftsmanship. When Mrs Oliver visits a flat in Borodene Mansions, she comes to a door marked 67 in metal numbers affixed to the centre of the door: 'The numeral 7 detached itself and fell on her feet as she arrived.'

Mrs Oliver (or, through her, Mrs Christie) also takes a dig at her publisher – 'I don't believe *you* know whether anything I write is good or bad' – and complains, of the things strangers say to her in public, such as 'how much they like my books, and how they've been longing to meet me'. Cynicism infects one or two of the other characters as well, among them the incredibly ancient ex-soldier, Sir Roderick Horsefield, who is engaged in writing his memoirs: 'All the chaps are doing it nowadays. We've had Montgomery and Alanbrook all shooting their mouths off in print, mostly saying what they thought of the other generals. We've even had old Moran, a respectable physician, blabbing about his important patient.' (Lord Moran, former President of the Royal College of Physicians, published his *Winston Churchill, the Struggle for Survival* in 1966.)

Several characters from *Third Girl* have appeared or will appear, in other works of Agatha Christie. Mr Goby had begun gathering information for Poirot as early as *The Mystery of the Blue Train* in 1928, and will be called upon again in *Elephants Can Remember* in 1972. Dr Stillingfleet, a friend of Poirot, appeared in the story, 'The Dream' (*The Adventure of the Christmas Pudding*: 1960). At the end of *Third Girl*, he is planning to go to Australia and marry someone he has met during Poirot's investigation of the murders in which Norma Restarick was involved. Chief Inspector Neele had become a friend of Marple in *A Pocket Full of Rye* (1953), at which time he held the rank of Inspector.

A 'ridiculous nursery rhyme' comes into Poirot's mind and helps him to find the solution to the *Third Girl* mystery, though exactly how 'Rub a dub dub, three men in a tub' manages to do this is not vouchsafed to the reader. *Third Girl* is more impressive as an elderly author's picture of the 'swinging sixties' than as a murder mystery. Some Christie commentators will not even allow it this merit. Robert Barnard[8] calls it 'one of Christie's more embarrassing attempts to haul herself abreast of the swinging sixties', and Barzun and Taylor[9] incline to the belief that 'admirers of the author will not blemish their vision of her by reading this late one.'

Admirers of Agatha Christie will doubtless make up their own minds. In the view of this writer, they would be unwise to ignore *Third Girl*.

Endless Night (1967)

It was in 1967 that a Swedish academic, Frank Behre, published *Studies in Agatha Christie's Writings*, a misleadingly titled philological treatise that can have been of very little interest to anyone who was not a grammarian, or deeply interested in linguistics. The following is a relatively readable excerpt from the book's introductory chapter (later on, the text becomes considerably less interesting or relevant to the non-specialist reader):

There are no doubt many other words that are particularly favoured by the characters at one time or another, maybe under the influence of the fashion prevailing at the time of the publication of the book in which the words occur. But to deal with them falls beyond the scope of the present study. By way of narrowing down the scope, let us instead compare our quantifiers and intensifiers A GOOD DEAL, A LOT, MUCH, PLENTY, (=set A) with a set of 'appreciatory intensives' such as *marvellous(ly)*, *amazing(ly)* (=set B). The comparison works as follows:

(1) In the pattern N+V+x(-*ly*) as measurers of degree the two sets may touch upon each other occasionally: 'he has improved marvellously (=very MUCH)' . . .

Why, you might wonder, did the learned Professor Behre pick on Agatha Christie? The lady herself certainly wondered why, and wrote to the author that, though she was charmed and flattered by his attention, she had not understood a word of his book. At the same time she described her own work as 'half-way between a crossword puzzle and a hunt in which you can pursue the trail sitting comfortably at home in your armchair.'

The 1967 Christie, *Endless Night*, triggered off one of Mrs Christie's frequent minor rows with her publisher. Her advance copies had not arrived before she left to go on a holiday trip to Spain, but when she got to London airport to board her plane she was astonished and irritated to see a huge stack of copies of the novel on display at the airport bookstall. Her own copies had arrived by the time she returned home a few weeks later but, as she pointed out to her publisher, these could hardly be called 'advance' copies!

'Usually I spent three to four months on a book,' Agatha Christie told an interviewer, 'but I wrote *Endless Night* in six weeks. If I can write fairly quickly, the result is more spontaneous.' The result, in the case of *Endless Night*, is a novel which, despite the fact that she resorts to one of her most impudent confidence tricks which she had already used many years earlier, is almost completely different from anything else she had written.

It is more than usually difficult to discuss *Endless Night*, other than in the most general terms, without revealing the identify of the murderer. What can be said, however, is that the novel is virtually unique in Mrs Christie's *oeuvre* in its portrait in depth of a psychotic killer, and in the manner in which it maintains suspense with the minimum of actual detection. The killer's plans do come unstuck, but through two instances of bad luck, not through any ingenious detective-work. There are, in fact, no investigators, or none who performs a significant role in the narrative.

Does the author play fair? This is a question which has been raised on earlier occasions, and Mrs Christie has always been given the benefit of the doubt. She does, it is true, keep the reader ignorant of certain facts until she is ready to reveal them, but that, surely, is a legitimate part of the game. It would even be a legitimate aspect of technique if *Endless Night* were a pure and simple murder mystery which, in a sense, it is not.

The character of Michael Rogers, the young narrator of the novel who falls in love and marries, is superbly presented, and his individualistic classlessness; his relationship with his mother, and his determination to make his own way in the world, are all perfectly conveyed. Michael's attitudes, you suspect, are shared in large part by the author:

They wanted me to go steady with a nice girl, save money, get married to her and then settle down to a nice steady job. Day after day, year after year, world without end, amen. Not for yours truly! There must be something better than that. Not just all this tame security, the good old welfare state limping along in its half-baked way! Surely, I thought, in a world where man has been able to put satellites in the sky and where men talk big about visiting the stars, there must be *something* that rouses you, that makes your heart beat, that's worth while searching all over the world to find!

Michael falls in love first with a piece of land, before he falls in love with a woman. Gipsy's Acre, as it is called in the novel, was a field which made a deep impression on Agatha Christie when she saw it on a Welsh moorland. She transferred it to the south of England in *Endless Night*. Another striking character in the novel is the architect genius Rudolf Santonix whom Michael commissions to build a marvellous house on Gipsy's Acre.

Ellie, the girl whom Michael marries, likes to sing to her own guitar accompaniment. One of Michael's favourites among her songs is a 'sweet-sad, haunting little tune' whose words are from Blake's *Auguries of Innocence*:

> Every Night and Every Morn
> Some to Misery are born.
> Every Morn and every Night
> Some are born to Sweet Delight,
> Some are born to Sweet Delight,
> Some are born to Endless Night.

The murderer in *Endless Night* is one of Mrs Christie's most interesting. In an essay, 'The Inheritance of the Meek: Two Novels by Agatha Christie and Henry James'[10] which appeared in an American magazine, *Endless Night* is compared with James's *Wings of the Dove* and the point is made that the message of the two novels is the same: 'that life and love built on victimized innocence cannot endure'.

There are links between *Endless Night* and several earlier works of Agatha Christie: with the story, 'The Case of the Caretaker', which is to be found in the volume, *Three Blind Mice* (published in the USA only); with *Death on the Nile* and with an earlier novel which it would be imprudent to mention here. The relationship between the wealthy Linnet Ridgeway and her American trustee 'Uncle' Andrew Pennington in *Death on the Nile*, is not dissimilar to that between Ellie and her solicitor-guardian. 'Uncle' Andrew Lippincott in *Endless Night*. Nor are the characters themselves dissimilar in certain respects.

This is one of the finest of the later Christie novels, and one with which the author herself was especially pleased. As the critic of the London *Sun* wrote, 'The best Christie since she used the basic plot gimmick in the 1920s. And if old crime hands think this is a clue, let me say that she fooled me this time too.' 'The crashing, not to say horrific suspense at the end is perhaps the most devastating that this suspenseful author has ever brought off,' said the crime writer Francis Iles in the *Guardian*. Another of her rivals, Edmund Crispin, writing in the *Sunday Times*, thought *Endless Night* 'one of the best things Mrs Christie has ever done'.

In 1972, *Endless Night* was filmed in England by United Artists. The director was Sidney Gilliat, who was also responsible for the screenplay which was reasonably faithful to the novel, and the leading players included Hywel Bennett (as Michael), Hayley Mills (Ellie), George Sanders (Andrew Lippincott), Per Oscarsson (Santonix) and Britt Ekland (Ellie's friend, Greta). Firmer direction, and perhaps a less emphatic musical score than that provided by Bernard Herrman, would have resulted in an excellent movie, for most of the performances were first-rate, and Harry Waxman's colour photography made the most of Gipsy's Acre. But, as Max Mallowan said in his memoirs, 'for Agatha and many of her readers all was ruined by the introduction at the end of an erotic scene altogether alien to Agatha's ideas.'

By the Pricking of My Thumbs (1968)

Though she was now in her late seventies, Agatha Christie continued to produce at least one new title each year. The 'Christie for Christmas' had become a tradition. Once or twice, her publishers feared that she might not produce her typescript in time. But the suggestion made to her one year, that they might bring out instead a 'Ngaio Marsh for Christmas' produced a novel from Agatha Christie, as Collins' Editorial Director put it, 'virtually by return of post'. There were no signs of flagging energy: she could no doubt have written more in her old age but she abhorred 'working for the taxman'. With an annual income now for each new title said to be approximately £100,000, but probably considerably higher, Mrs Christie had no need to exert herself. She told a friend, 'I only write one book a year now, which is sufficient to give a very good income. If I wrote more I'd enlarge the finances of the Inland Revenue, who would spend it mostly on idiotic things.'

In 1968, Max Mallowan was knighted, in recognition of his services to archaeology.

The title of the 1968 novel, a new Tommy and Tuppence adventure, derives from the Shakespeare play which Mrs Christie was most fond of quoting, Macbeth: 'By the pricking of my thumbs/Something wicked this way comes.' In a brief address to her readers the author writes: 'This book is dedicated to the many readers in this and other countries who write to me, asking "What has happened to Tommy and Tuppence? What are they doing now?" My best wishes to you all, and I hope you will enjoy meeting Tommy and Tuppence again, years older, but with spirit unquenched!'

Years older they certainly are. When last heard of, during the Second World War in N or M?, Tommy was in his forties and Tuppence must have been thirty-nine. Now, twenty-seven years later, Tommy is over seventy and Tuppence is sixty-six. Their man-of-all-work, the cockney Albert whom they first encountered when he was nine (in The Secret Adversary in 1922) is therefore now fifty-five. Yet Tommy and Tuppence still hanker after adventure, and go more than half-way to meet it. They decide that it is time to pay a visit to Tommy's aged Aunt Ada, who is in a nursing home, and while Tuppence is sitting in a reception room she meets another elderly inhabitant of the nursing home whose mind is clearly wandering, for she asks Tuppence: 'Was it your poor child?', with the implication that there is a child walled up in the fireplace.

This incident, or a variant of it, has already been used twice by Mrs Christie: in The Pale Horse (1961) and in a Miss Marple novel, Sleeping Murder, which she wrote during the forties but put aside for posthumous publication (see p. 239). It must surely have emanated from words overheard by the author, or perhaps spoken to her, which lodged in her mind because of their rather sinister connotation. In *By the Pricking of My Thumbs*, it is when Tommy's aunt dies some weeks later that Tuppence finds an excuse to make further inquiries about the old lady who had asked that odd question. The old lady has been taken away by a relative, and she is not easy to find. If the plot does not thicken, it certainly takes on some very odd aspects.

This is one of those novels about crimes in the past which Agatha Christie was fond of asking her sleuths to solve several years after they were committed. It is also one in which an air of inconsequentiality, which is found in some of her very late novels, tends to make itself felt. One of the virtues of early and middle Christie is the economy of the author's dialogue, which is always pointed and anything but inconsequential. But Tommy and Tuppence, in old age, tend to allow their conversations to meander (although less disastrously here than in their next, and final, adventure, *Postern of Fate*) and they are occasionally repetitious. What saves them, and saves *By the Pricking of My Thumbs*, is their author's sense of humour, to which she usually gave freer rein in the Tommy and Tuppence novels than in those involving Poirot or Miss Marple.

Tommy and Tuppence are more light-hearted about crime than Poirot or Jane Marple, relishing their adventures in a spirit of adolescent fun. And adolescents they remain in their old age. Their frivolity affects their author, leading her to an even more casual attitude to chronology than usual.

The ages of various characters in *By the Pricking of My Thumbs*, and the timing of some of the past events, do not bear too close an examination. The reader is advised not to attempt to fight Mrs Christie's assault upon his commonsense, but to lie back and enjoy it; allow Tommy to expatiate irrelevantly upon *Macbeth*, and Tuppence to indulge her highly unsuitable yearning for adventure. They are still, after nearly half a century, in love with each other and, although their bodies may be more than slightly arthritic, their spirits are, as their author says, unquenched. Think of *By the Pricking of My Thumbs* as Agatha Christie's comic dissertation on old age.

Hallowe'en Party (1969)

As she approaches her eightieth year, Agatha Christie was careful to conserve her energy. Public appearances, always infrequent, now became fewer, and her family, her garden, and her writing occupied most of her time. Writing remained enormously important to her. 'I am like a sausage machine,' she had told Francis Wyndham. 'As soon as one is made and cut off the string, I have to think of the next one.' But equally important to her was Max Mallowan's archaeology. 'I retreat into myself with fiction,' she said. 'I emerge from myself in my husband's work.'

In 1969, asked to contribute to *Adam*, a literary magazine, a short article on the French novelist Simenon, Agatha Christie wrote a very brief letter of refusal which the editor published: 'I do not really feel that authors should comment on their own opinion of other authors' work unless they are doing so as a professional reviewer, and I never review or criticize books. One talks about authors one likes to one's friends, but I never give my views professionally.'

In the autumn, the new Christie title was a Poirot crime novel, *Hallowe'en Party*, dedicated to P.G. Wodehouse 'whose books and stories have brightened my life for many years. Also, to show my pleasure in his having been kind enough to tell me that he enjoys *my* books.' That the most widely read novelist of all should want to boast of being praised by a fellow writer is touching, for it indicates, surely, that even at this late stage of her career she valued what might be called intellectual respectability. She must have known that her readers ranged from the near cretinous to the intellectually brilliant. Many, in both categories, were university professors, even more were shop assistants and factory hands. Among the geniuses, Sigmund Freud was a devoted reader of Agatha Christie (and, it must be admitted, of Dorothy L. Sayers as well),[11] as was the great orchestral conductor, Otto Klemperer.

At a Hallowe'en party attended by Mrs Ariadne Oliver, a thirteen-year-old girl who has been telling all and sundry she once witnessed a murder is drowned in a tub of floating apples. Mrs Oliver enlists the aid of her old friend Poirot in finding the murderer. Poirot discovers that his ex-colleague, Superintendent Spence, who had been involved years earlier in the Mrs McGinty affair (*Mrs McGinty's Dead*: 1952), is living in the district, and he asks Spence to provide him with information about the locals. He is unable to prevent a second murder (this is a not uncommon occurrence in Poirot's cases) but identifies the killer just as he is about to strike for the third time.

The characters in *Hallowe'en Party* are not all as sharply drawn as in vintage Christie, and although the plot is typically convoluted there are a number of careless loose ends which could easily (and should) have been attended to. The Poirot-Ariadne Oliver relationship, however, is engagingly described, and it is always fascinating to hear Mrs Oliver holding forth about her method as a crime novelist. We think we know what Mrs Oliver, and perhaps Dame Agatha Christie, think of Poirot. In *Hallowe'en Party* we find Poirot murmuring to himself about Mrs Oliver: 'It is a pity that she is so scatty. And yet, she has originality of mind.' This might almost be Agatha Christie's summing-up of herself.

In *The Secret of Chimneys* in 1925 the country of Herzoslovakia was invented. A story in *The Labours of Hercules* (1947) is set in the same country. In *Hallowe'en Party* (and in *Third Girl*: 1966) there is passing reference to a country called Her(t)zogovinia. The question of whether or not it is spelt with a 't' can be put down to the vagaries of transliteration from Balkan cyrillic script, but is this country a neighbour of Herzoslovakia, or the same country after a no doubt violent change of regime? Who can tell?

Hallowe'en Party is an odd novel. Perhaps it is not so odd that Poirot should have a close friend called Solomon Levy, though it would not have happened in the early Poirot stories of the 1920s. But it is curious that Poirot, as he grows older, should be so moved by male beauty. There was an instance in *Third Girl*, and now in *Hallowe'en Party* he is struck by

. . . a young man, so Poirot now recognized, of an unusual beauty. One didn't think of young men that way nowadays. You said of a young man that he was sexy or madly attractive, and these evidences of praise are quite often justly made. A man with a craggy face, a man with wild greasy hair and whose features were far from regular. You didn't say a young man was beautiful. If you did say it, you said it apologetically as though you were praising some quality that had been long dead . . .

Poirot goes on at some length about this young man who 'was tall, slender, with features of great perfection such as a classical sculptor might have produced.' We should probably remind ourselves at this point that, although Poirot is male, his author is female and is momentarily allowing herself to assess ideals of beauty in the nineteen sixties. And, in any case, appreciation of beauty is life-enhancing, whereas Poirot's views on justice and mercy have a certain Old Testament rigour about them: 'Too much mercy, as he knew from former experience both in Belgium and this country, often resulted in further crimes which were fatal to innocent victims who need not have been victims if justice had been put first and mercy second.' Surely, all that men can do is to act justly and leave mercy to God. If there should turn out to be no God, then the concept of mercy is without meaning.

Thirty and forty years earlier, Agatha Christie was extremely circumspect in dealing with sexual inversion. In the sixties, however, she begins to talk of 'queers' and even, in *Hallowe'en Party*, allows a discussion of a lesbian relationship. *Tempora mutantur, et nos mutamur in illis.*

A certain trick with a person's will in *Hallowe'en Party* has been used in an earlier Christie novel, but even if the reader happens to remember it he will not be helped thereby to discover the murderer. Although she may be beginning to fail in one or two other aspects of her craft, Dame Agatha retains her ability to surprise.

Passenger to Frankfurt (1970)

On 15 September 1970, Agatha Christie celebrated her eightieth birthday, and to mark the event Sir Max Mallowan produced an offering in the form of a pastiche of one of Agatha's Odes:

> Our Bingo has bitten the Mail and Express,
> For those two reporters there is no redress.
> But to bite Peter Grosvenor and nip Godfrey Winn
> Shall not be accounted to him as a sin:
> Tis better than when he indulges in passes
> At Cocoa's and Golly's protruding arses.
> But today all our dogs are joined in full amity
> To spare you the shame of such a calamity.
> Such conduct they say would now be atrocious;
> For this day at least we shall not be ferocious.

When Godfrey Winn's interview with Agatha Christie appeared in the London *Daily Mail*, three days before her birthday, it contained no mention of his having been nipped by Bingo. He described the house by the river Dart, and the lady herself, 'dressed in a becoming shade of red, her white hair full of vitality, who reminded me, sitting so upright, of one of the more aristocratic-looking members of my bridge club'. 'I once heard two women discussing me in a railway carriage,' Agatha Christie told him, 'both with copies of my paperback editions on their knees. "I hear she drinks like a fish," one said".'

When asked the expected question about the permissive society, the author replied, 'The old have been through too much themselves to be shocked by anything. It is the in-between generation, who throw up their hands and go through the motions of being outraged.' On the subject of marriage, she and Sir Max having now been married for forty years, she gave it as her view that mutual tastes were not necessary. 'Those of my husband are academic and intellectual, while mine could be described as frivolous and fictional. However, we seem to manage splendidly. Mutual respect. Now that *is* important. Equally so in all lasting relationships.'

'A writer,' she thought, 'must have a genuine respect for the intelligence of his or her readers. I myself never cheat. It is the one rule in writing that I have never broken.' She ended the interview by announcing that she would go to see *The Mousetrap* again on her birthday. 'I feel that would be only appropriate since I wrote the original story, "Three Blind Mice" to commemorate Queen Mary's own eightieth birthday.' 'Do you know,' she added, 'they change the cast of *The Mousetrap* every year to prevent staleness? But there is one character they have never succeeded yet in casting exactly right.'

'Which part is that?' Winn asked.

'Oh, it wouldn't be fair to say. It would be cheating.'

Though Agatha Christie referred to her tastes as frivolous and fictional, she asked her publishers to send her the titles in their paperback series, *Modern Masters*, edited by Professor Frank Kermode. These were scholarly and erudite introductions to the work of such intellectual giants as Freud and Wittgenstein and such fashionable gurus of the sixties as Chomsky and Marcuse. Hence the passing reference to Marcuse and three other key names in *Passenger to Frankfurt*, the Christie novel published to coincide with its author's eightieth birthday.

Near the desk [in a *Gasthaus* bedroom somewhere 'in the Tyrol or Bavaria'], by the stove of period porcelain, were paperback editions of certain preachings and tenets by the modern prophets of the world. Those who were now or had recently been crying in the wilderness were here to be studied and approved by young followers with haloes of hair, strange raiment, and earnest hearts. Marcuse, Guevara, Lévi-Strauss, Fanon.

It is as a desperate, indeed despairing warning against these modern prophets that *Passenger to Frankfurt* is to be read. The last of Agatha Christie's free-ranging thrillers (one more Tommy and Tuppence thriller was to follow), it is vague and disjointed, its plot so attenuated that at times its existence is difficult to discern. Her publishers had grave doubts as to the wisdom of publishing the novel, but there it was, the 'eightieth' Agatha Christie title to celebrate her eightieth birthday (though it took some Lewis Carroll-like counting to arrive at eighty as the number of titles, for Dame Agatha had produced considerably more than that, even if the count is limited to crime and thriller titles). There is no doubt that it must have seemed an extremely odd and highly disappointing typescript to whomever read it at Collins. Could it be called a novel at all? The author was persuaded to describe it on the title-page as 'an extravaganza'.

Passenger to Frankfurt introduces its most engaging character right at the beginning. He is the forty-five-year-old Sir Stafford Nye, who had failed to fulfil his early promise as a diplomat mainly because 'a peculiar and diabolical sense of humour was wont to afflict him in what should have been his most serious moments.' As Sir Stafford remarks later in the narrative, 'One cannot go entirely through life taking oneself and other people seriously.' How your heart warms to him.

Sitting in the transit lounge of the airport at Frankfurt, on his way back to England from a commission of enquiry in Malaya, Nye finds himself plunged into adventure when a young woman with a faintly foreign accent persuades him to relinquish his passport to her. Soon, he is pitting his wits against nothing so definite as an organization dedicated to world-wide anarchy but something infinitely more dangerous. The young woman has become his ally. Or perhaps she has not. Familiar figures from the worlds of espionage and international finance such as Colonel Pikeaway (from *Cat Among the Pigeons*) and Mr Robinson ('that yellow whale of a fellow' from *Cat Among the Pigeons* and *At Bertram's Hotel*) are encountered. Stafford Nye's elderly Aunt Matilda (Lady Matilda Cleckheaton) also plays a part in helping to keep the world on an even course for a little longer. The *Almanach de Gotha* is consulted, and the works of Wagner, with special reference to *Siegfried*, are of great significance to the events, if so solid a noun as 'events' is not inappropriate in a description of *Passenger to Frankfurt*. You sympathize with Nye when he quotes (in English) Hans Sachs's world-weary cry, 'Wahn, Wahn, überall Wahn' from *Die Meistersinger*.

Is the crux of what meaning there is to this extravaganza to be found in the statement of Henry Horsham, a Security man? 'There are bits of it sticking out, you know, like a badly done up parcel. You get a peep here and a peep there. One moment you think it's going on at the Bayreuth Festival and the next minute you think its tucking out of a South American estancia and then you get a bit of a lead in the USA.' You could, in fact, describe *Passenger to Frankfurt* unkindly as a badly done up parcel, but you would have to add, in all fairness, that it is a distinctly intriguing parcel. It contains, among other surprises, Adolf Hitler's marriage in South America, and the subsequent birth of a child, a child branded on the foot with the mark of the swastika.

To the sound of Siegfried's horn call, there appears through a doorway (we are in an 'Eagle's Nest in Bavaria') 'one of the handsomest young men Stafford Nye had ever seen. Golden-haired, blue-eyed, perfectly proportioned, conjured up as it were by the wave of a magician's wand, he came forth out of the world of myth.' This is Franz Joseph (also known as the Young Siegfried), presumably the child of Hitler, who is going to lead a super-race of heroic Aryan youth against the inferior races of mankind. 'It has to be Aryan youth in this part of the world,' a character remarks cynically.

Cynicism pervades the pages of this weird and absorbing *Pilgrim's Progress* of the modern world. 'Don't pass it on to any one of those idiots in the Government, or connected with government or hoping to be participating in government after this lot runs out,' Lady Matilda advises her nephew. And Colonel Pikeaway remarks: 'One of our politicians the other day, I remember, said we were a splendid nation, chiefly because we were permissive, we had demonstrations, we smashed things, we beat up anyone if we hadn't anything better to do, we got rid of our high spirits by showing violence, and our moral purity by taking most of our clothes off. I don't know what he thought he was talking about – politicians seldom do – but they can make it sound all right. That's why they are politicians.'

Passenger to Frankfurt, however, whatever else it is, is no simple-minded tract against the permissive society, or call to fascists of the world to unite against those who are 'arseing around with Russkies' (the language Dame Agatha uses in old age!). It is, rather, an appeal to the deeply frivolous of the world to join her in deploring extremism of all kinds. 'The news from Italy is very bad,' says Colonel Pikeaway. 'The news from Russia, I imagine, could be very bad if they let much out about it. They've got trouble there too. Marching bands of students in the street, shop windows smashed, Embassies attacked. News from Egypt is very bad. News from Jerusalem is very bad. News from Syria is very bad. That's all more or less normal, so we needn't worry too much. News from Argentine is what I'd call peculiar. Very peculiar indeed. Argentine, Brazil, Cuba, they've all got together. Call themselves the Golden Youth Federated States, or something like that. It's got an army, too. Properly drilled, properly armed, properly commanded. They've got planes, they've got bombs, they've got God-knows-what.'

This bleak vision of world anarchy is perfunctorily dispelled in the final stages by some John Buchan-type action which is singularly unconvincing. What remains with the reader, if he does not consider that the 'extravaganza' would have been more aptly named a farrago, is a pessimistic daydream of the futility of life and of endeavour. Nor is there much comfort to be derived from the Introduction, entitled 'The Author Speaks'. After describing how ideas for earlier books have come to her, through a cruise on the Nile, a journey on the Orient Express, a fight between two girls in a Chelsea café, Dame Agatha turns to what is going on in the world around her:

> What is everyone saying, thinking, doing? Hold up a mirror to 1970 in England.
>
> Look at that front page every day for a month, take notes, consider and classify.
>
> Every day there is a killing.
>
> A girl strangled.
>
> Elderly woman attacked and robbed of her meagre savings.
>
> Young men or boys – attacking or attacked.
>
> Buildings and telephone kiosks smashed and gutted.
>
> Drug smuggling.
>
> Robbery and assault.
>
> Children missing and children's murdered bodies found not far from their homes.
>
> Can this be England? Is England *really* like this? One feels – no – not yet, *but it could be.*

As epigraph, there is a line from Jan Smuts, which is also quoted by a character in the narrative: 'Leadership, besides being a great creative force, can be diabolical . . .'

Agatha Christie wrote *Passenger to Frankfurt* not as a diversion in the style of her earlier thrillers but as a serious picture of the world as she saw it, using the means of the thriller, just as Verdi made use of the operatic language he knew best when he came to compose his Requiem Mass. Her distrust of utopianism, her scorn for the inanities uttered by politicians of all hues, her firmly held belief that human nature is not to be changed, her horror at the cynical exploitation of youth by the commercial manipulators of 'pop' culture, all are balanced by a faith in the rare attribute of reason and the even rarer virtue of good will. Can those qualities win in the end? On the bad day, or in the bad six weeks, when Agatha Christie wrote *Passenger to Frankfurt*, she tended to think not.

Despite less than enthusiastic reviews,[12] this eightieth birthday extravaganza did well, no doubt because of the occasion with which its publication coincided. The largest printing ever of a Christie first edition, 58,000 copies, sold quickly. Four years later, on the occasion of the première of the film of *Murder on the Orient Express*, Agatha Christie told Lord Brabourne, the producer, that she thought *Passenger to Frankfurt* might make a good film. Brabourne disagreed.

The Golden Ball and other stories (1971)

The Mallowans were now dividing their time between three homes, one in Chelsea, another, Winterbrook House, in Wallingford, Berkshire, and, of course, Greenway House, on the river Dart in Devon. Agatha Christie found it easiest to write in Chelsea. 'In the country,' she told an interviewer, 'there's always some nice distraction, and I'm only too eager for any excuse to stop work.'

Max Mallowan had been knighted in 1968, for his services to archaeology, which entitled his wife to be called Lady Mallowan. Now, in 1971, Agatha Christie, who had been awarded the CBE in 1956, was given the Order of Dame Commander of the British Empire. Dame Agatha solved the problem of her two titles by deciding to be Lady Mallowan when she was being her husband's wife and Dame Agatha when she was being herself, the crime novelist!

The year 1971 had begun well, with the announcement of Agatha Christie's new honour on New Year's Day, but it continued less well when, in mid-June, Dame Agatha suffered a fall at her Berkshire home, and broke her leg. She was successfully operated upon at the Nuffield Orthopaedic Centre in Oxford, but for the rest of her life she usually walked with the aid of a stick. A happier event during the year was the painting of her portrait by the distinguished Austrian artist, Oskar Kokoschka, who was her senior by four years.

For the first time since *Rule of Three*, her three one-act plays of ten years earlier, Dame Agatha had written a new play, *Fiddlers Five*. It toured briefly in the provinces in the summer of 1971, but closed before reaching the West End. (After thorough revision, it was presented again the following year as *Fiddlers Three*: see p. 224.)

During the year, Agatha Christie contributed a story, 'The Harlequin Tea Set', to an anthology, *Winter's Crimes 3*, which was published by Macmillan. Two Christie volumes were published in 1971: *The Golden Ball* and *Nemesis*.

Published only in the USA, *The Golden Ball* contains fifteen stories, all but two of which had appeared in volumes published in Great Britain nearly forty years earlier. The title-story, as well as 'The Listerdale Mystery', 'The Girl in the Train', 'The Manhood of Edward Robinson', 'Jane in Search of a Job', 'A Fruitful Sunday', 'The Rajah's Emerald' and 'Swan Song' are all to be found in *The Listerdale Mystery* (1934: see p. 78). Five stories come from the 1933 volume, *The Hound of Death* (see p. 72): 'The Hound of Death', 'The Gipsy', 'The Lamp', 'The Strange Case of Sir Andrew Carmichael' and 'The Call of Wings'.

It is only the remaining two stories in *The Golden Ball* which are new, and they have still to be published in the UK. Neither is a crime story or a mystery, and both could almost be fragments from one of the Mary Westmacott novels. Perhaps they were originally intended by Agatha Christie to be Westmacott short stories, and were published under her own name simply because she had not written sufficient Westmacott stories to make up a volume by that author. 'Magnolia Blossom' is about a woman who has to make a difficult choice between her husband, to whom she wishes to remain loyal in his financial difficulties, and the man she loves. The behaviour of one of the two men removes some of the difficulty. In 'Next to a Dog', Agatha Christie indulges her well-known love of dogs, especially wire-haired terriers, in a story about a young woman who contemplates desperate measures in order not to be parted from Terry, 'an aged wire-haired terrier very shaggy as to coat and suspiciously bleary as to eyes'. A sentimental and attractive story.

Though the majority of the stories from the earlier two volumes are mysteries of a kind, most of them concern crimes considerably less reprehensible than murder. The operatic 'Swan Song' is a notable exception. Those of the stories which were first published in *The Hound of Death* are, in fact, not about crime but about the supernatural. All in all, the fifteen stories in *The Golden Ball* make up an extremely entertaining collection.

Nemesis (1971)

Nemesis is the last book that Agatha Christie was to write about Miss Marple. Two more titles were to be published posthumously, but one, *Sleeping Murder* (1976) had been written during the Second World War and deliberately put aside for posthumous publication, while the other, *Miss Marple's Final Cases*, contains stories also written earlier. *Nemesis* is not exactly a sequel to the 1965 Miss Marple novel, *A Caribbean Mystery*, but it does, in a way, grow out of the earlier book and out of Jane Marple's collaboration with the elderly, wealthy Jason Rafiel in the West Indies.

At the beginning of *Nemesis*, Miss Marple comes across Mr Rafiel's name in the Deaths column of *The Times*. A week or so later, the late gentleman's solicitors write to her with an offer of a legacy of £20,000 from Mr Rafiel on condition that she investigate a certain crime. Miss Marple is given no more detail than this, but some days later she is invited to join a tour of Famous Houses and Gardens of Great Britain, at the expense of the late Mr Rafiel. The hunt is on, and another of Agatha Christie's 'crime in the past' novels is off to a highly promising start.

Miss Marple mentions more than once that it is a year, or perhaps even two, since the Caribbean adventure during which she had met Mr Rafiel. However, *A Caribbean Mystery* was published in 1964, a good seven years before *Nemesis*. The reader should perhaps consider the events of *Nemesis* as occurring in 1968: either that or, as happens with the old, Miss Marple's memory has contracted periods of time.

Critics tend to be severe with the later works of Agatha Christie, and it has to be admitted that, now in her eighties, Dame Agatha is more careless than ever. Improbabilities are not explained, certain things do not quite add up, and it is as well, as far as *Nemesis* is concerned, not to worry unduly about how X knew that Y was investigating a death and would be at a certain place at a certain time, or why a somewhat anarchistic young man in his teens should join a tour of largely middle-aged people on a tour of historic homes and gardens.

Nevertheless, *Nemesis* is a highly enjoyable mystery novel, especially if you have recently read *A Caribbean Mystery*, two characters from which reappear briefly. Agatha Christie's observation is as sharp as Miss Marple's has always been, though both ladies are now grown somewhat frail. It is interesting, incidentally, to contrast the Old Manor House and its one elderly servant with Styles Court of *The Mysterious Affair at Styles* fifty years earlier, buzzing with servants. The decline of the upper-middleclass in England had occurred during those fifty years.

Miss Marple finds her thoughts wandering to the witches in *Macbeth*, and she imagines to herself how she would produce their scenes. This is not the first time Agatha Christie has addressed herself to this problem: there was a character who had appeared in *The Pale Horse* ten years earlier with precisely the same production ideas.

'I have never read books on criminology as a subject or really been interested in such a thing,' Miss Marple notes. 'No, it has just happened that I have found myself in the vicinity of murder rather more often than would seem normal.' In *Nemesis*, she confronts not only the challenge of a murder in the past which has first to be identified before it can be solved, but also a lesbian relationship which, as far as you know, is not something Miss Marple has previously known about at first hand. She copes with tact, sympathy and determination. The reader is almost surprised that she does not quote De La Mare's 'Everything human we comprehend', for she does indulge in rather more than her usual amount of quotation, from Longfellow's 'ships that pass in the night' through T.S. Eliot's 'moment of the rose' to the Bible's 'Let Justice roll down like waters'.

Mr Rafiel's interest in having the crime solved becomes understandable quite early in the narrative. It is not only murder which is involved, but rape, though as one of Miss Marple's companions, a criminologist and adviser to the Home Office, remarks: 'Girls, you must remember, are far more ready to be raped nowadays than they used to be. Their mothers insist, very often, that they should call it rape.' An interesting and, no doubt, to feminists an infuriating point of view.

Nemesis is by no means one of the best Jane Marple mysteries, but it is enjoyable, unusual, and as easy to read as the most successful of them.

Elephants Can Remember (1972)

In March, 1972, Dame Agatha was approached by the management of Madame Tussaud's Wax Museum in London, who wished to add her to their collection of wax figures. She allowed herself to be measured with tapes and calipers, and in due course a life-size figure of the author took its place in the Museum.

In the summer a revised version of the previous year's play was presented, as *Fiddlers Three*, and in November *The Mousetrap* celebrated its twentieth birthday.

A new Poirot novel, *Elephants Can Remember*, was published in time for

Christmas. The impresario Peter Saunders published his memoirs, *The Mousetrap Man*, and Agatha Christie wrote a friendly Introduction in which she recalled the many occasions on which they had collaborated.

Elephants Can Remember, although no one realized this at the time of its publication, was to be Poirot's penultimate case. It was, in fact, the last Poirot novel that Agatha Christie wrote, for the final Poirot, *Curtain*, which would appear in 1975, was one which she had written during the Second World War with the intention that it be published posthumously as the final case of Hercule Poirot. *Elephants Can Remember* also marks the last appearance of Ariadne Oliver, who plays a leading part in the investigation.

Mrs Oliver is at her most delightful, and most scatty, in this, her farewell appearance. Her similarity in some respects to her creator has been mentioned several times: like Dame Agatha, Mrs Oliver is no conventional feminist, for she is relieved when a luncheon in honour of celebrated female writers, which she is obliged to attend, turns out not to be confined to female writers. She is as vague as Agatha Christie, too, concerning Hercule Poirot's address. Dame Agatha has given it in the past both as Whitehaven and as Whitehouse Mansions. Miss Oliver thinks it might be Whitefriars Mansions. Now we shall never know for certain. (Mrs Oliver complains of her new secretary, Miss Livingstone, and bewails the loss of Miss Sedgwick, of whom we have never heard until that moment). Max Mallowan, in his memoirs, mentions that Mrs Oliver was 'a portrayal of Agatha herself', and adds, somewhat mischievously, that a pretended scattiness was one of Mrs Oliver's assets.

This is one of those stories about crime committed in the past. In this case, a girl's father murdered her mother, or perhaps it was the mother who murdered the father. All that is certain is that both parents died, the murderer having committed suicide immediately afterwards. Twelve years later, when the girl is now a young woman engaged to be married, her prospective mother-in-law thinks it important to know who killed whom. The elephants of the title are people whose memories of the events of twelve years earlier are accurate. Mrs Oliver goes on rather tiresomely about elephants never forgetting: it becomes a dreadfully winsome joke between her and Poirot, and at least five of the nine references to it ought to have been deleted.

This is one of the more meandering Christies. Elephants may never forget, but the author who is now over eighty frequently does. Her publisher ought to have provided her with an editor to help her deal with dates, ages and calculations, for these frequently go awry in *Elephants Can Remember*. At one point we are told that a man is twenty-five years older than his wife; later we learn that 'as a young man' he had been in love with his wife's twin sister. How young a man was he? If he was under forty, then she was under fifteen! No one is ever quite certain whether the deaths of Celia Ravencroft's parents occurred ten, twelve, fifteen or twenty years in the past. Poirot reminisces with his old friend Superintendent Spence about cases on which they have collaborated in the past, and gets an important detail about *Five Little Pigs* wrong. But then Poirot, too, is getting old. Even his author realizes this, and wittily reminds us of the fact:

Hercule Poirot stopped himself with a slight effort from saying firmly 'Most people have heard of me.' It was not quite as true as it used to be, because many people who had heard of Hercule Poirot, and known him, were now reposing with suitable memorial stones over them, in country churchyards.

Young Celia is made to say that she knows very little about the family tragedy, never having read any account of the inquest, and then two pages later says 'I think about it nearly all the time', and reveals that she is by no means ignorant of the details. These narrative weaknesses, infrequent in the earlier novels, make themselves particularly noticeable in the late Tommy and Tuppence adventures, *By the Pricking of My Thumbs* and *Postern of Fate*, as well as in *Elephants Can Remember*.

The story is actually an ingenious one, and the pace is not quite as leisurely as when the elderly team of Tommy and Tuppence amble into action. Also, it is enjoyable to encounter again such earlier colleagues of Poirot as Superintendent Spence and Mr Goby, the latter still gathering information for Poirot, forty-four years after his first appearance in *The Mystery of the Blue Train*. A certain premise is repeated from a story, 'Greenshaw's Folly' which appeared in the volumes *The Adventure of the Christmas Pudding* (UK: 1960) and *Double Sin* (USA: 1961). A final query: Why should a hand be covered with blood when all it has done is to push someone over a cliff?

Elephants can Remember was fortunate to collect some highly favourable reviews on its initial publication in London. 'A quiet but consistently interesting whodunit with ingenious monozygotic solution,' wrote Maurice Richardson in *The Observer*, adding cryptically, 'Any young elephant would be proud to have written it.' 'A beautiful example of latter-day Christie,' said the *Birmingham Post*, while the *Sunday Express* thought it 'a classic example of the ingenious three-card trick (now you see it, now you don't) that she has been playing on her readers for so many years'.

Fiddlers Three (1972)

No other writer on Agatha Christie makes any mention of her last play, and at least three of them state that Dame Agatha never wrote specifically for the stage after the comparative failure of *Rule of Three* in 1962. The final Christie play, nevertheless, is *Fiddlers Three* which was toured in 1971 by the actor manager, J. Grant Anderson, in its first version when it was called *Fiddlers Five*. The play had first been offered to Peter Saunders who had presented every new Christie play for more than twenty years, but Saunders thought the script disappointing and was reluctant to stage it.

He said later: 'I would, of course, have put it on out of gratitude to her, but felt it would not do her reputation any good. When it was tried out later on I think everyone agreed that it was not vintage Christie, and as far as I know it has not been done again.'[13]

Under the headline, 'Haggis in an Agatha Christie' the London *Sunday Telegraph* on 11 July 1971 told its readers:

Agatha Christie, who was made a Dame Commander of the British Empire in the New Year Honours, has written a new play, her first for ten years, at the age of 80.

The play is called *Fiddlers Five*. In it Dame Agatha has combined a thriller theme with comedy situations.

Among the questions posed are 'Who put the body in the deep freeze?' and 'Who choked to death on a haggis in the wilds of Scotland?'

The play is about a tycoon who reaches his 70th birthday and concerns a £100,000 inheritance. It is to be presented by Mr James Grant Anderson, the 74-year-old actor-manager who has been playing the judge in Dame Agatha's earlier play, *Witness for the Prosecution*, in a recent provincial tour.

Dame Agatha may have to miss the première of her play, which opens at the Arts Theatre, Cambridge, on 16 August, as she is recovering from a broken leg after a fall at her home at Wallingford, Berkshire.

Her last play to be staged was *Rule of Three* in 1960 [sic: actually 1962] but four months ago she went to Paris to see the French version of her perennial *The Mousetrap*, now in its nineteenth year in the West End.

Fiddlers Five goes to the Ashcroft Theatre, Croydon, from Cambridge, which is treating the production, by John Downing, as 'the theatrical event of the year'. Booking there opens tomorrow week.

Curiously, or you might even say mysteriously, the information given to the *Sunday Telegraph* by James Grant Anderson's press representatives proved to be inaccurate in several details, and had to be corrected in the following Sunday's edition of the newspaper. The play, it transpired, had already been touring for some weeks and without the haggis:

Fiddlers Five, the first Agatha Christie play in ten years, opens at Wimbledon Theatre tomorrow without the haggis claimed in a publicity handout.

The reference to the haggis was made in a leaflet distributed by a firm for the production company and referred to by the *Sunday Telegraph* last week. Dame Agatha's agent, Hughes Massie Ltd, said yesterday: 'There is no reference to a haggis in the play. In fact the food from which a character meets its death is a veal and ham pie.'

Dame Agatha, who saw the play at the King's Theatre, Southsea, on 7 June, despite pain from an injured hip, may attend tomorrow. Several West End managers are also expected.

Though the Ashcroft Theatre, Croydon, has been advertizing the thriller as a coming attraction, no contract has been signed yet for it to play there, its producer, Mr James Grant Anderson, said.

No West End management wanted to bring the play into London as it was, but Cameron Mackintosh took Alan Davis[14] to see it at Brighton in September, as a result of which Davis agreed, after a meeting with Agatha Christie in October at Winterbrook House, to redirect the play the following year for Lenver Theatre Productions, after it had been rewritten. Davis's suggestions for improving what he considered to be an entertaining but 'slightly broken-backed' play were accepted by Dame Agatha. These included turning two of the principal characters, 'a middle-aged and a younger woman who cancelled each other out', into one new character, and led in due course to a change of title to the familiar *Fiddlers Three* of the 'Old King Cole' nursery rhyme.

On 1 August 1972, *Fiddlers Three*, directed by Allan Davis, opened at the Yvonne Arnaud Theatre, Guildford, with a cast headed by Doris Hare, Arthur

Howard, Raymond Francis and Gabor Baraker. It toured quite successfully for several weeks, but did not succeed in finding a suitable West End theatre available, and eventually closed. In the opinion of Alan Davis today, the play's failure to reach London was due as much to bad luck as to anything else. He still thought it an entertaining comedy-thriller, though by no means one of Agatha Christie's best.

In *Fiddlers Three*, as distinct from *Fiddlers Five*, neither haggis nor veal and ham pie is mentioned: a character who does not appear in the play dies in Scotland from unspecified 'food poisoning'. The play, in two acts, the first set in a London office, the second a hotel in Bognor Regis, cannot really be described as a thriller or a murder mystery, though there is a murder towards the end of Act I and it is not until near the end of Act II that you discover who committed it.

Fiddlers Three combines crime and comedy in a somewhat inconsequential manner, with a plot concerning four collaborators who slip from deviousness into actual crime when they decide to conceal the identity of a corpse in order to get their hands on a large sum of money which they need for a legitimate business enterprise. They at first have no reason to suspect that their corpse achieved his status by unnatural means, and by the time they do realize that a murder has been committed, they are too deeply involved in their plot to pull out. There are four conspirators or four fiddlers, despite the title and the use, stipulated in the stage directions, of the tune of 'Old King Cole' (he called for, amongst other things, his 'fiddlers three') as music to accompany the rise and fall of the curtain.

The dialogue is light, rather than witty. The characters of Sam Fletcher and Sally Blunt, the chief conspirators, give some scope for players of strong personality without themselves being invested with much in the way of personality, for which Dame Agatha substituted a few characteristics. The dénuouement is rather flat, the final curtain comes down on a note of forced jollity, and it would require performances of extraordinary insouciance to keep *Fiddlers Three* alive in the theatre.

Agatha Christie was guest of honour at the opening night of *Fiddlers Three* at the Yvonne Arnaud Theatre, Guildford, on Tuesday, 1 August 1972. On 4 August, the *Surrey Advertiser* published this review:

The gods love the goddesses

In all the creative arts there are exponents who transcend the rules. That Dame Agatha Christie is among them was manifest at the Yvonne Arnaud Theatre, on Tuesday, where an audience which filled the auditorium gave her a standing ovation as she entered the theatre on the arm of Mr Laurier Lister, the director, and then spent two hours demonstrating its enjoyment of the latest brain-child of this still productive octogenarian.

The euphoria induced by the presence of greatness may well last until the run ends on 19 August for it was handsomely reinforced on the first night by a presence on the stage. Doris Hare would be justified in feeling (if she does so feel) that Dame Agatha's Sally Blunt is not the most rewarding role she has ever played, but she can seldom have encountered a friendlier audience. Indeed, all the players were bathing in the reflected warmth to some extent.

Despite her tremendous box-office successes, Agatha Christie has never been a favourite author of drama critics. Indeed, many theatre enthusiasts feel that most 'whodunits' make unsatisfactory plays because of the inevitable superficiality of the characterization. Her gifts as a storyteller, in print or on the boards, are, however, beyond challenge.

The great criticism of *Fiddlers Three*, alas, is that it fails to live up to the author's standards in this respect. A plot of mystifying complexity and total implausibility finds its development and resolution through coincidences which would be acceptable in farce, but rob the more sober medium of credibility.

It is all too easy to stop bothering about the play and sit back to enjoy the personalities and creative comedy touches of the players. Doris Hare is splendidly ebullient as the secretary in a real estate office, who draws on her experience as a petty crook, trained pharmacist and professional actress (quite a career!) to extricate the firm from a threat of bankruptcy. She even persuades a doctor to certify the cause of death without examining the corpse, and her employer to masquerade as the dead man.

The other fiddlers in the trio are played by Raymond Francis, whose firm and accomplished acting gives the production a stable hub, and Gabor Baraker, whose impish style of comedy accentuates the fun to be made of his immense girth.

Mark Wing-Davey, as a young man whose mental attributes are less obvious than his physical grace, reproduces the smile, and something of the style, of that firm favourite of Guildford audiences who is his mother, Anna Wing. He should not wish for better praise than this comparison. There are two very pretty girls involved, one a goodie, the other a baddie, but both adornments to the stage in their Bognor beach costumes – Julia Knight and Suzanne Barrett.

The play's dying moments are enlivened by an undertaker with a positively regal mastery of his craft, played, in an amusing cameo performance, by George Lacey. Arthur Howard, as the family solicitor, bears the burden of narrative development and makes light of it.

Alan Davis's production has the advantage of Anthony Holland's pleasing sets and Michael Saddington's lighting.

No one could disguise the play's basic weaknesses, but a playwright whose box office support outstrips that of Coward, Rattigan and Bolt, not to mention Shaw and Sheridan, can afford to make her own laws. And a mere journalist denigrates a cult goddess at his peril.

Poems (1973)

In May, 1973, *Akhnaton*, the play Agatha Christie had written in 1937 (see p. 99), was published for the first time. In November, *The Mousetrap* came of age with a lavish twenty-first birthday party given at the Savoy Hotel by Peter Saunders. On the day following the party all the major London newspapers carried photographs of it, among them a group photograph of all twenty-one actresses who had played the leading female role in *The Mousetrap*.

Asked whether she still enjoyed writing, Agatha Christie said, 'I wouldn't say that anyone enjoys their work. I mean, you have chosen something as your profession so you just get on with it. It's great fun thinking about writing, and planning it, and getting ready to do it, but when it gets down to the hard work it isn't so much fun.' She had got down to the hard work for the last time with *Postern of Fate*, which was published in the autumn. Also published during the year was a volume in which she collected together those of her poems which she wished to preserve.

Poems, a collection of 62 poems, is divided into two 'volumes'. Volume I, according to the verso of the title page, consists of the poems published in 1924 under the title *The Road of Dreams*, while the poems in Volume II are new. However, there are discrepancies between the contents of *The Road of Dreams* (1924) and Volume I of the 1973 *Poems*. 'Pierrot Grown Old', the final poem of the 1924 volume, is inserted in 1973, appropriately, into the opening sequence, 'A Masque from Italy'; an odd little poem of love's duplicity, 'Isolt of Brittany', is added in 1973 to the section of 'Ballads'; a poem called 'Beatrice Passes' has been removed from 'Dreams and Fantasies' and put among the new poems in Volume II of the 1973 book; 'A Palm Tree in Egypt' has been retitled 'A Palm Tree in the Desert'; and 'In a Dispensary', an engaging poem with a certain autobiographical interest, has been removed.

The poems in Volume II of the 1973 publication are presumably the only ones which Agatha Christie wished to preserve from her poetic output between 1924 and 1973. There are four sections, 'Things', 'Places', 'Love Poems and Others' and 'Verses of Nowadays'.

The four poems in 'Things' are of little interest, unoriginal in feeling and lacking the sense of form of much of Agatha Christie's earlier verse. The 'Places' of the next section include Baghdad, the Nile, Dartmoor, Calvary, an anonymous island, and a cedar tree in Lebanon. The best of the poems is 'Dartmoor', unambitious and inoffensive, making up in sincerity what it lacks in originality:

> I shall not return again the way I came.
> Back to the quiet country where the hills
> Are purple in the evenings, and the tors
> Are grey and quiet, and the tall standing stones
> Lead out across the moorland till they end
> At water's edge.

The reader has occasionally been asked to admire worse poems than this about Dartmoor.

'Love Poems and Others' begins with an imaginative little lyric, 'Count Fersen to the Queen', in which Count Fersen addresses Marie Antoinette. Among the twelve poems in this section are an odd love poem, 'The Lament of the Tortured Lover', written as though by a man to a woman:

> In twenty years your face will be haggard,
> Your eyes will be cold,
> Your sagging breasts will not stir my desire

and an affectionate sonnet, 'To M.E.L.M. in Absence', written to Max Mallowan, which begins:

Now is the winter past, but for my part
Still winter stays until we meet again.
Dear love, I have your promise and your heart
But lacking touch and sight, spring buds bring pain.

The final poem in this section is 'Jenny by the Sky', reprinted from the 1965 volume of stories and poems for children, *Star Over Bethlehem*.

The concluding section of the volume, 'Verses of Nowadays', consists of four poems, two of which are very slight, and one ('Picnic 1960) no less slight, perhaps, but of interest as being *à la* Betjeman:

Afternoon tea by the side of the road,
That is the meal that I love,
Hundreds of cars rushing past all the time,
Sunshine and clouds up above!

Get out the chairs and set up the tea,
Serviettes, too, are a must.
Never a moment that's quiet or dull,
Sausage rolls flavoured with dust!

Time to go home? Strew the orange peel round,
Leave paper and portions of pie,
Pack up the crocks and get into the queue,
Perfect picnic place, love, and goodbye . . .

Rather more strongly felt than its fellow in 'Verses of Nowadays' is 'Racial Musings', especially in the second of its two stanzas:

Some think, and more than one,
That coffee-coloured children meet the case,
It is our duty so to take one's fun
That the resulting mixture has a face
That nicely illustrates Mendelian lore.
Oh, coffee-coloured world,
You'll be a BORE.
Satiety but no variety,
A BORE. A BORE. A BORE.

However, the most touching poem in the book, presumably also privately addressed to Mallowan, is 'Remembrance' in which Agatha Christie envisages dying before her husband, which in due course she was to do. It ends with the lines,

I died – but not my love for you,
That lives for aye – though dumb,
Remember this
If I should leave you in the days to come.

The publication of *Poems* did not excite a great amount of critical interest. Several reviewers did not quite know what to make of Dame Agatha's verses, though William Weaver in the London *Financial Times* found them 'deft and ladylike and never cloying'.

Postern of Fate (1973)

The last of Agatha Christie's 'crime in the past' novels, *Postern of Fate* is also the last novel she wrote. Five more titles were to be published (two novels, two volumes of stories, and an autobiography), two of them posthumously, but all had been written earlier.

The eighty-two-year-old author's final novel was a mystery-thriller involving Tommy and Tuppence Beresford, now a somewhat arthritic but still young-hearted pair in their seventies. The title of the novel derives from James Elroy Flecker's poem, *Gates of Damascus*, some lines from which are printed as an epigraph:

> Four great gates has the city of Damascus . . .
> Postern of Fate, the Desert Gate, Disaster's Cavern,
> Fort of Fear . . .
> Pass not beneath, O Caravan, or pass not singing.
> Have you heard
> That silence where the birds are dead, yet something
> pipeth like a bird?

The aged Tommy and Tuppence have moved into a new house, and their faithful factotum Albert Batt is still with them. (We are told that Albert's wife, Amy, has been dead for some years; however, when she was alive her name, we were told in *By the Pricking of My Thumbs*, was Milly.) A number of popular novels and children's books have been left in the house, and as Tuppence is sorting them out, she notices certain letters underlined in red in a copy of Robert Louis Stevenson's *The Black Arrow*. The letters spelled out a message: 'Mary Jordan did not die naturally. It was one of us. I think I know which.' Naturally, Tuppence is determined to find out more; asking questions of a number of local and not so local people, they eventually arrive at – well, not exactly an answer, but something that might be thought to resemble, in other circumstances, an answer.

The circumlocutionary style of that last sentence is not unlike that of Dame Agatha in the highly self-indulgent *Postern of Fate*. After Tuppence's discovery of the marked copy of *The Black Arrow*, very little happens until eighteen chapters later, when a minor character is killed and it becomes clear that those spies or evildoers who were active fifty or more years ago when Mary Jordan died unnaturally are still in business.

Among those who give Tommy and Tuppence help, advice and encouragement in their quest are such characters from past Christie novels as Colonel Pikeaway, ex-head of the Special Branch, and the enigmatic financier, Mr Robinson. Neither has appeared in earlier Tommy and Tuppence adventures, but both were encountered in the Poirot mystery, *Cat Among the Pigeons*, and the thriller, *Passenger to Frankfurt*.

This is a rambling, highly self-indulgent and not always coherent novel: if it is readable, this is because of information it indirectly provides about Dame Agatha's view of the world in her last years, and about the books she loved as a child. Tuppence, browsing among the books she finds on the shelves in their newly acquired house, The Laurels, comments on several of them:

'Oh fancy! All these. I really have forgotten a lot of these. Oh, here's *The Amulet* and here's *The Psamayad*. Here's *The New Treasure Seekers*. Oh, I love all those. No, don't put them in shelves yet, Albert. I think I'll have to read them first. Well, I mean, one or two of them first, perhaps. Now, what's this one? Let me see. *The Red Cockade*. Oh yes, that was one of the historical ones. That was very exciting. And there's *Under the Red Robe*, too. Lots of Stanley Weyman. Lots and lots. Of course I used to read those when I was about ten or eleven. I shouldn't be surprised if I don't come across *The Prisoner of Zenda*.' She sighed with enormous pleasure at the remembrance. *The Prisoner of Zenda*. One's first introduction, really, to the romantic novel. The romance of Princess Flavia. The King of Ruritania. Rudolph Rassendyll, some name like that whom one dreamt of at night.'

Albert handed down another selection.

'Oh yes,' said Tuppence, 'that's better, really. That's earlier again. I must put the early ones all together. Now, let me see. What have we got here? *Treasure Island*. Well, that's nice but of course I have read *Treasure Island* again, and I've seen, I think, two films of it. I don't like seeing it on films, it never seems right. Oh – and here's *Kidnapped*. Yes, I always liked that.'

Amiable padding, but clearly this is Dame Agatha remembering her childhood, which she does at some length. Similarly, when a disproportionate amount of space is devoted to Tommy's thoughts on modern tradesmen, you have the feeling that the passage was inserted because Dame Agatha had just been let down by one of them:

Some days before he had had the same kind of trouble. Electricians arriving in a kindly tangle of optimism and efficiency had started work. 'Coming along fine now, not much more to do,' they said. 'We'll be back this afternoon.' But they hadn't been back that afternoon. Tommy was not precisely surprised. He was used, now, to the general pattern of labour in the building trade, electrical trade, gas employees and others. They came, they showed efficiency, they made optimistic remarks, they went away to fetch something. They didn't come back. One rang up numbers on the telephone but they always seemed to be the wrong numbers. If they were the right numbers, the right man was not working at this particular branch of the trade, whatever it was . . .

There is much more of this sort of thing in *Postern of Fate* than there is of mystery or action. There are also far too many meandering conversations about nothing very much at all, and some extraordinarily unlight banter:

'All right,' said Tommy. 'You were tempted. You felt it was a good buy.'
'Yes. At least – what d'you mean "a goodbye"?'
'I mean b-u-y,' said Tommy.
'Oh. I thought you were going to leave the room and were saying goodbye to me.'

Not surprisingly, in some of these conversations, Dame Agatha forgets who it is who is supposed to be speaking. For instance:

'I shouldn't think there would be anything hidden here, do you, Tommy?'
'It doesn't seem the sort of house where anything would have been likely to

be hidden. Lots of other people have lived in the house since those days.'
'Yes. Family after family, as far as I can make out. Well, I suppose it might
be hidden up in an attic or down in the cellar. Or perhaps buried under the
summerhouse floor. Anywhere.'
'Anyway, it'll be quite fun,' said Tuppence. . . .

The to-and-fro of conversation then proceeds as though the partners have
mentally changed step. As it happens, the conversational styles of Tommy and
Tuppence are so alike that it hardly matters which of them is speaking at any
given moment.

On one page Tommy sets out for an appointment in Harrow, and arrives
instead in Hampstead, at a house near the heath. No matter, it appears to be the
right place. Elsewhere, a twelve-year-old boy is given dialogue which would
sound impossibly stilted for an adult, and is simply impossible for a child.

Verbs are certainly more inclined to be passive than active in *Postern of Fate*.
Certain facts become known, certain actions are taken, several identities are
revealed. The dénouement is as vague as that. Some of the clues on a list which
Tuppence has compiled are explained – though we were not exactly on
tenterhooks to know whether Grin-hen-Lo would turn out to be *Lohengrin*
backwards. (It is from another Wagner opera, *Die Meistersinger*, that Mr
Robinson unexpectedly quotes Hans Sachs' 'Wahn, Wahn, überall Wahn', and
he is courteous enough to say it in English: 'Mad, mad, all the whole world is
mad.')[15] Unless this reader has missed it (and he has read the novel more than
twice), the reason why a certain greenhouse used to be known as 'KK' is never
explained. Since an Austrian spy is involved, can it be something to do with
'Königlich und Kaiserlich'? It is another of life's minor mysteries which will
remain unsolved.

By far the most engaging character in the book is Hannibal, the small, black
Manchester terrier who helps his master and mistress in their investigations, and
who has a nice line in dialogue and, for that matter, stream-of-consciousness
thought. Agatha Christie was always able to write about her canine characters
with insight and sympathy. Hannibal is one of her most successful dogged
detectives, and thoroughly deserves the honour accorded him in the closing lines
of the novel, when he is made a Count of the Realm. (Tuppence – and Agatha? –
had been re-reading Stanley Weyman's *Count Hannibal*.) Hannibal also deserves
the photograph of himself which appeared on the back of the dust-jacket of the
first edition of *Postern of Fate*. (The photograph is actually of the Mallowan's
Manchester Terrier, Bingo, whom they loved dearly. Sir Max revealed in his
memoirs that Hannibal was based upon Bingo: Agatha Christie, however,
dedicated the novel to 'Hannibal and his master'.)

There is not much point in listing all the inaccuracies and inconsistencies in
Postern of Fate; or the improbabilities, among them the Beresford grandchildren, aged fifteen, eleven and seven, two of whom are supposed to be twins! The
greatest improbability of all is that the novel should be, in spite of all, enjoyably
readable: at least to readers who have followed Agatha Christie through the
years. It is not, however, recommended as an introduction to her *oeuvre*. As
Tommy rather unwisely remarks in the penultimate chapter, in answer to his
daughter Deborah who doubts that his and her mother's latest adventure would
make much of a book, 'You'd be surprised what people *will* read and enjoy!'

A trace of cynicism from the distinguished author? Let us hope not. Her *credo*, in these her last years, would seem to be disillusioned rather than cynical. There are traces of it in the autobiography, finished eight years earlier, and surely also in these words of Colonel Pikeaway in this, Agatha Christie's last novel:

. . . big fortunes made out of drugs, drug pushers, drugs being sent all over the world, being marketed, a worship of money. Money not just for buying yourself a big house and two Rolls-Royces, but money for making more money and doing down, doing away with the old beliefs. Beliefs in honesty, in fair trading. You don't want equality in the world, you want the strong to help the weak. You want the rich to finance the poor. You want the honest and the good to be looked up to and admired. Finance! Things are coming back now to finance all the time. What finance is doing, where it's going, what it's supporting, how far hidden it is.

A final comment: the story 'The Herb of Death' from *The Thirteen Problems* (or *The Tuesday Club Murders*), written more than forty years earlier, contains material which is not altogether irrelevant to a consideration of *Postern of Fate*.

Poirot's Early Cases or *Hercule Poirot's Early Cases* (1974)

On Saturday, 23 March 1974, *The Mousetrap* closed at the Ambassadors Theatre, but only in order to move next door to the slightly larger St Martin's Theatre, where it opened on Monday the 25th, without missing a single night's performance.

The film version of Agatha Christie's 1934 novel, *Murder on the Orient Express*, opened in London in November at the ABC Cinema in Shaftesbury Avenue, its première attended by Her Majesty the Queen to whom Dame Agatha and the stars of the film were presented. After the screening there was a banquet at Claridge's, and this proved to be the occasion of the last public appearance which Agatha Christie, now approaching eighty-five, was to make in London. Max Mallowan in his memoirs recalled watching as Lord Mountbatten (whose son-in-law Lord Brabourne had produced the film) escorted Dame Agatha 'out of the dining-room at midnight and raising her arm in farewell. Shy as always, she enjoyed this occasion to the full.'

When A.L. Rowse sent her a copy of his book about his cat, *Peter the White Cat of Trenarren*, Agatha Christie wrote: 'I enjoyed your book about the White Cat so much that I really must ponder seriously about your suggestion of a little book about my cats and dogs, possibly in the Christmas season, though I rather doubt whether my publisher would care for the idea.'

As it seemed unlikely that Agatha Christie would find the stamina to complete another novel, her publishers issued, as the 1974 Christie, a collection of early Poirot stories, under the title of *Poirot's Early Cases*. (For America, this became *Hercule Poirot's Early Cases*.) All of the eighteen stories, fourteen of which are narrated by Hastings, had been written between 1923 and 1936, and most had appeared originally in magazines or newspapers. All but two were new to Great Britain in volume form, but none was new to the United States.

Three of the stories ('The Lost Mine', 'The Chocolate Box' and 'The Veiled Lady') had appeared in the US edition of *Poirot Investigates* in 1925 (though not in the 1924 original British edition, which contains three stories fewer than the American.) Two ('How Does Your Garden Grow?' and 'Problem at Sea') come from the 1939 American volume of stories, *The Regatta Mystery*. Two ('The Third-Floor Flat' and 'The Adventure of Johnnie Waverly') are to be found in *Three Blind Mice*, published in the USA in 1950. Three stories ('Double Sin', 'The Double Clue' and 'Wasps' Nest') come from the 1961 American volume, *Double Sin*. *The Under Dog* (USA only: 1951) finds its entire contents, with the exception of its title-story, reissued in (*Hercule*) *Poirot's Early Cases*: 'The Market Basing Mystery', 'The Lemesurier Inheritance', 'The Cornish Mystery', 'The King of Clubs', 'The Submarine Plans', 'The Adventure of the Clapham Cook' and 'The Plymouth Express'.

Comments on most of these stories will be found earlier in these pages. As already mentioned, although 'The Submarine Plans' had not appeared in an earlier British volume, an expanded version of the same story, entitled 'The Incredible Theft', was included in *Murder in the Mews* or *Dead Man's Mirror* (1937).

The only two stories in *Poirot's Early Cases* to have appeared earlier in a British volume are 'The Market Basing Mystery' and 'The Veiled Lady', both of which were in a volume of mystery stories for young readers, *Thirteen for Luck* (US: 1961; UK: 1966). This consists of stories from other collections, selected as being suitable for children. 'The Veiled Lady' had also appeared earlier in Great Britain, in the sixty-four-page booklet, *Poirot Lends a Hand*, which contained three Poirot stories (Polybooks: London and New York, 1946).

It is odd that, although most of these stories date from the same period as those in *Poirot Investigates* (1924), they were not published at that time in a volume, for they are certainly not inferior to the stories in *Poirot Investigates*. 'The Affair at the Victory Ball' would appear to be the earliest Poirot short story, narrated by Hastings shortly after the events related in Agatha Christie's first novel, *The Mysterious Affair at Styles*. 'Pure chance,' Hastings begins his narrative,

led my friend Hercule Poirot, formerly chief of the Belgian force, to be connected with the Styles case. His success brought him notoriety, and he decided to devote himself to the solving of problems in crime. Having been wounded on the Somme and invalided out of the Army, I finally took up my quarters with him in London. Since I have a first-hand knowledge of most of his cases, it has been suggested to me that I select some of the most interesting and place them on record.

'The Chocolate Box' is the famous quasi-failure, the only not completely successful case in Poirot's career. It took place during Poirot's early days on the Belgian police force, and he tells Hastings of it in order that, if he, Poirot, ever shows signs of becoming conceited, Hastings should murmur 'Chocolate Box' and recall him to a becoming modesty. Naturally, Poirot tells his story in such a way that, although he failed to solve the case at the time, ('My grey cells, they functioned not at all') he comes quite well out of the narrative.

This is one of two stories which are narrated not by Hastings to the reader but by Poirot to Hastings. The other is 'The Lost Mine'. Four of the eighteen stories are not first-person narrations by either Hastings or Poirot, and Hastings does not feature in them. They were written later than the others, after Agatha

Christie had tired of Hastings and banished him to South America, but before she had relented and brought him back again. These stories are 'The Third-Floor Flat', 'Wasps' Nest', 'Problem at Sea' and 'How Does Your Garden Grow?'.

Curtain: Poirot's Last Case (1975)

As her publishers had feared, Agatha Christie was no longer able to sustain the effort and concentration to complete another novel. She had, of course, no need to. She had gone on writing for as long as it remained not too difficult a task, but for many years now her income had been such that it was pointless for her to earn any more. A company, Agatha Christie Ltd, set up as long ago as 1955 to handle incoming royalties on all her works after that date, had been reorganized in 1968 when the firm of Booker McConnell bought a fifty-one per cent stake for an unspecified sum. Later, some pre-1955 Agatha Christie titles were taken under the wing of the company, and Booker McConnell extended its holding to sixty-four percent. It is now by far the major shareholder, the remainder of the company being partly owned by Agatha Christie's daughter and grandson and partly vested in various family and charitable trusts. In the year ending 31 December 1974, the income of Agatha Christie Ltd (i.e. the royalties accruing during that year on books, films and plays, less agents' commissions) was £366,000.

Agatha Christie and her family may have had no need of a new 'Christie for Christmas' in 1975, but her publishers, understandably, felt differently. Remembering the two crime novels (one featuring Poirot and the other Miss Marple) which their author had written during the Second World War and salted away for posthumous publication, her publishers, in the person of Sir William Collins, approached Dame Agatha with the request that she release one of the two novels for publication in 1975. She was at first reluctant to do so, but eventually agreed that *Curtain*, the earlier novel of the two, and the one in which Poirot conducts his final investigation, could appear in time for the Christmas season.

Agatha Christie had already assigned the author's rights in *Curtain* to her daughter Rosalind (and those in the Miss Marple novel, *Sleeping Murder*, to Max Mallowan). ('I thought it a useful way of benefiting my relations,' she explained to an interviewer. 'I gave one to my husband and one to my daughter – definitely made over to them, by deed of gift. So when I am no more they can bring them out and have a jaunt on the proceeds – I hope!'

Rosalind was able to have, or at least to begin, her 'jaunt on the proceeds' in her mother's lifetime, for the amount of money earned by *Curtain* was remarkable, even by Agatha Christie's standards. A first British edition of 120,000 sold out quickly, American hardback rights were sold for an advance of 300,000 dollars, and American paperback rights for one million dollars. No doubt Agatha Christie had not realized how generous she was being when she assigned those rights away in the forties; but her own earnings in 1975 were close to £1,000,000. (In the United States, the success of the film version of *Murder on the Orient Express* had resulted in sales of 3,000,000 copies of a paperback reprint of the novel.)

In *Curtain*, whose sub-title is 'Poirot's Last Case', Hastings returns as narrator for the first time since *Dumb Witness* in 1937 (except for a few short stories written earlier but not collected into volumes before the sixties), and immediately the problem of chronology arises. To some extent, Hastings' place as Poirot's colleague had been taken over in the post-war years by Ariadne Oliver. Now, at the end, Hastings comes back to visit his old friend Poirot who is staying at, of all places, Styles, the country house which had been the scene of their first case, *The Mysterious Affair at Styles*, published in 1920. But when is this end, when must this last case, in the course of which Poirot dies, be presumed to happen? We know that *Curtain* was written during the war years of the forties, but there is, of course, no reference to the war in the novel, for Agatha Christie had to remain vague as regards the year in which Poirot was to die. She had determined that it would be shortly after her own death, and she was, at the time of writing *Curtain*, a healthy woman in her early fifties.

This plays havoc with the ages of the characters in the novel, and not least with that of Poirot and Hastings. It must be assumed that the events in *Curtain* take place after those in *Elephants Can Remember*, Poirot's penultimate case in 1972. Hastings mentions that their earlier Styles adventure had been in 1916. He and Poirot are therefore fifty-six years older than they were in Agatha Christie's first novel. This would make Hastings eighty-six years of age, and Poirot at least one hundred and twenty! From what is often called internal evidence, however, the reader can work out Hastings' age in *Curtain* as being just over fifty, while the description of Poirot is of a man close to death, but nearer to eighty-five than to one hundred and twenty. We should simply be grateful that Agatha Christie, while the bombs were falling on London, gave thought to the rounding-off of Poirot's career, and refrain from looking a gift detective in the mouth.

Curtain is a sad, muted and nostalgic book. Sad, in that Poirot dies, and apparently without having brought the murderer to justice; muted, in that the inhabitants of Styles, no longer a country manor house but a private hotel or guesthouse, not unlike the one in *The Mousetrap*, are, with one or two exceptions, people who are old or disappointed or embittered; nostalgic, in that Hastings is continually aware of the wheel having come full circle, of Poirot and himself ending their long and productive collaboration in the house in which they had begun it. Hastings learns, or is at least momentarily aware, that nostalgia for the happy past is a snare and a delusion. The past, after all, is happy mainly because it is past, because it has been endured.

Hastings' wife has died in Argentina, but one of his four children, his daughter Judith, is among the guests at Styles. It is because of a problem concerning Judith that Hastings is driven to contemplate, and even to take steps to commit, murder. Poirot, during the course of events, fulfils a prophecy made jokingly by Inspector Japp forty years earlier in *The ABC Murders*.

Confined to a wheelchair, his face thin, lined and wrinkled, though with moustache (dyed) and hair (a wig) still as black as ever, Poirot has to rely more than ever on his little grey cells. 'This, Hastings,' he is forced to admit, 'will be my last case. It will be, too, my most interesting case – and my most interesting criminal. For in X we have a technique superb, magnificent, that arouses admiration in spite of oneself. So far, *mon cher*, this X has operated with so much ability that he has defeated me, Hercule Poirot! He has developed the attack to which I can find no answer.'

X, the murderer, does indeed operate in such a manner (a more than usually improbable manner, it must be confessed) that the law cannot touch him. Nor, it seems can Hercule Poirot. It is only four months after Poirot's death, when Hastings comes into possession of a manuscript bequeathed to him by his old friend, that the truth is revealed. A knowledge of Shakespeare's *Othello* and of the character of Iago, in particular, has helped Poirot considerably. In fact, he leaves Hastings, as clues, copies of *Othello* and of the play *John Ferguson* by St John Ervine, an interesting playwright of Agatha Christie's generation who is now almost forgotten. *John Ferguson* (which Christie misspells) is Ervine's finest play.

The ending of *Curtain* is one of the most surprising that Agatha Christie ever devised. If it somehow fails to make the effect that it ought to, this may be because the character of the murderer has been too lightly sketched throughout the novel, and his motivation not made sufficiently convincing. The basic idea behind *Curtain* had been adumbrated in one chapter of the 1932 novel, *Peril at End House*; had its characters been more fully developed, Poirot's last case could have become Christie's finest novel.

If *Curtain* is not Agatha Christie's finest, it is, surely, her saddest novel. Who among her readers could fail to be affected by the death of the lovable and infuriating Hercule Poirot? What other characters of fiction has had his obituary published on the front page of the *New York Times*?

HERCULE POIROT IS DEAD: FAMED BELGIAN DETECTIVE

Hercule Poirot, a Belgian detective who became internationally famous, has died in England. His age was unknown.

Mr Poirot achieved fame as a private investigator after he retired as a member of the Belgian police force in 1904. His career, as chronicled in the novels of Dame Agatha Christie, was one of the most illustrious in fiction.

At the end of his life, he was arthritic and had a bad heart. He was in a wheelchair often, and was carried from his bedroom to the public lounge at Styles Court, a nursing home in Essex, wearing a wig and false moustaches to mask the signs of age that offended his vanity. In his active days, he was always impeccably dressed.

The news of his death, given by Dame Agatha, was not unexpected. Word that he was near death reached here last May.

Dame Agatha reports in *Curtain* that he managed, in one final gesture, to perform one more act of cerebration that saved an innocent bystander from disaster. 'Nothing in his life became him like the leaving of it,' to quote Shakespeare, whom Poirot frequently misquoted.[16]

Sleeping Murder: Miss Marple's Last Case (1976)

The Mallowans and their family celebrated Christmas, 1975, in their Berkshire house at Wallingford. Dame Agatha was by now very frail, but she participated in the family Christmas and also observed Christmas as a religious festival when she insisted on being carried downstairs and placed on the sofa in the drawing-room in order to receive Holy Communion for what was to be the last time.

Ten years earlier, at the age of seventy-five, Agatha Christie had written:[17]

I am ready now to accept death. I have been singularly fortunate. I have with me my husband, my daughter, my grandson, my kind son-in-law – the people who make up my world. I have not yet quite reached the time when I am a complete nuisance to them all.

I have always admired the Esquimaux. One fine day a delicious meal is cooked for dear old mother, and then she goes walking away over the ice – *and doesn't come back* . . .

One should be proud of leaving life like that – with dignity and resolution.

It is, of course, all very well to write these grand words. What will *really* happen is that I shall probably live to be ninety-three, drive everyone mad by being unable to hear what they say to me, complain bitterly of the latest scientific hearing aids, ask innumerable questions, immediately forget the answers and ask the same questions again. I shall quarrel violently with some patient nurse-attendant and accuse her of poisoning me, or walk out of the latest establishment for genteel old ladies, causing endless trouble to my suffering family. And when I finally succumb to bronchitis, a murmur will go around of 'One can't help feeling that it really is a merciful relief . . .'

And it *will* be a merciful relief (to them) and much the best thing to happen.

It happened on 12 January 1976. Max Mallowan added this brief Epilogue to the book[18] he had just finished writing:

As I came to the last few pages of these memoirs my beloved Agatha died, peacefully and gently, as I wheeled her out in her chair after luncheon to the drawing-room. She had been failing for some time and death came as a merciful release, though it has left me with a feeling of emptiness after forty-five years of a loving and merry companionship. Few men know what it is to live in harmony beside an imaginative, creative mind which inspires life with zest. To me, the greatest consolation has been the recognition, which has come from many hundreds of letters, that admiration was blended in equal measure with love – a love and happiness which Agatha radiated both in her person and in her books. Requiescat.

Agatha Christie died in a week when *Curtain: Poirot's Last Case* was still heading the bestseller lists in the United Kingdom, the USA and Japan. Her death made front page news all over the world, and there were lengthy obituaries in the leading newspapers. The London *Daily Telegraph*[19] published two pieces whose titles indicate the two kinds of public interest in Agatha Christie: a literary appraisal whose headline was 'Like Poirot, Agatha Christie's Last Case is Over', and a financial report headed 'Richest Writer Britain Has Produced'. The front page of the newspaper also carried the story of Agatha Christie's death: 'Lights dimmed as Dame Agatha dies.' The two West End theatres in which her plays were running, the St Martin's and the Savoy, dimmed their outside lights as a mark of respect. At the St Martin's Theatre, *The Mousetrap* was in its twenty-fourth year, while at the Savoy a successful revival of *Murder at the Vicarage* was approaching its two hundredth performance.

The *Daily Telegraph* obituary thoughtlessly revealed the solutions of two of Dame Agatha's finest mysteries, as a result of which the Editor received a number of angry or indignant letters from Christie fans.

Agatha Christie was buried, on 16 January, in St Mary's churchyard, in the village of Cholsey, Berkshire, on a site which she had chosen herself ten years earlier, and where she is now joined by Max Mallowan who died on 19 August 1978. These lines from Spenser's *The Faerie Queen* are inscribed on her tombstone.

Sleepe after toyle, port after stormie seas,
Ease after war, death after life, does greatly please.

'She was beyond question,' as the London *Times* obituary claimed, 'one of the half-dozen best detective story writers in the world.' And she was, beyond any shadow of doubt, far and away the most popular. Though perhaps not in every part of the world. Several days after her death, *The Times*[20] printed this story under the heading, 'Agatha Christie denounced in communist press':

> The late Dame Agatha Christie has been denounced in Hongkong's communist press as a running-dog for 'the rich and the powerful'.
>
> In a rare and curious anti-British tirade in the party's leading daily, *Ta Kung Pao*, she is said to have 'described crimes committed by the middle and lowerclasses of British society but never exposed their social causes'.
>
> The newspaper's film critic writes: In her book *Witness for the Prosecution* she extolled the great lawyer and judge as 'the best people'. This explains clearly whom her works are serving and what political functions they are performing. Accordingly in 1971 the Queen made her a Dame Commander of the British Empire, the female equivalent of a knighthood.

In October, 1976, *Sleeping Murder: Miss Marple's Last Case* was posthumously published. This, the second of the two novels she had written during the Second World War, was the one Agatha Christie had made over, by deed of gift, to Max Mallowan. Until it appeared, a number of readers had continued to entertain the hope that, one day, their author would allow Hercule Poirot and Jane Marple to meet and to work together on a murder case. But this idea had never appealed to Agatha Christie. 'Why should they?' she wrote.[21] 'I am sure they would not enjoy it at all. Hercule Poirot, the complete egoist, would not like being taught his business by an elderly spinster lady. He was a professional sleuth, he would not be at home at all in Miss Marple's world. No, they are both *stars*, and they are stars in their own right. I shall not let them meet unless I feel a sudden and unexpected urge to do so.'

She never felt that urge. Unlike Poirot in *Curtain*, Miss Marple is allowed to survive her last case, but as with *Curtain* the chronology of *Sleeping Murder* will not bear too close a scrutiny. Although it was written in the early forties, the reader must imagine it is happening after 1971 and *Nemesis*, if he is to regard it as really being Miss Marple's last case. (A further posthumous volume, entitled *Miss Marple's Final Cases*, was to appear three years later, but would turn out to consist of stories written and previously published at least thirty years earlier.)

The heroine of *Sleeping Murder* attends a performance in London of Webster's *The Duchess of Malfi* with John Gielgud in the cast. This can only have been during the Gielgud repertory season at the Theatre Royal, Haymarket, in 1944, when Gielgud played Ferdinand to Peggy Ashcroft's Duchess, which makes it difficult not to envisage the events of the narrative as occurring in the mid-forties. And, indeed, Miss Marple is presented as 'an attractive old lady, tall and thin, with pink cheeks and blue eyes and a gentle, rather fussy manner'. There is no hint of that fragility of extreme old age which had crept up on her by the time of *At Bertram's Hotel* (1965), or *Nemesis* which, published in 1971, must be regarded as Miss Marple's real last case.

Towards the end of the performance of *The Duchess of Malfi*, when she hears the actor playing Ferdinand utter the famous line, 'Cover her face; mine eyes dazzle: she died young', Gwenda Reed reacts in an extraordinary manner:

> Gwenda screamed.
>
> She sprang up from her seat, pushed blindly past the others out into the aisle, through the exit and up the stairs and so to the street. She did not stop, even then, but half walked, half ran, in a blind panic up the Haymarket.

Yes, it was clearly the Theatre Royal, Haymarket (though Agatha Christie calls it His Majesty's Theatre, which is opposite). What, one wonders, can John Gielgud, who played Ferdinand, have thought? He is an actor who would have noticed a member of his audience walking, nay, running out on him.

Gwenda had experienced a sudden flash of revelation. She had heard that line before, as a child, and it had been accompanied by a vision of murder and of a murderer. Inexplicably, it seemed to have taken place in the house by the sea in South Devon which she, a young married woman of twenty-one and just arrived from New Zealand, had only recently bought.

Gwenda's husband Giles is a distant cousin of the well-known novelist Raymond West, and so it comes to pass that Raymond's aunt, Miss Marple, agrees to help Gwenda unravel her mystery. This is one of Agatha Christie's favourite 'crimes in the past', and it is one of the most baffling, for there are several questions to be answered. Who, if anyone, was killed, and where, and when, and, of course, why? Also, of course, by whom? There is one enormous coincidence to be swallowed, but Dame Agatha disarmingly dares the reader not to swallow it: 'It's not *impossible*, my dear,' Miss Marple says to Gwenda. 'It's just a very remarkable coincidence – and remarkable coincidences do happen.'

Does the line from *The Duchess of Malfi* offer too helpful a clue to those who know their Webster? Or is that merely a red herring? Incest does play a part in *Sleeping Murder* as well as in Webster's play. One or two characters from St Mary Mead make brief appearances, there is an enjoyable postscript set on the terrace of the Imperial Hotel, Torquay, and there is also an odd little mystery which has been referred to earlier. At the beginning of Chapter 10 of *Sleeping Murder* Gwenda visits a sanitorium in Norfolk, and has an odd, chance encounter with an old lady while she is sitting in a waiting-room:

> Her eyes rested thoughtfully on Gwenda and presently she leaned forward towards her and spoke in what was almost a whisper.
>
> '*Is it your poor child, my dear?*'
>
> Gwenda looked slightly taken aback. She said doubtfully: 'No – no. It isn't.'
>
> 'Ah, I wondered.' The old lady nodded her head and sipped her milk. Then she said conversationally, 'Half past ten – that's the time. It's always at half past ten. Most remarkable.' She lowered her voice and leaned forward again.
>
> 'Behind the fireplace,' she breathed. 'But don't say *I* told you.'

In *Sleeping Murder* this leads to nothing, and we are to assume that the old lady is merely a senile patient of the nursing home. But perhaps she is the Julia Lancaster who in 1968 will say (or has said?) very much the same thing to Tuppence Beresford in *By the Pricking of My Thumbs* (see p. 213). A similar incident is referred to by a character in *The Pale Horse* of 1961 (see p. 194). Is there some deeper meaning to this recurrent Christiean motif? Should research students be set to work on it? Or is it, as seems most likely, based on something once said in the waiting room of a nursing home to Agatha Christie, and never forgotten by her? But could she really have used it for the second and third times without realizing that she had already made use of it? Again, did no editor at her publishers' ever draw her attention to it? Let it remain 'a marvel and a mystery to the world'.

Once again, life chose to imitate Agatha Christie's art. The following news story from its Washington correspondent appeared in the London *Times* on 17 December 1979, under the heading 'Visions find an "Agatha Christie" murderer':

A particularly gruesome murder has been uncovered in North Carolina, in circumstances very similar to Agatha Christie's last novel, *Sleeping Murder*. In the book, a woman returns to her childhood home, where events trigger memories long suppressed of the time when she saw. . . .[22]

In the North Carolina case, Mrs Annie Perry recently started having 'visions' of the time her father disappeared in April, 1944. She was then 10. She told the police last week that 'on Easter morning she saw her mother in the kitchen and the sink full of pots and pans of bloody water.'

Later that day she saw her father's body almost naked in an unused room. During the night she heard 'butchering sounds'.

The family lived on a farm, and had an outside privy. In the following week, when using the privy she looked down the hole and saw her father's face floating.

Her mother, Mrs Winnie Cameron, reported her husband missing and in due course obtained a divorce, on grounds of desertion.

When the daughter recently began to have 'visions', she went to a psychiatrist who sent her to the police.

They took the matter seriously enough to obtain a search warrant. She took them to the site of the privy, where they dug and found human bones.

On Friday afternoon the police found Mrs Cameron. She had shot herself, leaving a suicide note in which she confessed to the murder of her husband.

Sleeping Murder: Miss Marple's Last Case was enormously successful, attracting more favourable reviews than had been accorded to Poirot's last case. The *Chicago Tribune* put it succinctly: 'Agatha Christie saved the best for last.'

An Autobiography (1977)

Published posthumously, *An Autobiography* by Agatha Christie was begun in Iraq in 1950 and finished in England in 1965. It is a very long book, and although it is but intermittently revealing it is immensely readable. What it fails, no doubt deliberately, to reveal, except very occasionally, is the kind of intimate detail of personal relationships which so many memoirs, and certainly biographies, do nowadays delight in presenting. Agatha Christie was essentially a private person. She enjoyed, in this volume, sharing with her readers a huge amount of detail concerning her childhood and youth, her family life in the early years of the century, her parents and grandparents, but she tells only what she wants to tell, she remembers a great deal, and she conveniently forgets much else.

Three-quarters of the book's length is devoted to the first forty years of the author's life, of which she seems to have had almost total recall. The second forty or more years are squeezed into the remaining and more reticent quarter, and you are given the distinct impression that, as she grew older, it is those early years that Agatha Christie most enjoyed recalling and writing about. 'What I plan to do,' she noted in her Foreword which, unlike most Forewords, was written at the outset and not after completion of the rest of the book, 'is to enjoy the pleasures of memory – not hurrying myself – writing a few pages from time to time. It is a task that will probably go on for years.' And so it did.

Though you cannot completely trust the elderly author's memory, *An Autobiography* is valuable not only for the information it provides but also for revealing Agatha Christie's opinions on a number of important issues; opinions which she had often attributed to Poirot or Miss Marple or Mrs Oliver in the novels and which it is fascinating to find repeated by the author *in propria persona*. Equally valuable are her comments on her own working methods. 'Plots,' she reveals, 'come to me at such odd moments: when I am walking along a street, or examining a hatshop with particular interest, suddenly a splendid idea comes into my head, and I think, "Now that would be a neat way of covering up the crime so that nobody would see the point." Of course, all the practical details are still to be worked out, and the people have to creep slowly into my consciousness, but I jot down my splendid idea in an exercise book.'

An Autobiography has proved to be as popular as any Christie murder mystery. 'Agatha Christie has done it again,' said *The Times*, '. . . a book that is wonderfully easy to read and as engrossing as *Ten Little Niggers*'.

Miss Marple's Final Cases and two other stories (1979)

Miss Marple's Final Cases was published in the UK only, for the stories were already available in other volumes published in the USA. Two of the stories, 'The Dressmaker's Doll' and 'Sanctuary', are to be found in *Double Sin* (1961: see p. 193); four stories, 'Strange Jest', 'Tape Measure Murder', 'The Case of the Perfect Maid' and 'The Case of the Caretaker', are from *Three Blind Mice* (1950: see p. 153); and the remaining two stories, 'Miss Marple Tells a Story' and 'In a Glass Darkly', come from *The Regatta Mystery* (1939: see p. 114).

Of the eight stories, two ('The Dressmaker's Doll' and 'In a Glass Darkly') are not Miss Marple adventures. The remaining six ought not really to have been called *Miss Marple's Final Cases*, for they are examples of that redoubtable lady in mid-career. The publisher's justification for putting together a collection of them was that, although they had appeared in magazines in the past, the stories were being published in volume form for the first time in Great Britain. A statement to this effect appeared in the 'blurb' on the inside of the front jacket. It is, however, slightly inaccurate, for 'Tape-Measure Murder' had found its way into *Thirteen for Luck*, 'a selection of mystery stories for young readers' which Collins had published in 1966.

Unless a few fugitive stories are collected to make a further volume, *Miss Marple's Final Cases* is the final book to appear by the most widely read British author of all time. Let the last comments be statements of a contrasting character from Dame Agatha's agent, Edmund Cork, and from the author herself. Mr Cork was quoted[23] in 1975 as saying: 'Her sales go up every year. A million-and-a-half paperbacks a year in Britain alone. She is unquestionably the bestselling author of all time. Every estimate of her sales I have seen is a gross underestimate.' Fair enough: that is the language of agents. Interviewed by Lord Snowdon[24] who asked her what she hoped to be remembered for, Agatha Christie replied: 'Well, I would like it to be said that I was a good writer of detective and thriller stories.'

Agatha Christie was an exceptionally good writer of detective and thriller stories.

Notes to pp. 201–243

1 In Earl F. Bargainnier: *The Gentle Art of Murder* (1980). Barzun and Taylor wrongly identify Colin as Japp's son, in *A Catalogue of Crime*.

2 Agatha Christie: *An Autobiography*.

3 *An Autobiography*.

4 Or monkey puzzler, a popular name for the Araucaria tree.

5 Quoted in 'The Algebra of Agatha Christie' by Francis Wyndham (London *Sunday Times* 17 February 1966.

6 In *Mallowan's Memoirs*.

7 Quoted in the Francis Wyndham article in the *Sunday Times*, 27 February 1966.

8 In *A Talent to Deceive* (1980).

9 In *A Catalogue of Crime* (1971).

10 By Abigail Ann Hamblen, in *Discourse* (Summer, 1969).

11 'Jones was disheartened to hear from Anna Freud of Freud's great love for detective stories, especially following operations'. Agatha Christie and Dorothy Sayers were special favourites.' Paul Roazen: *Freud and His Followers* 1974.

12 Not all the reviews were unfavourable. The *New York Times* complimented the author on her topicality: 'Last week, with attention still fixed on the airplane hi-jackings in the Middle East, Miss Christie came out with *Passenger to Frankfurt*, which just happens to include four hi-jackings.' And Maurice Richardson in the London *Observer* thought the novel 'marvellously entertaining', though he added that 'at moments one wonders whether the old dear knows the difference between a hippie and a skinhead'.

13 Letter from Peter Saunders to Charles Osborne, 24 November 1981.

14 A well-known stage director whose production of the comedy *No Sex Please, We're British*, was, in 1982, in its twelfth year at a London theatre.

15 Stafford Nye quotes the same phrase in *Passenger to Frankfurt* (1970).

16 *New York Times*, 6 August 1975. There are three inaccurate or misleading statements here: Styles was not 'a nursing home' but a guesthouse; it is by no means certain that Poirot retired from the Belgian police force as early as 1904; and Poirot cannot fairly be said to have 'frequently' misquoted Shakespeare.

17 In *An Autobiography*.

18 *Mallowan's Memoirs*.

19 On 13 January 1976.

20 On 22 January 1976.

21 In *An Autobiography*.

22 Remainder of sentence suppressed by C.O.

23 *Atlanta Journal and Constitution*, 3 August 1975.

24 *Toronto Star*, 14 December 1974.

Numbers 1 and 2 of the lists below are arranged alphabetically. Numbers 3 to 6 are chronological lists.

1 Crime novels and short story collections
2 Short stories
3 Other titles by Agatha Christie
4 Novels published as by Mary Westmacott
5 Plays
   (a) Plays written or adapted by Agatha Christie herself
   (b) Plays adapted by others from works by Agatha Christie
6 Films based on works by Agatha Christie

1. Crime novels and short story collections
(A indicates a novel or story collection in which Hercule Poirot appears; B=Jane Marple; C=Tommy and Tuppence Beresford)

The ABC Murders (1936) (A)
The Adventure of the Christmas Pudding (1960) (A, B)
After the Funeral or *Funerals are Fatal* (1953) (A)
And Then There Were None see *Ten Little Niggers*
Appointment with Death (1938) (A)
At Bertram's Hotel (1965) (B)
The Big Four (1927) (A)
Blood Will Tell see *Mrs McGinty's Dead*
The Body in the Library (1942) (B)
The Boomerang Clue see *Why Didn't They Ask Evans?*
By the Pricking of my Thumbs (1968) (C)
Cards on the Table (1936) (A)
A Caribbean Mystery (1964) (B)
Cat Among the Pigeons (1959) (A)
The Clocks (1963) (A)
Crooked House (1949)
Curtain (1975) (A)
Dead Man's Folly (1956) (A)
Dead Man's Mirror see *Murder in the Mews*
Death Comes as the End (1944)
Death in the Air see *Death in the Clouds*
Death in the Clouds or *Death in the Air* (1935) (A)
Death on the Nile (1937) (A)

Destination Unknown or *So Many Steps to Death* (1954)
Double Sin (1961) (A, B)
Dumb Witness or *Poirot Loses a Client* (1937) (A)
Easy to Kill see *Murder is Easy*
Elephants Can Remember (1972) (A)
Endless Night (1967)
Evil Under the Sun (1941) (A)
Five Little Pigs or *Murder in Retrospect* (1943) (A)
The Floating Admiral (by Agatha Christie and others) (1931)
4.50 From Paddington or *What Mrs McGillicuddy Saw* (1957) (B)
Funerals are Fatal see *After the Funeral*
The Golden Ball (1971)
Hallowe'en Party (1969) (A)
Hercule Poirot's Christmas or *Murder for Christmas* (1938) (A)
Hercule Poirot's Early Cases see *Poirot's Early Cases*
Hickory, Dickory Death see *Hickory Dickory Dock*
Hickory, Dickory Dock (1955) (A)
The Hollow or *Murder After Hours* (1946) (A)
The Hound of Death (1933)
The Labours of Hercules (1947) (A)
The Listerdale Mystery (1934)
Lord Edgware Dies or *Thirteen at Dinner* (1933) (A)
The Man in the Brown Suit (1924)
The Mirror Crack'd see *The Mirror Crack'd from Side to Side*
The Mirror Crack'd from Side to Side or *The Mirror Crack'd* (1962) (B)
Miss Marple's Final Cases (1979) (B)
Mr Parker Pyne, Detective see *Parker Pyne Investigates*
Mrs McGinty's Dead or *Blood Will Tell* (1952) (A)
The Mousetrap see *Three Blind Mice*
The Moving Finger (1942) (B)
Murder After Hours see *The Hollow*
Murder at Hazelmoor see *The Sittaford Mystery*
The Murder at the Vicarage (1930) (B)
Murder for Christmas see *Hercule Poirot's Christmas*
Murder in Mesopotamia (1936) (A)
Murder in the Calais Coach see *Murder on the Orient Express*
Murder in Retrospect see *Five Little Pigs*
Murder in the Mews or *Dead Man's Mirror* (1937) (A)
Murder in Three Acts see *Three-Act Tragedy*
A Murder is Announced (1950) (B)
Murder is Easy or *Easy to Kill* (1939)
The Murder of Roger Ackroyd (1926) (A)
Murder on the Links (1923) (A)
Murder on the Orient Express or *Murder in the Calais Coach* (1934) (A)
Murder with Mirrors see *They Do It With Mirrors*
The Mysterious Affair at Styles (1920) (A)
The Mysterious Mr Quin (1930)
The Mystery of the Blue Train (1928) (A)
N or M? (1941) (C)

Nemesis (1971) (B)
One, Two, Buckle My Shoe or *The Patriotic Murders* (1940) (A)
Ordeal by Innocence (1958)
The Pale Horse (1961)
Parker Pyne Investigates or *Mr Parker Pyne, Detective* (1934)
Partners in Crime (1929) (C)
Passenger to Frankfurt (1970)
The Patriotic Murders see *One, Two, Buckle My Shoe*
Peril at End House (1932) (A)
A Pocket Full of Rye (1953) (B)
Poirot Investigates (1924) (A)
Poirot Loses a Client see *Dumb Witness*
Poirot's Early Cases or *Hercule Poirot's Early Cases* (1974) (A)
Postern of Fate (1973) (C)
The Regatta Mystery (1939) (A, B)
Remembered Death see *Sparkling Cyanide*
Sad Cypress (1940) (A)
The Secret Adversary (1922) (C)
The Secret of Chimneys (1925)
The Seven Dials Mystery (1929)
The Sittaford Mystery or *Murder at Hazelmoor* (1931)
Sleeping Murder (1976) (B)
So Many Steps to Death see *Destination Unknown*
Sparkling Cyanide or *Remembered Death* (1945)
Taken at the Flood or *There is a Tide* (1948) (A)
Ten Little Indians see *Ten Little Niggers*
Ten Little Niggers (*Ten Little Indians*) or *And Then There Were None* (1939)
There is a Tide see *Taken at the Flood*
They Came to Baghdad (1951)
They Do It With Mirrors or *Murder With Mirrors* (1952) (B)
Third Girl (1966) (A)
Thirteen at Dinner see *Lord Edgware Dies*
The Thirteen Problems or *The Tuesday Club Murders* (1932) (B)
Three-Act Tragedy or *Murder in Three Acts* (1934) (A)
Three Blind Mice or *The Mousetrap* (1950) (A, B)
Towards Zero (1944)
The Tuesday Club Murders see *The Thirteen Problems*
The Under Dog (1951) (A)
What Mrs McGillicuddy Saw see *4.50 From Paddington*
Why Didn't They Ask Evans? or *The Boomerang Clue* (1934)
Witness for the Prosecution (1948) (A)

2. **Short Stories**
(The letter after the title indicates the volume in which the story has been collected.)
A *The Adventure of the Christmas Pudding*
B *Double Sin*
C *The Golden Ball*
D *The Hound of Death*

A Christmas Tragedy (o)
The Clergyman's Daughter (k)
The Coming of Mr Quin (i)
The Companion (o)
The Cornish Mystery (m, q)
The Crackler (k)
The Cretan Bull (e)
The Dead Harlequin (i)
Dead Man's Mirror (Expanded version of 'The Second Gong') (h)
Death by Drowning (o)
Death on the Nile (j)
The Disappearance of Mr Davenheim (l)
The Double Clue (b, m)
Double Sin (b, m)
The Dream (a, n)
The Dressmaker's Doll (b, g)
The Erymanthian Boar (e)
The Face of Helen (i)
Finessing the King (k)
The Flock of Geryon (e)
Four-and-Twenty Blackbirds (a, p)
The Four Suspects (o)
The Fourth Man (d, r)
A Fruitful Sunday (c, f)
The Gate of Baghdad (j)
The Gentleman Dressed in Newspaper (k)
The Gipsy (c, d)
The Girdle of Hyppolita (e)
The Girl in the Train (c, f)
The Golden Ball (c, f)
Greenshaw's Folly (a, b)
The Harlequin Tea Set (Published in *Winter's Crimes 3*, 1971, and *Ellery Queen's Murdercade*, 1975)
Harlequin's Lane (i)
Have You Got Everything You Want? (j)
The Herb of Death (o)
The Horses of Diomedes (e)
The Hound of Death (c, d)
The House at Shiraz (j)
The House of Lurking Death (k)
How Does Your Garden Grow? (m, n)
The Idol House of Astarte (o)
In a Glass Darkly (g, n)
The Incredible Theft (Expanded version of 'The Submarine Plans') (h; but in the UK edition only)
Ingots of Gold (o)
Jane in Search of a Job (c, f)
The Jewel Robbery at the Grand Metropolitan (l)
The Kidnapped Prime Minister (l)

The King of Clubs (M, Q)
The Lamp (C, D)
The Last Seance (B, D)
The Lemesurier Inheritance (M, Q)
The Lernean Hydra (E)
The Listerdale Mystery (C, F)
The Lost Mine (L, M)
The Love Detectives (P)
Magnolia Blossom (C)
The Man from the Sea (I)
The Man in the Mist (K)
The Man Who Was No. 16 (K)
The Manhood of Edward Robinson (C, F)
The Market Basing Mystery (M, Q)
The Million Dollar Bond Robbery (L)
Miss Marple Tells a Story (G, N)
Mr Eastwood's Adventure (F)
Motive vs. Opportunity (O)
Murder in the Mews (H)
The Mystery of Hunter's Lodge (L)
The Mystery of the Baghdad Chest (N)
The Mystery of the Blue Jar (D, R)
The Mystery of the Spanish Chest (Slightly expanded version of 'The Mystery of the Baghdad Chest') (A)
The Mystery of the Spanish Shawl (Alternative title of 'Mr Eastwood's Adventure') (R)
The Nemean Lion (E)
Next to a Dog (C)
The Oracle at Delphi (J)
The Pearl of Price (J)
Philomel Cottage (F, R)
The Plymouth Express (M, Q)
Problem at Pollensa Bay (N)
Problem at Sea (M, N)
The Rajah's Emerald (C, F)
The Red House (K)
The Red Signal (D, R)
The Regatta Mystery (N)
Sanctuary (B, G)
The Second Gong (R)
The Shadow on the Glass (I)
The Sign in the Sky (I)
Sing a Song of Sixpence (F, R)
SOS (D, R)
The Soul of the Croupier (I)
The Strange Case of Sir Arthur Carmichael (C, D)
Strange Jest (G, P)
The Stymphalean Birds (E)
The Submarine Plans (M, Q)

The Sunningdale Mystery (K)
Swan Song (C, F)
The Tape-Measure Murder (G, P)
The Theft of the Royal Ruby (Version of 'The Adventure of the Christmas
   Pudding') (B)
The Third Floor Flat (M, P)
Three Blind Mice (P)
The Thumb Mark of Saint Peter (O)
The Tragedy of Marsdon Manor (L)
Triangle at Rhodes (H)
The Tuesday Night Club (O)
The Unbreakable Alibi (K)
The Under Dog (A, Q)
The Veiled Lady (L, M)
The Voice in the Dark (I)
Wasps' Nest (B, M)
Wireless (or Where There's a Will) (D, R)
The Witness for the Prosecution (D, R)
The World's End (I)
Yellow Iris (N)

3. Other Titles by Agatha Christie (excluding plays)

The Road of Dreams (poems) (1924)
Come, Tell Me How You Live (1946)
Star Over Bethlehem (1965)
Poems (1973)
An Autobiography (1977)

4. Novels published as by Mary Westmacott

Giant's Bread (1930)
Unfinished Portrait (1934)
Absent in the Spring (1944)
The Rose and the Yew Tree (1948)
A Daughter's a Daughter (1952)
The Burden (1956)

5. Plays (The dates are those of the first productions)

(a) *Plays written or adapted by Agatha Christie herself*

Black Coffee (1930)
Akhnaton (written 1937; published 1973; not professionally staged)
Ten Little Niggers or *Ten Little Indians* (1945)
Appointment with Death (1945)
Murder on the Nile (1945)
The Hollow (1951)
The Mousetrap (1952)
Witness for the Prosecution (1953)
Spider's Web (1954)

Towards Zero (adapted by Agatha Christie and Gerald Verner) (1956)
Verdict (1958)
The Unexpected Guest (1958)
Go Back for Murder (1960)
Rule of Three (three one-act plays: 'The Rats', 'Afternoon at the Seaside' and
    'The Patient') (1962)
Fiddlers Three (1972)

(b) *Plays adapted by others from works by Agatha Christie*
(The names in brackets are those of the adaptors)

Alibi (Michael Morton) (1928)
Love From a Stranger (Frank Vosper) (1936)
Peril at End House (Arnold Ridley) (1940)
Murder at the Vicarage (Moie Charles and Barbara Toy) (1949)
A Murder is Announced (Leslie Darbon) (1977)
Cards on the Table (Leslie Darbon) (1981)

6. Films based on works by Agatha Christie

Die Abenteuer Gmbh (*Adventures Ltd*) (1928)
The Passing of Mr Quinn (1928)
Alibi (1931)
Black Coffee (1931)
Lord Edgware Dies (1934)
Love from a Stranger (1937)
Ten Little Niggers or *And Then There Were None* (1945)
A Stranger Walked In or *Love From a Stranger* (1947)
Witness for the Prosecution (1957)
The Spider's Web (1960)
Murder, She Said (1962)
Murder at the Gallop (1963)
Murder Most Foul (1964)
Murder Ahoy! (based on Miss Marple and other Christie characters, but with an
    'original' screenplay) (1964)
Ten Little Indians (1965)
The Alphabet Murders (1965)
Endless Night (1972)
Murder on the Orient Express (1974)
And Then There Were None or *Ten Little Indians* (1975)
Death on the Nile (1978)
The Mirror Crack'd (1980)
Evil Under the Sun (1982)

≡ILLUSTRATION ACKNOWLEDGMENTS≡

Numbers refer to the position of each picture in sequence.
Between pp. 64–65: BBC Hulton Picture Library 4, 5, 6, 7, 9, 10, 17; John Topham Picture Library 8, 15, 16; Keystone 13, 32, 36; Kobal 23; Mander and Mitchenson 2, 11, 12, 21, 28, 31, 34; Popperfoto 20, 24, 25, 26, 27, 35; Gerd Treuhaft 29, 30, 33; Kenneth Thomson 18, 19; Rainbird 14.

Between pages 160–161: Central 39, 46, 66, 67, 69; John Topham Picture Library 60, 61; Keystone 54, 56, 57, 58, 68; Kobal 38, 48, 49, 59, 64; Popperfoto 40, 41, 42, 43, 44, 47, 50, 51, 52, 55, 65; Gerd Treuhaft 37, 53; Kenneth Thomson 62, 63.